An Agenda for Regional History

Edited by Bill Lancaster,
Diana Newton & Natasha Vall

Published by Northumbria University Press
Trinity Building, Newcastle upon Tyne NE1 8ST, UK

First Published 2007
© Northumbria University Press 2007

British Library Cataloguing in Publication Data. A Catalogue Record for
this book is available from the British Library.

ISBN 978-1-904794-24-0

Designed and printed by External Relations, Northumbria University
Typeset in Adobe Garamond

Northumbria University is the trading name of the
University of Northumbria at Newcastle. NG–190301C/11/07

Contents

Part Two
Region and Empire

Part Three
Region and politics

Part Four
Region and City

Part Five
Region and Culture

Foreword

The emergence of regional history in Britain during the last two decades was endorsed by the AHRC's funding of the Centre for North East England History between 2000–2005. The Centre's main concern was the history of regional identity since the late medieval period, but as the project evolved links were established with other scholars and institutions in Britain and Europe. Historians from outside the North East were closely involved with both the management and the intellectual development of the Centre and the need for comparative work was recognised early in the Centre's life. The annual conferences of the AHRC Centre increasingly highlighted the need for a major international conference that would bring together scholars from a variety of institutions, countries and disciplines. The conference had several aims. One was to present a wide variety of regional history from different periods and countries. Another was to try and map the parameters of what is proving to be a growing sub-discipline in historical scholarship. Many were aware of the similarities between contemporary regional history and the position of the infant urban history during the late 1960s and accept that the newcomer faces equally daunting methodological and conceptual problems. We were aware from the early period of the Centre that if regional history was to put down firm roots the subject would have to engage with scholars working in cognate disciplines, particularly geographers and political scientists. The conference held in the autumn of 2004 did succeed in achieving some of these objectives. Our proceedings were enlivened by the contributions of scholars from other disciplines and the dialogue across subject boundaries was of high order. The conference attracted nearly fifty contributions from a wide range of European countries, but we are aware of the need to engage with scholars from other continents. Regional history is maturing conceptually and readers will notice the trend amongst contributors to seek out themes and analytical frameworks that will serve to provided deeper understanding of the regional historical process and facilitate meaningful comparative work. This book does not provide the tantalising prize of a 'regional variable', but it does offer a number of pathways which have the potential to bring rigour and broader conceptual horizons to the study of regional history.

This book is organised thematically and to this end hopes to address some of the issues at stake for the historical study of regions. This also means that a chronological approach is eschewed. Whilst we remain committed to understanding the region over time, its development has not been linear, either in Britain, across Europe, or beyond. Chapters are structured around five organising themes, but are published in the format that they were presented to the conference and the idiosyncrasies in style also reflects the diverse range of international and subject perspectives.

The contributions to **Region and Space** all address the question of space and its temporal experience: in terms of the experience and response to regional spaces by migrants in Britain by Colin Pooley; or comparatively, as proposed by Charles Phythian-Adams, through the spaces variously structured and humanized by successive regional societies in contrasted English contexts; or in Bill Lancaster's exploration of different regional geographical constructs in North East England; as well as Brian Roberts who probes links between the physical environment of Northumbria and the cultural responses to it.

In **Region and Empire** the question of overlapping and contested identities that are formulated in response to a 'host' or 'patron' as represented by a range of international empires since the early medieval period is consistent across a diverse range of chapters: Peter Wilson's contribution concerns the notion of regionalism in the context of the Holy Roman Empire and asks how far the experience of imperial hierarchy may account for territorial mobilization in the early modern region; David Saunders similarly explores the question of negotiating resources and power in an imperial context by focussing on the experience of the Andreevskoe in the late Russian Empire; in Thomas Granier's contribution we see how the experience of being part of a prestigious Empire impinged upon the various scales – local, regional and universal – in which identity was expressed in early medieval Italy; Tony Hepburn's chapter, whilst focussing upon modern Ulster, draws comparisons with regions ranging from the Basque Country to the Punjab, asking how Empire-led boundary reformulation has impacted upon national and regional identities.

Region and Politics offers several perspectives of the relationship between the region and state formation in central Europe: Michael Keating's wide-ranging contribution explores the usefulness of the history of regions in the context of the current reconsideration of national histories; meanwhile, Patrick Gilli's piece reflects upon the importance of the regional construct for state-formation in Italy at the end of the Middle Ages; whilst Ian Farr and Graham Ford's chapter on the construction of a Bavarian regional identity by the CSU between 1950 and 1970 attests to the endurance of the regional construct for political mobilisation to the late modern period.

Region and City reminds us of the importance of interaction between the city and its regional hinterland: Ranald Michie's long established expertise on the City of London examines the ongoing dynamic between metropolitan and regional financial centres; by contrast John Belchem's contribution on Liverpool investigates the relationship between Britain's most self-consciously 'peripheral' city and the North West region; Alistair Thompson's chapter meanwhile explores both the connections and dissonance between city and region, as well as the clashing interests of the state and municipality as experienced in Berlin at the end of the nineteenth century.

This book's final theme examines **Region and Culture** and all the contributions are united by their focus on the complex and varied cultural response to the regional construct in Britain and Europe: Peter Aronsson's exploration of the development of cultural regionalism in Sweden offers perspectives of regional negotiating strategies that are arguably equally useful in analysing regions elsewhere; likewise, Philip Payton's chapter on Cornwall examines the various strategies deployed in the reformulation of Cornish identity against the backdrop of British imperialism, first as 'frontier folk' and more recently as Celtic revivalists; Dave Russell's focus is on the dynamic relationship between cultural practices, texts and institutions, and the formation of modern northern English identities; John Walton meanwhile compares the experience of regional culture in the recent creation of 'North-West England' to that of more established regions including the Basque Country in northern Spain; Matt Holford's concern is with continuity and change in North English identities during the late medieval period.

It is inevitable that this book will raise more questions than it answers. Such a range of scholarship bodes well for the future of regional history, but we need to bear in mind that our subject's conceptual project is at an early stage. Many geographers share similar interests and political scientists have widened their horizons towards regional topics. We can only benefit from dialogue with scholars from these disciplines. Above all, even a cursory read of this book indicates the need to develop a comparative approach to the study of regional history. Hopefully this book will stimulate such work and help set an agenda for regional history.

Part One

Region and Space

Chapter One

Differentiating provincial
societies in English history: spatial
contexts and cultural processes

Charles Phythian-Adams

Some premises

The analysis of regional differentiation in England has been handicapped not only by the splintered nature of established approaches to agrarian, urban, and regional history, but also by the failure to integrate these (and other) themes sub-nationally, nationally, and internationally. What follows simply represent in outline some personal responses to what should be a challenge.[1]

There are three broad standpoints from which regions may be differentiated: those of contemporary insiders or outsiders (including immigrants), and that of retrospective commentators. The further back we historians probe, however, the more all of us are forced to replace the competing contemporary perceptions of the first two with surrogate measures: that is by generalizing ways in which regions separately internalized activities and attitudes. This said, whether they existed on the ground or in the mind, historic "regions" have always been experienced by those inhabiting them as parts of a larger whole. No one has put this better than Edmund Burke:

> *We begin our public affections in our families... We pass on to our neighbourhoods, and our habitual provincial connections. These are inns and resting places. Such divisions of our country as have been formed by habit, and not by a sudden jerk of authority, were so many little images of the great country in which the heart found something which it could fill.*[2]

So if we are to discover how the many divisions of the "great country" may have contributed to the composition of the whole, they will need to be identified, and then systematically compared within that wider context. And if treated comparatively, as far as possible like must be contrasted to like. In an ideal world, to cherry-pick criteria according to localized preference should be inadmissible *unless those adopted are also consistently applicable to other regions of the country.* An important proviso here is that due allowance should always be made for degrees of interpenetration or of constantly redefined overlap. Surely no one assumes that the parts of a social whole are ever inflexible or hermetically sealed. There is thus a paramount need for at least an initial model of the English regions in their national context which might be submitted to detailed discussion, testing, and revision in the hope of its replacement by something better.

Any such model would need to take account of certain considerations. The foremost, historically, must be chronological. Do we see "regions" contingently: as relatively short-lived, specialized sub-divisions of some wider plane of *national* activity that often turns out to be economically categorized in terms of farming, marketing, industry or finance?[3]   If so, not only would this temporary character need to be recognized, but so too would the particularized identities of these "regional" types; the relatively restricted areas they appear to occupy; and, in the narrowest cases, the frequent discontinuities between them on the ground.

Or should we adopt a long-term perspective: one that is evolutionary rather than episodic? Insofar as a degree of underlying stability is in question, it could be that spatially more extensive regional areas in well-defined permanent, geographical contexts might be relevant here. Transitory specialist "regions" would then be accommodated within such wider territories as *sub*-regions – or occupational neighbourhoods – and the older arrangements of the *pays* be seen to coexist alongside the new.[4] These localities would now be related specifically to a more enduring regional level, intermediate between them and the nation, rather than directly to the nation itself. Whatever a region's extent, it is still undeniable that its identity is essentially a function of a long-accumulated past as that is retained selectively in the "social memory"– from myth to institutions to iconic buildings, let alone glorious industrial episodes or devastating disasters.

The second problem that needs to be recognized, however, is the elusive nature of the evidence for so-called "regional cultures" especially over time. The danger of retrospectively inferring the extents of whole "cultures" simply from the distributions of a few cultural idioms, selected because of their survival rate and normally of a material and sometimes transitory kind, is all too obvious if sometimes overlooked. It may be true that the interior of a *pays* could have boasted a degree of cultural consistency, through the imprecise coexistence of specific occupational customs, diet, craft techniques, building materials, settlement and field patterns and so on. Beyond such spatial levels, however, homogeneity is less to be expected as the distinguishing mark of a "region", even if there were ever available all the evidence from which such a judgement ought to be made. Least of all would this be so over a wider region containing more than one *pays* and a range of towns. Cultures are invariably multiplex and internally variegated not only according to ethnicities, social statuses and religious affiliations, but also in terms of cultural densities relative to contrasted concentrations of population, whether urban or agrarian, and their immensely varied occupational activities.

Significantly too, mapped distributions of cultural idioms are rarely, if ever, either uninterrupted or coextensive. Often, in fact, they are better taken to reflect the spread of particular new ideas, trends, or persisting influences from *beyond* the region in question – even from overseas. When assessing the indigenous culture of a region, such cultural imports, including those from London, must surely always be regarded (other than in the relative timing and intensity of their assimilation) as of secondary significance. Without exploring how far beyond an area they may also reach, indeed, we cannot simply assume that combinations of even select cultural idioms coincide only within it as opposed to a social group, as David Hackett Fischer appears to do in his enterprising *Albion's Seed*.[5]

A third matter for consideration stems directly from the inevitably physical nature of regional space as that is inhabited, tempered, and redefined by human residence. The incorporation of geographical considerations into historical appraisals of what conditions human decisions in a landscape, however, should never be confused with environmental determinism. Settlement involves *continuing* interaction between man and his habitat, and may be limited, but not necessarily inhibited by poor soils, water scarcity, and physical barriers (though social contact will be facilitated in their absence). Human "regions" are defined by their occupancy, and so through the patterns of settlement within them. These represent both the transformation of natural habitats by those inhabiting them, and their investment with cultural meanings. It is surely inconceivable that the definition of an historic region could exclude the spatial distribution of people on the ground, their communication patterns, or their identification with their topographical context.

Differing forms of association with particular areas, indeed, comprise a fourth, human factor to be disentangled when seeking to define provincial divisions. For years historical thinking has tended to give priority in this respect to more *formal* modes of regional association with sub-national, institutionalized spaces: from shires to dioceses, and usually with little systematic reference to geographical context. One historian, however, has recently gone so far as to relegate both these factors as too simplistic: "Mapping the regions of medieval England, *except on crude geographical or administrative criteria*," he writes, "is an extraordinarily complex task" (my emphasis).[6] If that were all, one might agree, but in characterizing regions through their complexity at any period – especially given the disturbing problems surrounding cultural distributions already discussed – geographical or administrative criteria can hardly be disregarded as insignificant elements, especially when taken together. After all, administrative units usually owe something to the ways in which past societies adapted themselves to physical conditions. Their successors then found many of their social interactions focused thereby, and to some extent regulated, by the very jurisdictions previously originated. What should be more at issue, surely, is whether the administrative units usually chosen (commonly the single county) are too artificial or too small to be also reasonably convincing as settlement areas.[7] Though county historians consistently ignore the fact, shires whose landscape edges "bleed" uninterruptedly across their boundaries into their neighbours' territories, as most do in more than one direction, can hardly be characterized as unambiguously discrete arenas for past social interaction.

Clearly relevant here too is the weight that has been lent over the last few years to *informal* factors arising from sentiments of familiarity or belonging: "where the heart found something it could fill". At one variously understood, and so imprecise, level this sentiment was commonly expressed by contemporaries through a terminology that evoked their native or residential vicinity or district: the Old English *eard* (effectively a kindred neighbourhood to judge from the Laws of Æthelstan)[8] ; the Latin *patria*; the early-modern notion of one's "country"; or Burke's "habitual provincial connections". Such language strongly suggests that a sense of shared identity over a whole locality was in question here rather than an egocentric view. In his "Portrait of England", composed in Italian by George Rainsford in 1556, the gentry are said to "consider it more precious to have the friendship and hearts of the region (*provincia*) in which they live,… than all the honours that the court can give".[9]

How distantly such loyalties ranged according to different levels of social standing, is far from clear. It seems highly probable that for most people, in proportion to their capacity for spatial mobility and the range of their informants, areas of immediate belonging and instant familiarity were surrounded by zones of wider association. Clearly there will have been differences here between actors on the national stage – with extra-regional marital alliances – and those operating within their regional or neighbouring arenas. The former residents more probably absorbed many of the latter's traditional horizons in addition to their own wider concerns, than *vice-versa*. In reconstructing broad regional perceptions, therefore, historians may well need to discriminate in favour of the majority view so that the tiny minority may be measured against it. It would be misleading, however, to regard popular sentiments of association as wholly divorced from diverse administrative and geographical realities, not least during the great age of rebellions in defence of provincial interests (c.1381–1569). *Inter alia*, it was surely the rough and ready, subconscious blending of sentiment with the other two factors that mattered, especially where the formal boundaries of shires ambiguously divided rather than delimited the continuous areas of *pays*.

The underlying moral of all this seems plain. Regional cultures, administrative settings, and sentiments of locational belonging, never define themselves; they can only be understood specifically as long-term *reflections* of past and present societies inhabiting particular contexts. In such a space a society evolves its own specific "mix" of cultural idioms, whether or not some of these idioms might also be found alternatively combined in an adjacent society. It is, then, on the particularized ways in which provincial societies differentiated themselves, both individually and as integrated elements of the "great country", that regional historians should focus. To attempt this, we must first take account of societies as processes unfolding over time: how, *inter alia*, each society was disposed across its own unique landscape in recognizably interconnected patterns of settlement that continued to expand, in-fill, or contract, and so always in relation to what was already there.[10]

Distinguishing regional societies for comparison

On the ground, therefore, it is societies that define themselves. *Formal* societies in the mid-Anglo-Saxon period, for example, comprised specific peoples who were ethnically – as opposed to racially – distinct with individual names, their own royal dynasties, and constituent tribes, in recognized, often still broadly reconstructable, territories. Within these regional kingdoms or subkingdoms, their subdivisions, and their central places, were internalized the functioning of royal governance, jurisdiction, religion, economy, and kinship.

In subsequent times, following the unification of the realm and the rejection of regional sovereignties, a pre-modern society is definable through what I can only express as the more *informal* degree of "interiority" that now marked its arrangement and functioning. Seven key features may be briefly proposed if it is to merit the status of an informal, largely agrarian, "regional society":

(1) It needs to have comprised a recognizable concentration of population, but one large enough to reflect the multi-dimensional characteristics appropriate to the complexity of a major social division of the nation.

(2) Such a population will have been articulated on the ground through its individual settlement hierarchy, including a (commonly) enduring, regional primate town with its own dependent urban network, and seats of power at estate centres.

(3) In every case, this deployment of settlement will have directly expressed the economic *intra*-dependence of the region through the internal exchange of a

range of contrasting natural resources between its constituent *pays*. Between its towns, the internal disposition of a network of road and water linkages with greater or lesser access to the sea, will have reflected and enabled the functioning of an identifiable regional economy (by which I intend not a specialized sub-set of the national economy, but an economy in the round generated specifically by and for the regional society in question). This would have been capable both of creating product surpluses for internal circulation, consumption, and export, and of importing further needs by land or water. It would thus have been independently connected to both national and international markets as well as working through London.

(4) This extensive character should have meant further that every society reflected a range of individually self-identifying – but nonetheless inter-locking – agrarian, industrial, and commercial neighbourhoods, the peculiar mixture of which lent each region much of its economic and cultural particularity.

(5) Such a society would not exclude non-English ethnic presences, and would include a more or less proportional cross-section of national social statuses. Especially significant here would be the presence of sufficiently numerous figures of economic or political weight to counter-balance provincial interests against national power structures of different kinds.

(6) Given what we know about the preponderance of short-range migration even during industrialization, a demographic concentration structured in the ways described would thus be distributed widely enough across, and sufficiently enclosed within, its region for it to be perpetuated over generations largely, but not exclusively, through the internal replacement and circulation of indigenous families.

(7) A regional sense of "belonging" to such a broadly shared context would be cross-cut not only by customary ways passed on by these core families, but also by recognizable, but not necessarily coincident complexes of association. These might include shared religious *foci*, the implicit acknowledgement of particularized ethnic origins, and a contextual cultural topography, as this might be expressed *inter alia* in place-naming traditions or landscapes with commonly "owned" superstitious identities.[11]

On this basis, therefore, each "society" may be regarded as concentrating in itself a unique blend of regionally particular structures and cultural traits and, as we shall see later, a more diffused set of characteristics that derived from its wider national location.

For the moment it needs to be seen, all too briefly, how this national model for pre-modern times might be applied consistently to realities on the ground. It seems clear, for example, that for these purposes some conventionally understood "regions", like *pays* or ancient counties, are really too small in compass. Instead, therefore, wider units still should be recognized to allow for the sufficient heterogeneity that the model demands.

The least ambiguous point in the scheme outlined concerns the location, national spacing, and – until the rise of Salisbury or Birmingham – the long-lasting nature of earlier, regional primate centres. Most of these regionally unrivalled centres remained amongst the top twenty or so towns in any national urban ranking down to early modern times; others, equally unrivalled, nevertheless continued to dominate regions of more modest wealth. Ignoring minor – usually transitory – fluctuations in regional importance, centres of both Roman origin and repeated significance thereafter, comprised London, York, Lincoln, Winchester, Exeter, Chester, and Carlisle. To them, in the Anglo-Saxon period, were added Norwich (which conceivably superseded *Venta Icenorum* at Caistor S. Edmund), and Bristol (though there is a case to be made for linking it initially with ex-Roman Bath). Subsequently included were Coventry, Newcastle and King's Lynn (and Salisbury instead of Winchester). Eleven became sees (that is including the chequered history of Chester) while secular Newcastle/Gateshead was complemented by nearby ecclesiastical Durham, and Lynn by Ely. Further candidates for primacy but in regionally peripheral locations, were nevertheless overshadowed by one or other of the preceding, as in the most extreme cases were Canterbury, Oxford, and Colchester by London.

Of the primate centres, nearly all were sited on what were almost certainly navigable rivers originally (or their estuaries), many of them also developing international out-ports. River-crossings, as points of interchange *between* land and water, also encouraged the development of many other secondary towns in regional urban hierarchies. All told, indeed, between the fourteenth and the seventeenth centuries, around thirty-five of the forty most significant urban centres were sited on or near navigable rivers or estuaries. Then there were numerous minor lading points at other river-crossings, which often evolved formal or informal trading functions and even generated so-called "linear" communities of boating people along navigable waters.[12] The arable vales that so comprised the topographical cores of most such settings, moreover, were also the very areas that attracted closely spaced, rural forms of nucleated settlement (including key market towns). Dense, lower-lying, urban and rural populations hence contrasted with those of the adjacent, more sparsely inhabited, pastoral *pays* of dispersed settlement and lighter nucleation that tended to delimit the upper flanks of major valleys. These were often settled later (and more usually depopulated subsequently) than their better situated neighbours.[13] To that extent regional concentrations of population, their settlement patterns, and – to judge from the known trading hinterlands of major ports between the fourteenth and seventeenth centuries – their economies, were commonly focused broadly towards and along the floors of major river-drainage systems, or athwart major estuaries. Later river navigation schemes and regional canal linkages thus helped to intensify provincial economic patterns and identities rather than otherwise.

As we might have expected from the antiquity and siting of the early primate towns, such informal contexts remind us too that river basins seem to have previously accommodated the formal, core settlement areas of tribal kingdoms before some of them absorbed neighbouring peoples located in similar settings. That was broadly the case for the Deirans, the West Saxons (after the expansion of the *Gewisse* out of the upper Thames area into the wider "Hampshire" basin), the early Mercians, the *Hwicce* and others. In the east, such settings – like the Yorkshire Ouse, the navigable lower Trent, and the Middle Anglian Wash region – were simply perpetuated by the Scandinavians. It is thus highly relevant that north of Thames, the same ethnic heartlands were eventually partitioned by county groupings which conformed to much the same physical settings as before. Component shires in these groupings were individually arranged around the existing regional centres and leading second rank towns of urban networks that had already developed by the early eleventh century. Here then are clear signs that regional economies were in the making.[14] Although now fragmented, collectively the new administrative arrangements nevertheless still broadly coincided spatially with those of the polities that had preceded them around their respective riverine trading arteries. A number of these now divided entities, moreover, retained an important facet of former territorial unity in the arrangement of such sees as Durham, Norwich and Worcester. Regional ethnic allegiances, indeed, can be shown to have survived by name well into the twelfth century, often then being reformulated as origin myths associated with the same settings. They so furnished one crucial element of later provincial identities.[15]

To this inevitably generalized model of regional structures, three out of four necessary modifications must now be made. First, within the most extensive

settings in particular, room has to be left for what might be described as semi-independent sub-regional neighbourhoods that either lay at some distance from their primate towns and/or boasted their own port outlets. Those dependent on Canterbury, Oxford, and Colchester have already been mentioned in relation to London, but those surrounding inland Hereford or Beverley with outports at Chepstow and Hull respectively, or inland from Barnstaple or Poole, are other examples of contrasted extents and importance. In all such cases however they remained within the economic and sometimes ecclesiastical ambit of much more important regional centres – Bristol, York, Exeter or Salisbury (as the supplanter of Winchester) – to which recourse still had to be made for different purposes.

A second, related, point should be made about inland areas, such as Hallamshire or the Cirencester textile neighbourhood, which lay above easy reach of navigable river waters, and where choices had consequently to be made between cartage to ports (even beyond the parent region) and overland carriage to London. The latter factor was of especial significance on either side of the Watling Street line (or its diversion) between Chester and London, even though the more southerly societies concerned were often within reach of the waterways of the fenland area. Most seriously affected were the areas dependent therefore on Bedford; to some extent Northampton; and Leicester. Coventry (the only landlocked, provincial primate centre) probably captured much of the trade of its immediate inland region and some control of overland carriage between Ireland, Wales, and London, let alone the supply of the Midlands from Bristol. In medieval times such areas away from navigable rivers now look to have been characterized by greater price volatility than those within direct reach of water transport.[16]

A third sophistication of the model thus relates to what might be described as "frontier areas" between regions, where the interests of neighbouring urban networks overlapped to varying extents. Most frequently these borderlands lay along and across under-populated watershed zones or, less frequently, along such features as the lowland/upland juncture at the easternmost edge of the Cheshire plain or the chalk rim of the Channel region, and what I have described elsewhere as the "frontier valleys" of the Tees, Welland, and Suffolk Stour.[17] Such frontiers comprised broad belts of interpenetration between neighbouring provincial societies and cultures and, as was the case at inland *national* edges, may have sometimes evolved differing degrees of economic and cultural detachment from the contiguous parent heartlands concerned as a result.

Borderlands were often marked out by ragged lines of usually modest market towns. In the case of a watershed zone these could sometimes be found along major inter-regional routeways in complementary pairs on opposite sides of the divide with their market places aligned accordingly, and so placed to function as mediators between adjacent economies. More important towns, like Banbury, singly controlling the gap between the upper Thames valley region and that of the Warwickshire Avon, may have exerted cultural influences some distance along the major thoroughfares linking them to neighbouring societies. In the north, similarly sited towns at higher altitudes represented the means whereby the Pilgrimage of Grace was channelled westwards through the Pennines to the societies of the Irish Sea and Solway regions respectively.

In all of these cases a highly generalized coincidence between geographical and administrative borders is conspicuous. It must be stressed, however, that these outer limits to regional urban networks were influenced more by physical constraints on communication than by purely cultural factors. That was as true of the Wash region where the western towns of East Anglia were linked by water not to Norwich, but to King's Lynn on the estuary of the Great Ouse, as it was of the absorption of east-facing, Welsh Marcher towns into the ambits of English Shrewsbury or Hereford. Borderlands were sometimes distanced from formal boundary lines.

Wider contexts of association

The internally comparable, but individual, regional societies into which the English are here seen as subdivided, need also to be understood in their contrasting, external, cultural contexts: and hence as parties to differing zones of yet wider contact or association. For these purposes England is best understood as falling into broad, diagonal bands which reflected a distinction between, first, all those regional societies that interacted closely with neighbouring nations in the British archipelago and, secondly, all those that related to the nearest continental mainland; with, thirdly, an important, residual division of the nation between them. (This suggestion respects obvious geographical obstacles to easy cultural diffusion in the interior, like scarp lines, as well as the inwardly convergent pattern of the country's river valleys as channels for cultural transmission from contrasted foreign origins.) In respect of both cultural bias and broadly shared self-interest, three distinct, but also permeable, "Englands" may thus be distinguished:

(1) An "*Archipelago*" division comprising all the western and northernmost county groups that inter-related by land or sea with neighbouring Celtic cultures, including Brittany, and beyond them with the south European Atlantic littoral. With this zone should be understood those informal areas of economic and cultural influence where the edges of English-based urban networks overlapped national boundaries: the inner Solway region of Scotland, the northern and southern coasts of Wales and the Marches of Wales. Overlaps between national cultures, especially in the absence of natural barriers, are surely as relevant as those between regional societies.

(2) A "*European*" division defined by areas adjacent to the northern European mainland and so comprising a generous SE, broadly delimited inland by Dorset, and Wiltshire, Oxfordshire, and Northamptonshire inclusively.

(3) A narrowly defined "*Inner*" division lying between the other two: from the basins of the lower Severn/Avon and the upper Trent in the west as far as the coasts of Lincolnshire and Yorkshire in the east and north. This division looks both west and east, but across more tightly drawn maritime frontiers than the other two.

The most significant element in this pattern was the off-centre siting of London in a south-eastern recess of the European division. Here it acted as a communications node, not only for Britain and its SE in particular, but also within a wider European network of Roman roads linked by cross-Channel ferries. A circle describing a radius of 200 miles around London, indeed, demonstrates that Cornwall, Lancashire, Cumbria, Northumberland and Durham in the Archipelago division were all further away from the capital than Paris or the mouth of the Rhine. Before the turnpikes and the railways it could take nearly a week of forced riding to reach Berwick, 4 to 5 days to Exeter, yet under 2 days from London to cross the Channel, over which urgent news could anyway be signalled by beacon fires.[18]

That said, it must be stressed that the proposed European division cannot be seen, as it so often is, simply in terms of the capital and its fluctuating function as "national" port outlet. Down to the seventeenth century London was simultaneously the focus of the society resident within its own supply region, broadly comprising the Thames valley and its estuary. Beyond that, the city long reached more indirectly in rather specific ways: topping up its supply needs; trading in scarce commodities; lending to scattered landholding elites and

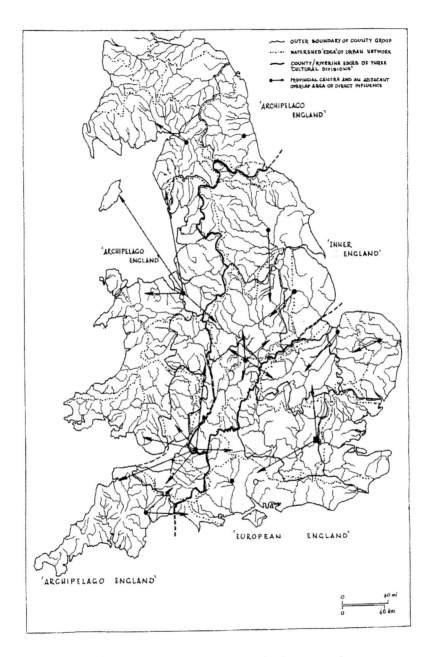

Pre-modern provincial centres and their suggested urban-network areas in relation to associated county-groupings and three cultural divisions of England. (Drawn by Kenneth Smith)

provincial merchants; and selling rare craft skills.[19] Its neighbouring regional societies to north and south – including the economically infiltrated Channel region – nevertheless retained quite distinct identities, specific concerns (such as in defence matters), and particular overseas trading partners, while also acting as exporters to London in their own rights.

These three divisions may be quickly characterized. European England was the most convenient first target for conquests, initial colonization and subsequent migrations from the continental seaboard, while its eastern and southern littorals functioned as front-lines of defence against later invasion or raids from Europe. It boasted all the favourite, provincial, royal residences of medieval and later England, two successive cities of government, archiepiscopal Canterbury and Lambeth, and Oxford, Cambridge, and the Inns of Court. Long claiming political aspirations across the Channel, this zone was also closely connected to Europe early on by its international fairs in the economically precocious Wash region especially. Medieval London is rightly regarded nowadays as a significant outlier of the early urban system of the mainland. In Reformation times, the court, the universities, London, and notably other coastal frontier towns from Southampton to Sandwich, to Ipswich, to Yarmouth, represented the immediate conduits for European migrants, ideas, technologies, and religious allegiances. It was not until the seventeenth century that the development of European England was overshadowed by the accelerating ability of the capital to engorge this zone's economy.

In Archipelago England, Anglo-Saxon settlement had tended to be late and sometimes tenuous. Here Scots, Welsh, and Cornish long perpetuated "remembered frontiers" that substantially overlapped English territory (well beyond the international, upland Marcher areas) through linguistic reminders and the survival of Celtic saints' cults or administrative practices. Only in this division too did the fourth, necessary modification to the model apply. Variously mixed ethnicities (and national defence needs) here lent specific identities to geographically delimited, modest territories (N. Cumbria, Shropshire, Herefordshire, and Cornwall) with their adjacent areas of national overlap. Boasting focal, second-rank towns of their own, with unique inter-cultural functions, these places tended locally to displace much of the influence exerted elsewhere by major primate centres in their wider vicinities. The trade networks of Bristol, Chester, and eventually Liverpool, however, ensured that this zone as a whole continued to belong firmly to an Irish Sea, and increasingly Atlantic, community within which inter-national migration was common. (Newcastle alone looked east to Scandinavia, but in terms of human contact and migration, it needs to be recalled that there its nearest port was Stavanger, some 400 miles away.)

Inner England was mostly situated over 80–90 miles away from the capital, and so outside its immediate supply region, and could look independently in opposite directions in external trading terms through Bristol, or through Hull and Boston towards northern Europe. It was also subdivided between a traditionally anglicized west, and an east – reaching from Tees to Welland – that had comprised the Scandinavian core of the Danelaw. Its unifying feature was the line of the Fosse Way – the only cross-country route to strike diagonally from SW to NE through the road network emanating from London. Given the relevance of settlement patterns as societal indicators, this zone broadly but not exclusively coincided with the concentrated *national* distribution of rural nucleated settlement.[20] If it was more like the European division with respect to its complex urban hierarchies; with Archipelago England, it had in common that long, discontinuous belt of metalliferous and carboniferous resources that stretched from Cornwall to the northern coal-fields. Uniquely it contained until the Reformation for the most part, the only centres of dioceses that overlapped extensively into one or other of the remaining two divisions.

I suggest that these divisions of England help to bridge the crude polarization of *Britain* – as between English core and Celtic periphery – and the equally distortive bisection of England itself into over-generalized Highland and Lowland zones. As we shall see, to some extent it helps even to blunt the continuing over-emphasis on the core/periphery model as applied within England either to the so-called North/South divide or to the tensions between "London" and "the provinces".

Societies, divisions and processes

The *typical*, pre-modern provincial society of the model, then, was defined on the ground by thinness of population at its higher inland margins, and by the corresponding convergence of its residential organization around a well-populated, vale-focused, core area (or narrowly separated core areas). Each whole was structured around a primate centre by a distinct urban network with its own riverine and maritime outlets. Its composition was never homogeneous, containing – as all did – its own peculiar combination of different neighbourhoods and sub-regions, and each was further differentiated according to its unique national location and aspect. Unlike a traditional "community" in which adult membership was usually a matter of choice, more transient, and predominantly *intra*-generational; membership of a regional "society" was based primarily on birth, and so functioned *inter*-generationally; hence the remarkable survival of personal names in the male line that may be associated with many regions even over centuries. A regional society conducted its own economy. Partially penetrated, it may be, by alien merchants or Londoners (some of them even regional kindred or contacts), it still exported and imported on its own account, both in partnership with the capital and elsewhere whether at home or overseas. An intra-dependent economy in turn made for a sense of association and an identity that reflected the cultural mix and wealth of its inhabitants. Its most regular foreign trading partners were the carriers of new fashions, techniques, or ideas from quite specific neighbours, with visual or other effects on the cultural image or identity of the society in question.

Provincial societies naturally persisted over time by continuously adapting to new circumstances, so it is the underlying continuities of their infra-structures that need to be isolated if we are to distinguish processes of change. The most enduring new element to be identified here for pre-modern times was the ordering of settlement in effectively fixed regional patterns – bar relatively minor internal adjustments – of siting and spacing. Established in essence as early as Domesday Book, the minutely detailed definition and organization of public and private spaces to which it bears witness, can hardly be divorced from the new social and economic circumstances that had recently generated such developments. This surely suggests that genuine transformations of regional societies involved (a) fundamental redistributions of populations, the accompanying re-disposition of their residential arrangements on the ground, and fresh definitions of territorial spaces; together with (b) new internal lines, or modes, of communication. Down to the eighteenth century by contrast, change measured by expansions and contractions of regional populations within established limits, served if anything to perpetuate, rather than to alter, the internalized extent and balance of arrangements previously constituted.

We might thus claim that sufficiently radical transitions occurred over only two, widely spaced, historical episodes, each taking time to complete, evidently at varying rates and to varying stages of accomplishment, in different regions. The first extended from c.875 to c.1225, and superseded previous "ethnic" patterns of shifting settlement organized around a scattering of permanent key places within tribal territories. The second has lasted since c.1660 and is presumably not finished yet, to judge from the way in which earlier processes of urban agglomeration are now being replicated on a more modest scale amongst a range of formerly small towns with their own commuter territories.

It is thus possible to distinguish seismic shifts from those less radical processes of alteration that occurred at two, sometimes inter-related, spatial levels. In the cases of regional societies, these constituted continuing, internal processes of adjustment whereby periods of expansion or decline in separate *sub*-regional elements (whether agricultural *or* industrial) involved a tilting towards every fresh area of regional prosperity. The resulting coexistence of degrees of novelty and anachronism, indeed, has ever been a further mark of differentiation – not least in building terms – both within regions and between them. Such differences have never been more conspicuous than in distinguishing those provinces that urbanized dramatically from those that did not.

But what needs to be stressed here is the fact that both radical transformations and the internal re-positioning of sub-regions usually seem to have occurred within enduring provincial frameworks. In the terminology used by Anglo-Saxonists, indeed, one might even describe the processes of eighteenth- and nineteenth-century urbanization (when many traditional primate centres were of course displaced) as generally involving the exaggerated, urbanized "fission" of existing settlement arenas albeit up to their lowland edges. Except in the West Midlands or perhaps the Humber area, former frontier zones still tended to separate re-defined societies one from another. Those who question this should drive or walk in such open landscapes to experience their relative emptiness – not least along the rims of the lower Thames basin – or, in its room, their very recent adaptation for airports, new towns and reservoirs.

At the wider level represented by "divisions" of cultural association, by contrast, deeper issues affecting change were clearly in play. Here an alternating balance between London/European England and the rest of the country may first be recalled simply as a broad context. In *both* the fourteenth and the nineteenth centuries, the provincial share of the nation's overseas trade may have been as high as two-thirds, and the population of London could have been equalled or even exceeded by the combined total of the top five provincial cities or major conurbations. Between the fourteenth and nineteenth centuries, the position was effectively the reverse: with London by 1700 exceeding the populations of the top thirty-two leading towns combined and engorging some three quarters of the nation's overseas trade. Space precludes a discussion of the accompanying, narrower alignments and realignments of the cultural divisions suggested, but what is clear is the way in which the experiences of Inner England – and its component regional societies – alternated in line with first one and then the other of its neighbouring divisions, as the balance periodically shifted. Especially conspicuous here was the eventual stitching together from the eighteenth century of Archipelago England (as far north as Tyneside) and the western edges of its Inner neighbour through networks of invention and entrepreneurship; the conspicuously detailed, new web of communications by turnpike, canal, and railway that linked them; and the shared experience of industrialization and urbanisation along much of the carboniferous and metalliferous belt. Above all, of course, was the opening up of the Irish Sea and Atlantic economies together with the association of all the regions involved, including Cornwall, in a newly integrated zone of activity. This eventually inter-related the urbanizing national littorals of the entire western archipelago not only through Manchester/Liverpool and Bristol, but also through Glasgow (and its links to Edinburgh), Belfast, Dublin, Cork and eventually Cardiff; and so created temporarily – through inter-regional migrations in particular – what might be regarded as an international zone of association – a maritime province of the Irish Sea – that was now effectively "British" rather than English. Perhaps this new "Inner *Britain*", rather than the so-called North/South divide of England, was why in 1912, Sir Laurence Gomme was gloomily predicting that "someone will one day shift the English capital northwards, and the government will follow the London newspapers, which have already opened their offices in Manchester."[21] Ironically this was perhaps too why what was now sentimentally idealized as the quintessential "England" tended frequently to be restricted to the ancient, southern chalk country of its "European" division.

Identities, then, clearly "moved" at different spatial levels, or may have been stretched, or even redefined, for particular purposes. Yet to sustain "regional" logics beyond their former limits, such floating perceptions still had to be – as it were – tethered to where their disseminators, or their forebears, originated: that is, to entrenched and collectively apprehended patterns of interdependency within congeries of places in contrasted landscape arenas. For periods before the demise of inland water transport, that is why – to my view – our understanding of these infrastructures as anciently evolved within nationally inter-linked, but physically exclusive, settings should remain central to any generally derived definition of the

English region. Occasionally glimpsed in the distance from within, it was physical horizons that represented the ultimate visual signifier of "otherness" beyond.

Notes

1. Full-length treatment will be found in *The Provincial Roots of England. A History since the Roman Occupation* (in preparation). An inevitably compressed case-study complementing this paper is "The Northumbrian island", *New History of Northumbria*, ed. Rob Colls (forthcoming). Fieldwork across England and mapping (by Kenneth Smith) were enabled by a grant from The Leverhulme Trust. Dr David Postles commented helpfully upon the first draft of this chapter.
2. Edmund Burke, *Reflections on the Revolution in France*, ed. Connor Cruise O'Brien (Harmondsworth, 1969), p.315.
3. 'Introduction', *Regions and Industries. A Perspective on the Industrial Revolution in Britain*, ed. Pat Hudson (Cambridge, 1989), p.3.
4. Alan Everitt, 'Introduction' to his *Landscape and Community in England* (London, 1985), pp.6–7.
5. David H. Fischer, *Albion's Seed: Four British Folkways in America* (New York, 1989).
6. Derek Keene, 'National and Regional Identities', *Gothic Art for England* 1400–1547, ed. Richard Marks and Paul Williamson (London, 2003), p.50.
7. *Cf.* the ten regions into which the country is divided in *A Regional History of England* (series), ed. Barry Cunliffe and David Hey (Harlow, 1986-).
8. *Cf.* V Æthelstan 1, 2, 3, and IV Æthelstan 3, *The Laws of the Earliest English Kings*, ed. F.L. Attenborough (Cambridge, 1922), pp.146–47, 152–53.
9. P.S. Donaldson, 'George Rainsford's *Ritratto d'Ingliterra* (1556)', *Camden Miscellany*, XXVII, Camden Fourth Series, 22, (1979) pp.76, 94–95.
10. For the reasons sketched in this section, it should be apparent why – as a matter of terminology only – the author now prefers to substitute for the insufficiently precise description 'cultural province', the 'regional society' that defined the cultural space in question from within. Some measures of contrasted cultural 'mix' in such regional contexts are mapped in Phil Withington, *The Politics of Commonwealth: Citizens and Freemen in Early Modern England* (Cambridge, 2005), figs. 2.2, 2.3, 2.4, 2.5, and 2.5.
11. Charles Phythian-Adams, 'Environments and Identities: Landscape as Cultural Projection in the English Provincial Past', *Environments and Historical Change. The Linacre Lectures 1998*, ed. Paul Slack (Oxford, 1999), pp.118–46.
12. Mary Prior, *Fisher Row: Fishermen, Bargemen, and Canal Boatmen in Oxford, 1500–1900* (Oxford, 1982), pp.136, 167, 316, 318; *Miners and Mariners of the Severn Gorge: Probate Inventories for Benthall, Broseley, Little Wenlock and Madeley 1660–1764*, ed. Barrie Trinder and Nancy Cox (Chichester, 2000), p.13.
13. H.S.A. Fox, 'The People of the Wolds in English Settlement History', *The Rural Settlements of Medieval England: Studies Dedicated to Maurice Beresford and John Hurst*, ed. Michael Aston, David Austin, and Christopher Dyer (Oxford, 1989), pp.77–101.
14. D.M Metcalf, *An Atlas of Anglo-Saxon and Norman Coin Finds 973–1086* (London, 1998), pp.192–248; Charles Phythian-Adams, '"Small-scale Toy-towns and Trumptons"? Urbanizations in Britain and the new *Cambridge Urban History*', *Urban History*, 28, 2 (2001), p.264.
15. n. 11 above.

16. M. Bailey, 'Peasant Welfare in England, 1290–1348', *Economic History Review*, 51 (1998), p.236; James A. Galloway, 'One Market or Many? London and the Grain trade of England', *Trade, Urban Hinterlands and Market Integration c.1300-1600*, ed. James A. Galloway, Centre for Metropolitan History Working Papers Series, no. 3 (Institute of Historical Research, 2000), pp.28–29, 34–36.

17. Charles Phythian-Adams, 'Frontier Valleys', *The English Rural Landscape*, ed. Joan Thirsk (Oxford, 2000), pp.236–260 (republished in 2002 as *Rural England: an Illustrated History of the Landscape*).

18. C. A. J. Armstrong, 'Some Examples of the Distribution and Speed of News at the Time of the Wars of the Roses', *Studies in Medieval History Presented to Sir Maurice Powicke*, ed. R.W Hunt, W.A. Pantin, and R.W. Southern (Oxford, 1948), pp.445–46, 452, 450.

19. Derek Keene, 'Changes in London's Economic Hinterland as Indicated by Debt Cases in the Court of Common Pleas', *Trade, Urban Hinterlands and Market Integration*, ed. Galloway, pp.72–79.

20. Brian K. Roberts and Stuart Wrathmell, *Region and Place: A study of English rural settlement* (English Heritage, 2002), figs. 1.1, 1.5, 5.4, and chapter 5.

21. Quoted in Donald Read, *The English Provinces c.1760–1960: A Study in Influence* (London, 1964), pp.272, 313.

Chapter Two

The North East, England's most distinctive region?

Bill Lancaster

One of the purposes of this book is to map out parameters, identify challenges and set agendas for future research. We must maintain an open approach that embraces many perspectives and engages with and listens to other disciplines that share our interest. We need to see the region as consisting of people and space that is frequently in flux in a series of internal relationships with individual groups and processes and externally interacts with metropolitan, national and transnational forces. It is vital that comparative models that facilitate analysis between regions both in space and time are developed. Above all we need to recognise that regions are constructs that are created both by people who live in them as well as those who observe them externally and that it is the act of reflection on this process that constitutes the formation of the region. Moreover, the creation of a region is never clear cut: space; language; culture; economic society; political movements and traditions and the changing relationship to the nation state all can play a part. As Aronsson's work on Sweden shows the construction of the region can take different forms and pursue different agendas. His insistence on context and process and the recognition of distinctive types, such as the "landscape", "resistance" and "winning" region, is a useful corrective to simplistic approaches that are often applied to the subject. This chapter will explore the emergence of North East England as an identifiable region during the modern period, a region that has claimed to be "England's most distinctive" and the one with the strongest identity.[1] This survey will examine a range of factors that are often singled out as keys to the region's particularity: the economy, cultural and political traditions and one that in the British context is often ignored, patterns of consumption. We will explore the multiplicity of agendas, some contradictory, which created and shaped the North East over the last two centuries and the process of reflection where the agenda setters created the region to their own accord.

All of these share a territorial dimension although this is never fixed and is constantly subjected to change. Our agenda is further complicated by the tendency prior to the 1920s to include the North East inside a more generalised "North" that was never clearly defined. The work of David Levine and Keith Wrightson has emphasised the remarkable transition in North East England from an agrarian to an industrial economy during the seventeenth and eighteenth centuries which set the region apart as a distinctive economic system. Levine and Wrightson's study of the early years of the coalfield carefully observed the emergence of a collective identity amongst the North East's coalminers, a consciousness which transcended individual communities and identified with and sought to embrace all those who laboured in the "Great Northern Coalfield".

Michael Flinn's work on the region's early iron industry confirms Levine and Wrightson's argument that Britain's first proletariat were to be found in early eighteenth-century County Durham and on Tyneside.[2] It should come as little surprise that the first working class employed in the mines and iron works of Tyneside and Wearside were often perceived as a "race apart" from the rest of the English population – even though they were generally in this period much better paid than other workers. The colliery village with its "pit row" housing stock, smoke and heaps was an alien landscape that usually shocked visitors. The growth of lead mining in the nearby North Pennines and coalmining and iron making in West Cumberland was often presented as parts of a common economic system. The government's mining inspectorate treated this as a single area; the new profession of mining engineer adopted the same territory and Lord Lonsdale in 1829 made a payment to the Newcastle based Natural History Society to include Cumberland, where he had extensive coal interests, in the Society's project to produce a geological map of the region.[3] The common feature of this economic system was that it was based upon the extraction of minerals, a system which required a particular type of worker who was often directly or indirectly employed by a member of the land owning elite. The relationship between this elite and the transformation to an economy that converted minerals into metal and machines – referred to in this study as carboniferous capitalism – is well known and has been the subject of scholarly research.[4] Britain's first industrial society was located on the surface of the region's mineral wealth and this geographical reality was inescapable.

The geography of the traditional administrative system was little affected by industrialisation. The counties continued to function along traditional lines during the process of industrialisation and the diocese ecclesiastical courts were often involved in disputes concerning mineral extraction. The fact that the coalfield was largely confined to Northumberland and Durham, which was also broadly in line with the Diocese of Durham, meant that the burgeoning coal trade could utilise the existing forms of administration. Interestingly the miners themselves were to use the county format when they finally established permanent trade unions during the nineteenth century.[5] County institutions were further strengthened after the 1860s army reforms which emphasised the importance of the county regiments.

The nineteenth century often displayed the amalgamation of regional and county terminology. The region's gentlemanly and business elite socialised in the Northern Counties Club located in central Newcastle. The charitable organisations which established schools for the blind and the deaf formally adopted the title of Northern Counties School. One of the region's premier institutions of teacher training was Newcastle's Northern Counties College. The new profession of mining engineer when granted their royal charter in 1872 chose as their organisation's name "The North of England Institute of Mining Engineering".[6] And as the emerging middle and working classes developed their political voice during the nineteenth century, one of their most formidable organisations was the Northern Political Union of the early 1830s.[7] Yet many of the people who were members of these organisations also formed the Northumberland, Durham and Tyneside Natural History Society in 1838 which quickly became one of largest middle- and upper-class institutions in the region. Thus the middle classes were perfectly at ease in slipping from county to regional nomenclature and rarely worried about geographical boundaries. What is interesting is that during the long nineteenth century of economic expansion extra-county regional institutions evolved which widened cultural horizons, promoted professional efficiency and realised more effective forms of charity. They were generally concerned with their own particular area of activity and although it has been claimed that the same members of the local elite dominated the economic and charitable institutions it is difficult to discern the emergence of a common regional agenda.[8]

Up until the twentieth century a variety of terms were used to designate the region's territory and during the nineteenth century we see the growing use of "Northumbria". The region could draw upon a distant history to claim the dignity of a former kingdom with a noble heroic heritage and during the modern period this occurred in a frequent, if uncoordinated manner. The industrial elite by the 1870s were abandoning Tyneside for the hills, peel towers and abandoned castles of Northumbria. Sir William Armstrong the region's major industrialist moved to Rothbury in Northumberland and later refurbished Bamburgh Castle and when the confiscated Langley Barony, with its castles and bastle house farms and its romantic association with the executed young Derwentwaters, was auctioned by the Greenwich Hospital in 1882, the lots were keenly contested by the coal owning and industrial elite, including James Joicey, W. D. Cruddas and the coal owning antiquarian Cadwallader Bates.[9] In their retreat from the industrialised conurbations these magnates created a new "Landscape Region" well away from the grime of Tyneside and the mess for which they were largely responsible. Armstrong's Northumbrian enthusiasms were further displayed in the street names of the Newcastle suburb of Heaton built upon land which he owned.[10] Whilst the elite created their pastiche Northumbria from derelict buildings, with the re-establishment of the Catholic hierarchy we see Northumbria being appropriated to form a religious landscape. The Catholic Diocese of Newcastle and Hexham was obviously anxious to reconnect with Saint Wilfrid's Hexham and numerous Catholic Churches built during the second half of the nineteenth century were dedicated to the four great Northumbrian saints of Aidan, Cuthbert, Oswald and Wilfrid.

So far we have seen a variety of names and constructs, created by diverse groups, used to describe and define regional territory. There is no evidence that people objected to any of them. This is not surprising as the region has lacked exact boundaries since the tenth century. Counties, dioceses, coalfields, administrative, charitable and professional boundaries have been established since the Middle Ages, but have never coincided to form a precise area. Such loose definition has been joined during the twentieth century by the usage of the term "North East". It needs to be underlined that the term "North East" to describe the area roughly covered by Northumberland and Durham was virtually unknown prior to the 1930s. True there was a North East Railway Company, but its headquarters were in York. The term first receives wide regional and national coverage in 1929 when the North East Coast Shipbuilders and Engineering Institute organised an exhibition in order to attract business for the region's rapidly ailing heavy industrial economy.[11] Thus the "North East" became synonymous with the inter-war depression as the term was increasingly adopted in government literature and the press. J.B. Priestley, Bill Brandt, the Pilgrims Trust and the Jarrow March developed an iconography for this post-1929 de facto region, which was quickly embedded into the national imagination. The region in the 1930s was given its new name as part of a national agenda set up to address the concerns of the government, industrialists and intellectuals on the plight of the "Special Areas".

Shifting geographical boundaries have fuelled internal and external debates on the lineaments of the region. Fawcett's map of the early twentieth century was a response to Churchill's call for "Home Rue all Round" – a proposal for strong, large regional political and administrative units for Britain and Ireland – as a solution to the "Irish Question".[12] *The Provinces of England* remains a challenging book where the author attempts to establish regions that would have a geographic, economic and cultural logic. Fawcett, hailing from Barnard Castle and acutely aware of the problems faced on Teesside by separate county administrations, was anxious to establish "provinces" that were untrammelled by medieval patterns of political and ecclesiastical governance. Viable provinces for Fawcett required an economic and social rationale, a shared culture and a readily identifiable capital. The Great Northern Coalfield, Newcastle's cultural and economic dominance, and the close economic connections with parts of Cumberland and Westmorland were the features which readily defined what Fawcett called the "North".[13] Fawcett's map was adopted, with some amendments, by the government after the First World War. Beginning with Civil Defence regions other ministries used the map as the basis of administrative areas.[14]

The increasing complexity of twentieth-century society required units of administration that connected with economic and social reality. The inter-war depression as well as being of interest to metropolitan artists and anthropologists also provoked political action. The Jarrow March was just one of many that originated in the region and the rising fortunes of the Labour Party locally were a similar response to economic turbulence. We begin to see the emergence of what Aronsson has described as a "resisting" region. The war provided a temporary respite to the long decline of carboniferous capitalism and by the 1950s stubbornly high levels of unemployment were being recorded. The sense that the region was not sharing in the post-war boom served to boost Labour support during the period.[15]   The Conservative government responded to this development by giving one of its major cabinet figures, Quentin Hogg, the task of reversing the region's comparative decline. Hogg's arrival at Newcastle Central Station wearing a cloth cap perfectly encapsulated the negotiation that was underway between central government and the resisting region. The victory of the Labour Party at the General Election in 1964 saw an even greater commitment from the government to meet the demands from the North East. The establishment of the Northern Development Council to plan and promote regional regeneration was the resolution of this negotiation. Spatially following Fawcett's province, the new body included industrialists, trade unionists and was headed by T. Dan Smith, arguably the first major political figure produced in the region since Joseph Cowen. This external construct proved to be relatively enduring and interestingly provoked no internal opposition. The charismatic T. Dan Smith rose to fame as "Mr Newcastle", spearheading the far reaching re-development of the regional capital. The Development Council was legitimised by his presence and in return he used his new position to transform himself into "Mr North". His longstanding interest in the arts was demonstrated by his role in establishing the Northern East Arts Association which became the template for Northern Arts and other regional arts organisations; whilst his leadership of the Blaydon Races Centenary Celebration served to transform the region's popular culture from its latent torpor into a phase on manifest vigour. Smith's genius was his ability to link the region's nascent cultural identity with the new Labour Government's modernisation ambitions. A natural ally of George Brown and his National Plan, Smith slipped easily into corporativist clothes. Dan the moderniser dazzled many with his grandiose development plans and his seat on the board of the newly formed Tyne Tees Television Company alongside such leading regional figures as Carr Ellison, Pease and Ridley, personified the broad appeal for the regional project.[16] His reign, however, was brief and by the time he fell from grace the deep rooted economic problems were getting worse. The period of optimism during the 1960s disappeared with Smith's demise and the corporate region became the domain of bureaucrats. The cultural genie could not be put back into the bottle and whilst the political vision became lost in the fog of Quangoland the region embarked upon a journey of cultural self-awareness that to outsiders can appear as self-obsession.

Since 1929 other definitions and names devised by non-governmental agencies and institutions have emerged in the cultural sector. A variety of institutions, personalities and movements have helped to create a cultural landscape that is quickly recognisable. The modern media has been particularly active in providing new regional descriptors. Asa Briggs in 1966 predicted that broadcasting regions could serve to redefine England's regional map.[17] Donald Read made similar comments in his classic *The English Provinces*.[18] The "North" as a BBC region was based in Manchester from 1929 and covered an area from Nottingham to Scotland. Transmission difficulties necessitated the establishment of a local station in Newcastle. Initially called Radio Newcastle, when the station was given a wider remit in the 1930's the corporation managers toyed with the idea of calling the station Radio Bernicia! Significantly the possibility of a Radio North East was never raised.[19] The original BBC "North" has proved enduring both as an institution with its orchestra and extensive production facilities based in Manchester. Recent mergers and takeovers between independent television companies have given rise to "Granadaland", a region similar to the BBC that stretches from the Scottish and Welsh borders to the Midlands.[20]

The television "North" needs to be placed alongside and compared with other cultural boundaries, particularly those that are generated internally. Dialect, for many, is the region's most distinctive feature. In recent years it has undergone scholarly scrutiny by Bill Griffiths who has shown that the inheritance of Old English is the basic ingredient of North East regional dialect – despite claims of profound difference between Tynesiders and Wearsiders.[21] This revival of interest in dialect is similar to that of the Victorian period when working-class songsters and their audiences revelled in the musical potential of the local tongue whilst middle-class antiquarians obsessively compiled wordlists, many of which were published in Cowen's local popular press. The material culture of the region displayed at Beamish Museum and its presentation is largely representative of the coalfield, which takes pride of place in the Museum's theme year of 1913. The region's notable tradition of comedy was personified by Bobby Thompson from Shildon, in County Durham and the star of *Wotcher Geordie*. This highly successful regional radio show attracted over one million listeners during the 1950s, but famously flopped when broadcast to a wider audience.[22] Thomson's humour lost its meaning once he travelled beyond the working men's clubs of Teesside and his fan base remained obdurately regional. Football is another cultural activity that thanks to the longevity of the Northern League still displays its roots in the geography of carboniferous capitalism.[23] Folk music is similarly located in this territory, but with a propensity to meld and connect with older rural traditions.[24] These are all examples of phenomena which can only be historically analysed in a regional context. Many are the product of the long dominance of carboniferous capitalism, with the exception of dialect which found the transition to an industrial society remarkably easy.[25] Even the large influx of Irish, into the dialect heartland of Tyneside, estimated by one scholar to account for over 20% of the conurbation's population, had little impact with a virtual absence of words that are specifically Irish.[26]

Patterns of consumption can be equally revealing, yet remain under-researched. As long ago as 1739 David Hume noted that:

> *Men are also vain of the temperature of the climate, in which they were born; of the fertility of their native soil; of the goodness of the wines, of the fruits or victuals, produced by it; of the softness or force of their language...*[27]

Britain, unlike France, lacks a historiography of *terroir* yet the notion that we "eat our region" was familiar to Hume. A passion for "stottie" bread and "savaloy dips" is in noticeable decline as North East cuisine and eating habits become increasingly global. Griffiths' research into the dialect history of North East cooking did reveal a distinctive style that unsurprisingly was high in carbohydrate but that also reflected the domestic arrangements of a large mining workforce.[28] Leek growing and showing remains a regional pastime, albeit amongst older members of the working class. The nationalisation and globalisation of food production and preparation is pushing aside regional cuisine in Britain, unless it is championed by a celebrity television chef! Yet well into the nineteenth century regional cuisine would have dominated most people's diets. Poorer folk were well aware of the distinctively parochial origins of their ingredients: Holy Island rabbits, Shields white fish, Tyne and Tweed salmon and North Sea Coast oysters were staples of Newcastle's markets and local market gardeners supplied fruit and vegetables.[29] The region may have lacked vineyards but its beer inspired many popular poems and songs. Dress and style could also be distinctively regional. The Bonnie Pit Laddies and Lassies who graced the quays and streets of Newcastle at weekends with their multi-coloured silk waistcoats contributed to a famously lively street life.[30] It was not until the 1870s that the working-class male uniform of the cloth cap, dark woollen suit and white muffler replaced the silk waistcoats and bright blues of the keelmen and pitmen as the dominant popular male style.[31] This rich material was to provide many of the ingredients for the cultural revival in the 1960s.[32]

Regions can also play an important role in patterns of shopping and distribution. The proximity of the Scottish Border and Edinburgh tea smuggling gangs limited the number of small shops in the North during the eighteenth century.[33] The pattern of mining settlement in the coalfield with colliery villages beyond the passenger railway lines encouraged vigorous forms of retail self-help. Rochdale was the oldest surviving retail co-operative society, but Blaydon established in 1858 was the second. The co-operative movement rapidly dominated the world of shopping in the region where, by 1900, society membership levels were the highest in Britain.[34] Bainbridge of Newcastle is arguably the world's first department store which served the needs of that new social strata created by industrialisation in the region, the lower middle class. Binns of Sunderland established similar institutions in other northern towns and cities, and Fenwick of Northumberland Street in Newcastle became Britain's first "walk round" Parisian style *Grand Magasin* in 1900.[35] This readiness to adopt new retail systems is underscored with the construction of the Grainger Market in 1835, Britain's second indoor market and the first to be architecturally designed.[36] Geography clearly was a factor in this retail institutional precociousness. The isolation from metropolitan markets; with ports that generally imported ballast rather than goods; the rise of a lower middle class commercial bureaucracy; the scattered, but relatively permanent nature, of mining settlements with their own particular class structure resulted in a propensity for retail innovation all served to shape a distinctive shopping culture whose scale often surprises visitors.

Alcohol and sociability are well known hallmarks of consumption and popular culture in North East England. Newcastle, with its free wine "pants" on royal birthdays and coronations, located on the Quayside and Bigg Market, paid for by the Corporation, was a magnet for revellers during the eighteenth and early nineteenth century.[37] Artisans from Tyneside and Wearside would assemble in large crowds and march through Newcastle displaying examples of their craft ranging from glass to footwear and conclude with concerts in public houses. Trains filled with passengers from Blyth, Sunderland and beyond poured into mid-nineteenth century Newcastle to watch the famous Tyneside rowers compete with their Thames rivals, events that attracted much gambling and as they were often organised by local publicans prodigious consumption of alcohol.[38] Horseracing had a similar association with drink and the Newcastle Hoppings, the largest travelling funfair in Europe, was set up as a temperance festival, strategically located on the Town Moor, to divert the regional crowd on their way to the new racecourse at Gosforth, during "Race Week", the traditional June coalfield holiday.[39] Recent research on the "Big Night Out" confirms that these traditional patterns of sociability continue, with the exception that Newcastle now attracts national and international revellers and Wearsiders have during recent years preferred to stay in Sunderland.[40] This distinctiveness in various forms of consumption is rooted in the particular patterns of industrialisation. The geography of industrial settlements, the peculiarities of class structure and importantly the continuation of an economy that produced a workshop and mining culture rather than a factory one, assured the longevity of a raucous plebeian culture.[41]

Sunderland's often commented upon hostility to Newcastle, a point used by some as a counter to claims that the North East has a strong identity, is recent in origin. For much of its history Sunderland was administratively and politically part of Chester le Street and since the industrial revolution has shared many links to Newcastle. Jack Commons' tongue-in-cheek comments on Tyne Wear differences, written in the early 1950s, were aimed at a regional audience that was close enough to be able to laugh at each other without feeling offence. Bobby Thompson's humour often drew upon this collective form of self-deprecation and expressed through the region's brand of dialect humour, a phenomena analysed by Tom Hadaway who dubbed it "...a language within a language."[42] But it cannot be denied that in recent years a gulf has opened between the two cities. In some ways this is puzzling: both rivers lost their shipbuilding and mining industries; levels of poverty and deprivation have been strikingly similar and politically both have been bastions of "Old Labour". The origins of recent Tyne Wear hostility undoubtedly lies in post-1960s football rivalry. A survey of more than a century of Newcastle United versus Sunderland derby matches reveals that the games were for most of the century manifestations of what the *Evening Chronicle* described as a "Neighbourly rivalry", conducted by fans who "erected a holiday atmosphere with bugles, bells and rattles."[43] The North East along with the rest of the country experienced the onset of football violence during the late 1960s, the game at Roker Park in late December 1967 is the first where violence between fans is reported, setting a trend which has continued with varying degrees of intensity.[44] What is interesting and requires more investigation is that hostility between rival groups of mainly young people at football matches has become a trigger for a generalised antipathy between two cities. Perhaps 40 years of fear amongst young men in visiting their neighbouring city has entered the collective psyche of both places. The explanation must acknowledge that this hostility is rooted in two places in the *same* region and its existence does not deny, but rather reinforces the reality of the region.

Patterns of regional consumption and leisure invariably connect to social class. Three centuries of heavy industrial dominance created mining and engineering settlements that to outsiders could appear monocultural in their social structure and manifestations of sociability. The labour history of the region's mining industry has been well documented by Levine, Wrightson and Colls and requires little further comment.[45] Shipbuilding, iron and steel making, heavy chemicals and engineering have had less historical attention.[46] Women in the region await their historian. But whether on the coalfield, or in the heavy industrial districts of the three north eastern rivers, the working-class ethos of the region is often overwhelming. Aspects of working-class life can be endearing, but for some the industrial heritage can be a curse. Health statistics have for long been the poorest in England and the North East is one of the nation's poorest regions for educational achievement. This has been traced back to poor rates of literacy during the nineteenth century and commentators have frequently noted the tradition in carboniferous capitalism of training young workers on the job.[47] The weakness of the North East's enterprise culture, measured by the lowest rate of new business start-ups in Britain, is attributable to the tradition of large units of production within carboniferous capitalism and in mining in particular; the persistence of absentee owners and their replacement by a management of industrial professionals rather than entrepreneurs.[48] The region's middle class are predominantly found in the public sector and there is a remarkable indifference to the world of business.

The rise of class society was a two way process. Northern magnates were pioneers of the English tradition of the industrial and commercial upper class sending their sons to southern boarding schools. The Carr-Ellisons and the Coatsworths were fearful of their sons talking like pitmen which resulted in their withdrawal from local grammar schools such as Keppier's In Houghton le Spring, the traditional academy for the region's young male elite.[49] The expansion of colliery villages and the growth of industrial suburbs accelerated the separation of the classes. The regional grand families abandoned their large homes near their economic interests and were in rapid retreat to rural areas of Northumberland and Durham, the Tyne valley being particularly favoured. The middle classes were equally prone to social separation. The Parliamentary enquiry into local government on Tyneside in the late 1930s was shocked to discover the conurbation's middle class huddled in their ghettoes of Gosforth and Jesmond and the unusual high level of spatial separation between social classes. Gosforth, then a separate Urban District Council, notoriously pumped its sewage north, at great expense, rather than have its effluent flow through Newcastle.[50] This desire to keep popular culture at arms length is underlined by the propensity of the region's middle and professional classes to send their children to private schools.[51] This interplay of economic society, social class and culture played out on the North East stage is an example of the usefulness of the regional historical method. Moreover, the regional format is well suited to the comparative approach. British industrialisation *must* be studied in its regional contexts in order to fully grasp its complexities. Why, for instance, did Lancashire cotton entrepreneurs take pride in retaining their dialect and using it for communicating with their workers for more than half a century after North East businessmen had abandoned theirs?[52] Answering such a question will involve the analysis of historical factors well known to historians, and the regional comparison may help reveal the complex process of causation.

The region does not always provide a neat template of interaction between spatial and temporal processes. Politics and the region can confound the predictions of those who read too much into cultural particularity. The North was famous for its nineteenth century radicalism from the reform movement of the 1830s, through Chartism, the Republicanism of the Cowenite Liberals of the 1860s and the widespread support for foreign liberation movements.[53] During the twentieth century much of the region became one of the staunchest centres of Labour Party support and its safe seats are still much prized by major party figures.[54] What is, and has been, notably absent in North East politics for much of the modern period is a regional agenda. The radical and reform movements of the nineteenth century were quintessentially national in their objectives, and when not concerned with parliamentary issues they were championing European ones. Regions, for nineteenth-century English radicals, were synonymous with backward area of *ancient regime* Europe, places whose salvation lay in the hands of the modernising liberal republic. Despite the economic turbulence of the twentieth century the North East continued to seek solutions in Westminster. T. Dan Smith, arguably Britain's most prominent twentieth-century regional political leader, at the height of his influence, placed his faith in government funded regional development agencies and Scandinavian public sector architecture and social housing.[55] Despite Smith's fall from grace his period of power heralded the plethora of agencies and "quangos" that have been largely responsible for the region's subsequent development. It is little wonder that after four decades of governance by bureaucratic elite, and the often cynical erosion of local government by Westminster, the region's electorate lost its ability to imagine change being realised by grassroots political processes. The politically correct world of "partnerships" and "stakeholders" has failed to rejuvenate a faith in local politics, a point demonstrated by the abysmally low participation rates in local elections and the resounding "No" to the Regional Assembly at the 2004 referendum.[56]

The debacle of the North East Assembly referendum is a salient lesson in the shifting interplay of regional factors. The Assembly campaign was conceived in the first storms of Thatcherite economic reforms, a process that hit the North East hard. The region was one of the first to suffer the effects of what was to be a fundamental transformation of the British economic system. The North East was also one of the last to feel the benefits of restructuring. But, during the years of the Assembly campaign unemployment fell sharply, living standards rose, the urban landscape was transformed, coal mining and much of carboniferous capitalism disappeared, the region's head was turned by rapid rises in house values and "New Labour" with many of its leaders holding seats in the North East all served to put a spring in the local step. More importantly were changing generational experiences. Most people live and experience the world within their generational cohort. Some undergo dramatic turn of events whether contemporaries of the Romantics during the late 1780s, young socialists during the early twentieth century, or 1960s "baby boomers". Few under forty in North East England today have any experience of working within or besides the noise and dirt of carboniferous capitalism. In recent decades in Britain and elsewhere there has been a major move away from industry and manufacturing towards a concentration upon retailing and services. The rise of this new economy has largely been

concentrated in cities and this has had an impact upon the utilisation of regional space. Former mining villages and industrial towns are being transformed into commuter settlements and what one social scientist described as the "colliery aesthetic" is disappearing fast as "pit rows" sprout bright white conservatories and nature reserves and commercial garden centres are found in former colliery yards.[57] The concentration of retail and leisure in Newcastle/Gateshead has seen the reduction of these functions in towns such as Consett and Stanley which were formerly largely self-sufficient.[58] Northumberland Street and the riverside in Newcastle and the Metrocentre in Gateshead form the new epicentre of the regional economy. Consumption and education – Newcastle alone has over fifty thousand students in further and higher education – have redefined the relationship between the city and its hinterland.[59]

The rejection by England's "most distinctive region" of a modicum of political devolution is really not surprising. As we have seen popular politics in the North East have usually been part of national movements and campaigns; when they have taken a regional turn such as in the 1930s and 1980s, the region took on its resistance apparel. Yet an agenda structured as "defensive" is always vulnerable to economic upturns. It also does not follow that a "cultural region" is a "political region"– the reality is more complex.[60] A sense of difference is not necessarily a sense of separation and it could be argued that north easterners have a strong sense of *national* identity. Britain's most martial region needs the nation's armed forces as much as its major football teams need the Premier League and rising levels of home ownership towards the national average, and increasing prosperity, along with the virtual disappearance of the old industrial economy, have serve to weaken traditional forms of working-class identity.[61]

When Fawcett drew his map of the "North" he was at pains to point out that Newcastle was an ideal type for his model of "Regional Capital". It was, in the early twentieth century, the centre of an industrial region and its functions included servicing the North's economy commercially and culturally. Today, greater Newcastle accounts for, according to one estimate, over sixty five per cent of jobs in the North East and the region is increasingly clustering into two "city regions", with Middlesbrough as the other centre.[62] Newcastle's ascendancy and the rejection of the Assembly in 2004 has prompted some analysts and institutions to see the City Region as the form of governance that is most suitable to the contemporary North East, a point underlined by the recent OECD report on Newcastle. This report formed part of an international series on city regions that includes Öresund (Malmö/Copenhagen), and Mexico City, argues that they constitute a growing trend in terms of social and economic development and offer the best form of political and administrative governance. What is striking in these developments is the speed with which the political and bureaucratic elite have been able to redefine the region's territory in little more than a decade. In 1999 the old regional development area was reduced from roughly Fawcett's "Province", to Durham Northumberland and the Tees Valley and less than 7 years later serious discussion now centres around the concept of the two cities. Popular indifference to these boundary changes might suggest that their impact upon the consciousness of ordinary folk is limited. On the other hand, this acceptance could also be said to reflect the realities of day to day living, or at least contemporary patterns of work, consumption and leisure concentrated in these urban areas.

For the development of a methodology appropriate to the historical study of regions the experience of the North/North East offers several useful reflections. Our first point of note is the distinction between internal and external definitions. National organisations and institutions including government ministries, the BBC, international bodies such as the EU and the OECD, have served up different geographies often based upon their own internal concerns. Metropolitan cultural elites have since the late 1950s held a fascination with the nation's northern "other", but have often imposed their own caricatures of people and space.[63] Recent national media attention on cultural developments and sociability add to this package. But attempted definitions often end up as dialogues. To what extent does the contemporary North East create its own identity and how much of this process of representation is a response to external expectations of North East authenticity?[64] What unites the Bonnie Pit Laddie and Lassie with the Bigg Market revellers is the extent to which their urban sartorial performance was for an external as much as an internal audience. The often commented upon tendency for dialect to develop extremes of impenetrability when outsiders are within earshot can be another example of this phenomenon and in some cases a form of social exclusion.[65] Such processes are not, however, exclusive to the North East and, as Philip Payton's chapter on Cornwall in this volume demonstrates, are likely to be found in other English regions. Further comparison with other European regions may help to establish how far the creation of an identity in response to external expectations is a peculiarity of English regional culture. For the historical study of regions we need to avoid an all encompassing conceptual formulation of the "Region" and instead approach it as a process which contains a range of elements and practices. Geography, culture, the economy, language, consumption, politics all make up the region but they are all in a constant state of flux, often at very different tempos and directions. Recent geographical work on "Scales Theory" emphasises the differential that exists between peoples' perceptions of space, culture and everyday life within the same region.[66] Nonetheless in the North East there have been specific points at which convergence between these different elements appears to have been significant for regional self consciousness. The popularisation of dialect during the Victorian period is one instance, and the 1960s renaissance of regional self-awareness witnessed an unprecedented degree of affinity between politics and culture. The temporal and spatial complexities that the term "the North East" embraces, indicates that we need a conceptual approach that recognises and can serve to capture the regional dynamic and probe those moments of change which witness the emergence of the reflective and conscious region. Finally, we need to recognise that historians are part of the process, and that our role as makers and breakers of "myths" is often integral to the regional project!

Notes

1. A. Green and A. Pollard, *Regional Identity in North East England*, Woodbridge, 2007.
2. M. Flinn, *Men of Iron The Crowley's in the Early Iron Industry*, Edinburgh, 1962.
3. T. Russell Goddard, *History of the Natural History Society of Northumberland, Durham and Newcastle upon Tyne*, Newcastle upon Tyne, 1929.
4. A.W Purdue, *Merchants and Gentry in North East England*, Sunderland 1999; E. Hughes, *North Country Life in the Eighteenth Century*, Durham, 1952.
5. Rob Colls, *Pitmen and the Northern Coalfield*, Manchester, 1987.
6. The British Association's *Industrial Guide*, published in 1889 to accompany their Newcastle conference discusses the geography of Northern mining engineering and safety inspection.
7. D.Ridley, 'The Spital Field Demonstrations, 1832', *North East Labour History Society Bulletin*, 26, 1992.
8. *The Making of the Ruling Class*, Benwell CDP, Newcastle upon Tyne, 1978.
9. D. Telford, 'The Barony of Langley and the Lordship of Haydon Bridge', *Haydon News*, July 2007.
10. Coquet, Meldon, Tosson, Simonside, Rothbury, etc. are a few examples of Heaton street names which were built in the 1890s and early 1900s.
11. J.F. Clarke, *Building Ships on the North East Coast*, Whitley Bay, 1997; *A Centenary of Service to Engineering and Shipbuilding. A Centenary History of the North East Coast Institute of Engineering and Shipbuilding*, Newcastle upon Tyne, 1984.
12. C.B. Fawcett, *The Provinces of England, A Study of Some Geographical Aspects of Devolution.*, revised with a new preface by W. Gordon East and S. W. Wooldridge, London, 1961.
13. It is interesting to note that Fawcett's region is quite similar to the government's mining inspectorate region of the 1860s.
14. *Ibid.* Editors preface to the second edition.
15. The Conservatives lost control of Newcastle to Labour in 1957.
16. N. Vall, 'Regionalism and Cultural History. The Case of North East England 1918–1976', in A. Green and A. J. Pollard, (eds), *Regional Identity in North East England*, Woodbridge, 2007.

17. A, Briggs, 'Themes in Northern History', *Northern History*, Volume 1, 1966.

18. D. Read, *The English Provinces*, London, 1964.

19. See N. Vall, 'Regionalism and Cultural History'.

20. *Granada Television, The First Generation*, J. Finch, (ed), Manchester, 2002.

21. Bill Griffiths, *Dictionary of North East Dialect*, Introduction, Newcastle upon Tyne, 2005.

22. N. Vall, 'Regionalism and Cultural History'.

23. B. Hunt, *Northern Goalfields, Official Centenary History of the Northern League*,1889–1989, Newcastle upon Tyne, 1989.

24. Judith Murphy, 'The Folk Music Revival on Tyneside', Northumbria University, PhD. Thesis, 2007.

25. Bill Griffiths, *Pitmatic: the talk of the North East Coalfield*, Newcastle upon Tyne, 2007.

26. D.Byrne, 'Immigrants and the Formation of the North East Working Class', *North East Labour History Society, Bulletin*, 30, 1996. Bill Griffiths, *Dictionary of North East Dialect*, Introduction.

27. David Hume, *A Treatise on Human Nature*, Oxford, 2000.

28. Bill Griffiths, *Stotty 'n' Spice Cake:The Story of North East Cooking*, Newcastle upon Tyne, 2006.

29. *The Picture of Newcastle upon Tyne*, D. Akenhead, Newcastle upon Tyne, 1807.

30. I have discussed this further in 'Sociability and the City', in R. Colls and B. Lancaster, (eds) *Newcastle, A Modern History*, Chichester, 2001.

31. The *Newcastle Weekly Chronicle*, April 1873, commented on this shift in their lengthy article on the miners' suffrage demonstration.

32. Frank Graham's local publishing business was partly based upon reproducing nineteenth century works. Other local publishers enjoyed a boom in reprinting traditional regional songs. See J. Murphy, 'The Folk Music Revival on Tyneside', Northumbria University, PhD. Thesis, 2007.

33. H. and L. Mui, *Shops and Shopkeeping in Eighteenth Century England*, London, 1989.

34. See J. Hugman, 'Joseph Cowen and the Blaydon Cooperative Society: A North East model', in B. Lancaster and P. Maguire, (eds), *Towards the Co-operative Commonwealth, Essays in the History of Co-operation*, Manchester, 1996.

35. B. Lancaster, *The Department Store*, A Social History, London, 1995.

36. See B. Lancaster, 'Shopping in Newcastle', *North East History*, 2000.

37. 'Pant' is a regional term for fountain. See the author's 'Sociability and the City', in Colls and Lancaster, *Newcastle, A Modern History*.

38. *Ibid*. See also H. Taylor, 'Sporting Heroes', in Colls and Lancaster, *Geordies, Roots of Regionalism*, Newcastle upon Tyne, 2006.

39. V. Toulman, 'Temperance and Pleasure at the Hoppings: A History of Newcastle's Town Moor Fair', *North East Labour History Society Bulletin*, 28, 1995.

40. North East Regional Information Partnership, *City Region Profile Report*, Newcastle upon Tyne, 2007.

41. See R. Samuel, 'The Workshop of the World', In *History Workshop Journal*, volume 3, 1978; E. P. Thompson, 'Eighteenth century English Society: Class Struggle without Class?', *Social History* Volume 3,2, 1978.

42. T. Hadaway, 'Comic Dialect', in Colls and Lancaster, *Geordies, Roots of Regionalism*, Newcastle upon Tyne, 2006.

43. *Evening Chronicle*, March 26, 1956. I am indebted to Tom Lynch for this reference.

44. *Evening Chronicle*, December 30, 1967. Again thanks to Tom Lynch for this information. There is a scholarly debate on the origins of football violence in Britain, see E. Dunning, P. Murphy, J. Williams, *The Roots of Football Hooliganism*, London, 1988, R. Holt and T. Mason, *Sport in Britain 1945-2000*, Oxford, 2000.

45. D. Levine and K. Wrightson, *The Making of Industrial Society*, Oxford 1991; R. Colls, *The Pitmen of the Northern Coalfield*, Manchester, 1987.

46. A. Potts, (ed.), *Shipbuilders and Engineers*, North East Labour History Society, Newcastle upon Tyne, 1989.

47. R. Houston, 'Illiteracy amongst Newcastle Shoemakers', *Archaeology Aeolia*, 1982; W.B. Stephens, 'Illiteracy in the North East Coalfield', *Northern History*, Volume 37, 2000.

48. IPPR, *State of the Region*, November, 2005.

49. A.W. Purdue, *Merchants and Gentry in North East England*, E. Hughes, *North Country Life in the Eighteenth Century*.

50. D. M. Goodfellow, *Tyneside: The Social Facts*, Newcastle upon Tyne, 1940.

51. See *The State of the Region* for a survey of the region's education.

52. P. Joyce, *Work, Society and Politics, The Culture of the factory in Late Victorian England*, Hassocks, 1980.

53. For the reform movement see D.Ridley, 'The Spital Fields Demonstration and the Parliamentary Reform Movement in Newcastle', *North East Labour History*, 26, 1992; Chartism is discussed in Colls, *Pitmen*; see Joan Hugman, 'Joseph Cowen and Radical Liberalism', Northumbria University, PhD thesis, 1992, for the most complete analysis of Joseph Cowen and Northern radical politics.

54. James Ramsay MacDonald, Sydney Webb, Hugh Dalton were notable local MPs during the first half of the twentieth century. More recently local members to grace Westminster include Alan Milburn, Peter Mandelson, Mo Mowlem, David Milliband and Tony Blair.

55. N. Vall, *Cities in Decline Comparative History of Malmö and Newcastle after 1945*, Malmö, 2007; T. Dan Smith, *Dan Smith, an Autobiography*, Newcastle upon Tyne, 1970.

56. C. Foote-Wood, *The North East England, Land of the 100 Quangos*, Bishop Auckland, 2002; K. Knock, 'The North East Referendum: Lessons Learnt?', *Parliamentary Affairs*, Volume 59, No. 4, 2005; 'Why The North East said No', *ESRC Devolution Briefings*, Briefing No. 19, February 2005.

57. The former mining communities of Clara Vale and Quaking Houses are examples of this trend.

58. M. Benney, in his post-war ethnographic study of *Charity Main, A Coalfield Chronicle*, London, 1946 – a fictitious name for part of Stanley, County Durham – he noted how infrequently the inhabitants visited Newcastle.

59. The best source for contemporary statistical data on the region is North East Institute for Public Policy Research, *The State of the Region*, Newcastle upon Tyne, 2005.

60. See M. Archer, *Culture and Agency. The Place of culture in Social Theory*, Cambridge, 1988, for a cogent critique of social science models that fail to recognise the force and independence of cultural factors.

61. The region's martial tradition is discussed in D. Jackson, 'Two Black Eyes and a Broken Nose...', *Northern Review*, Volume 15, 2005.

62. North East Regional Information Partnership, *City Region Profile Report*, Newcastle upon Tyne, 2007; OECD, *Territorial Reviews, the Case of Newcastle in the North East of England*, OECD, 2006.

63. D. Russell, *Looking North, Northern England and the National Imagination*, Manchester, 2004, presents a useful survey of this phenomenon.

64. For an interesting discussion of 'authenticity' and regional culture, see, N. Vall, 'Bohemians and Pitman Painters in North East England', 1930–1970, *Visual Culture in Britain*, Volume 5, issue 1, 2004.

65. J. Ardargh, *A Tale of Five Cities Life in Provincial Europe*, London 1979.

66. See 'The Significance of Scale in Cross Border Interaction: The Case of Catalonia', in *Borders Matter: Transboundary Regions in Contemporary Europe*, Institut For Graenseregionsforsking, Aabenraa, Denmark, 2001.

Chapter Three

Time and tide in North Eastern England

Brian K. Roberts

The view from the former Roman signal station at Goldsborough, above Kettleness, on the Yorkshire coast is singularly thought provoking; it overlooks a wide expanse of sea, notably northwards to Sunderland in Durham. The former tower was part of a chain, extending southwards from the line of the wall to Scarborough and ultimately Filey just north of Flamborough Head (Jones and Mattingly, 1990, 131–140, map 4:67). Archaeological opinion holds that these stations contained structures of the order of 30 meters high, and that they were used to co-ordinate the movements of Roman fleets based on the Humber, the Tees and the Tyne (Frere, 1998, 344–45; Salway, 1981, 383–84; Haywood, 1999, 69–70). This may be so, but there are two questions here: firstly, what were the coastguards on the lookout for? The level of investment suggests that this was for rather more than "three men in a boat". And secondly, what sort of boats and in what numbers? Post-dating the barbarian attacks in the wall line and populated lands to the south in AD 367 these watch-towers – and here we by-pass the national question of Roman coastal defences to focus regionally – suggest both maritime movement and maritime threat, while the scale of the system put into place suggests state-sponsorship. Without spreading to speculation about the signals exchanged between the coastal towers and any inland garrisons, we must accept that the menace from the sea was either directed at Roman coastal trade, and/or against local farming populations. Seafarers simply do not come on cattle-raids: they seek tradable movables such as precious objects and slaves. For a Pictish warrior's wife, a Romano-British girl represented the equivalent of being brought a washing machine today, offering, in addition, some consolation to the disposer of the gift for the effort involved. There is a very serious point here: the offspring of such unions is one way in which northern tribal societies developed internal social differentiation and slavery was a deeply ingrained custom. Of course, the concept of seaborne invasion – a sort of Picto-Scottish-Saxon Operation Overlord – is improbable, but centralized states take action when a threat damages large-scale economic interests of powerful people. South of the Wall, itself a fundamental and effective barrier to cattle raiding, this meant the taking of movable goods and slaves, for establishing sustained settlement footholds were not likely to have been the object of raids.

The very name Lindisfarne, perhaps, contains the Old English *faran*, "travellers" (Eckwall, 1970, 298–99), in this case coming from Lindsey, further south. If, next, we think of boats, vital amid the liminal zones between land and river, port and sea-highway, Seán McGrail presents two fundamental points. Firstly, that wooden plank boats built around skeleton frames were used in North West Europe during the early centuries AD and that secondly, seagoing vessels constructed of hides stretched over some form of framework, as seen in the Inuit *umiak* and the Irish *curach*, were also used (McGrail, 1998, 104–05, 184–86). Forty foot in length was perhaps an optimum for such boats, 20 to 30 feet was normal, while an upper practical limit may have been 60 feet. Caesar's account of the vessels of the Venetii of Brittany was reflected in the construction of the London Blackfriars ship of around AD 130, a decked, plank-built vessel some 18 metres (60 feet) in length, using a sail for propulsion and able to cope with Atlantic weather (Christensen, 1996, 68–71). Without going further into this technology, where words such as "seaworthy" and "sea kindly" loom large, we have here invoked icons of a vast range of accumulated and interlocking skills concerning construction and seamanship, with roots deep in prehistory (Gifford and Gifford, 1999, 83–85). Should this be doubted, consult McGrails and others' discussions of seamanship, pilotage and navigation (McGrail, 1998, 258–85; Christensen 1996, 120–28; Haywood 1999, 102–03). Also in my mind when writing these words is the powerful image of the surf-riding *curachs* of Robert Flatherty's *Man of Arran*, filmed in the 1930s. The north-eastern coast has always been ship-rich, with fishing, trade, travel and warfare. Tim Severin's reconstruction of a 36 foot skin boat, *The Brendan*, took fifty ox hides (Severin, 1978, 280–92): this was no small expense, even without the complexities of tanning and sewing. However, we should remember that Seebohm tells us that the *galenas* or honour price of a free tribesman in Wales was 120 cows and 180 for a chief of kindred, while in early Scottish law the hints available suggest *wergilds* of at least 100 and possibly 180 cows. Such numbers were raised by the kindred rather than the individual manslayer and all seem to have been productive cows, possibly with followers, the most expensive beasts of all. In the light of these figures, a raiding boat using fifty steer hides was well within the capacity of a single kindred (Seebohm, 1911, 42–49, 296–318).

As we look out from Goldborough we can only ask how many boats and how many men? Why were they on the move? In this, one must suspect that local population pressures played a part. The period between AD 100 and 400 saw some recovery of warmth and a tendency to be drier than in the period between 500 BC to AD 100, while this was followed by a distinct reversion to colder and wetter weather between AD 400 and 800 (McGrail, 1998, 259; Lamb, 1985, 373–74, 425). Do such details matter? Yes, for slight adjustments in summer temperatures and wetness can affect the base temperature or growth temperature of 4.4 degrees Celsius for cereals and 6.0 degrees Celsius for grasses (Parry, 1978,

80), while the effect of weather on a grain harvests has been amply demonstrated by the wet and stormy summers of recent times. The numbers of days in which such temperature levels are exceeded, expressed as day-degrees are, when applied in northern uplands, indicators of marginality and the potential for harvest failure (Parry, 1978, 74–85, 96–105: see figs 19 and 27) and hence the people-carrying capacity of the land. Thus, the spatial complexities and temporal variations of climate change, when average weather alters notably and perceptibly from satisfactory or good to appreciably worse, or indeed vice versa, can significantly affect the economic viability of local and regional agricultural populations in contexts when marginal land is present in substantial amounts. Often this impact may be quite local. This argument applies to much of the northern Britain and better weather, better harvests, creating local overpopulation may have been be one crucial push factor in seaborne raiding.

If this introduction to scholarly pedantry is insufficient, I have always wondered why go to Whitby? Some travellers in the autumn of AD 663 or the spring of AD 664 journeyed to debate the celebration of Easter and we can reflect on this. Two kings and contingents of clergy of the Roman and Celtic traditions assembled at *Streaneshalh*, identified with Whitby by early tradition (Smith, 1928, 126), a location chosen with sea travel in mind. While Wilfrid's journey from Ripon must have been by land, perhaps – to speculate – via the northern edge of Deira, between the cultivated lands of the edges of the Vale of Pickering and the moors to the north, but Colman of Lindisfarne, recently arrived from Ireland, may well have taken a sea route as might Cedd, Bishop of the East Saxons. Peter Hunter-Blair grasped the point when he noted that not only did Bede understand the significant aspects of the theory of tides, Northumbrian monks and bishops needed to have the a pragmatic knowledge of the sea; what we may term the sea-cunning of the fisherman, the sea-going Irish churchman and the trader-cum-pirate. Figure 1 shows two views, of coastal profiles, in impossibly good weather, produced in the 1930s and derived from the *North Sea Pilot* of 1960. This formal publication catches something of the transition from traditional knowledge, passed from father to son and grandson to the more formalized and scientific procedures outlined in the *Fisherman's Pilot* of 2002 (North Sea Pilot, 1960, 393 and 398; Admiralty-Kingfisher 2002, 3-52 to 3.57). Landsmen – perhaps we should now say "landspersons" – can only speculate upon the hazards of taking a small vessel, skin-built or planked, into Whitby harbour, with a tidal range of up to five and a half metres. Sometimes this had to be done in the face of a strong outflow from the River Esk. Bede's comment, that the original name

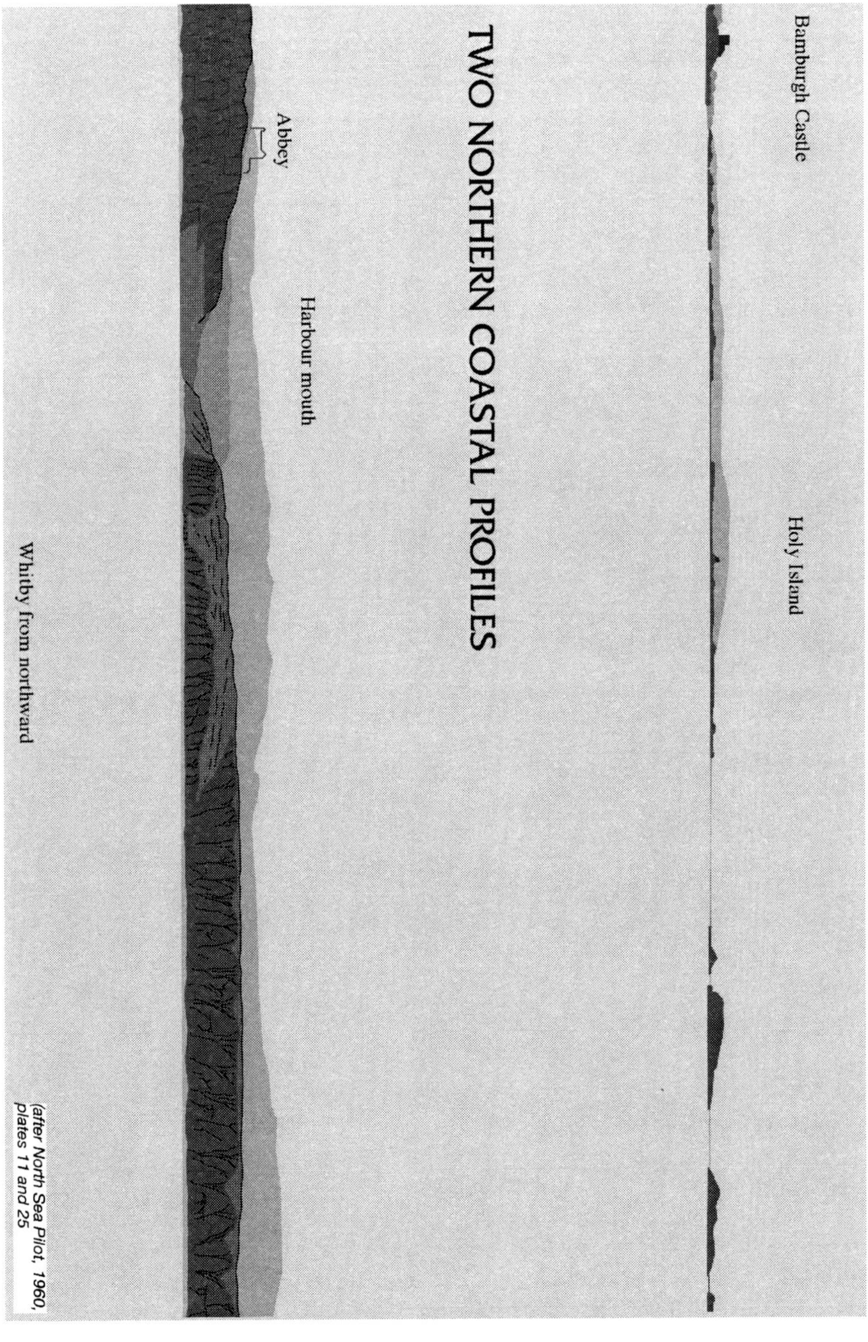

TWO NORTHERN COASTAL PROFILES

Bamburgh Castle

Holy Island

Abbey

Harbour mouth

Whitby from northward

(after North Sea Pilot, 1960, plates 11 and 25)

Figure 1. Two northern coastal profiles: the approaches to Holy Island and Whitby seen in clear weather.

Streanaeshalch means "the bay of the lighthouse" must give us pause for thought (HE, III, 25). In passing we must wonder if the two kings were taking advantage of hunting the fat autumn deer and boar available amid the local wood pastures. One doubts that they sought the dubious pleasures of gut-wrenching small boat journeys, so that it was sensible to make the churchmen do such travelling!

The form of the land and its regions

The Pennines comprise an uplifted block, highest in the west, where the broken edge forms the Fell Edge and overlooks the softer red rocks of the Vale of Eden (Figs 2 and 3). Older, generally rather hard, rocks from the region's basement rise to appear in the mountains of the Lake District and in splinters beneath Cross Fell, the Pennine summit. South of the Scottish border hard volcanic rocks give the mass of the Cheviots. Around these three upland masses far younger rocks are arranged rather like material draped on a vast uneven table top, forming a series of swashes, with harder bands giving ridges and softer bands the lower areas. On the eastern side of the Pennines eastwards flowing rivers reflect the uplift of the basement masses, with flow down the dip of the rocks, from west to east. This creates a powerful patterning on the eastern slopes of the Pennines with west to east valleys, themselves cut across by north to south and north-east to south-west valley lines following the strike of the softer rocks. This leads to large-scale changes in river direction, resulting from the capture of the headwaters of some streams by stronger rivers, and is seen in the courses of both the North and South Tyne and the Wear. Glaciations, with flows of ice from the east, north and west, have accentuated these basic forms. The uplands have been smoothed and masses of till – unsorted materials – deposited over the Northumberland coastal plain, the Durham and Yorkshire coast, with materials from the basin of the North Sea being pushed into the Tees Valley, across the Cleveland bench and southwards into the Vale of York. Finally, water-sorted materials, the products of vast and complex melt water flows, have cut into the drifts and country-rocks of much of the region, and deposited gravels and sands and clays in temporary lake basins. Ultimately, the lower Vale of York and the great gash of the Humber result from these watery outflows.

Can we say what this meant in cultural terms? Firstly, in these forces we have the definition of a basic stage, a physical environment that must be set in the context of a large island, off the north-western coasts of Europe. The North Sea basin is a newcomer, the result of the post-glacial flooding of the mouth of a great river

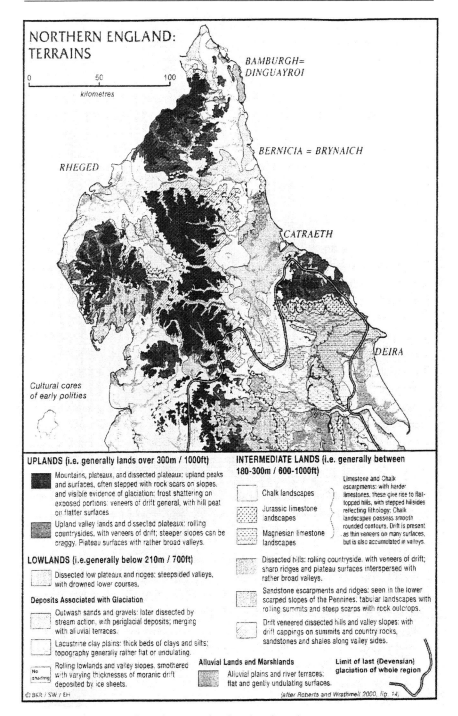

NORTHERN ENGLAND: TERRAINS

0   50   100
kilometres

BAMBURGH=
DINGUAYROI

BERNICIA = BRYNAICH

RHEGED

CATRAETH

DEIRA

Cultural cores
of early polities

UPLANDS (i.e. generally lands over 300m / 1000ft)

Mountains, plateaux, and dissected plateaux: upland peaks and surfaces, often stepped with rock scars on slopes, and visible evidence of glaciation; frost shattering on exposed portions: veneers of drift general, with hill peat on flatter surfaces

Upland valley lands and dissected plateaux: rolling countrysides, with veneers of drift; steeper slopes can be craggy. Plateau surfaces with rather broad valleys.

LOWLANDS (i.e. generally below 210m / 700ft)

Dissected low plateaus and ridges; steepsided valleys, with drowned lower courses.

Deposits Associated with Glaciation

Outwash sands and gravels: later dissected by stream action. with periglacial deposits; merging with alluvial terraces.

Lacustrine clay plains: thick beds of clays and silts: topography generally rather flat or undulating.

Rolling lowlands and valley slopes, smothered with varying thicknesses of moranic drift deposited by ice sheets.

INTERMEDIATE LANDS (i.e. generally between 180-300m / 600-1000ft)

Chalk landscapes

Jurassic limestone landscapes

Magnesian limestone landscapes

Limestone and Chalk escarpments: with harder limestones, these give rise to flat-topped hills, with stepped hillsides reflecting lithology. Chalk landscapes possess smooth rounded contours. Drift is present as thin veneers on many surfaces, but is also accumulated in valleys.

Dissected hills: rolling countryside. with veneers of drift; sharp ridges and plateau surfaces interspersed with rather broad valleys.

Sandstone escarpments and ridges: seen in the lower scarped slopes of the Pennines. tabular landscapes with rolling summits and steep scarps with rock outcrops.

Drift veneered dissected hills and valley slopes: with drift cappings on summits and country rocks, sandstones and shales along valley sides.

Alluvial Lands and Marshlands

Alluvial plains and river terraces: flat and gently undulating surfaces.

Limit of last (Devensian) glaciation of whole region

© BKR / SW / EH

(after Roberts and Wrathmell 2000, fig. 14)

Figure 2. The terrains of northern England and early polities.

system that encompassed the Rhine and its tributaries. Lying east of the North Atlantic, south of the Norwegian Sea, and under the influence of the Gulf Stream and at latitude between 50 and 60 degrees north, the influence of the sea looms large. Sir Cyril Fox's well-known division of Britain into a Highland Zone and a Lowland Zone is now "unfashionable" in scholarly circles – but try telling a farmer that the very real contrasts implied do not matter. In short, the essential qualities of the north-east as a broad cultural region derive from the fact that it lies where Lowland Zone meets Highland Zone, and while lacking the drama of the stark mountain front of Wales when approached from the Midlands, this distinctive location has always had implications for living and winning a living here. We started with a Roman signal tower and a church synod at Whitby, and both have meaning amid the fundamental physical facts of local regional contrasts.

Secondly, glaciation may seem a long way from culture, but let us put it this way: if we add the limits of the last glacial advance onto a simplified map of terrain – for there is always more detail than the mind can take in, and generalization is essential – then we can see a very simple fact (Fig.2). After the melt the areas north and south of this ice limit were left a wilderness of tundra, with temporary lakes, slumping permafrost, and ground – not soil – of water-sorted gravel, sand and clay, all set upon on a general matrix of often stony drift resulting from unsorted glacial deposition. Further to the south of this line, when the last ice advance never reached, the melting waters had more time to sift and sort the immediate surface materials and the existing tundra vegetation changed more rapidly. In a nutshell, the drainage system was more mature, helped by the spring melt of winter snows. Of course, earlier ice advances had reached the Thames and the Bristol Channel, so that the great river systems of England and the great plains of the Midlands reflect earlier glacial events. In short, from the farming viewpoint and irrespective of latitude, recently glaciated lands present more problems of agricultural reclamation than do lands with older, deeper more mature drainage systems and long-developed soils.

Thirdly, soils were not, to use Demangeon's words, "delivered from the hand of nature". The 8,000 or so years between the disappearance of the ice and the arrival of farming communities had indeed seen the development of soils and the spread of extensive woodlands. At this time perhaps even the Pennine tops carried birch and pine woodlands, but the transition from a natural soil and a natural vegetation to farmland, or even rough pasture, is a labour-intensive step. Farmed – *husbanded* – soils are *made* by farming communities, slowly, so slowly, in the face of all nature can throw at them. I owe my own perception of this to Axel Steensberg, a man

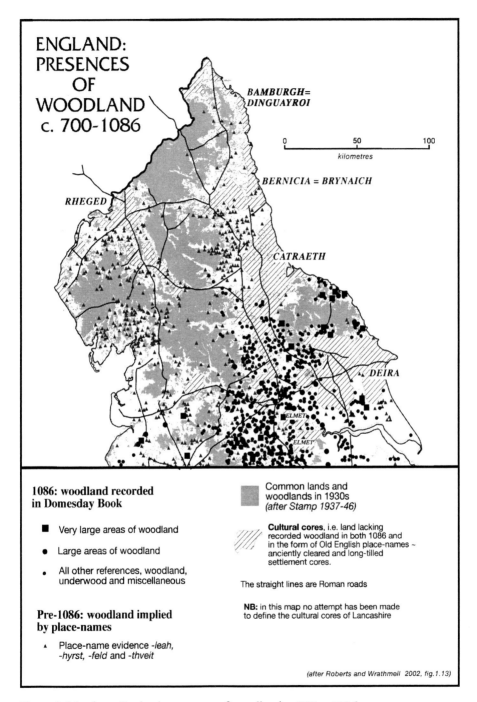

Figure 3. Northern England, presences of woodland c. 700 – 1086.

and scholar with practical contact with the land. Tree felling, shrub clearance, root-removal, stone picking, boundary definition, and ploughing must all precede sowing and harvesting. Sustained soil productivity, in contrast to slash and burn, is the result of labour and time (Proudfoot, in Buchannan, 1971, 8–33). Of course, sustained cropping invariably results in nutrient depletion, but fallowing, resting the soil, offers one solution in a system where manure was not present in sufficient quantities to replace what was taken out by crops, while any inflow of lime, that intermediary between plants and soil nutrients, resulted in areas attractive to agricultural settlement – once they had been identified. The availability of this lime is also a reflection of country geology and rainfall. Furthermore, the north-eastern region spans yet another physical boundary: most of England has between 7–8 months with a mean temperature above 6 degrees Celsius, a generally accepted index of plant growth, while in the northern foothills and uplands this falls to 5 and 6 months. Even if such data cannot be mapped in great detail, anymore than the mysterious isophrenes, lines telling of the arrival of spring, the north-east of England is in a zone of transition. To put it simply, climatic variations, greater wetness, greater cold, better summers, and the like, in many combinations, all have a more noticeable impact at the margins, where height of land and latitude combine, as Parry has shown in some detail in the Lammermuir Hills further north. Of course, these comments ignore the powerful but later impact of coal, a fundamental regional moulding force from the sixteenth century onwards.

Cultural cores and rimlands

Physical regions are a contemporary way of perceiving the land, but we can only speculate on how people saw these landscapes in the past. An elegiac poem of the post-Roman times speaks of land that was:

> *Between the brine and the high ground and the fresh stream water.*
> (John T. Koch, 1987, Translation of an awdl from *Marwnad Cunedda, xxxvii*)

This shows that both the singer – for the elegy was sung or chanted – and his listeners were well aware of the fundamentals of terrain contrasts; in a few words we are given a sharp and accurate image of north-eastern England. Wood and plain, mountain land and marsh, arable and waste, are also present as words in later documents. However, a map of the distribution of woodland in times past allows us to achieve a more fine-grained image of former regional contrasts. An account of the making of the map appearing as Figure 3 has already been published, the problem with the north being that the record of the Domesday Book ends at the Tees and is essentially discontinuous throughout Lancashire (Roberts and Wrathmell, 2002, 21–31). Nevertheless, place-name evidence continues the picture beyond the threshold of the record of 1086, and the general close *in-situ* correlation between Old English "woodland" names and recorded woodland in 1086 is a sound foundation for building hypotheses. For Durham detailed work by Simon Harris and Helen Dunsford confirms the presence of a band of open fell containing place-names indicative of woodland at an earlier time (Roberts and Wrathmell, 2002; Dunsford and Harris, 2003; Watts, 2002, xiii–xix). In spite of all the caveats to be made about the chronology and character of this evidence this distribution does give clues concerning the dispositions of waste, woodland and settled land in, and probably long before, the Anglo-Saxon period, although the possibility of some post-Roman regeneration of woodland should not be excluded (Dark, 2000, Fig. 5.6).

Figure 3 can be approached in two ways: firstly, it can be seen as a map of open pastures, recorded in the 1930s – a map of them throughout the north in the later eighteenth century has to be created – together with former woodlands, evidenced by the records of place-names and the Domesday Book of 1086. The collated image is one of open land, pasture and woodland before 1086, a fundamental tripartite division of both the natural and cultural environment. Although a little out of focus and needing many qualifications this map is nevertheless a powerful tool. However, it is on the negative areas, the areas *not* containing large amounts of recorded woodland or surviving common waste, and diagonally shaded in Figure 3 and visible as transparent over shading in Figure 2, on which discussion must now concentrate. These are anciently cleared zones that bear a heavy imprint of many centuries of occupation and agriculture. Ignoring Lancashire, the Eden Valley and Solway Plain to the west, to the east of the Pennines four cleared zones can be identified north of the Humber, and it will be noted that this analysis breaks free of the constraints of county divisions, the frames for so much historical and archaeological investigation.

- Firstly, there is a south-eastern zone, centering on the chalk wolds, the limestone hills and the lake basin lowland south of the North York Moors, the Yorkshire Wolds, the Tabular Hills and the Vale of Pickering.

- Secondly, is the Tees Valley, together with its flanking lowlands, and extending northwards to the dip slopes of the Magnesian Limestone. Focusing on the Tees, this extends southeast into the Vale of York.

Two negative zones separate these two, the upland pastures of the moors and wood-pastures, heaths and marshlands of the Vale of York.

- Thirdly, is a zone north of the Tyne, extending along the Tyne Valley to the junction with the North Tyne and northwards of this junction. From this core a band of cleared land, judging by place-names, also extends along the Northumbrian coastlands, probably with inland outliers along the Wansbeck and Coquet, cultivated areas barriered inland by extensive wastes.

- Fourthly, a major zone comprises the coastal lowlands north of the Aln, the Till valley, and extending into the Tweed valley. Here the wholly artificial Scottish border, the limit of this mapping, masks our perception, for the region extends northwards into Berewickshire to the slopes of the Lammemuirs.

Between the Tees and the Tyne valleys, lies the great wedge of former woodland and rough pasture documented by Watts, Dunsford and Harris, while further north sandstone hills bring the fingers and outliers of the great wastes of the northern Pennines and Cheviots to the coast.

The north-western boundary of the second of these regions – termed *Catraeth*, after the early name for Catterick – deserves comment. It appears to lie along the western boundary of the Magnesian Limestone escarpment where it cuts across County Durham, but in fact is set rather to the west of this. This is an important boundary in Durham, being essentially marked by the line of towns or quasi-towns, Barnard Castle, Staindrop, Bishop Auckland, Durham, Chester-le-Street and Gateshead, (Roberts *et al.* in Britnell and Liddy, 2005, 221–37). But this is to assume that such boundaries are indeed lines; in fact the "line" is a short-distance transition between one type of countryside and another, and is cultural in character, not corresponding closely to any physical division. There is indeed a nationally important cultural break along this line. To the south there emerged large scale communally cultivated townfield systems that eventually came to dominate a great tract of countryside, extending from the Tees Valley, across the Midlands of England to the south coast, while to the north these were significantly smaller, mere islands in a sea of waste (Wrathmell and Roberts, 2000). Post-seventeenth century agricultural improvements and enclosures now conceal this former contrast.

If we can accept that the imperfect reconstruction seen in Figure 3, does indeed reflect a real situation in – say – the middle Saxon period, 750–850, then we have a picture of large islands of improved land – what I will term *core zones* – between the pasture wastes to the west and the salt wastes of the east. Both presented economic possibilities, but both were untamed, chancy and fraught with dangers. The world was physically as large as it is today, but horizons differed and regional perception differed, for the landscapes of fell and sea are physically dominant. The warmth and homely smells of the steadings and hamlets, hallgarths, monasteries and ports, with men, women and children, growing crops, stock and barns, were indeed islands set between two wastes. We should also remind ourselves that even within well-settled areas these activities did not at first form a continuous spread of equally spaced settlement of equal density, but in Paul Barford's nice image, "formed clusters resembling a leopard's spots" (Barford, 2001, 129).

Regional analysis

The old chestnut "compare and contrast" applies to the analysis of the regional pattern of core zones that have been defined, but no one interested in the past could create Figures 0.2 and 0.3 and escape perceiving *Deira* in the south-east, with *Bernicia* immediately to the north of the Tyne and extending into the middle Tyne and North Tyne valley. In the far north is the polity centred upon Bamburgh/*Dinguayroi*, and it was Nick Higham who saw the middle area and with sharp perception grasped that this must be *Catraeth*, centering on Catterick (Higham, 1986, Fig. 6.2). I am here ignoring the questions about *Elmet* and indeed the trans-Pennine polities – *Rheged and Lyvenneth* – but they are part of the wider picture and can be detected in the general map. What follows can only be seen as selective and as such only has a brief commentary – highlighting important questions from work in progress.

Prehistoric and Roman material

There is a clear tendency for prehistoric and Romano-British sites to be concentrated outside the cultural cores. Of course, in upland Northumberland the survival of sites is noteworthy, and wholly to be expected on land that has long remained in pastoral usage, even if settled and ploughed occasionally. In the lower lands the evidence is largely based on photographs taken from the air, reflecting the attrition of sites by subsequent ploughing. We face the possibility that the north-western limit of the core zone running parallel with the Magnesian Limestone escarpment was in fact the northern territorial limit of the Iron Age Brigantes rather than the Tyne, with a no-mans-land, occupying the lower Tyne area, a river mouth shattered by the insertion of Hadrian's Wall. Far to the north lay the main locus of the Votadini, prosperous and well able to occupy and use the vast reserves of upland pastures for cattle production. These provided a notable contrast to the uplands of Durham where, while there was some occupation, and certainly a great deal of clearance, the overall density of known native sites is very low. The author believes this contrast: you fall over the sites further north, but not in the Durham uplands. Work by Margaret Faull and others of *The West Yorkshire Archaeological Survey* suggests that in Yorkshire, Roman and pre-Roman sites lie in some numbers along the margins of the townfield-dominated townships of the Vale of York (Faull and Moorhouse, 1981; Faull, 1983, Fig. 3). The extensive prehistoric linear dyke systems of the Tabular Hills to the north of the Vale of Pickering, not only lie just above the levels of townfield cultivation but may well have a degree of relationship to the historic township boundaries (Spratt, 1989, Figs 1, 4 & 8). Here, there must be a probability that the main foci of prehistoric and Romano-British activity lay down-slope of the medieval upper limits of cultivation and improvement, namely the head dykes set at about 300 metres throughout this northern region. In the Tabular Hills of East Yorkshire we are dealing here with the northern edge of the territory of the Parisi, an Iron Age group who successfully developed the territory later to become Deira (Halkon, 1989), whose out-pastures and marchlands lay on the North York Moors. The relative absence of small hill forts in the lands of the Brigantes and the Parisi do suggest developed and well-populated polities, even though there are no indications of the existence of any coinage. Cattle and slave-girls no doubt served this purpose – and here I have in mind the Irish *cumal*, a slave-girl worth three dairy cows with their followers (Kelly, 1998, 33, n. 53; 620): both were high value stock, but there was more potential work in the lass, a grim but realistic view of the period!

There are many questions; the site at Stanwix in north Yorkshire was an northern Iron Age *oppidum* if there ever was one, and lies at the western edge of the core zone to be identified with *Catraeth* (Catterick, itself a few miles to the south), the point from which cattle raids coming from the north and west could be challenged. If the later Brigantian locus was indeed at Aldbrough on the Ure, *Isurium Brigantum*, then this suggests a settlement axis along the eastern slope and dales of the Pennines, avoiding the wash lands of the vale proper. Marijke van der Veen (1992, *passim*) tells us that the later prehistoric agriculture of the Tees Valley component of this zone differed from that further to the north and west which was characterized by small-scale intensive subsistence cultivation contrasting with material from Thorpe Thewles, Stanwix and Rock (just south of Stanwix) where larger scale arable cultivation was present. Paradoxically the Romano-British agriculture of this same area appears to have more resembled the small-scale intensive subsistence cultivation found further north in later prehistoric times, implying at least a degree of recession under the stress of conquest (van de Veen, 1992, 157–59). Clearly mapping this core zone opens a window upon reassessments of a large *corpus* of existing evidence, but we are here touching here long and uncomfortable chains of temporal continuity and discontinuity.

Place-names

Victor Watts' mapping of English habitation names in County Durham confirms the presence of the northern wedge of settled land in the east and south of the county and the mixing of habitation and woodland names in the wedge between the lower Tyne and lower Wear raises interesting questions about the chronology of names in -*tun* (Watts, 2002, xiv). In the North Riding of Yorkshire – and how easily we revert to county terminology, an administrative framework that post-dates the foundation of English settlement – Gillian Fellows-Jensen's map of early Anglo-Saxon burial sites and early "Anglian" (strictly Old English) place-names differs in detail from Sam Lucy's (see later) but reveals an undoubted concentration in the south-eastern core zone. There is some penetration of the Tees Valley cultural core – one is tempted to add via the line of the Dere Street – but it is not until the appearance of place-names in -*tun* in the eighth century that the vale of York and Cleveland plain are infilled by Old English settlement names (Fellows-Jensen, 1972, Figs. 1 & 2). It is clear from this account that existing evidence needs reassessing and collating to create a synoptic distribution map, and that this would open the possibility of furthering our understanding of local place-name chronologies. This work is in progress. A similar problem exists north of the Tyne, although Nicholaisen's map of Anglian names containing, amongst others – *ingtun and-ingham* – reveals the Bernician cultural core and the fact that the Bamburgh cultural core does indeed extend north of the Tweed (Nicholaisen, 1976, Fig. 2).

Burial material before AD 750

Sam Lucy, in a cogent analysis of burial rites in the region between AD 500 and 750, touches on many of the issues being raised here, namely the correlation between often intractable and imperfect archaeological evidence and the environmental contexts that nurtured and sustained early societies. In an introduction Lucy isolates key problems issuing from previous debates, namely the numbers involved in an incoming Anglo-Saxon population and whether they were merely an incoming elite, the degree to which burial practices, and indeed grave materials, do indeed reflect ethnic groups, and the issue of the boundary between Bernicia and Deira. Side-stepping the detail of burial practices and grave goods, the concentration of fifth and sixth century burials within the south-eastern core zone, Deira, is notable and geographically significant, while a second less intense concentration occurs in the Tees Valley core zone, concentrated north of the river, and north of the best well-drained soils of the middle Tees. This was an area, spreading from the northern flank of the Tees Valley to the crest of the Magnesian Limestone, where the thin soils the plateau surface carried much open moor, while the dip slope boulder clays give soils that can be too wet to work in the spring. It may be no accident that this same area experienced extensive village depopulation between the sixteenth and the nineteenth century (Roberts in Britnell and Liddy, 2005, Fig. 14.5) and indeed Scandinavian settlement (Higham, 1986, Fig 7.3). This was perhaps a slightly more marginal zone for lowland settlement. The best soils and better local climate lies south of the Tees, a large tract where Anglo-Saxon burials have in general not been found, and it is possible that we should think of dense Romano-British populations in this area. Lucy's maps of seventh and eighth century burials and finds contain numbers that are not easily amenable to geographical analysis, while throughout the whole period burials with "prehistoric and Roman associations", which, as Lucy asserts, reflect the choices of mourners rather than geographical factors. What is notable, however, is that association with prehistoric features, usually secondary internments in barrows, is noteworthy in the south-eastern core zone, i.e. the incipient Deira. This is a reflection of the long period of occupation in this heartland zone, with its noteworthy concentration of Langdale Pike axes of the Neolithic period, surely here indicative of clearance, as well as grooved ware and other Neolithic monuments (Edmonds, 1995, Figs 27, 62 and 77). Furthermore, York, the eventual regional capital, is seen to be peripheral to this long established territory. This is not to say that there are not internal divisions within Deira, to mention only the Chalk Wolds, the Vale of Pickering, the drift-covered wold dip slope, and the ring of limestone hills to the north-west and north. This diverse physical area, a key cultural core, shows signs of a sustained continuity in which the Parisi were but one incident. This brings us back to Lucy's question about the nature of local regional populations and their rulers in a region linked to the south by an impressive series of prehistoric Humber ferries.

Where does this take the argument? The woodland map of the period between about 700 and 1086 provides a base-stable and reliable image, whatsoever its imperfections, for it is strongly supported by a detailed Durham map for the period c.1150–1350 (Dunsford and Harris, 2003), we are then forced to assess earlier distributions in the light of the cultural frame developed from it (Fig. 0.3). Of course, there are often clear correlations with what is to be seen in Figure 0.2, but by thinking in this way we have moved beyond geology, soils and relief – important as these can be – into a soundly based assessment of culture zones and what one can succinctly term *landscape continuities*. To comment upon one example that has already been slipped in: the great concentration of Langdale Pike axes in this Deiran zone is so great that it can hardly be wholly the result of the activities of a few antiquaries and archaeologists. What then are we to make of a subsidiary concentration of such axes in the Bernician zone to the north of the Tyne, with a marked thinning out of the evidence in the "Catraeth" zone between the two? Without digressing here into the deeper obscurities of the *Gododdin*, a praise poem based upon sixth century warfare and a raid south by the post-Roman descendants of the Votadini, the *Gododdin*, it is Deira and Catraeth who appear as the "enemy" not Bernicia. The real nature of the Catraeth zone, with its *oppidum* at Stanwix and links with the Brigantes, emerges as a significant research problem (Koch, 1997). Was Higham wrong in seeing this Tees valley core zone as an identifiable cultural "region" for want of a better term? This evidence suggests he was right. To be linking Neolithic axe distributions to the obscurities of an early elegiac poem may appear perverse, but it is the logical concomitant of an awareness of landscape continuities.

Anglo-Saxon stone sculpture

The find loci of Anglo-Saxon stone sculpture are not randomly distributed. Comparison with Figure 3 – which must be done orally for a map-synthesis is in preparation – emphasises the essential liminality of these artefacts; they either lie close to the sea or close to the boundaries between the bulk of cleared and settled land and the inland seas of waste to the west. Coastal sites at Lindisfarne, Tynemouth and Hartlepool are also well known, with Whitby being part of the chain of monastic foundations in this liminal zone of sea communications. Escomb, Hexham, Falstone and Rothbury in the "early" period, and Gainford, Auckland, Durham, Chester-le-Street, Hexham, Chollerton and Birtley, Bolam and Bothel in the "later" period, lie to the west. Again these are set in a liminal zone, but in this case between the leopard spots of improved and cultivated lands and a great western sea of waste (Cramp, 1984, Figs 2 & 3). By this later period the richness of the core zone of Catraeth is noteworthy. At this time, in spite of ongoing grants of land, County Durham did not exist, so that the much-examined sites at Jarrow and Monkwearmouth have a triple liminality. They lie between the sea and the land, between the cultivated lands and the great tracts of fell, and between two core cultural zones, that of Bernicia to the north and that of Catraeth to the south. Jackson concluded that the name Bernicia implied the "land of the mountain passes": in fact Bernicia, perhaps with local power set in the Corbridge-Hexham area, controlled the eastern end of *the pass*, the gap through the Pennines, namely the Tyne-Irthing route between the Solway Firth and the North Sea (Jackson, 1953, 704–05) as well as key north to south routes.

Concluding comments

While "regions" undoubtedly have a presence in the real world, giving rise to different countrysides, differences in place, whose characteristics may, as the French concept of the "pays" recognises, permeate life-style and even language, regions are also tools for organizing our perception of the world (Braudel, 1988, 41–50). Their definition is part of the way the human mind make sense of terrestrial space, and while we do get indications from earlier authors that such perceptions have long been part of human thinking, they are merely tools, so that the areas we define and the boundaries we select are based upon varied criteria, sometimes long-lasting, and sometimes wholly ephemeral. Much scholarly ink has been invested in such matters, but the regions defined here are created for two reasons, first, to communicate what the author believes he sees amid the North of England, and second, as ways of formulating questions about historical and archaeological evidence, issues that will be examined in future publications.

The definition of the cultural cores was derived from the *positive* mapping of woodland and pastures and then using these to identify *negative* areas, i.e. those areas where there was less likely to be large quantities of woodland or pasture. These areas are then, perhaps unsurprisingly but convincingly, found to correlate with other indicators of cultural activity seen on archaeological distribution maps. Nevertheless, this way of identifying cultural cores is important for several reasons: it is possible, with something approaching confidence:

• to note presence or absence of other elements, burials or monasteries, distinctive place-names or random archaeological discoveries in the interior or on the periphery of the cores.

- to examine the internal diversity of the cultural cores, with variable terrains: they are not in any sense based on physical regions, but include and use a variety of terrains, indeed may be using land qualities not revealed by the maps we have available.

- to be aware of the "rimlands", the surrounding environments of marsh, pasture and woodland. These were in no way unoccupied, or indeed unused – offering grazing lands and other products – but they were less densely populated and served as separators, marchlands, dividing polity from polity.

- to suggest that the cultural cores were the more densely populated zones, even though they varied internally, possessing a "leopard spot" pattern of internal development, even though, and this is an important point for the emergence of polities, they differed from each other in the intensity of their development.

- to postulate sustained archaeological destruction within these cultural cores, for they were areas of the most intense land usage, with successor developments and sustained arable use tending to remove antecedent traces.

To recall Kitson Clark's acid test, what has come out of this analysis that is new? Fundamentally there are two issues: firstly, the concept of positive and negative evidence, with a spatial distribution being reversed to ask about the negative spaces and what they mean, has been the basis of this work. This is most viable as a technique when applied to an excellent and "complete" data set, but with care, and using "complete" data sets as a control, more partial distributions can be assessed in this manner. Secondly, the use of maps demonstrated here is as research tools, not mere illustrations or end-products, and while this analysis is based upon maps, some already committed to the computer and others in books, the lines of enquiry formulated here will continue by building all the evidence into computer maps so that extended "compare and contrast" exercises become possible.

References

Admiralty-Kingfisher, 2002 *Fisherman's Pilot – North Sea, Lowestoft to Peterhead* (United Kingdom Hydrographic Office, Taunton and Hull).

Braudel, F. 1988, *The Identity of France: History and Environment* (vol. I, Fontana Press, London, translated by S. Reynolds).

Christensen, A.E. (ed.) 1996, *The Earliest Ships* (Conway Maritime Press, London).

Cramp, R. 1984, *Corpus of Anglo-Saxon Stone Sculpture, vol. 1, County Durham and Northumberland,* in two parts (The University Press, Oxford, for the British Academy).

Dark, P. 2000, *The Environment of Britain in the First Millennium A.D.* (Duckworth, London).

Dunsford, H. and Harris, S.J. 'Colonisation of the wasteland in County Durham, 1100-1400', *Economic History Review* LVI, no. 1, 34-56.

Eckwall, E. 1970, *The Concise Oxford Dictionary of English Place-Names* (The Clarendon Press, Oxford).

Edmonds, M. 1995, *Stone Tools and Society* (B.T. Batsford Ltd., London).

Faull, M. L. and Moorhouse, S.A. 1981 *West Yorkshire Archaeological Survey to AD 1500*, 3 vols. and maps (West Yorkshire Metropolitan County Council, Wakefield).

Faull, M. L. 1983, 'Roman and Saxon Settlement Patterns in Yorkshire: a Computer Generated Analysis', *Landscape History*, 5, 21-40.

Frere, S. 1998, *Britannia, a History of Roman Britain* (Pimlico, London).

Gifford, E. and J. 1999, 'The Art of Anglo-Saxon Shipbuilding' in Hawkes, J. and Mills, S. *Northumbria's Golden Age* (Sutton Publishing, Stroud, England).

Halkon, P. (ed.) 1989, *New Light on the Parisi* (East Riding Archaeological Society and School of Education, University of Hull).

Haywood, J. 1999, *Dark Age Naval Power* (Anglo-Saxon Books, Hockwold-cum-Wilton, Norfolk, England).

Jackson, K. 1953, *Language and History in Earl Britain* (reprinted 2000, Four Courts Press, Dublin).

Jones, B. and Mattingly, D. 1990, *An Atlas of Roman Britain* (Basil Blackwell Ltd., Oxford).

Kelly, F. 1998, *Early Irish Farming* (School of Celtic Studies, Dublin).

Koch, J.T. 1997, *The Gododdin of Aneirin: Text and Context from Dark-Age North Britain* (University of Wales Press, Cardiff)

Lamb, H.H. 1985, *Climatic History and the Future* (University Press, Princeton).

Lucy, S. 1999, 'Changing Burial Rites in Northumbria AD 500-750 in Shipbuilding' in Hawkes, J. and Mills, S. *Northumbria's Golden Age* (Sutton Publishing, Stroud, England).

McGrail, S. 1998, *Ancient Boats in North-West Europe* (Longman, London).

Nicholaisen, W.F.H. 1976, *Scottish Place-Names* (B.T. Batsford, London).

North Sea Pilot, 1960, *Comprising the East Coast of England from Berwick to North Foreland including the Rivers Thames and Medway*, vol. 3 (Hydrographic Department of the Admiralty, London, Twelfth Edition).

Parry, M.L. 1978, *Climatic Change, Agriculture and Settlement* (Dawson, Archon Books, Folkestone).

Proudfoot, B. 1971, 'Man's Occupance of the Soil' in Buchannan, R.H., Jones, E. and McCourt, D. (eds.) *Man and His Habitat* (Routledge and Kegan Paul, London).

Roberts B.K. and Wrathmell, B.K. 2002, Region and Place: *a Study of English Rural Settlement* (English Heritage, London).

Roberts, B.K., Dunsford, H. and Harris, S.J. 2005, 'Framing Medieval Landscapes: Region and Place in County Durham' in Britnell, R.H. and Liddey, C. (eds.) *North-East England in the Later Middle Ages* (Boydell Press), 221-237.

Salway, P. 1981, *Roman Britain* (Clarendon Press, Oxford).

Seebohm, F. 1911, *Tribal Custom in Anglo-Saxon Law* (Longmans, Green and Co, London).

Severin, T. 1978, *The Brendan Voyage* (Hutchinson, London).

Smith, A.H. 1928, *The Place-Names of the North Riding of Yorkshire* (English Place-Name Society, vol. V. University Press, Cambridge).

Spratt, D.A. 1989, *Linear Earthworks of the Tabular Hills of Northeast Yorkshire* (Department of Archaeology and Prehistory, University of Sheffield).

Van der Veen, M. 1992, *Crop Husbandry Regimes: an Archaeobotanical Study of Farming in northern England 1000 BC – AD 500* (Sheffield Archaeological Monographs 3, J.R. Collis Publications, University of Sheffield).

Chapter Four

The role of migration
in constructing regional identity

Colin G. Pooley

Introduction

> *... this leaving our own Countery was a great cross to my mother, for she was greatly attached to her Native town, & had she known what would follow, I am sure that she never would have left her relations & country on any account.*[1]

> *I wonder why all the girls here are simply dying to get home for good? I see only a few advantages and a whole lot of disadvantages. The chief is, I think, that I would not be able to do exactly as I like.*[2]

These quotes, the first relating to movement within North-west England in the late eighteenth century and the second to migration from Northern Ireland to London in the first half of the twentieth century, give two very different perspectives on the links between migration and regional identity. Whilst Isabella Shaw was reluctant to move a relatively short distance and missed her hometown, Rhona Little quickly adapted to her new life in London and saw no advantages in returning home to Northern Ireland despite the imminent threat of war. Such contrasting images occur commonly in accounts of migration found in diaries and life histories, and emphasise the complex relationships that existed between the process of migration and the construction and retention of regional identities. This chapter explores links between migration and the construction of regional identities, and examines the factors that influenced connections between the two.

Much historical and contemporary research on migration and identity tends to focus on distinctive groups of migrants, who have usually moved a long distance, and with characteristics that are very different from those of the society that they are entering. There are thus numerous studies of the Irish and Jews in nineteenth-century Britain[3], of South Asian and Caribbean migrants to Britain from the 1940s,[4] and of refugees and asylum seekers in contemporary Europe.[5] Such studies usually emphasise the ways in which migrants construct new identities following relocation. There is also a large literature on transnational migration, in which migrants retain an association with more than one place, possibly moving between the two on a regular basis.[6] However, a strong place identity is not unique to long distance migrants. To some degree everyone develops associations with places in which they have lived, and identity with a place or region may be affected by most everyday migration experiences. This chapter focuses on everyday migration experiences of people who have moved voluntarily over both long and short distances, and who do not have any especially distinctive characteristics, to explore the ways in which migration and regional identity may influence each other.

Concepts of both region and identity are hard to define precisely. As other contributors to this book also stress, regions may be constructed at a variety of spatial scales, for different purposes, and with overlapping or permeable boundaries. Regional identity, or a sense of belonging to a particular place, relates to many different characteristics and attributes of both the place and the people involved, including factors such as family, neighbourhood, community, occupation and workplace, class, ethnicity, gender, language and religion. All these, and more, interact to construct regional identities, or the ways in which people feel about particular locations. Some inkling of the significance and meaning of regional identity can be discerned by posing two related questions. Firstly, what are the factors that make a region distinctive and different from other regions for a particular individual? Secondly, why does an individual like a region and what benefits does association with that region convey?[7] This chapter uses specific case studies to explore these questions, to uncover the multi-layered nature of regional identities, and the complex relationship of regional or place identity with migration. Evidence is drawn from a variety of sources utilised in recent research. Most emphasis is placed on the testimonies of migrants recorded in a number of (mostly unpublished) diaries and life histories collected by the author as part of a recent project on migration in Britain. However, firstly, a larger data set of individual migration life histories collected from family historians is used to outline the key characteristics of inter-regional migration in Britain.

Migration and region in Britain

It is now well established that internal migration within Britain was dominated by short-distance moves in which most people stayed within a well-known locality or moved only to an adjacent area. Although longer-distance movement did take place, this was rarely speculative or unplanned. Most migrants followed a well-prepared route and had contacts in the place to which they moved. This can be illustrated by evidence culled from 16,091 individual migration life histories gathered from family historians.[8] Data are analysed within four time periods from the eighteenth to the twentieth century (Table 1). In each time period over half of all recorded moves were less than 10 km, one quarter were under 1 km, and the mean distance moved was around 35 km from 1750–1919, rising to 55 km in the twentieth century. Given that very short-distance moves were almost certainly under-recorded before the twentieth century, these data suggest that although residential migration was quite frequent (on average approximately five recorded moves per individual but with a large variance around this mean) most people did not stray far from their region of origin. Not only did most individuals remain in the same locality, but also over several generations most members of the same family remained in the same region. In most families there were, of course, some who moved further from home, but on average around 75% of all family members remained within the same locality.

Regression analysis was used to identify the variables that best "explained" variations in distance moved.[9] A variety of models were applied, all with broadly similar results. This chapter reports results from a logistic regression model that treated distance moved as a dichotomous variable divided into those that remained within the same settlement and those that moved elsewhere. Ten independent variables were added to the model: age at move; reason for moving; occupation before the move; settlement size of origin; settlement size of destination; companions during the move; gender; relation to household head; marital status and region of origin. The technique seeks to evaluate the relative importance of the above variables in determining whether someone remained within the same settlement or moved to another locality.

Table 1. Migration distances within Britain, 1750–1994 (% in each distance band)

Distance (km)	Time period			
	1750–1839	1840–1879	1880–1919	1920–1994
<1	24.5	40.5	43.7	35.5
1–4.9	14.7	13.2	11.8	9.9
5–9.9	14.1	9.3	7.9	8.5
10–19.9	12.3	8.3	7.0	8.3
20–49.9	15.4	11.0	9.5	10.1
50–99.9	8.6	7.2	7.7	9.0
100–199.9	5.8	6.1	6.8	9.2
200+	4.6	4.4	5.6	9.5
Mean distance (km)	37.7	33.7	38.4	55.5
Total number of moves	8,199	19,656	20,934	17,864

Source. 16,091 migration life histories provided by family historians

Table 2. Factors influencing distance migrated within Britain, 1750–1994: change in –2 log likelihood if each term is removed from the logistic regression model

Variable	Change	Significance (p)	Degrees of freedom
Age at moving	35.5	<0.001	1
Marital status	20.2	0.001	5
Region of origin	1425.3	<0.001	19
Size of origin settlement	333.6	<0.001	1
Size of destination settlement	223.7	<0.001	1
Companions	99.9	<0.001	6
Relationship to household head	57.0	<0.001	4
Reason for move	5094.5	<0.001	19
Occupation prior to move	475.6	<0.001	19
Gender	-	not significant	1

Source. 16,091 migration life histories provided by family historians

Overall, the model correctly predicted 75% of the cases, with reasons for the move and region of origin the two most significant factors. This is shown by the large change in the model log likelihood indicated in Table 2. Taking all cohorts together, all other variables except gender were also significant (though of much lesser importance than reasons and region of origin), and when broken down by time period differences between cohorts were relatively small. In summary, the model shows that moves for job-related reasons, and also (predictably) for emigration, education, war service and apprenticeship were most likely to be to a new settlement, and that migration to and from London was different to that of other regions. Analysis of the other (and less significant variables) shows that movement to another settlement was also most likely to be undertaken by younger migrants (but not children), male household heads, single migrants, and (obviously) migrants from smaller settlements (with the exception of moves from London).

Although a necessarily rather crude analysis of aggregate data, the regression analysis shows that the minority who left their community of origin, and thus who were most likely to change their regional identity following migration, were mainly young, single males, moving for work either from small settlements or from London. Other large towns were more likely to retain their population, with a high incidence of inter-urban mobility; and women, children, older migrants and those moving for housing and family reasons were all more likely to move within their settlement of origin. None of this is especially surprising, and it confirms contemporary observations on migration, later local studies, and most migration theory.[10]

However, scale is a crucial factor in any consideration of regional identity, and the discussion so far has evaded the question of precisely how distance and regional identity interact. It has been assumed that if migrants stay broadly within the same area (north-east England or south-west England for instance), or within the same settlement, then migration is unlikely to have affected their identity with region. However, we should beware of attributing modern concepts of distance to the past when the ability to travel was very different, and individuals from contrasting backgrounds may have viewed distance rather differently. This can be illustrated from nineteenth-century literature as, for instance, in this interchange between Mr Darcy and Elizabeth Bennet in Jane Austin's novel of 1813, *Pride and Prejudice*:

> *"It must be very agreeable to her to be settled within so easy a distance of her own family and friends."*
>
> *"An easy distance do you call it? It is nearly fifty miles."*
>
> *"And what is fifty miles of good road? Little more than half a day's journey. Yes, I call it a very easy distance."*
>
> *"I should never have considered the distance as one of the advantages of the match,"* cried Elizabeth. *"I should never have said Mrs. Collins was settled near her family."*
>
> *"It is a proof of your own attachment to Hertfordshire. Any thing beyond the very neighbourhood of Longbourn, I suppose, would appear far."*
>
> *"I do not mean to say that a woman may not be settled too near her family. The far and the near must be relative, and depend on many varying circumstances. Where there is fortune to make the expence of travelling unimportant, distance becomes no evil. But that is not the case here. Mr. and Mrs. Collins have a comfortable income, but not such a one as will allow of frequent journeys – and I am persuaded my friend would not call herself near her family under less than half the present distance."* [11]

Further examination of the links between migration and regional identity must thus be focused on the individual to assess the extent to which people felt an association with particular places at a variety of scales, and the ways in which migration may have affected regional identity: this can best be done by focusing on personal diaries, autobiographies and life histories. The following section explores these concepts through the eyes of five individuals whose life histories cover the eighteenth to the twentieth centuries.

Migration and identity: five case studies

The opening quotation relates to Isabella Shaw (née Noddle) born in Dent (Yorkshire) in 1751. After her marriage to Joseph Shaw in 1771 (in Dent) she moved home some eleven times around the Yorkshire/Lancashire/Cumbria borders before settling with her husband in Preston (Lancashire) in 1795. She died in Preston in 1798. The longest move she undertook was some 80 km from Milthrop in south Cumbria (close to Dent) to Preston, but most moves were only a few km and she remained within a clearly defined region of North-west England. However, the life history written by her son Benjamin suggests that Isabella had a very strong attachment to her home area, and was reluctant to travel even a short distance from Dent. Thus in 1773 the Shaw's moved some 25 km from Dent to the small market town of Kendal in Cumbria, ostensibly to enable Joseph to seek more work in his trade as a weaver, but they left after only a year and returned to Dent. Benjamin writes: "It seems that my mother was very Partial to the Place of her nativity".[12] Thus although remaining well within what should have been a familiar and comfortable region, Isabella had a very precise identity with the village of Dent and the family and friends that she had there, and found it difficult to relocate even a short distance. It is thus not surprising that the longer moves of some 50 km to Dolphinholme (Lancashire) in 1791 (referred to in the opening quotation) and eventually to Preston, were disliked by Isabella, and it can be suggested that dislocation from the place of her birth played a role in her rapidly declining health in Preston.[13]

Although the life history written by Benjamin Shaw does not provide a detailed window into his mother's life, in answering the questions posed in the introduction, it can be suggested that it was a combination of locality and community that made Dent a special place for Isabella Shaw, and that this provided her with support and comfort that she could not get elsewhere despite the presence of her immediate family. In contrast, Isabella's husband, Joseph, was happy to move frequently. His natural reaction to adversity was to seek his fortune elsewhere, and there is no indication from the autobiography that he ever felt uncomfortable moving to different places within a North-west region that became quite familiar to him. It can be suggested that his identity was focused much more on work, especially the availability of appropriate employment, and that he would have felt equally at home almost anywhere within the textile districts of northern England.

Amos Kniveton was born in the village of Astley Green, near Manchester, in 1835. After some early mobility in the local area he served his apprenticeship as a boot and shoemaker with his father, and remained at home until the age of twenty-two when he married a local girl. Initially he continued to work for his father but later established his own business in the village. However, in 1863 he decided to move away from Astley Green: the reason given in his autobiography being the fact that the village could not sustain two shoemakers and he did not wish to compete with his father. Amos then moved four times within Lancashire, before in 1867, he moved back to the locality of his birth and established his own business in Leigh, just 4 km from Astley Green where his family still lived. In moving elsewhere Amos seemed prepared to go anywhere, at least within Lancashire which he appeared to view as his home territory, and the two factors that seemed to give him place identity were his occupation and his religion. Both his work as a boot and shoemaker, and his religion (as a Methodist) were transferable almost anywhere within Britain, and thus he had a large community of interest with which he could identify. In fact he never moved outside Lancashire, which suggests a loyalty both to the North-west and to his family, and it is clear that he took the opportunity to move back to his home locality as soon as he could. However, his first move away from home, some 70 km to Morecambe in north Lancashire, was effected by answering an advertisement in the Methodist recorder for a "bootmaker and manager" that stated that a teetotaller and local preacher would be preferred.[14] It can be suggested that it was this community of work and religion that sustained Amos and provided him with identity for the 4 years that he was away from his home locality, extended family and friends.

Both Amos Kniveton and the Shaw's moved over relatively short distances and remained within the same corner of England. Yet they also had well developed but different place identities that seemed to be based on a range of factors, but which encouraged them to remain relatively close to their community of origin. In contrast, we now consider two men, both born in the 1820s, who migrated overseas, but who also retained strong links to their local communities. These examples demonstrate the ways in which identity with a local region may remain strong, or even be intensified, after long-distance migration.

George Osborne was born in Northampton in 1820, and at the age of sixteen was apprenticed as an agricultural implement manufacturer in Essex. However, he did not like the iron trade and at the age of twenty-one decided to emigrate to Australia. He sailed from Portsmouth to Sydney Cove on the 13 May 1841 and in his journal described himself as:

> … *ready for any kind of employment for a living and having a desire to see and experience more of the ways and customs of the world than he could do behind a counter at home.*[15]

However, his experiences in and around Sydney did not live up to his expectations. He encountered some illness, described his initial job as "very dull" and then spent several weeks picking up whatever work was available in and around Sydney. By mid-January 1842, only 4 months after he had arrived, George decided to return home. His journal recorded:

> *I thought of getting work in an engine factory but found my health so indifferent that my mind was soon made up to leave this horrid hole at once and once more see the only bit of earth in my estimation worth living for and I sincerely hoped there to spend the rest of my days for I felt it was better to live upon bread & water in the midst of one's Friends than to live independent in a country where I had not yet seen a soul that I knew at home.*[16]

George could not afford the fare home so signed on as a seaman and left on the 17 February 1842 when he wrote: "This day I took my last look at detestable Sydney".[17]

When he arrived back in England he went first to his hometown of Northampton, but remained there only a couple of years before taking a job as clerk in an iron works in Staffordshire where he married and lived for 30 years.

Certainly in his younger days George Osborne was someone who viewed his home region as more attractive when he was away from it than he did when he lived there. He was clearly dissatisfied with his life in England when he decided to emigrate, but he had little knowledge of what to expect in Australia, and no family or friends in Sydney. His initial impression of Australia was negative and he gave it little chance to improve. From a distance friends and family in Northampton were much more attractive than they had been 6 months earlier. It can thus be suggested that for George Osborne migration to an alien environment led him to exaggerate all the positive aspects of his home region and to play down the negative factors that encouraged him to leave in the first place. The advantages of home, familiarity, friendship and comfort far outweighed the perceived hardships and inconveniences of Sydney in the 1840s. The fact that on his return he did not stay long in Northampton, but moved to Staffordshire to seek new work, suggests that once back in England many of his original reservations about his home region returned. We only have a detailed journal for his voyage to Australia, but the fact that he subsequently remained for 30 years in the same town in Staffordshire suggests that at the age of twenty-four he transferred his regional identity to this area, with marriage and his own family possibly providing the key settling factor.

In contrast, John James, born in Sithney, Cornwall in 1822, had a very different experience of travel overseas. He was a skilled tin miner and during his life rose to the position of mine manager, but for long periods found it impossible to find work in Cornwall. In addition to moving within Cornwall, at various times he worked in Newcastle upon Tyne and Garston (near Liverpool) in Britain, and overseas in North America (in Tennessee and Newfoundland), Ireland and, more briefly, in Norway and Belgium. The main motive for movement cited in the journal of John James was the need to find employment. It is clear that by preference he would have remained in Cornwall, but the uncertainty of work in the Cornish tin industry forced him to take his skills elsewhere, often for long periods. On some such trips he took members of his family with him, but at other times he was away from his family for a substantial amount of time.

His close affinity with Cornwall as a place, with his friends and family members that were still there, and with the community of Cornish tin miners comes through in many diary entries. Thus in 1869 after moving to Newfoundland he wrote:

> *After having been home from Norway near two months with but little prospect of a situation. Trying to help bring out New Rosewarne Mine but without success, everthing in the mining world being dull, I accepted the offer of a situation in this place – Burtins Pond – Notre Dame Bay, Newfoundland. This is through my friend Mr. Pike. Went to Liverpool, engaged with C J Browning Esq. the head of the firm. My salary £250 per annum, taking with me my son & seven others as miners at £8 per month, also a smith at £10 per month. Also took with me wife & three daughters, leaving home three others. This course would never have been adopted if I could have seen any other source. I have left friends whom I hope to meet again. It seems I must follow what I hope are providential openings. We left on 4th August 1869 via Bristol and Liverpool.*[18]

He remained in Newfoundland for two years but on returning home again found it hard to find work in Cornwall. One journal entry read:

We have been home about three months. I have had much anxiety. I have had no situation, have travelled many miles & made many inquiries after mine situations etc, but have not succeeded to anything as yet. There are some friends who would help me when opportunity offers & I hope to succeed soon. I have no desire to leave home & home comforts again.[19]

He did remain in Cornwall for a couple of years, though to find work he was forced to travel widely in the county and often lived away from home. However, in 1873 lack of work again forced him to travel overseas, this time to work as a mine manager at Ballycastle coal and iron mine in Ireland. Initially he travelled alone and wrote in his diary: "...was very sorry to have again to leave home, but it seemed I had no alternative."[20] The following year he gave up his home in Cornwall and his wife joined him in Ireland. His diary entry recorded rather ruefully: "It seemed as if I could not stay at home ... It is a new line of life to me, this management of coal and Iron mines ... I shall soon get used to it."[21]

Towards the end of his journal he looked forward to his return to Cornwall, stressing the climatic advantages of the south west:

I think it is time for me to leave this strong Northern atmosphere. If my life be spared until the end of March next I hope to go to Cornwall and try the effect of a warmer climate and my native air.[22]

He viewed all his moves as temporary and despite 10 years in Ireland from 1873–83, he returned to Cornwall at the age of sixty-one where he died some 2 years later.

John James was skilled and well travelled, but it is clear from his diary that despite living elsewhere for long periods he never lost his Cornish identity. For John there were a number of elements that made Cornwall special: the climate and landscape; the employment in tin mining that he knew so well; and his family, friends and comforts of home. However, although people were important to John James, even when most members of his family were with him overseas he still retained a strong identity with Cornwall and a desire to return to the part of England that he called home. It is clear that for John James Cornwall offered something that was special and distinctive, and that could not be replicated elsewhere even when he had his immediate family with him.

The final case study moves into the twentieth century, and focuses on the way in which a teenage girl who moved from Londonderry (Northern Ireland) to London (England) in the 1930s constructed a new identity in the city. Rhona Little left

Londonderry in January 1938 at the age of eighteen to take up work as a typist with the Inland Revenue in London. She had never travelled outside Northern Ireland before and this was her first experience of independent living outside the parental home. However, she quickly settled into her new life in London, she adopted deliberate strategies to explore the city, and her diary gives no evidence that she missed her home unduly, although in March 1938 she commented on other girls in her hostel who did display feelings of homesickness: "The new girl S had an attack of homesickness at breakfast, she had one yesterday too. I wouldn't like to be homesick."[23]

The only times that she seemed to miss her home and family was after she had direct contact with them. Thus despite living happily in London for 6 months after she had been home for 2 week's annual leave in July 1938 Rhona recorded her departure to London as follows:

Round about this time I lost control of my feelings and felt altogether dreadful. I said goodbye to everyone... It was awful having to go away... I felt like weeping when I said goodbye to Daddy.[24]

Thus whilst she lived in London, and was busy with her everyday life, she seemed not to miss home and family, but when reminded directly of them through visits after 6 months in London this rekindled a strong sense of identity with her home in Londonderry. However, only 2 months later in September 1938 with the threat of war becoming imminent, Rhona recorded the sentiments outlined in the opening quotation. Despite the opportunity to return to the relative safety of Northern Ireland, she felt as though she had transferred her life to London and saw no advantages in returning home. This is reinforced by views expressed in an interview with Rhona conducted in 1996, where she stressed that by this time her place identity had been fully transferred to London:

Oh after a year or so. When the war came I never thought of going home.

I don't remember anyone at home saying why aren't you coming home...

I would have said I was beginning to become a native, yes, I liked London.[25]

For Rhona Little long distance migration led to the quite rapid adoption of a new place identity, with London providing a number of key advantages in terms of employment, new sets of friends and, especially, independence. In contrast to John James, who despite widespread travel retained a strong Cornish identity, after 6 months or so in London Rhona Little entertained no desires to return home and seemed to lose her affinity with Londonderry as a place. However, she retained her personal identity as a Northern Irish Protestant with a distinctive accent, and she continued to value family and retained relatively close contact with them through letters and occasional visits.[26]

Discussion

The principal argument advanced in this chapter is that the links between migration and regional identity are complex and can manifest themselves in a variety of ways. It has been demonstrated that most migration took place over short distances, that those who moved further mostly had particular characteristics, and that individual case histories indicate the ways in which regional identity operated at a variety of spatial scales and had multiple layers of interpretation. For some, links to a local community inhibited migration and led to return movement; for others long-distance migration led to exaggeration of the virtues of their home area and a heightened sense of identity; yet other migrants quickly adopted a new place identity after migration, though this did not necessarily alter significantly their personal identity. The factors that constructed

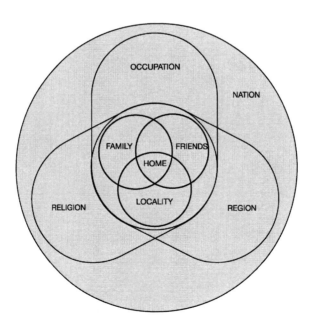

Figure 1.

regional identities, and that made a particular region distinctive and of value to an individual, were also varied. Whilst some migrants identified with the characteristics of place (landscape, climate); others emphasised people (family, friends and community); whilst others identified with activities, opportunities and special interest groups that were available within a locality (employment, religion).

These factors, that made a region distinctive and offered advantage to particular people, can be summarised as a series of overlapping sets (Figure 1). Locality, family and friends were likely to be the most close-knit influences on identity, and were usually focused on a specific area, though some migrants could take at least part of their family and friendship group with them on their travels. These factors may have sat within broader characteristics that overlapped within a region of identity but were not peculiar to it. Thus it was possible to move over quite a wide area and to remain attached to a particular community of employment or religion. Beyond this, overseas migrants might have retained their identity with a large region or even the nation. Many other factors could be incorporated into the schema. Ethnicity was obviously an important factor for some migrants, though not for the categories examined in detail in this paper, and for some gender-based communities may have been important. However, although opportunities for female employment did vary spatially in the past, gender-based communities were unlikely to exhibit strong regional differentiation and, in any case, are likely to be reflected in family and friendship networks.

In conclusion, it is argued that it is hard to produce any more meaningful generalisations about the links between migration and regional identity, or to relate it simply to one over-arching theoretical or conceptual framework. Not only were the links between migration and regional identity complex and multi-faceted, but also they depended heavily on individual circumstances and individual personality. Whilst it is possible to identify the sorts of factors that affected regional identity and how it was changed during and after migration – variables such as ties to family and friends, communities of occupation or religion and particular landscape preferences – it is much less easy to say what factors were important for individual migrants and how migration and regional identity may be linked. In most cases, the nature of the relationship, and the ways in which regional identity was formed and changed related to a combination of particular circumstances and personality characteristics, which themselves could change over time.

This is not to argue that regional identity is unimportant. Rather it is suggested that it should be viewed as one of a set of variable characteristics that can only be understood in the context of an individual's life course and within the framework of all the other circumstances that affected life course decisions. In one sense it is hardly original to suggest that identity is a highly variable and personal phenomenon, but this obvious point is sometimes overlooked in historical analyses. Because individual-level information about identity with place or region is rarely available for the past, there is a strong temptation to infer associations from general social and cultural theories. However, these tend to emphasise large group characteristics or identities related to factors such as nationality, ethnicity, gender, class or community.[27] This chapter argues that for most people regional identity was much more complex and permeable than this, and that there is a need to balance such generalisations with a fuller understanding of how individual migrants constructed, changed and used their regional identities.

Acknowledgements

The original research on migration in Britain since 1750 on which much of this chapter is based was funded by the Economic and Social Research Council and was carried out in collaboration with Dr Jean Turnbull. Many thanks to all the family historians who provided migration life histories and especially those who gave access to family diaries and life histories. Thanks also to Cleo Small for research assistance with the regression analysis.

Notes

1. Family History of Benjamin Shaw, Preston Record Office, DDX/1154/1, 27 (July 1791). See also Crosby, A. (Ed.) (1991) *The Family records of Benjamin Shaw Mechanic of Dent. Dolphinholme and Preston, 1772–1841* (The Record Society of Lancashire and Cheshire, CXXX).
2. Unpublished diary of Rhona Little, 15 September 1938. Copy held by C. Pooley, Department of Geography, Lancaster University.
3. Williams, B. (1976) *The making of Manchester Jewry* (Manchester: Manchester University Press); Swift, R. & Gilley, S. (Eds) (1989) *The Irish in Britain, 1815–1919* (London: Pinter); Davis, G. (1991) *The Irish in Britain, 1815–1914* (Dublin: Gill and MacMillan); Holmes, C. (1991) *A tolerant country? Immigrants, refugees and minorities in Britain* (London: Faber). MacRaild, D. (Ed.) (2000) *The Great Famine and beyond: Irish migrants in Britain in the nineteenth and twentieth centuries* (Dublin: Irish Academic Press); Endelman, T. (2002) *The Jews of Britain, 1656 to 2000* (Berkley, Ca: University of California Press).
4. Krausz, E. (1971) *Ethnic minorities in Britain* (London: MacGibbon and Kee); Rex, J. & Tomlinson, S. (1979) *Colonial immigrants in a British city: a class analysis* (London: Routledge); Walvin, J. (1984) *Passage to Britain: Immigration in British History and Politics* (Harmondsworth: Penguin); Robinson, V. (1989) 'Economic restructuring: the urban crisis and Britain's Black population' in Herbert, D. & Smith, D. (Eds) *Social problems and the city.* (Oxford: Oxford University Press) 247–70; Rex, J. (1991) *Ethnic identity and ethnic mobilisation in Britain* (Coventry: Centre for Research in Ethnic Relations, University of Warwick).

5. Joly, D. & Cohen, R. (Eds) (1989) *Reluctant hosts: Europe and its refugees* (Aldershot: Gower); Castles, S. & Miller, M.J. (1993) *The Age of Migration* (London: Macmillan); Black, R. & Robinson, V. (Eds) (1993) *Geography and refugees* (London: Belhaven); King, R. (Ed.) (1993) *Mass migrations in Europe* (London: Belhaven); Al-Ali, N., Black, R. & Khoser, K. (2001) 'The limits to transnationalism: Bosnian and Eritrean refugees in Europe as emerging transnational communities', *Ethnic and Racial Studies* 24, 578–600.

6. Vertovec, S. & Cohen, R. (Eds) (1999) *Migration, diasporas and transnationalism* (Cheltenham: Edward Elgar); Castles, S. (2000) *Ethnicity and globalisation: from migrant worker to transnational citizen* (London: Sage); Vertovec, S. (Ed.) (2001) 'Transnationalism and identity', Special Issue, *Journal of Ethnic and Migration Studies*, 27, 573–748; Yeo, B., Charney, M. & Kiong, T. (2003) *Approaching transnationalisms: studies in transnational societies, multicultural contacts and imaginings of home* (Boston: Kluwer Academic).

7. These issues are discussed in the context of contemporary Canadian regional identity in: Bickerton, J. (2001) *The political voice of Canadian regional identities.* (http://www.mta.ca/faculty/arts/canadian_studies/english/about/study_guide/regional/index.html)

8. Pooley, C. & Turnbull, J. (1998) *Migration and mobility in Britain since the eighteenth century* (London: UCL Press).

9. Griffith, D. & Amrhein, C (1997) *Multivariate statistical analysis for Geographers* (Prentice Hall: Upper Saddle River, NJ).

10. Danson, J. & Welton. T. (1857–60) 'On the population of Lancashire and Cheshire and its local distribution during the fifty years 1801–51', *Transactions of the Historic Society of Lancashire and Cheshire*, 9, 195–212; 10, 1–36; 11, 1–70; 12, 35–74; Ravenstein, E.G. (1885 and 1889) 'The laws of migration', *Journal of the Royal Statistical Society*, 48, 167–227; 52, 214–301; Redford, A. (1926) *Labour migration in England*, 1800–1850 (Manchester: Manchester University Press); Lee, E. (1966) 'A theory of migration', *Demography*, 3, 47–57; Friedlander, D. & Roshier, R. (1966) 'A study of internal migration in England and Wales', *Population Studies*, 19, 239–79; Darroch, G. (1981) 'Migrants in the nineteenth century: fugitives or families in motion', *Journal of Family History*, 6, 257–77; Pooley, C.G. (1983) 'Welsh migration to England in the mid-nineteenth century', *Journal of Historical Geography*, 9, 287–305; Woods, R. (1985) 'Towards a general theory of migration', in White, P. & van der Knap, P. (Eds) *Contemporary studies of migration*, (Norwich: Geobooks) 1–5; Schurer, K. (1991) 'The role of the family in the process of migration'. In Pooley, C. & Whyte, I. (Eds) *Migrants, emigrants and immigrants: a social history of migration* (London: Routledge), 106–142; Southall, H. (1991) 'The tramping artizan revisits: labour mobility and economic distress in early Victorian England', *Economic History Review*, 44, 272–91; Reay, B. (1996) *Microhistories: demography, society and culture in rural England*, 1800–1930 (Cambridge: Cambridge University Press).

11. Jane Austin (1813) *Pride and Prejudice* Volume II, chapter 9 (chapter 32),

12. Family History of Benjamin Shaw, Preston Record Office, DDX/1154/1, 21 (July 1791). See also Crosby, A. (Ed.) (1991) *The Family records of Benjamin Shaw Mechanic of Dent. Dolphinholme and Preston*, 1772–1841 (The Record Society of Lancashire and Cheshire, CXXX).

13. See also Pooley C. & D'Cruze S. (1994) 'Migration and urbanization in North West England, circa 1760–1830,' *Social History*, 19, 339–58.

14. Life History of Amos Kniveton, 1835–1927, provided by Mr W Melling. Copy held by C. Pooley, Department of Geography, Lancaster University.

15. Journal of George Osborne, 1841–42, provided by Mrs S. A. Moyle. Copy held by C. Pooley, Department of Geography, Lancaster University.

16. *Ibid.*

17. *Ibid.*
18. Journal of John James, 1847–80 provided by Mr M. D. Smith. Copy held by C. Pooley, Department of Geography, Lancaster University. A transcript of this journal is also available in the Cornish Studies Library at Alma Place, Redruth.
19. *Ibid.*
20. *Ibid.*
21. *Ibid.*
22. *Ibid.*
23. Diary of Rhona Little, 1932–59, provided by Mrs R.M.I. Ward. Copy held by C. Pooley, Department of Geography, Lancaster University.
24. *Ibid.*
25. Interview with Rhona Ward (née Little), London, 1996.
26. See also Pooley, C. (1999) 'From Londonderry to London: Identity and sense of place for a Protestant Northern Irish woman in the 1930s', *Immigrants and Minorities* 18, 189–213; Pooley, C. (2004) 'Getting to know the city: the construction of spatial knowledge in London in the 1930s', *Urban History*, 31.
27. Hobsbawm, E.J. *Nations and nationalism since 1780* (Cambridge University Press, 1990); Engman, M., Carter, F., Hepburn, A. & Pooley, C. (Eds) (1992) *Ethnic identity in urban Europe* (Dartmouth, 1992); Colley, L. (2003) *Britain: forging the nation, 1707–1837* (London: Pimlico).

Bibliography

Al-Ali, N., Black, R. & Khoser, K. (2001) 'The limits to transnationalism: Bosnian and Eritrean refugees in Europe as emerging transnational communities', *Ethnic and Racial Studies*, 24, 578–600.

Bickerton, J. (2001) *The political voice of Canadian regional identities.* Available at: (http://www.mta.ca/faculty/arts/canadian_studies/english/about/study_guide/regional/index.html)

Black, R. & Robinson, V. (Eds) (1993) *Geography and refugees* (London: Belhaven).

Castles, S. & Miller, M.J. (1993) *The Age of Migration* (London: Macmillan).

Castles, S. (2000) *Ethnicity and globalisation: from migrant worker to transnational citizen* (London: Sage).

Colley, L. (2003) *Britain: forging the nation, 1707–1837* (London: Pimlico).

Crosby, A. (Ed.) (1991) *The Family records of Benjamin Shaw Mechanic of Dent. Dolphinholme and Preston, 1772–1841* (The Record Society of Lancashire and Cheshire, CXXX).

Danson, J. & Welton. T. (1857–60) 'On the population of Lancashire and Cheshire and its local distribution during the fifty years 1801–51', *Transactions of the Historic Society of Lancashire and Cheshire*, 9, 195–212; 10, 1–36; 11, 1–70; 12, 35–74.

Darroch, G. (1981) 'Migrants in the nineteenth century: fugitives or families in motion', *Journal of Family History* 6, 257–77.

Davis, G. (1991) *The Irish in Britain*, 1815–1914 (Dublin: Gill and MacMillan).

Endelman, T. (2002) *The Jews of Britain*, 1656 to 2000 (Berkley, Ca: University of California Press).

Engman, M., Carter, F., Hepburn, A. & Pooley, C. (Eds) (1992) *Ethnic identity in urban Europe* (Dartmouth).

Friedlander, D. & Roshier, R. (1966) 'A study of internal migration in England and Wales' *Population Studies*, 19, 239–79.

Griffith, D. & Amrhein, C (1997) *Multivariate statistical analysis for Geographers* (Prentice Hall: Upper Saddle River, NJ).

Hobsbawm, E.J. (1990) *Nations and nationalism since 1780* (Cambridge University Press).

Holmes, C. (1991) *A tolerant country? Immigrants, refugees and minorities in Britain* (London: Faber).

Joly, D. & Cohen, R. (Eds) (1989) *Reluctant hosts: Europe and its refugees* (Aldershot: Gower).

King, R. (Ed.) (1993) *Mass migrations in Europe* (London: Belhaven).

Krausz, E. (1971) *Ethnic minorities in Britain* (London: MacGibbon and Kee).

Lee, E. (1966) 'A theory of migration', *Demography*, 3, 47–57.

MacRaild, D. (Ed.) (2000) *The Great Famine and beyond: Irish migrants in Britain in the nineteenth and twentieth centuries* (Dublin: Irish Academic Press).

Pooley, C.G. (1983) 'Welsh migration to England in the mid-nineteenth century', *Journal of Historical Geography*, 9, 287–305.

Pooley, C. (1999) 'From Londonderry to London: Identity and sense of place for a Protestant Northern Irish woman in the 1930s' *Immigrants and Minorities*, 18, 189–213.

Pooley, C. (2004) 'Getting to know the city: the construction of spatial knowledge in London in the 1930s', *Urban History*, 31.

Pooley C. & D'Cruze S. (1994) 'Migration and urbanization in North West England, circa 1760–1830', *Social History*, 19, 339–58.

Pooley, C. & Turnbull, J. (1998) *Migration and mobility in Britain since the eighteenth century* (London: UCL Press).

Ravenstein, E.G. (1885 and 1889) 'The laws of migration', *Journal of the Royal Statistical Society*, 48, 167–227; 52, 214–301.

Reay, B. (1996) *Microhistories: demography, society and culture in rural England, 1800–1930* (Cambridge: Cambridge University Press).

Redford, A. (1926) *Labour migration in England, 1800–1850* (Manchester: Manchester University Press).

Rex, J. & Tomlinson, S. (1979) *Colonial immigrants in a British city: a class analysis* (London: Routledge).

Rex, J. (1991) *Ethnic identity and ethnic mobilisation in Britain* (Coventry: Centre for research in ethnic relations, University of Warwick).

Robinson, V. (1989) 'Economic restructuring: the urban crisis and Britain's Black population', in Herbert, D. & Smith, D. (Eds) *Social problems and the city* (Oxford: Oxford University Press), 247–70.

Schurer, K. (1991) 'The role of the family in the process of migration', in Pooley, C. & Whyte, I. (Eds) *Migrants, emigrants and immigrants: a social history of migration* (London: Routledge), 106–142.

Southall, H. (1991) 'The tramping artizan revisits: labour mobility and economic distress in early Victorian England', *Economic History Review*, 44, 272–91.

Swift, R. & Gilley, S. (Eds) (1989) *The Irish in Britain, 1815–1919* (London: Pinter).

Vertovec, S. & Cohen, R. (Eds) (1999) *Migration, diasporas and transnationalism* (Cheltenham: Edward Elgar).

Vertovec, S. (Ed) (2001) 'Transnationalism and identity' Special Issue, *Journal of Ethnic and Migration Studies*, 27, 573–748.

Walvin, J. (1984) *Passage to Britain: Immigration in British History and Politics.* (Harmondsworth: Penguin).

Williams, B. (1976) *The making of Manchester Jewry* (Manchester: Manchester University Press).

Woods, R. (1985) 'Towards a general theory of migration', in White, P. & van der Knap, P. (Eds) *Contemporary studies of migration*, (Norwich: Geobooks), 1–5.

Yeo, B., Charney, M. & Kiong, T. (2003) *Approaching transnationalisms: studies in transnational societies, multicultural contacts and imaginings of home* (Boston: Kluwer Academic).

Part Two

Region and Empire

Chapter Five

Regions and regionalism in early modern German history

Peter H. Wilson

The Holy Roman Empire has been presented recently by a German historian as an early modern "Central Europe of the regions". Its constitution fostered and protected "cultural diversity", stimulating activity and progress through economic interchange and cultural cross-fertilisation, whilst leaving niches in which minorities could preserve their own distinctiveness.[1] This positive image stands in stark contrast with the earlier depiction of the Empire as a symbol of German national disunity and political impotency. Supposedly lacking both a clear centre of power and the infrastructure necessary to make firm government effective, the Empire gradually fell apart, particularly after confessional conflict arising from the Reformation tainted the efforts of the Catholic Habsburg emperors to assert greater authority. Following the turmoil of the early seventeenth century, the Empire allegedly fragmented into a loose federation of independent principalities after 1648 until it was pushed aside by Napoleonic France in 1806.[2] Few would now accept this condemnation of the Empire as a failed nation state. Four decades of careful research have shown that its institutions continued to function, even in the late eighteenth century. However, some bold claims have been made recently, pushing the positive reappraisal in two different directions. One completely overturns the earlier critique by suggesting the Empire was the first German nation state.[3] The other goes still further and presents it as a model for current European integration.[4]

The recent trend raises some important questions about the place of regions in early modern German history. Firstly, how should we interpret regions within German history at a time when "Germany" did not exist? Though the appellation "of the German nation" was tacked onto the formal title of the Empire in the late fifteenth century, this First, or "old" Reich was never synonymous with a nation state. Not only did other cultural and linguistic groups, like Czechs, Slovaks and Poles, form a significant proportion of its population, but the early modern sense of belonging cannot be reduced to nineteenth-century "blood and soil" criteria.[5]

Secondly, what is the place of a region in a country that lacks an established tradition of strong central government? The experience of the Second (1871–1918) and Third Reichs (1933–45) rather obscures that of the First, which lacked firm hereditary rule from its foundation in 800 and formally adopted elected succession by the thirteenth century. Monarchy remained itinerant throughout the middle ages as the sovereign governed by royal progress, dispensing justice, rallying support and punishing opponents as he travelled across his vast, sparsely inhabitant realm.[6] Power remained diffuse despite the transition to imperial rule based on hereditary dynastic possessions in the fourteenth century.

The Habsburg *de facto* monopoly of the imperial title after 1438 did not change this, since they had to bargain for each succession with the key princes, who could, as they demonstrated in 1742, elect a rival instead.[7] Moreover, centralised rule emerged relatively late in the Empire's component territories. The Habsburg monarchy remained a composite state into the nineteenth century, and while that of their Hohenzollern rivals developed central institutions somewhat earlier, these were never as comprehensive or effective as depicted by patriotic Prussian historians.[8]

Finally, there is the more theoretical issue of a region's place in the process of state formation. State formation is generally presented as a violent process in which regions are forcibly incorporated within an expanding nation state. In Norbert Elias' model, for instance, local and regional power-holders are reduced through a series of "elimination contests" to leave a single victor. In Stein Rokkan's centre-periphery analysis, states emerge through competition between border areas and heartlands. More generally, regions are simply gobbled up as successful war-making states seek fresh resources.[9] Discussions are frequently coloured by ideologically-charged interpretations of the State as either benevolent or repressive. In the former, mainly conservative model, state expansion offers regions the benefits of protection, administration and development through integration within wider markets. In the latter, largely critical view from the left, expansion deprives regions and their inhabitants of their autonomy and identity. Either way, regions are presented as acted upon, rather than actors in the process of state development. They can either collaborate or resist, but rarely do they contribute anything beyond additional resources.

The German case offers an especially fruitful point of departure for these questions, because there was no exact match between what are commonly considered its regions and the main political sub-divisions of the Empire into territories like Brandenburg, Austria and Bavaria. The Empire thus differed from the western European norm where regions generally corresponded with older kingdoms, duchies and counties that were subsumed within national monarchies, as in England, Spain and France, or survived as independent mini-states as in Italy. This chapter will explore these questions in two sections, beginning with the place of the region in the writing of the early modern German past. The second analyses the *Kreise*, or "imperial circles", which represented the main areas for regional politics within the Empire after 1500. The conclusion will address the more theoretical issue of how we might conceive a region within early modern politics.

The region in medieval and early modern German history

The idea of a region as a political entity scarcely figures in German historiography prior to the later twentieth century. Central European development was viewed through the lens of the nineteenth-century ideal of the nation state and the old Reich presented as a "German Empire". Political development was thought to be advancing at two levels with some form of nation state as the inevitable outcome. One possibility was that the emperor would subordinate the territorial princes and create a national monarchy, thus permitting Germany to reach modernity by the route taken in France, Spain and Britain. Alternatively, the princes would wrest sufficient power from the emperor to achieve independence as sovereign rulers of miniature centralised monarchies. These would then eliminate each other in a Darwinian struggle of the fittest to create a single nation state. This is indeed what happened according to the Prussian Historical School of the mid-nineteenth century that ascribed a "historic mission" to the Hohenzollern dynasty to unite the country by defeating the Catholic multicultural Habsburg monarchy.

This twin-track history left little room for regions. The national perspective concentrated on high politics, chronicling what was thought to be a series of failed attempts by successive emperors to impose central control. What might be considered regional history in other countries was subsumed within what Germans call *Landesgeschichte*. Though sometimes translated as "regional history", the word Land means territory as distinct from the vaguer term *Region*. The latter was introduced through the social sciences since the 1970s, along with Raum, or space. The more recent theoretical discussion distinguishes between usage of these terms as analytical constructs imposing coherence on social and economic activity, and as political products and the result of sentimental identification with a given area.[10] The term *Land* encompassed territorial rights, such as jurisdictions, customs, and other prerogatives. These were often shared between different lords, especially in southern, western and central Germany where fragmented, overlapping lordship prevailed throughout the middle ages and the early modern era. The nature of lordship changed, particularly with the transition from rule over people to that over land, as well as the emergence from the twelfth century of a distinct group of territorial princes standing above a lengthening hierarchy of other nobles.[11] It was logical to concentrate on political history, chronicling territorial development as the accumulation of land and rights and their concentration in the hands of a single, princely family. The fortunes of Germany's princely dynasties have thus imposed their own boundaries and hierarchy on *Landesgeschichte*. The dominant traditions are those associated with the thirty or so dynasties that survived the Empire's collapse in 1806 and emerged as kings or grand dukes thanks to French or Russian patronage. Most of these were still on the throne when historical societies and journals were founded between the 1830s and 1880s. These organs survived the vicissitudes of the twentieth century and still overshadow the journals and societies dedicated to the lands of the 200 or so dynasties that lost their autonomy in the territorial redistribution between 1803 and 1806.[12]

However, newer forms of social, economic and cultural history have transformed *Landesgeschichte*, enabling it to shed its earlier antiquarianism and political conservatism. The reorganisation of Germany into sixteen *Bundesländer*, begun in 1949 and completed with reunification in 1990, encouraged this since the new areas bear only a passing resemblance to the old dynastic states and imposed new geographical parameters onto the past.[13] Local history also emerged from the dynastic shadow, starting life as the *Landesgeschichte* of those territories that failed to develop beyond 1806, and evolving through patriotic accounts of home towns to incorporate the new methodology of microhistory.[14] Though it remains a subdiscipline, *Landesgeschichte* continues to thrive and seems to have absorbed attempts to create a distinct economic and social "regional history" that started in the 1970s. Regional political history meanwhile took a new direction with the renewed interest in the *Kreise* as intermediary subdivisions within the Empire between the central imperial institutions and the myriad of princely territories. It helped that the *Kreise* resembled the *Bundesländer* more closely in name and location, but also that their consultative institutions and federal elements represented a more acceptable past than the dynastic states.[15]

The Kreise in German politics

Though they were not constituted until 1500–12, the *Kreise* rested on over six centuries of medieval development. Their structure was influenced by the pattern of medieval settlement that concentrated the Empire's population in numerous fragmented territories long-established in the south and west, with the remainder scattered across newer, larger and more contiguous principalities in the north and east. While clearly influenced by physical geography, this process was determined primarily by the political evolution of the Empire as a feudal hierarchy subordinate to the emperor's jurisdiction, but not to his direct authority. This was given definitive shape through a combination of internal and external pressures between 1480 and 1520 that forced lords to define their relationship to the wider imperial structure. Though holding a bewildering variety of titles, territorial rulers emerged as a princely elite under the emperor's immediate jurisdiction and, together with the free cities, secured a say in the management of the Empire through their representation in the *Reichstag* (imperial diet) and other imperial institutions. Other lords and towns fell under the jurisdiction of one of these "imperial estates" (*Reichsstände*) and were only indirectly subject to the emperor's authority.[16] The *Kreise* were inserted as an intermediary level between emperor and territories to assist in the maintenance of public order and external security. The imperial estates – with some minor exceptions – were incorporated within one of the ten *Kreise* by 1512 in a process that owed more to prevailing politics than to the legacy of the medieval economic and political zones within the Empire.

Four factors proved decisive. The first was the Habsburg's desire to keep their own hereditary lands outside the jurisdiction of the new imperial institutions. Habsburg imperial rule rested on their extensive dynastic possessions that were concentrated north of the Alps from the Upper Rhine to the Hungarian Plain. Their inability to subdue the Swiss split these lands after 1499 and ensured that Switzerland remained outside the *Kreis* structure.[17] The other parts became the Austrian *Kreis* in 1512, even though those in Alsace and the Upper Rhine were physically separate from Austria itself. While Austria was indisputably part of the Empire, uncertainty surrounded the Burgundian lands that straggled down the Rhine into the modern Netherlands. France disputed the Habsburg inheritance of Burgundy in 1477 and many princes were reluctant to be drawn into what they saw as the emperor's private affair. The Habsburgs were also keen to limit princely interference in Burgundian affairs, particularly once the northern Netherlands rose in revolt after 1568. Consequently, the Burgundian lands were grouped into a separate *Kreis* that was transferred to the Spanish branch of the Habsburgs after 1548 and only returned in truncated form to Austria in 1700.[18]

Habsburg-Wittelsbach rivalry was a second decisive factor. Emperor Maximilian I (1493–1519) was determined to weaken the Wittelsbachs who had already provided two recent emperors and were the Habsburg's main rivals. By intervening in an inheritance dispute between Bavaria and the Palatinate, he managed to keep the family divided and entrenched this by ensuring that, unlike Habsburg territory, Wittelsbach land was split between several *Kreise*. He also balanced the rising power of Bavaria by grouping it with Salzburg, one of the most powerful ecclesiastical principalities, in the Bavarian *Kreis*.[19] Traditional imperial clientele amongst the smaller cities and counties were insulated from Wittelsbach interference by placing them in the Franconian and Swabian Kreise that together evolved from the earlier Swabian League founded by Maximilian's predecessor as a means of managing the south-west of the Empire.[20]

Disputes within the imperial hierarchy determined the shape of the *Kreise* to the north. Seven princes acquired exclusive rights as "electors" to choose each emperor by the mid-fourteenth century.[21] The three ecclesiastical electors and their leading secular colleague, the elector Palatine, were concerned to preserve their "electoral pre-eminence", and only accepted incorporation by grouping their lands as a distinct Electoral Rhenish *Kreis*. This split the Rhineland. The southern part became the Upper Rhenish *Kreis* that nominally included the duchy of Savoy, the only part of northern "imperial Italy" to be included within the new structure. The rump of the lower Rhine was combined with the rest of Westphalia as a separate *Kreis* that only became fully distinct from the Burgundian lands in 1548.[22] These decisions also reflected the emperor's concern to marginalise princes that could disrupt Habsburg plans. The powerful landgraviate of Hessen was distracted by internal problems and was assigned to the Upper Rhine, rather than forming the core of an alternative central German region. Likewise, the Thuringian duchies were given to a new Saxon Kreis that encompassed the north and eastern territories that had been on the periphery of imperial influence since the 1430s. Establishing a working relationship with the elector of Saxony gave the Habsburgs a measure of influence here after 1547, by which time this unwieldy area had split into eastern, Upper, and western, Lower, halves.[23]

The final piece of the puzzle was placed by reactions to the Hussite insurrection in the Bohemian lands in 1419–34. Bohemia already held a special place within the medieval Empire through its possession of its own royal title, as well as relatively clear frontiers and a distinct language, culture and economy. While the Bohemian king was recognised as an elector in 1356, he kept his lands largely beyond imperial jurisdiction. Bohemia became more closely involved in imperial politics as its crown passed to the Luxembourg dynasty which held the imperial title between 1347 and 1437. The Hussite insurrection was perceived as a common threat and was only subdued with great difficulty. Most princes were happy to keep the land at arms' length as the *Kreise* were being established, and the Habsburgs were content to perpetuate this arrangement when they inherited the crown in 1526.[24] Other German-ruled lands beyond the imperial frontier escaped incorporation, notably Prussia that emerged from the wreckage of the Teutonic Order state in 1525.

The internal structure of the *Kreise* also reflected the Empire's uneven development. The Habsburgs had exclusive possession of the Burgundian *Kreis*, and dominated the Austrian *Kreis* that had only three other members. Both organisations existed only on paper, but could be invoked whenever the Habsburgs wished to act in concert with neighbouring regions. The other eight *Kreise* developed formal institutions that roughly replicated the distribution of power between emperor and Reichstag on a regional basis. Each *Kreis* was headed by one or two "convening princes" (*Kreisausschreibenden Fürsten*), who summoned the assembly (*Kreistag*) and acted as the formal conduit for all correspondence with higher institutions. The assembly did not replicate the Reichstag's tri-cameral structure, but instead gave each member an equal vote regardless of size or status.[25] The *Kreise* were initially established to select judges for the *Reichskammergericht*, or new supreme court established in 1495 to arbitrate political disputes within the Empire. They acquired additional functions as subsequent legislation consolidated the public peace and linked it to new mechanisms for the Empire's collective security.[26] Recent research has done much to demonstrate their continued vitality despite the mounting confessional tension within the late sixteenth-century Empire and the subsequent Thirty Years War.[27] The Peace of Westphalia assisted in their renewal by extending their functions to maintain peace and assist in external defence. The latter assumed greater significance with the imperial defence reform of 1681–82 that enabled the Empire to resist the dual threat of Louis XIV's France and the Ottoman empire.[28]

The broader impact of the *Kreise* was to secularise regional politics and sustain the traditional imperial hierarchy, thus prolonging the Empire's existence. For the first development it is important to remember that the *Kreise* were established in 1500–12, before the onset of the religious schism after 1517 and that they were linked to the secular public peace. In their attempts to find a workable solution to religious discord, Emperor Charles V (1519–58) and his successors tried to isolate the theological difficulties by treating the crisis as a secular dispute over rights and property. The Empire renounced the option pursued by western European monarchies of imposing a single faith by force, and instead adopted an uniquely multi-confessional framework in 1555, granted toleration initially to Lutherans and then to Calvinists after 1648. Territorial rulers were free to remain Catholic or accept Lutheranism after 1555. Problems with this arrangement prompted the Peace of Westphalia to identify each territory permanently with whatever faith that had predominated in 1624. Minorities received formal protection and the right of dissenters to emigrate was extended.[29]

The territorial character of this settlement removed religion as a basis for an alternative regional sentiment. Having failed to establish a national organisation, Protestant rulers founded their own territorial churches (*Landeskirchen*), while the Catholics remained within their universal structure. Territories provided the basis of all confessional leagues from that of Dessau in 1524 to the Protestant Union and Catholic League on the eve of the Thirty Years War. Though radical Protestants sometimes invoked the higher authority of their evangelical faith, they followed the Catholics in anchoring their organisations firmly in the imperial constitution. Leagues occasionally exhibited a potential for real institutional growth, but usually relied on the *Kreis* structure to underpin their organisation.[30] Secular associations followed the same route, such as those of the imperial counts who combined for mutual protection and to secure recognition as full imperial estates.[31] Acceptance of confessional diversity within the Reich meant that most *Kreise* contained territories of differing faiths whose rights were protected by imperial law. Religious tension could impair the *Kreis* assemblies, just as it periodically paralysed the Reichstag, encouraging the search for confessionally neutral solutions that gradually took religion out of regional politics.

The growth of the *Kreise* confirmed the decline of the medieval diocese as an element of regional organisation. Catholic rulers had already secured some control over their clergy prior to the Reformation and extended this through further concordats with the papacy and German archbishops. Some dioceses disappeared or were truncated by the secularisation of a significant proportion of the ecclesiastical territories that collectively comprised the Catholic imperial church (*Reichskirche*). The remainder survived after 1648, thanks to the protection of imperial law, until they were annexed in the territorial reorganisation following 1801 Diocesan jurisdiction was an important element in Catholic reform efforts from the 1580s, but played little part in wider imperial politics. Other ecclesiastical and spiritual institutions exhibited even less potential as alternatives: the network of papal nuncios, and the provinces of the Jesuits and other religious orders, broadly followed the same political boundaries that underpinned the *Kreis* structure.

The role of the *Kreise* in sustaining the traditional imperial hierarchy was related to their part in the systems of conflict resolution and external security that were anchored in the public peace legislation. These systems received renewed interest from historians after the 1950s as potential antecedents to West German federal politics and defence policy. The defence reforms of 1681–82 entrusted the *Kreise* with coordinating contingents provided by the territories to repel French and

Ottoman attacks. The defensive character of this structure lent itself to being presented as a form of deterrence or collective security.[32] The political dimension was derived from the role of the *Kreise* in coordinating other activities and their potential for curbing the harmful consequences of dynastic ambition. The *Kreis* structure compensated for the extreme territorial fragmentation of the west and south by offering the numerous territorial governments a forum for addressing common problems like vagrancy, epidemics, currency and tariff regulation.[33] The assemblies permitted weak, but more numerous lesser territories to outvote their larger neighbours who were more inclined to engage in international conflict. By providing a regional forum for legislation and decision-making, they also counter-balanced the Reichstag that was dominated by the electors and major princes. This has led one historian to equate the Bavarian *Kreis* assembly with the modern *Bundesrat*.[34]

However, interest centres on the possibilities for cross-regional collaboration through *Kreis* Associations, or alliances.[35] Confusion over their role and potential has arisen through a failure to appreciate that political development within the Empire ran along multiple, often conflicting paths, rather than scoring a single trajectory either towards, or away from, a nation state.[36] The predominant trend was concerned with the strengthening the complex feudal hierarchy that underpinned the entire Empire which assumed its definitive shape in the constitutional reforms of 1480 to 1520. The Peace of Westphalia renewed this structure which, far from ossifying, continued to evolve into the eighteenth century. The other two trends bent this imperial spinal cord in opposite directions. The repeated efforts of successive emperors to achieve their dynastic and imperial goals pushed the Empire towards a unitary monarchy, even though few emperors intentionally sought this. Meanwhile, attempts by territorial rulers and other corporate groups to defend and extend their rights created opportunities for a more federal organisation. The princes emerged as the principle carriers of this trend following the defeat of earlier attempts by peasants and nobles to establish cross-regional associations.

Like many imperial institutions, the *Kreise* had the potential to assist any one of these paths. They provided the emperor with the means to rally support for his objectives. The power of medieval emperors had varied across the Empire depending on the location of their hereditary possessions, those of their relations and the distribution of the surviving crown lands.[37] The *Kreis* structure imposed a more formal framework by identifying regional leaders, creating assemblies and defining relations with the emperor and central institutions. The Habsburgs were quick to appreciate this and, having segregated their own lands into the Austrian and Burgundian *Kreise*, tried to use the others as a means to manage imperial politics. Emperor Charles V came the closest to realising this in 1548 when he attempted to impose a tripartite division of the Empire. Though it remained part of the Empire, government of Burgundy was assigned to Charles' son Philip, who founded the separate Spanish Habsburg branch on his father's death ten years later. Austria and Bohemia were entrusted to Charles's brother Ferdinand who continued the Austrian line after 1558. The remaining eight *Kreise* were to be used to rally the princes behind Habsburg objectives by marshalling the emperor's clientele into an "imperial alliance" (*Reichsbund*). This part of the programme was derailed by Charles's insistence on linking it to a controversial attempt to settle the religious controversy, largely in favour of the Catholics.[38] This did not prevent his successors using the *Kreise* as a means of raising men and money for their campaigns against the Ottomans whenever the Reichstag proved uncooperative. Ferdinand I (1619–37) tried to formalise this after 1630 by persuading the electors to agree regular war taxes to be collected through the *Kreise*. Inability to achieve military preponderance during the later stages of the Thirty Years War prevented this from being fully implemented.[39] The Peace of Westphalia restored the hierarchical structure by entrenching the Reichstag as the forum for national debate. Leopold I (1658–1705) accepted this after 1663 and agreed the defence reforms of 1681–2 that consolidated the traditional structure. However, the *Kreise* remained an option since the emperor could always appeal for the support of particular regions when other princes opposed his national demands in the Reichstag.

The *Kreis* Associations emerged in the 1650s as a response to Habsburg manipulation of the constitution. Few territorial rulers wanted to risk involvement in European conflicts after the Thirty Years War and saw collaboration through the *Kreise* as a means of maintaining armed neutrality. This was permissible under the imperial constitution that bound territories to keep the peace and prevented the emperor from starting a war on behalf of the Empire without the *Reichtag's* agreement. Continual French aggression and the growing Ottoman threat removed simple neutrality as an option by the 1670s and encouraged the use of the Associations as a way of influencing imperial military and foreign policy. By mobilising respectable collective forces, the *Kreise* gave weaker territories a voice and the Swabian-Franconian Association of 1691 proved that even the most fragmented part of the Empire could play a part in European diplomacy. The emperor and the more ambitious of the major princes were swift to appreciate the implications of these developments and both tried to bend the Associations to their ends. The shift towards a Europe of sovereign states was forcing the German princes to define their place in the new international order. The more senior dynasties and those with sizeable lands were not prepared to sink to the ranks of simple Central European aristocrats and sought royal titles and other foreign recognition of their distinctive status. As ambition drove them into military alliances with powerful states, they tried to find additional resources within the Empire by encroaching on their neighbours. The *Kreis* structure offered an ideal framework for this, especially as weaker territories often found the provision of military contingents too difficult and were prepared to pay others to field substitutes. Brandenburg used this to extend its influence in Westphalia and Lower Saxony. Electoral Saxony did the same in Upper Saxony, as did Bavaria in its own *Kreis*, while both Hessen-Kassel and Mainz attempted to dominate the Upper Rhine.[40]

Two distinct federal options emerged. The Associations had the potential to shift power away from central institutions like the Reichstag in favour of the *Kreis* assemblies that could bargain bi- or multi-lateral agreements within the Empire. Equally, ambitious princes could raise their profile by emerging as regional spokesmen, using *Kreis* institutions to draw on their neighbours' resources and political influence. What happened depended much on the prevailing balance within each region. The first option prevailed in the south and west, whereas the northern and eastern *Kreise* tended to become vehicles for one or two regional powers.

Some have argued recently that the *Kreise* and leagues of lesser princes had the potential to reinvent the Empire as "a federal state, compatible with the rational constitutionalism and respect for regional individualism that were the hallmarks of Enlightened thought", and so offered a third way to modernity between the twin poles of unitary national monarchy and a confederation of enlarged, sovereign principalities.[41] This greatly overestimates their potential. Modern federalism was inherently at odds with the Empire's feudal hierarchy and political culture, since it involved the interaction of equals. The lesser rulers simply wanted to safeguard their collective constitutional rights and, where possible, enhance their own personal status. It is no coincidence that the Reich collapsed precisely when this hierarchy was dismantled through the annexation of the minor territories by the more powerful princes who had become impatient with the limited potential of the *Kreise* and other institutions. Over 100 ecclesiastical and civic territories disappeared after 1801, followed by most of the minor secular ones in 1806. Though sanctioned by the *Reichstag*, this process was driven by naked force, in complete contravention of the imperial political culture that sanctified ancient rights and safeguarded the weak against the strong. The way was clear for the federal option of medium-sized kingdoms and principalities, grouped first in Napoleon's Confederation of the Rhine (1806–13) and then in the German Confederation (1815–66). The fact that discussions to re-establish the *Kreise* persisted into the 1840s simply underscores the conservatism of the old Empire. The reform debates of the late eighteenth century, in which the lesser princes participated, failed to produce any alternatives to the traditional imperial hierarchy and instead centred on plans to revive existing institutions, like the *Kreise*.[42]

Conclusions

The German experience indicates the difficulty of defining a region within early modern European politics. Regions are to a large extent historical constructs without permanent size and shape, despite the consistency of certain geographical features. They are variables that depend on prevailing transportation and communications technology, and on the forms of political interaction. Within the Empire, such interaction took place both through the formal constitutional framework and less well-defined forms of patronage and clientelism. The *Kreise* represented the principal regional institution throughout the entire early modern era, but they were not clearly aligned with any one of the three main trends in political development. The Empire's peculiar constitution limited their potential as autonomous actors, and Germany's future federal development stemmed from inter-territorial competition rather than as an outgrowth of regional politics. This suggests that we should regard regions as politically ambivalent elements in the state formation process, neither automatically retarding or fostering it, but acting according to the interplay of local, national and international influences.

Notes

1. P.C. Hartmann, *Kulturgeschichte des Heiligen Römischen Reiches* 1648 bis 1806 (Vienna, 2001), esp. pp.5–7, 19–21, 448.
2. The historiography of the Empire is reviewed by P.H. Wilson, *The Holy Roman Empire 1495–1806* (Basingstoke, 1999); H. Neuhaus, *Das Reich in der frühen Neuzeit* (Munich, 1997). See also, P.H. Wilson, 'Still a monstrosity? Some reflections on early modern German statehood', *The Historical Journal*, 42 (2006).
3. G. Schmidt, *Geschichte des alten Reiches. Staat und Nation in der frühen Neuzeit 1495–1806* (Munich, 1999).
4. This has been apparent since the early 1990s: P.C. Hartmann, 'Bereits erprobt: ein Mitteleuropa der Regionen', *Das Parlament*, nr.49–50 (3/10 Dec.1993), p.21; M. Hughes, *Early modern*

Germany 1477–1806 (Basingstoke, 1992).

5. R. Stauber, 'Nationalismus vor dem Nationalismus? Eine Bestandaufnahme der Forschung zu "Nation" und "Nationalismus" in der frühen Neuzeit', *Geschichte in Wissenschaft und Unterricht*, 47 (1996), 139–65.

6. J.W. Bernhardt, *Itinerant kingship and royal monasteries in early medieval Germany c.936–1075* (Cambridge, 1993).

7. H. Duchhardt, *Protestantisches Kaisertum und altes Reich* (Wiesbaden, 1977).

8. See for instance, P. Dwyer (ed.), *The rise of Prussia 1700–1830* (London, 2000).

9. N. Elias, *The civilising process* (Cambridge, 1994); P. Torsvik (ed.), *Mobilization, center-periphery structures and nation building* (Bergen, 1981). See also B.M. Downing, *The military revolution nd political change in early modern Europe* (Princeton, 1991); T. Ertman, *Birth of the Leviathan. Building states and regimes in medieval and early modern Europe* (Cambridge, 1997); A. Giddens, *The nation state and violence* (Berkeley, 1985); F.C. Lane, *Venice and history* (Baltimore, 1966); M. Mann, *The sources of social power* (2 vols., Cambridge, 1986–93); C. Tilly, *Coercion, capital and European states* AD990–1992 (Oxford, 1992), and his 'War making and state making as organised crime', in P. Evans et al (eds.), *Bringing the state back in* (Cambridge, 1985), pp.169–91.

10. I. Veit-Brause, 'The place of local and regional history in German and French historiography', *Australian Journal of French Studies*, 16 (1979), 447–78. For the theoretical debate see G. Brunn (ed.), *Region und Regionsbilduung in Europa* (Baden-Baden, 1996); P. Schöller, 'Traditionsbezogene räumliche Verbundenheit als Problem der Landeskunde', *Berichte zur deutschen Landeskunde*, 58 (1984), 31–6; P. Weichhart, *Raumbezogene Identität. Bausteine zu einer Theorie räumlich-sozialer Kognition und Identfikation* (Stuttgart, 1990); B. Werlen, Sozialgeographie (Bern, 2000); H.W. Wollersheim et al (eds.), *Region und Identifikation* (Leipzig, 1998).

11. M. Innes, *State and society in the early middle ages. The middle Rhine valley 400–1000* (Cambridge, 2000); B. Arnold, *Princes and territories in medieval Germany* (Cambridge, 1991), and his German knighthood 1050–1300 (Oxford, 1985).

12. Major journals include *Zeitschrift für Bayerische Landesgeschichte, Zeitschrift für Württembergische Landesgeschichte, Hessisches Jahrbuch für Landesgeschichte, Neues Archiv für Sächsiche Geschichte.* Others dovetail more closely with the new *Bundesländer* like the *Niedersächsisches Jahrbuch für Landesgeschichte.*

13. Major examples include *Das Land Baden-Württemberg* (issued by the state archive administration since 1974); K.S. Bader, *Der deutsche Südwesten in seiner territorialgeschichtlichen Entwicklung* (2nd ed., Sigmaringen, 1978); M. Braubach (ed.), *Rheinische Geschichte* (Düsseldorf, 1976); K. Demandt, *Geschichte des Landes Hessen* (3rd ed., Kassel, 1980); W. Kohl (ed.), *Westfälische Geschichte* (Düsseldorf, 1983); H. Patze/W. Schlesinger (eds), *Geschichte Thüringens* (6 vols., Cologne, 1982); M. Spindler (ed.), *Handbuch der Bayerischen Geschichte* (2 vols., Munich, 1988).

14. J. Schlumbohm (ed.), *Mikrogeschichte – Makrogeschichte: komplementär oder inkommensurable?* (Göttingen, 1998).

15. The literature on the Kreise is summarised by W. Dotzauer, *Die deutschen Reichskreise in der Verfassung des alten Reiches und ihr Eigenleben* (1500–1806) (Darmstadt, 1989), that was revised and expanded as *Die deutschen Reichskreise* (1383–1806) (Stuttgart, 1998). Note that the early modern Kreise should not be confused with the modern *Landkreis* which is an administrative sub-unit of a *Bundesland.*

16. For the *Reichsstände* see J.J. Moser, *Neues Teutsches Staatsrecht* (23 volumes in 42 parts, Frankfurt/Main, 1766–82), vol.III parts 1 and 2. Medieval development is summarised in B.

Arnold, *Medieval Germany 500–1300* (Basingstoke, 1997), and P. Moraw, *Von offener Verfassung zu gestalteter Verfassung. Das Reich im späten Mittelalter 1250 bis 1490* (Berlin, 1985).

17. It remained formally part of the Empire until 1648: P. Stadler, 'Die Schweiz und das Reich in der frühen Neuzeit', in V. Press (ed.), *Alternativen zur Reichsverfassung in der frühen Neuzeit?* (Munich, 1995), pp.131–41.

18. A.K. Mally, 'Der Österreichische Reichskreis', in W. Wüst (ed.), *Reichskreis und Territorium. Die Herrschaft über die Herrschaft?* (Stuttgart, 2000), pp.313–31; N. Mout, 'Die Niederlande und das Reich im 16. Jahrhundert (1512–1609)', in Press (ed.), *Alternativen*, pp.143–68.

19. P.C. Hartmann, 'Der Bayerische Reichskreis', in Wüst (ed.), *Reichskreis und Territorium*, pp.297–311.

20. H. Carl, *Der Schwäbische Bund 1488–1534* (Leinfelden-Echterdingen, 2000); A. Laufs, *Der Schwäbische Kreis* (Aalen, 1971).

21. A. Gotthard, *Säulen des Reiches. Die Kurfürsten im frühneuzeitlichen Reichsverband* (Husum, 1999).

22. W. Dotzauer, 'Der Kurrheinische Reichskreis in der Verfassung des alten Reiches', *Nassauische Annalen*, 98 (1987), 61–104; P. Casser, 'Der Niederrheinisch-westfälische Reichskreis', in H. Aubin/E. Schulte (eds.), *Der Raum Westfalen*, vol. II (Berlin, 1934), pp.35–72.

23. J. Vötsch, Kursachsen, *das Reich und der Mitteldeutsche Raum zu Beginn des 18. Jahrhunderts* (Frankfurt/Main, 2003).

24. J. Pánek, 'Der böhmische Staat und das Reich in der frühen Neuzeit', in Press (ed.), *Alternativen*, pp.169–78.

25. See Moser, *Neues Teutsches Staatsrecht*, X 171–244 for the convenors, and pp.285–445 for the assemblies. General development is covered by P.H. Wilson, *From Reich to Revolution: German history 1558–1806* (Basingstoke, 2004), pp.183–90.

26. Recent literature on this is summarised by H. Neuhaus, 'Reichskreise und Reichskriege in der frühen Neuzeit', in Wüst (ed.), *Reichskreis und Territorium*, pp.71–88.

27. See especially F. Magen, 'Die Reichskreise in der Epoche des Dreissigjährigen Krieges', *Zeitschrift für Historische Forschung*, 9 (1982), 408–60.

28. M. Fimpel, *Reichsjustiz und Territorialstaat. Württemberg als Kommissar von Kaiser und Reich im Schwäbischen Kreis (1648–1806)* (Tübingen, 1999); P.H. Wilson, *German armies: war and German politics 1648–1806* (London, 1998).

29. These rights are summarised (with a Protestant bias) by Moser, *Neues Teutsches Staatsrecht*, VII and supplementary vol. III 506–607. Amongst the many important interpretations, see M. Heckel, 'Autonomia und Pacis Compositio', *Zeitschrift der Savigny-Stiftung für Rechtsgeschichte, Kanonistische Abteilung*, 45 (1959), 141–248.

30. Useful introductions to these issues in T.A. Brady, 'Phases and strategies of the Schmalkaldic League', *Archiv für Reformationsgeschichte*, 74 (1983), 162–81; M. Kaiser, 'Ständebund und Verfahrensordnung. Das Beispiel der Katholischen Liga (1619–1631)', in B. Stollberg-Rilling (ed.), *Vormoderne politische Verfahren* (Berlin, 2001), pp.331–415.

31. G. Schmidt, *Der Wetterauer Grafenverein* (Marburg, 1989); J. Arndt, *Das Niederrheinisch-westfälische Reichsgrafenkollegium und seine Mitglieder (1653–1806)* (Mainz, 1991).

32. For example, P.C. Storm, *Der Schwäbische Kreis als Feldherr* (Berlin, 1974).

33. For example, J.A. Vann, *The Swabian Kreis. Institutional growth in the Holy Roman Empire, 1648–1715* (Brussels, 1975).

34. P.C. Hartmann, 'Die Kreistage des Heiligen Römischen Reiches – Eine Vorform des Parlamentarismus?', *Zeitschrift für Historische Forschung*, 19 (1991), 29–47.

35. Differing perspectives in H.H. Hofmann, 'Reichskreis und Kreisassoziationen', *Zeitschrift für*

Bayerische Landesgeschichte, 25 (1962), 377–413; B. Wunder, 'Die Erneuerung der Reichsexekutionsordnung und die Kreisassoziationen 1654–1674', *Zeitschrift für die Geschichte des Oberrheins*, 139 (1991), 494–502; K.O. Freiherr v. Aretin (ed.), *Der Kurfürst von Mainz und die Kreisassoziationen 1648–1748* (Wiesbaden, 1975), and his *Des Reich. Friedensgarantie und europäisches Gleichgewicht 1648–1806* (Stuttgart, 1986), pp.167–208.

36. Fuller discussion in Wilson, *From Reich to Revolution*, pp.1–17.

37. P. Moraw, 'Landesgeschichte und Reichsgeschichte im 14. Jahrhundert', *Jahrbuch für Westdeutsche Landesgeschichte*, 3 (1977), 175–91.

38. V. Press, 'Die Bundnispläne Kaiser Karls V. und die Reichsverfassung', in his *Ausgewählte Aufsätze* (Berlin, 1997), pp.67–127.

39. H. Haan, 'Kaiser Ferdinand II. und das Problem des Reichsabsolutismus', *Historische Zeitschrift*, 207 (1968), 297–345.

40. Details in Wilson, *German armies*, pp.165–201.

41. M. Umbach, 'History and federalism in the age of nation-state formation', in her (ed.), *German federalism. Past, present and future* (Basingstoke, 2002), pp.42–69 at 42, and her *Federalism and Enlightenment in Germany 1740–1806* (London, 2000) and H. Wellenreuther (ed.), *German and American constitutional thought* (New York, 1990). More critical comments from A. Kohler, 'Das Heilige Römische Reich – Ein Föderativssystem?', in T. Fröschl (ed.), *Föderationsmodelle und Unionsstrukturen* (Munich, 1991), pp.119–26.

42. W. Burgdorf, *Reichsknostitution und Nation* (Mainz, 1998); P. Burg, *Die deutsche Trias in Idee und Wirklichkeit* (Stuttgart, 1989).

Chapter Six

Local or regional identity in early medieval Latin Southern Italy?

Thomas Granier

Is there a sense of regional identity expressed in Latin Southern Italian sources in the eighth to eleventh centuries? Is region, when dealing with issues of identity, a relevant concept for writers and their ecclesiastical, intellectual audiences? This connects to another, more general debate: what is and what makes a region in a given moment in history? Do people and writers living in a given region automatically feel they have something in common?

The region considered here is Latin Southern Italy as a whole, the scale above that of each different political unit; this region comprises the *Longobardia Minore*, heir to and successor of the Northern Lombard kingdom after the Frankish conquest of 774 (that is the duchy and subsequently principality of Benevento, and its offspring, the principalities of Salerno and Capua) and the formerly Peribyzantine coastal duchies of Naples, Amalfi and Sorrento. Latin language and civilization and the Beneventan script give this region a genuine geographical, human, linguistic and cultural identity even across the Romanobyzantine-Lombard divide. This region has no institutional coherence as it does not match the territory of any one political or religious unit. Its heart, roughly what is now Campania, where human settlement – Latin and Lombard – is the densest, includes all political and religious centres: the main cities and their territories (except for Benevento and Salerno, the territories of which extend into Calabria and Puglia) and the Benedictine abbeys of Montecassino and San Vincenzo al Volturno. Byzantine areas proper – the rest of Calabria and Puglia – are excluded on grounds of their different language and civilization and because their political and religious centre lies overseas. This region is never comprehensively included in either the Lombard then Carolingian kingdom or the Roman *patrimonium* or the Byzantine Empire; so, it is not a part in a whole, but the scale above local or subregional distinct and independent units frequently at war with each other; it is not a specific part of a State because there is no State.[1]

Because this region concentrates centres of settlement, power and religious authority over a limited territory identified by both insiders and outsiders, it is a rewarding field in which to investigate the relationship between space and identity, and it produces many sources which address precisely this issue, predominantly history and hagiography. Asking the question of regional identity when there is no integrated regional political unit directly addresses the issue of region and regional identity as an ongoing process.

In order to identify the basis of eighth- to eleventh-century writers' and their audiences' sense of regional identity and to consider on what level any sense of identity functions and why, firstly their attitudes towards the contemporary geopolitical landscape are analysed. When writing about Italy and the South, authors tend to acknowledge the region as a valid geographical concept and to clearly differentiate its inhabitants from the outsiders. Secondly, they also demonstrate that many political and religious features used to fuel particularism are indeed common throughout the region. Yet, finally, they predominantly express a sense of identity on either a local, subregional scale (each city or political unit), or as a specific metaregional, universal identity, that is belonging to the Christian Church.

The sources clearly reveal the basis for a regional identity: they attest some sense of region, but above all consider outsiders as wholly different from insiders. The Latin South has some geographical coherence inasmuch as it is part of Italy. Introducing the peninsula conquered by the Lombards around 570, Paul the Deacon, in his *History of the Lombards* written in the 790s, gives a digest of Late Antique cosmography in which Italy is divided into eighteen provinces.[2] Paul's account is antiquarian and out of date, but similar geographical views are featured at the beginning of the *Vita* of Bishop Athanasius of Naples, written in 872–877, in a panegyric to the city of Naples, birthplace of both saint and writer. The author gradually narrows the focus from Italy to Naples itself:

> *Nobody with even the slightest knowledge of cosmography ignores that Italy is the noblest and richest part of Europe. It is divided into two islands and sixteen provinces, the seventh of which is named Campania (…). Campania hosts the noblest and richest of cities. One of which is Naples…*[3]

This careful interlocking of scales (Europe, Italy, Campania, Naples) reveals a precise geographical consciousness. In the *Chronicon Salernitanum* written in 974–980, *Italia* means the peninsula, from a geographical or political viewpoint: it refers to the area conquered by the Lombards, and thus the kingdom, before and after 774, and to the geographical unit as opposed to North Africa, Sicily and the Balkans.[4] To describe the area governed by Sicardus of Benevento in the 830s, the ninth- or tenth-century hagiographer of Trophimena of Minori uses the highly literate and archaistic word *Ausonia*: here, the principality of Benevento and its area of influence are almost identified with Italy itself.[5] Such instances are rare however, and the region is not viewed as a uniform unit, since it contains some distinct areas, such as the *Terra di Lavoro* shared between Naples, Benevento and Capua. Other areas are clearly differentiated from Campania proper, such as the *fines Lucaniae*, south of the principality of Salerno; sometimes the archaistic word *Samnium* is used to name the area around Benevento.[6] These examples show that the writers acknowledge Latin Southern Italy, but more as a part of Italy than as a free-standing, distinct regional unit.

Above the local scale, ethnicity, as far as the Lombards are concerned, is a strong criterium for regional identification. Whatever city or political unit they belong to, the Lombards – and only them among the insiders – are also wholly referred to as a people, a *gens*, the *Longobardi*, both from within and from outside, for example by the Lombard-Cassinese monk Erchempert in his *History of the Lombards of Benevento* and by the Neapolitan deacon John in his *History of the bishops of Naples*, both in the 890s.[7] The word *Longobardi* can also be used in a highly literate and solemn context, as in epitaphs, for instance those of Prince Sico of Benevento (817–832) and Duke Bonus of Naples (832–834).[8] This Lombard consciousness survives in the South long after centuries of social integration. It can even be traced, after the eleventh- and twelfth-century Norman conquest and the fall of the last independent Lombard power in 1077, in the revolt of the "Lombard" aristocracy in Salerno against King William I's government reform in 1160–1162.[9]

There is only very scarce evidence for such a sense of ethnic identity in the coastal cities: phrases like *quidam uero uir, genere Amalfitanus* or *populus Neapolitanus*, as found in the subdeacon Peter's tenth-century *Miracles* of Agnellus of Naples, are indeed extremely rare.[10] Yet, the early medieval Lombard areas are inhabited by a mixture of people, and the Southern *Longobardi* are no less multi-ethnic than their neighbours.[11] Ethnicity thus appears as a relevant criterium for the Lombards, but generally not to the people in the coastal cities in the same context at the very same time, where identity is mostly rooted in a consciousness of Roman-Byzantine origins and the use of late Roman law. The sense of ethnicity and its display in the sources is a specific construction of the Southern Lombards themselves: writers think of them as a *gens* not so much because of their biological identity (anthroponymical studies even reveal the Southern ethnic stock to be somewhat different from the Northern one[12]) but rather because of a political ideal, carrying on Lombard rule after 774.[13] This sense of ethnic identity is a basis for regional identity throughout the various Lombard units.

Although the sources clearly differentiate the Lombards from others on ethnic grounds, they also attest a common attitude towards outsiders in this region, considered both as ethnically coherent *gentes* and different from the Latin

Southern Italians themselves. First of all, local Latin peoples clearly differentiate themselves from the Italian Byzantines, the *Greci*. This word refers to people living anywhere within the Empire, to people from Byzantine areas having settled in the Latin areas, or to people speaking Greek and observing the Greek rite even if their ethnic origin is unspecified.[14] The *Miracles* of Agnellus mention one man from Reggio Calabria for instance, and clearly define him as Greek: *in Italiae partibus erat uir quidam, natione Graecus, nomine Leo, apud Regium ciuitatem*.[15] The sources never refer to people from the coastal cities, Neapolitans, Amalfitans and so on, as *Greci*.[16] In the *History of the bishops of Naples, Greci* clearly refer to the Byzantines. The Neapolitan writer thus gives the word exactly the same meaning as the Lombard Erchempert does in the same period.[17]

The same ethnic differentiation is used about the Franks in the eighth and ninth centuries and their German successors in the tenth, named *Franci* or *Galli*. *Galli* is for instance used by Erchempert, and *Galliarum gens* in the ninth- or tenth-century Neapolitan *Homily* on the miracles of Januarius. *Franci, Galli* and *gens Francorum* appear several times in the *Chronicon Salernitanum*. Eleventh-century Neapolitan *Miracles* refer to the German Empire and Imperial troops as *Theotonici*, carrying on the same feeling of opposition to people North of the Alps. *Gallia* can even mean Carolingian Northern Italy as opposed to the South, especially when referring to the time when Emperor Louis II (855–875) wages war in the South with his Italofrankish armies (866–873).[18]

As soon as they cease to be mere mercenaries in traditional local conflicts and begin displaying their own power in the second half of the eleventh century, the Normans are referred to as a people as well, as *Normanni*, in the twelfth-century *Chronicle* of Montecassino as well as in various Neapolitan charters. And among the eleventh-century Norman writers, "us", "our people" mean the Normans.[19]

This overview illustrates that all this might be characterised as a kind of negative identity: writers and their audiences do not consider people from early medieval Latin Southern Italy as one, yet all are equally distinct from clearly identified outsiders. However different among themselves, all are equally non-Frank, non-Greek, non-Norman. The main reason for this shared clear-cut differentiation lies in these outsiders' general attitude: placed halfway between the two Empires, Southern Italy is target to the ambitions of both. So these outsiders are primarily seen as conquerors at worst, burdensome allies at best.[20] This region does not try to acquire or defend any form of autonomy from a State controlling it on grounds of right or strength, but from various separate external powers trying to enforce nominal rights: Byzantium still considers the territories reconquered by Justinian in the mid-sixth century as part of the Empire and the Franks interpret their conquest of the Northern kingdom in 774 as grounds for legitimate authority over the Southern Lombards. Local powers often formally submit to one of these external powers to get formal and, they hope, physical protection against the others if the need arises.

Ethnicity aside, one of the main factors usually acknowledged as fuelling early medieval local particularism is a consciousness of local political and religious traditions and especially the cult of certain saints.[21] However, many of these features are indeed common throughout the region.

Southern Lombards are usually opposed to the Peribyzantine coastal duchies on the criterium of the existence of links with Byzantium or not. These duchies of Byzantine origin are, however, genuinely independent in the period considered here. They are ruled by local aristocratic families whose members are no longer imperial officers. In Naples, the process of independence gains momentum in the 750s and is complete in 840. In Amalfi, an independent series of *comites* and then *praefecti* begins in 839.

These political units are frequently at war with each other. Yet war is just one side of complex relationships, usually supplemented by peace and alliances. These are exemplified by the marriage links between Naples and the Lombards of Capua and Benevento in the second half of the ninth century.[22] According to a very commonplace practice, rulers of these various rival units are related, which helps to create and maintain personal, social, cultural and political links on a regional level.

The links with Byzantium are shared by both the coastal cities and the Lombards. Lombard princes sometimes imitate Byzantium, starting with Prince Arechis (758–787) in 774 who orders the building of a church and monastery to Haghia Sophia.[23] Local rulers often receive Byzantine titles from the emperor: *imperialis spatarius candidatus and protospatarius* in Amalfi, *protosebastos* in Naples, and *anthypatus* and *patricius* in Amalfi, Benevento, Capua, Naples and Salerno.[24] Further, like the Byzantine emperors, these rulers frequently associate their sons and successors in their own rule: for example, in Naples, Dukes Stephen II and his son Gregory II (before 766), Sergius I and his son Gregory III (850–864), Gregory III in turn and his son Sergius II (864–870), or as late as Sergius VI and his son

John VI (1090–1107); in Amalfi, Mastalus and his son Leo in the 920s. In Lombard Salerno, the practice is documented from 861 to 1077.[25]

Stressing links with the Eastern Empire is thus a common feature, even when none of these local rulers, chiefly the Lombards, recognize themselves as institutionally subordinate to the Byzantine court. Bearing Byzantine titles is above all a way to enhance their dignity and stress their independence from the Western Empire.

In the religious field, almost all local Latin churches use a bilingual liturgy mixing Greek and Latin. This is well-known in Naples for example, but is also featured in the Beneventan liturgy.[26]

The cult of saints is an issue closely linked to local identity, cities having special *patroni*, protectors, often expected to protect them against outsiders. However, several cases of cults venerated in more than one city can also be pointed out. The *History of the bishops of Naples*, for example, mentions the piety and generosity of Prince Arechis towards the cemeterial church of saint Januarius in the late eighth century. This particular devotion is easily explained: Januarius is an ancient bishop of Benevento, and in 831 Prince Sico takes away (part of?) his relics to Benevento. A charter issued on November 20th, 975 by Duke Marinus II for the monastery of Saints-Severinus-and-Sossius in Naples also states that it received gifts from Lombards donors.[27]

Southern Italian churches carry on Mediterranean traditions through the spectactular amount of Oriental and African saints they worship. There is an exceptional interest in ninth- and tenth-century Naples for the *passiones* and *vitae* of Oriental saints, almost thirty of these texts being translated or rewritten there over the course of seventy to eighty years,[28] and African worship traditions are also noteworthy in Naples. Yet, most of these texts have come to us through Beneventan-Cassinese manuscripts, proving the sheer interest in those texts in the Lombard area in the eleventh and twelfth centuries.[29] Further, the Lombards themselves are keenly interested in the cult of African and Oriental saints: the *gastald* Gualtari, back from a diplomatic mission in Constantinople, brings relics of saint Helianus (one of the 40 Martyrs of Sebastes) to Benevento in 763. In 768, Prince Arechis has relics of saint Mercurius, one of Constantinople's greatest military saints, transferred to their own altar in Saint-Sophia. Mercurius' cult in Benevento, unparalleled by a similar interest in Naples, is a case of genuine original Lombard interest in a Byzantine saint.[30] In the eleventh century there is a widespread veneration for the cult of Saint Nicolas throughout Southern Italy, fuelled by the arrival of relics in Bari in 1087, a cult the origins of which lie in the *Life* translated in Naples at the end of the ninth century and widely circulated. Here, therefore, is another element of regional commonality.[31]

In spite of these common features, however, identity is mainly expressed as a local particularism, modelled after each *civitas* which men and women belong to. Lombards are first and foremost described as *Beneventani*, "men from Benevento", *Capuani* or *Salernitani* by Erchempert and in the *History of the bishops of Naples*.[32]

People from the coastal cities are named in the very same way: in the *History of the bishops of Naples* is the phrase *Tunc Sergius consularis una cum Amalphitanis Caietanisque ac Surrentinis*, "then the consul Sergius with the men from Amalfi, those from Gaeta and those from Sorrento…".[33] Sorrento is, at the time, not yet independent from Naples: *Surrentini* does not refer to men from an independent unit, so that its meaning is not political but geographical. There even are references to the civic status of men, as in the case of *quidam uir nobilis, nomine Iohannes, ciuis Neapolitanus,* or even women, as *quaedem paralitica, ciuis Neapolitana* in the *Miracles* of Agnellus.[34]

In the 830s, Prince Sicardus of Benevento tries to conquer Amalfi and to merge its inhabitants with the Salernitans in order to control Amalfitan trade. This effort to extend a regional political unit over another major *civitas* fails because of Sicardus' death in 839. Some Amalfitans settle near Salerno, and then within the city, but remain named after the city they first came from, as *Atranenses*, until the eleventh century: local origin, a different law and inhabiting a specific part of the city around a church dedicated to their Amalfitan patron saint, Trophimena, still prevail over generations of settlement and intermarriage in Salerno.[35]

This prominence of local, civic identity is reflected in the expression of us-ness. In most cases, phrases meaning "us" or "our folk" refer to this or that political unit: *concives nostri* and *nostrates* mean the Beneventans in the *capitula* issued in 866 by Prince Adelchis of Benevento (853–878); *quidam nostratium*, "some of us", means Neapolitans in the *Translation* of Athanasius written in 877.[36] So, the city, and its territory inherited from the ancient *civitas*, appears to be the predominant level at which men are identified. This fits a clear consciousness of the many political divisions throughout the region and is a consequence of it.[37]

At the other end of the scales spectrum to the city, however, the sources attest a clear sense of religious, Christian identity, Christendom being the real common ground for all the men and powers discussed here. In contrast to the expressions of us-ness discussed above, in the *Translation* of saint Severinus, written in Naples in 902/903, *quidam nostratium*, "one of us", refers to someone from Naples, but qualified as Latin and Christian, as opposed to the Saracens of whom he is a prisoner.[38] An even clearer example is featured in the *Chronicon Salernitanum*, where two duels between Saracen and Salernitan champions are recorded, dated 871/872. The word *christianus* is, in some instances, enough to mention either of the two Salernitans, and the citizens as a whole are then identified as *Christiani*.[39] A part of the Neapolitan *Miracles* of Agrippinus goes even further: a Greek (*Eolico genere*) prisoner of the Saracens complains about an Arab attack against Naples in 956/957, "because I am a Christian and cannot bear the destruction of my people" (*quia christicola sum, nec possum sustinere necem populi mei*).[40] There is thus a genuine consciousness of a *populus christianus* that supercedes even the nation one belongs to, here the Greek *genus*; according to context and purpose of the narrator, identity can sometimes be expressed according to this religious factor, which is of course common to all Christians.

These latest examples refer to the clearest-cut of all oppositions, that between Saracens and everyone else, expressed in both ethnic and religious terms. The Saracens are described as a people, and named after ancient biblical models. *Agareni* or *gens Agarenorum* are for instance used in the *Miracles* of Agnellus, *Hismahelitae* by both John the Deacon and Erchempert, and *Saraceni* by John, Erchempert and Peter, and all by the *Chronicon Salernitanum* as well.[41] Besides this ethnic naming, the Muslim Saracens are qualified as pagans. This general designation as one pagan people simply eliminates all perception of ethnic diversity among the attackers and shows that Southern Italians, as almost everyone else in the Christian world, refuse to understand Islam for what it is.[42] To express global rejection, authors can therefore call enemies pagans like the Saracens, like some Lombard sources do about the Neapolitans – by no means pagans – in the context of war.[43]

The strength of this clear-cut opposition in terms of region and identity is best understood if we note that, unlike the reaction to Frankish or Norman conquerors, which is always individual (except for the Civitate league in 1053), the only regional-wide unions are antisaracen coalitions: Amalfi and Gaeta supply ships to the Byzantines in 812; Amalfi, Gaeta, Naples and Sorrento ally at Licosa in 843; Amalfi, Capua-Benevento and Naples again in 905 and the pope,

Byzantines, Capua, Gaeta, Naples, Salerno and Spoleto for the great Garigliano attack in 915.[44] Only in these instances do we witness effective action bringing together Southern Christians on a regional scale towards a common goal.

Latin Southern Italy in the eighth to eleventh centuries thus appears to produce a large amount of sources addressing, in various specific ways, an issue that seems chiefly important in the regional context, that of identity. There are geographical, political and religious grounds for a consciousness of regional identity, plus also ethnic grounds for the various Lombards. Yet, by far the largest part of the sources point out local particularism, and writers never identify people as a regional community. Region, although acknowledged, is therefore not a valid scale in order to understand and express identity and belonging, and this can be explained by three groups of factors:

Lombard specificity is the first key issue: after 774 and until the fall of the last independent Lombard power in 1077, due to a political ideal, rulers and writers think of the Southern Lombards as specific and thus different from everyone else, and their contemporaries also feel like this. This ethnic sentiment creates a genuine sense of regional identity uniting the *Longobardia Minore* as a whole and clearly differentiating it from the Northern kingdom, even before the Frankish conquest.[45] This is a discourse about ethnicity rather than a fact, as it is impossible to view any political unit as biologically, linguistically, culturally and juridically both coherent and absolutely different from the others. According to each local context, this ethnic discourse is chosen and used by some and not by others. Then, from the late ninth century onwards, the great Southern Benedictine houses, chiefly Montecassino, use the Lombard heritage as a key to their own monastic identity, survival and privileges.[46]

Then is the issue of the permanent political break-up of the region. Until Norman rule is finally laid down in the twelfth century, the area is made up of different political units clashing with each other. Identification is therefore felt according to the unit one belongs to, be it one city and its tiny territory (Amalfi) or a major subregional area (the principality of Benevento until 849, extending into Puglia and Calabria). Although all stress common opposition to outsiders, all react differently and separately to their threats, and these outsiders use these divisions to their own profit, in turn exaggerating them. Particularism, as a defensive discourse, is especially appropriate and efficient in this violent context. The sources point out differences more than common factors, which proves that this is the result of the writers' choice, even the common factors are stressed as grounds for particularism and not as grounds for community.

Finally there is also the strength of the two other levels of identification, local and universal: the *civitas* on one side, Christian belief and Roman authority on the other. Landscape, patterns of human settlement and urban civilization are the key reasons for the strength of local particularism – even with scarce references to the civic status of the people. Only the sense of being fellow Christians appears strong enough to balance it, hence the clear common identity-based opposition to the Saracens. On some rare occasions, it even leads to common anti-Saracen military expeditions.

The conjunction of these three groups of factors leaves no room for a true feeling of common identity on a regional scale. Region and regional identity are not *a priori* defined realities, set once and for all in history, but are constantly ongoing creations. The case of early medieval Latin Southern Italy places the concept of region in history in an especially original perspective: it is one phase in this process of creation when region and regional identity could have been shaped but were not, allowing scholars a glance at why it was not, at whether or not, how, and why writers of the past and their audiences think of region as a valid concept.

Acknowledgement

It is my great pleasure to warmly thank my dear friend Clare Pilsworth, University of Manchester, for her very kind and efficient proofreading of my English text.

Notes

1. Chris Wickham, *Early Medieval Italy. Central power and local society. 400-1000*, New Studies in Medieval History 4 (London-Basingstoke, 1981); *Italy in the Early Middle Ages. 476–1000*, ed. Cristina La Rocca, Short Oxford History of Italy 5 (Oxford, 2002).
2. Paolo Diacono, *Storia dei Longobardi*, ed. Lidia Capo, Scrittori Greci e Latini (Rome-Milan, 1992), 2, 14–24, pp. 94–105; About Paul's writing context, see Rosamond McKitterick, 'Paul the Deacon and the Franks', *Early Medieval Europe* 8 (1999), pp. 319–339.
3. *Vita et Translatio s. Athanasii Neapolitani episcopi (BHL 735 e 737). Sec. IX.*, ed. Antonio Vuolo, ISIME. Fonti per la Storia dell'Italia Medievale. Antiquitates 16 (Rome, 2001), 1, 1–6 p. 115.
4. *Chronicon Salernitanum*, ed. Ulla Westerbergh, Studia Latina Stockholmiensia 3 (Stockholm, 1956), p. 1 l. 12 & 25, c. 9, p. 11 l. 14 & 20 & c. 88, p. 89 l. 3.
5. *Historia inventionis ac translationis sanctae Trophimenae (BHL 8316–8318)*, ed. *AASS Julii II* (Paris-Rome, 1867), pp. 231–240, c. 13 p. 236B.
6. Jean-Marie Martin, *Guerre, accords et frontières en Italie méridionale pendant le haut Moyen Âge. Pacta de Liburia, Divisio principatus Beneventani et autres actes*, Sources et Documents d'Histoire du Moyen Âge publiés par l'EFR 7 (Rome, 2005), pp. 101–138; Huguette Taviani-Carozzi, *La*

principauté lombarde de Salerne (IXe–XIe siècle). Pouvoir et société en Italie lombarde méridionale, Collection de l'EFR 152, 2 vol. (Rome, 1991), vol. 1 pp. 502–514; *Chronica sancti Benedicti Casinensis*, ed. Georg Waitz, *Monumenta Germaniae Historica. Scriptores Rerum Langobardicarum et Italicarum saec. VI.–IX.* (Hannover, 1878) [*MGH. SRLI*], pp. 467–489, c. 25, p. 487 l. 17; c. 26, p. 488 l. 15 & *Catalogus regum Langobardorum et ducum Beneventanorum, ibid.*, p. 490–497, p. 495 l. 14 & 32.

7. Erchempert, *Ystoriola Langobardorum Beneventi degentium, MGH. SRLI*, pp. 231–264, c. 1 p. 234 l. 28, c. 2, p. 235 l. 14 & c. 4, p. 236 l. 14–15; *Gesta episcoporum Neapolitanorum, ibid.*, pp. 398–436, c. 57, p. 431 l. 43 & c. 64, p. 434 l. 41–42.

8. *Epitaphium Siconis principis, MGH. Poetae Latini Aevi Carolini*, ed. Ernst Dümmler, t. II (Berlin, 1884), l. 23–24 p. 650 *& Bonus consul et dux, ibid.*, l. 1–2 p. 651.

9. Errico Cuozzo, 'À propos de la coexistence entre Normands et Lombards dans le Royaume de Sicile: la révolte féodale de 1160–1162', *Peuples du Moyen Âge. Problèmes d'identification*, ed. Caude Carozzi & Huguette Taviani-Carozzi (Aix-en-Provence, 1996), pp. 45–56.

10. *Una testimonianza agiografica napoletana: il 'Libellus miraculorum s. Agnelli' (sec. X)*, ed. Antonio Vuolo (*BHL* 150–152), Università degli Studi di Salerno. Sezione di Studi Storici 4 (Naples, 1987), mir. X, p. 171 l. 2 & mir. II, p. 156 l. 10.

11. Stefano Palmieri, 'Le componenti etniche: contrasti e fusioni', *Storia del Mezzogiorno*, ed. Giuseppe Galasso & Rosario Romeo (Rome, 1994), Vol. III. *Alto Medioevo*, pp. 43–72.

12. Elda Morlicchio, *Antroponimia longobarda a Salerno nel IX secolo. I nomi del* Codex Diplomaticus Cavensis, Romanica Neapolitana 17 (Naples, 1985), p. 14.

13. Walter Pohl, 'Memory, identity and power in Lombard Italy', *The uses of the past in the Early Middle Ages*, ed. Yitzhak Hen & Matthew Innes (Cambridge, 2000), pp. 9–28; Claudio Azzara, 'Il ducato di Benevento e l'eredità del regno dei Longobardi', published on-line at http://centri.univr.it/RM/biblioteca/scaffale/a.htm #Claudio%Azzara

14. Stefano Palmieri, 'Le componenti etniche', *cit.*, pp. 53–59.

15. *Libellus miraculorum s. Agnelli, cit.*, mir. XIX, p. 186 l. 3–4.

16. Thomas Granier, 'Napolitains et Lombards aux VIIIe–XIe siècles. De la guerre des peuples à la 'guerre des saints' en Italie du Sud', *MEFRM* 108 (1996), pp. 403–450, pp. 408–409.

17. *Gesta, cit.*, c. 41, p. 424 l. 42; c. 54, p. 429 l. 25; Erchempert, *cit.*, c. 38, p. 249 l. 14; c. 39, p. 249 l. 18.

18. Erchempert, *cit.*, c. 34, p. 247 l. 23; *Homilia de miraculis sancti Ianuarii* (*BHL* 4138), ed. *AASS Septembris VI* (Paris-Rome, 1867), pp. 884–888, c. 11 p. 886C; Thomas Granier, 'Un miracle accompli par le contact d'une effigie de saint Janvier à Naples au IXe siècle', *Revue belge de Philologie et d'Histoire* 75 (1997), pp. 957–966, pp. 962–963; *Chronicon Salernitanum, cit.*, c. 10, p. 13 l. 28, c. 11, p. 17 l. 18, c. 108, p. 121 l. 9 & c. 109, p. 122 l. 3 & 5 for *Gallia* about Northern Italy; *Miracula sancti Severi episcopi Neapolitani* (*BHL* 7677), ed. *AASS Aprilis III* (Paris-Rome, 1866), pp. 779–781, c. 10 p. 779E; Carlrichard Brühl, *Naissance de deux peuples. Français et Allemands (IXe–XIe siècle)* (Paris, 1994), pp. 67–117; Huguette Taviani-Carozzi, 'Une bataille franco-allemande en Italie: Civitate (1053)', *Peuples du Moyen Âge, cit.*, pp. 181–211.

19. *Die Chronik von Montecassino*, ed. Hartmut Hoffmann, *MGH. SS* 34 (Hannover, 1980), *Capitula libri secundi*, p. 159 l. 9 & 11; ms A 2, 37, p. 236 l. 3; mss CDMSW 2, 37, p. 236 l. 16–18 & 20 & p. 237 l. 13; ms C 3, 35, p. 411 l. 21; charters of May 2nd, 1043 (*RN* 478), *Monumenta ad Neapolitani Ducatus Historiam Pertinentia*, ed. Bartolomeo Capasso, 2 t. in 3 vol. (Naples, 1881–1892) [*MND*], 2-1, p. 292; August 14th, 1078 (RN 528), p. 321; December 10th, 1087 (RN 541), p. 326; June 19th, 1130 (*RN* 646), p. 402; Norman writers: Huguette Taviani-Carozzi, *La terreur du monde. Robert Guiscard et la conquête normande in Italie. Mythe et*

histoire (Paris, 1996), p. 20.

20. Walter Pohl, 'Invasions and ethnic identity', *Italy in the Early Middle Ages, cit.*, pp. 11–33, p. 32.

21. Paolo Golinelli, *Città e culto dei santi nel Medioevo italiano*, Biblioteca di Storia Urbana Medievale 4b (Bologna, 1996); Hans C. Peyer, *Città e santi patroni nell'Italia medievale*, ed. Anna Benvenuti, Le Vie della Storia 35 (Florence, 1998) and Giovanni Vitolo, *Tra Napoli e Salerno. La costruzione dell'identità cittadina nel Mezzogiorno medievale*, Immagini del Medioevo 5 (Salerno, 2001), pp. 52–63 & 163–183.

22. Erchemp*ert, cit.*, c. 53 p. 256; *Chronicon Salernitanum, cit.*, c. 152 pp. 160–161; Nicola Cilento, 'La Cronaca dei conti e dei principi longobardi di Capua dei codici Cassinese 175 e Cavense 4 (815–1000)', *Bullettino dell'ISIME e Archivio Muratoriano* 69 (1957), pp. 1–67, genealogical chart; Paolo Bertolini, art. 'Cesario', *DBI* t. 24 (Rome, 1980), pp. 205–210; Patricia Skinner, *Family Power in Southern Italy. The Duchy of Gaeta and its Neighbours, 850–1139*, Cambridge Studies in Medieval Life and Thought. Fourth Series 29 (Cambridge, 1995), pp. 46–49.

23. Hans Belting, 'Studien zum Beneventanischen Hof im 8. Jahrhundert', *Dumbarton Oaks Papers* 16 (1962), pp. 141–196 + 6 plates, pp. 175–193 & Thomas S. Brown, 'Ethnic independence and cultural deference: the attitude of the Lombard principalities to Byzantium c. 876–1077', *Byzantium and its neighbours. From the mid-9th to the 12th centuries*, ed. Vladimír Vavrínek, Byzantinoslavica LIV–1 (1993), pp. 5–12.

24. *Diplomata ducum*, n. 5 (November 20th, 975), *MND*, 2–2, p. 15; n. 21 (January 12th, 1097), p. 61; n. 22 (September 2nd, 1107), p. 64; Ulrich Schwarz, *Amalfi im frühen Mittelalter (9.–11. Jahrhundert). Untersuchungen zur Amalfitaner Überlieferung*, Bibliothek des Deutschen Historischen Instituts in Rom 49 (Tübingen, 1978), pp. 31 & 33–34; Huguette Taviani-Carozzi, *La principauté, cit.*, vol. 2 p. 1125; Thomas S. Brown, 'Ethnic independence and cultural deference', *cit.*, p. 8.

25. Huguette Taviani-Carozzi, *La principauté, cit.*, vol. 1 p. 362.

26. Naples: *Vita sancti Athanasii, cit.*, 1, 32 p. 118; *Translatio sancti Athanasii Neapolitani episcopi (BHL 737), ibid.*, 7, 1 p. 150; *Translatio sancti Severini (BHL 7658), MND*, 1, pp. 291–300, c. 13 p. 296; *Translatio sancti Sossii* (BHL 4134–4135), ed. *AASS Septembris VI, cit.*, pp. 874–884, c. 32 p. 881D. Benevento: Thomas F. Kelly, *The Beneventan Chant* (Cambridge, 1989); Roger E. Reynolds, 'The Greek liturgy of St. John Chrysostom in Beneventan script: an early manuscript fragment', *Mediaeval Studies* 52 (1990), pp. 296–302.

27. *Gesta, cit.*, c. 44, p. 426 l. 34–36; *Diplomata ducum*, n. 5 (November 20th, 975), *MND*, 2–2 p. 16.

28. Paolo Chiesa, 'Le traduzioni dal greco: l'evoluzione della scuola napoletana nel X secolo', *Lateinische Kultur im 10. Jahrhundert*, ed. Walter Berschin, *Mittellateinisches Jahrbuch* 24–25 (1989–90), pp. 67–86 and Thomas Granier, 'L'hagiographie napolitaine du haut Moyen Âge: contexte, corpus et enjeux', *Bulletin du CRISIMA* 2 (2001), pp. 13–40.

29. Thomas Granier, 'Les échanges culturels dans l'Italie méridionale du haut Moyen Âge: Naples, Bénévent et le Mont-Cassin aux VIIIe–XIIe siècles', *Les échanges culturels au Moyen Âge*. XXXIIe Congrès de la SHMES, Histoire Ancienne et Médiévale 70 (Paris, 2002), pp. 89–105.

30. Hans Belting, 'Studien zum Beneventanischen Hof', *cit.*, p. 157; Antonio Vuolo, 'Agiografia beneventana', *Longobardia e Longobardi nell'Italia meridionale: le istituzioni ecclesiastiche*, ed. Giancarlo Andenna & Giorgio Picasso, Bibliotheca Erudita. Studi e Documenti di Storia e Filologia 11 (Milan, 1996), pp. 199–237, pp. 202–217.

31. Antonio Gambacorta, 'Culto e pellegrinaggi a San Nicola di Bari fino alla prima Crociata', *Pellegrinaggi e culto dei santi in Europa fino alla Ia Crociata*, Convegni del Centro di Studi sulla Spiritualità Medievale IV (Todi, 1963), pp. 485–502; Agostino Pertusi, 'Ai confini tra religione e

politica: la contesa per le reliquie di san Nicola tra Bari, Venezia e Genova', *Quaderni Medievali* 5 (1978), pp. 6–56; Antonio Vuolo, 'Agiografia beneventana', *cit.*, pp. 231–233.

32. Capuani: Erchempert, *cit.*, c. 32, p. 247 l. 1; Beneventani: *ibid.*, c. 32, p. 246 l. 38 & c. 34, p. 247 l. 23 and *Gesta, cit.*, c. 51, p. 428 l. 25.

33. *Gesta, cit.*, c. 60, p. 432 l. 42.

34. *Libellus miraculorum s. Agnelli, cit.*, mir. III, p. 158 l. 2 & mir. II, p. 155 l. 2–3.

35. Ulrich Schwarz, *Amalfi im frühen Mittelalter,* *cit.*, pp. 18–20; Huguette Taviani-Carozzi, *La principauté, cit.*, vol. 2 pp. 800–837.

36. *Capitula domni Adelchis principis,* ed. *Claudio Azzara & Stefano Gasparri, Le leggi dei Longobardi. Storia, memoria e diritto di un popolo germanico,* Altomedioevo 4 (Rome, 2005), pp. 306–313, p. 308; *Translatio sancti Athanasii, cit.*, 2, 3 p. 146.

37. Walter Pohl, 'Invasions and ethnic identity', *cit.*, p. 32; Thomas Granier, 'Napolitains et Lombards', *cit.*, p. 409.

38. *Translatio sancti Severini, cit.*, c. 16–17 p. 297; Thomas Granier, 'Le peuple devant les saints: la cité et le peuple de Naples dans les textes hagiographiques fin IXe–début Xe s.', *Peuples du Moyen Âge, cit.*, pp. 57–76, p. 59.

39. *Chronicon Salernitanum, cit.*, c. 113–114 pp. 127–128.

40. *Miracula sancti Agrippini (BHL* 174–177), ed. *AASS Novembris IV* (Paris-Rome, 1925), pp. 118–128, c. 12 p. 127BC.

41. Erchempert, *cit.*, c. 29, p. 245 l. 18 & c. 33, p. 247 l. 18; *Gesta, cit.*, c. 54, p. 430 l. 4 & c. 57, p. 431 l. 22; *Libellus miraculorum sancti Agnelli, cit.*, mir. I, p. 152 l. 10, mir. II, p. 156 l. 13 & mir. VIII, p. 168 l. 2; *Chronicon Salernitanum, cit.*, c. 79, p. 77 l. 5, c. 117, p. 130 l. 22 & p. 131 l. 5.

42. *L'Occidente e l'Islam nell'Alto Medioevo,* CISAM. Settimane 12, 2 vol. (Spoleto, 1965); Luigi Andrea Berto, 'I musulmani nelle cronache altomedievali dell'Italia meridionale *(secoli IX–X)*', *Mediterraneo medievale. Cristiani, musulmani ed eretici tra Europa ed Oltremare (secoli IX–XIII)*, ed. Marco Meschini, Scienze Storiche 74, (Milan, 2001), pp. 3–27; Walter Pohl, 'Invasions and ethnic identity', cit., p. 31.

43. Thomas Granier, 'Napolitains et Lombards', *cit.*, pp. 430 & 444–446.

44. Jules Gay, *L'Italie méridionale et l'Empire byzantin depuis l'avènement de Basile Ier jusqu'à la prise de Bari par les Normands (867–1071),* BEFAR 90 (Paris, 1904), pp. 22, 55, 159 & 161–163.

45. Walter Pohl, 'Le identità etniche nei ducati di Spoleto e Benevento', *I Longobardi dei ducati di Spoleto e Benevento*. Atti del XVI Congresso Internazionale du Studi sull'Alto Medioevo (Spoleto, 2003), 2 t., t. 1, pp. 79–103.

46. Walter Pohl, *Werkstätte der Erinnerung. Montecassino und die Gestaltung der langobardischen Vergangenheit,* Mitteilungen des Instituts für Österreichische Geschichtsforschung. Ergänzungsband 39 (Wien-München, 2001).

Chapter Seven

Contested regions in the nineteenth
and twentieth centuries:
Ulster in comparative perspective

A.C. Hepburn

There is no absolute difference between a regional and a national consciousness. Regions have become nations, and nations have become regions. Just as a language has been defined pragmatically as "a dialect with an army", so a state is more literally "a region with an army". A region may be delineated in various ways, which can be either mutually reinforcing or cross-cutting. Physical geography – sea and rivers, the nature of the terrain, even climate – may define a region's character or borders. Some regions have evolved as distinct economic units, often related to the discovery or development of natural resources. Human agency may also play a central role in fashioning a region: sometimes it may come to be differentiated on the grounds of its strategic importance, for example a "buffer region"; more frequently it has been distinguished by cultural or historic factors related to the people who live there – a shared sense of history or a common language, dialect or religion which is specific to that region.

Although Bill Lancaster's work has shown that North East England was not conceptualised as a region distinct from "the North" until the 1920s, it does meet these objective criteria.[1] The physical boundaries, the heritage of heavy industry, and the distinctive group of north-eastern dialects all support this view, notwithstanding the following passage from Jack Common's autobiographical novel of his youth, *Kiddar's Luck*:

> *My Uncle Will …used to make this point with all the reiterated dogmatism natural to a Sunderland man supporting a Sunderland thesis. Listening to him I felt he certainly had an argument, though couched in curiously uncouth speech. At that time I was accustomed to hearing only the pure English spoken in Northumberland and on the Tyne and did not know that as you get deeper into Durham a tykey element creeps into the dialect as a sort of warning to the sensitive traveller that the bottomy dumps of Yorkshire are, indeed, imminent.*[2]

Sunderland and Newcastle are not renowned for camaraderie, especially where sport is concerned. But sub-regional divisions co-exist with, rather than override, a strong sense of regional identity. Whereas forces of nature or history, or some more specific intervention, have decreed that a certain territory constitutes a region, the inhabitants thereof do not necessarily regard themselves as a homogeneous group of people. As with nation-states, a regional identity may be contested. A contested region may take one of two forms: on the one hand it may have a population which perceives itself as homogeneous but a territory which is contested between two states; alternatively, the identity and rightful state affiliation of the region itself may be a matter of dispute between its inhabitants.

"Ulster", the north-east quarter of Ireland, is an example of a contested region of the latter sort. This paper will explore elements of that conflict, and seek to set it in the broader context of contested regions as a whole.

Part I

In some ways the territory known since 1921 as Northern Ireland is very clearly a region. It has a high level of geographic distinctness provided by mountains and rivers. By the late eighteenth century it had developed an economic distinctness from the rest of Ireland which then widened substantially, so that by the early twentieth century the eastern part of the region at least was dominated by large-scale industrial manufacture supplying global markets, whereas the rest of Ireland, outside the administrative capital of Dublin, was dominated by farming and agricultural products. By the mid-nineteenth century English was the first language of the overwhelming majority of Ulster's people, while sub-regional dialects of Ulster English were defined by territory rather than ethnicity, and all had more in common with one another than with any other Irish or British dialects. Ethnic groups in Ulster's population are not differentiated by physical appearance or dietary preferences. Likewise surnames are an unreliable guide to ethnic difference. Yet notwithstanding this absence of objective ethnic delimiters, it is of course the case that the population of this particular region regards itself as one of the most sharply divided in Europe. The real badge of ethnic difference is religious denomination – Roman Catholic on the one side and what is called simply "Protestant" on the other – and these in turn serve as markers identifying people who perceive themselves to be descended from either a Gaelic, native-Irish population or from Anglo-Scots settlers. A sense of these identities can to some extent be traced back to the period of the Ulster Plantation in the seventeenth century, but "Protestant" as an ethnic identity owes much more to political and social developments which occurred between the 1780s and the 1830s: many middle-class Nonconformist Protestants in Ulster, as in Britain, identified with the ideals of the French Revolution and some died for them, but the survivors recoiled from the violence and repression which beset Ireland in 1798. As intra-Protestant ideological differences were narrowed in the interests of "Protestant unity" and the Orange Order helped to spread this through the working class and among small farmers, Irish nationalism also retreated from the secular ideals of the radical Enlightenment to become increasingly concerned with Catholic civic rights, Catholic organisational exclusivity and, later, a Gaelic cultural revival which was permeated at the popular level by Catholicity. Its political demand became for some form of termination of the Act of Union which had taken Ireland into the United Kingdom in 1801 – either through legislative devolution or through sovereign independence.

By the late nineteenth century this conflict between Unionism and Nationalism pervaded the whole island. But as the introduction of manhood suffrage appeared to bring Nationalist victory closer, so Unionism adopted an increasingly territorial focus. The north-east of the country had since the seventeenth century been distinguished as the area of mixed religion in Ireland, the territory where Protestants comprised local majorities, or large minorities, rather than just a narrow elite as in most of the rest of the country. Between the 1880s and 1920 Unionism came to define the Ulster region with increasing specificity. Strictly speaking Ulster was a nine-county "historic province" with no administrative significance in the modern period, though with clearly marked boundaries. Once the British Liberal Party embraced the cause of home rule for Ireland, Ulster Unionism began to emerge as a distinct regional movement, aimed at preserving what it saw as "their region" from the concessions to nationalism which were happening in the rest of the country. In 1912, through the so-called "Ulster Covenant" the movement collected signatures and organised armed resistance to home rule throughout the nine counties of Ulster. As the crisis deepened successive British governments sought to explore the possibility of temporary exclusion of (in 1914) four counties, and (in 1916) six counties, from a home rule settlement. By 1919 the Ulster Unionists – to the great anger of Unionists/Protestants in the other three counties – had accepted that a six-county "Ulster" was the largest "region" which they could defend and secure.

This was the territory which became the devolved region of "Northern Ireland", within the United Kingdom, in 1921. It had no previous rationale as a territory, lacking both the historic status of the nine-county Province of Ulster, and the democratic logic of "county option", for while four of the six counties had clear Unionist majorities, the counties of Tyrone and Fermanagh had narrow Catholic majorities. What the British Government, in tacit agreement with the Ulster Unionists, had chosen to define as "Northern Ireland" was in fact simply the largest easily-designated area within which the Unionist side could still be confident of sustaining a large voting majority. It also meant that the territory so designated was a good approximation to what may be called "the area of mixed religion" in Ireland. Protestant leaders since 1921 have habitually used the term "Ulster" with more affection than "Northern Ireland" to describe the territory, while "the Ulster people" tends to be used by them to mean, implicitly "the Ulster

Protestant people". By contrast "the Northern Irish people" trips less easily off the tongue. It was used briefly and unsuccessfully during the late 1970s by well-meaning centrist journalists and others seeking to build an inter-communal identity.[3] In 1945–47 the Unionist Government of Northern Ireland attempted to have the name of the province changed formally to "Ulster" and, more tentatively, to seek dominion status with a view to avoiding the "socialistic measures" anticipated from the new Labour Government at Westminster. These ideas were briskly dismissed by a British government which otherwise proved remarkably sympathetic to the Ulster Unionist position.

Both the new states in Ireland after 1921 acted as if they each represented a single culture. In essence the organisational reforms introduced into the Irish Catholic Church by Cardinal Paul Cullen (Archbishop of Dublin, 1852–78) and the Gaelic cultural revival of c.1890–1914 had both assumed that an independent Ireland would be essentially a Catholic state. This sat uneasily with the standard nationalist claim for "the island of Ireland".[4] As Eamon de Valera sought to consolidate the independent Ireland of the 1930s into precisely such a conservative, Catholic and Gaelic state, in the north Lord Craigavon famously declared that "we are a Protestant Parliament for a Protestant State".[5] The chief author of the 1921 settlement, Lloyd George, also suggested that it was in this sense even-handed. The problem of course was that the northern state, in particular, was not a Protestant state but a state within which one-third of the population were Catholics and nationalists. Nonetheless the outcome of 1921 (and the fruitless boundary commission which followed in 1925) fit neatly the theory of the contemporary American political scientist Ian Lustick concerning state expansion and contraction: "Different borders", he wrote, "have different demographic implications... The territorial shape of the state thus helps determine what interests are legitimate, what resources are indivisible."[6] A nine-county Ulster might promptly have voted itself into the Irish Free State; a six-county Ulster was assured of a pro-Union majority while embracing a Nationalist minority large enough – in the context of the first-past-the-post electoral system which operated between 1929 and 1973 – to encourage the continuation of "Protestant unity" in support of the Ulster Unionist Party.

The Irish Boundary Commission established under the 1921 Treaty reported confidentially to the British Government in 1925, although the Report was not made public until 1968.[7] It was, however, leaked in the contemporary press, the Free State commissioner resigned and the proposals – minor adjustments which would have transferred 31,000 people to the Free State and 7,000 to Northern

Ireland – were not implemented. Many on the Nationalist side had expected a much larger award from a brief which required the Commission to take account of "the wishes of the inhabitants", insofar as they were "compatible with economic and geographic factors". But in its economic assessment of the Catholic-majority border towns of Derry and Newry the Commission laid more stress on their links to the north and east than on their cross-border associations. The wider economic links between the north and south of Ireland had always been limited during the industrial era, while commercial and small business links had been further damaged by Sinn Féin's boycott of "Belfast" goods during the troubles of 1920–22. Likewise the Commission chose to consult "the wishes of the inhabitants" along a narrow border strip, rather than take a poll of larger units such as Counties Tyrone and Fermanagh, which might well have voted wholesale to join the Free State.

As we shall see below, the context of the struggle in some contested regions has been altered at particular points by such factors as demographic change and linguistic shift. The Irish context has been relatively unchanged by such factors, the sole historical exception being the relative rise of the Catholic population of Belfast – from around 10 % to 34 % – during the first half of the nineteenth century, and its relative decline – to 24 % – during the second half. The years since 1971 have seen a more general increase in the Catholic population of the region, from barely one-third to more than two-fifths, due to changes in the patterns of emigration to Britain and elsewhere, but the political implications of such a trend have yet to emerge. Other issues which have frequently impacted on regional ethnic conflicts elsewhere have, likewise, had little significance in Ulster. These include the failure of cross-cutting ideologies or other factors to modify or blur the ethnic divide at all. Socialism and the organised labour movement in Ulster quickly divided along the same lines as middle-class nationalism. An ethnic divide which depended so strongly, in the absence of other convincing objective factors, on religious denomination was far less likely than a divide based on language difference to develop any middle ground or third force. The location of the Ulster region on the fringe of Europe meant that international interventions were unlikely to be of major significance, while the relatively untrammelled power of the United Kingdom in the region meant that large-scale communal violence was unlikely to run sufficiently out of control for a long-term political refugee problem to become an issue. It is true that the famine of the 1840s produced a massive exodus of economic refugees, creating an enormous Irish diaspora which was later to have a significant political impact on Ireland's development. While the Ulster

Scot diaspora is also very large it is so long-established in America, without recent replenishment, that its political links are very weak. Evangelical Protestantism has been a somewhat more effective link between Protestant Ulster and the "Scotch-Irish" heartlands of the southern United States. But neither of these diasporic interventions has created the direct political effect which a large refugee community of Ulster Catholics in Dublin, or of Ulster Protestants in Glasgow, might have done.

A final feature of the Ulster case to which we need to draw attention is the role of the regional metropolis. Large cities have often been of particular significance in regions of conflict. Even the few great primate cities of early modern Europe punched far above their weight in societies where their numbers were greatly exceeded by those of the rural community. Some sub-state nationalisms in the late nineteenth century, in contrast, drew their energy far more from the responses of recently-fractured rural communities. Dublin's prominence in Irish nationalism, for instance, was a matter of occasional moments in the spotlight rather than regular leadership of a movement whose values were essentially rural. Belfast, on the other hand, is an example of a metropolis which was of crucial importance to its region. Demographically its large Protestant majority tipped the overall balance of the regional population firmly in favour of the Union. Politically its fierce reputation for sectarian rioting, especially its potential for holding the Catholic minority of the city as surety for the behaviour of Nationalists elsewhere, meant that the British Government in 1914, and again in 1974, flinched rather than attempt to impose its previously-declared policies on a resistant city.

Part II

This has been a brief overview of the modern ethnic history of the Ulster region. How might it contribute more broadly to the study of regions and regionalism? The second half of this chapter will draw out some of the main themes discussed above, and analyse them in a comparative context. The aims of regional movements have varied not only between cases but also across time, as Lustick's theory would suggest. The strategic aim of the Ulster movement shifted between 1880 and 1920 from using its regional power as a weapon for maintaining the status quo throughout Ireland to accepting devolved self-government within the UK for six of the nine Ulster counties. The Catalan movement sought devolved regional powers and was confident in its ability to absorb large numbers of economic migrants from other regions of Spain, whereas the Basque movement underwent a much more sudden industrialisation and accompanying population inflow in the late nineteenth century. It has sought to use its inaccessible language and militant policies to maintain an ethnic identity based on blood, and to achieve total separation from Spain. Quebec nationalism likewise sought for two centuries to preserve its culture by insulating itself from modernising influences. Since 1960 it has modified this, using the power of the regional state to seize the economic high ground and to impose Francophone linguistic policies on incomers. But its followers continue to have as to whether or not they need full sovereign independence from Canada in order to secure this.

Some regions have been contested because of their strategic or economic significance. It has long been part of the Irish republican credo that Britain wanted Ireland, or in the twentieth century Northern Ireland, for security reasons. From Perkin Warbeck in the 1490s through the Spanish invasion of 1603 to Pitt's famous comment during the French revolutionary period, there was some truth in this.[8] The dispute over the "treaty ports" in the Free State between 1921 and 1938, and the role of Northern Ireland as a base during the Second World War suggest that this continued to be a factor, although it has ceased to be of significance during the past half-century. The Saarland was excluded from Germany between 1919 and the plebiscite of 1935, not because there was any real doubt about the wishes of its people but because France wanted the security of its coal deposits and its borders.[9] Kashmir is perhaps the most serious contemporary example of this type of contested region. Partitioned since 1947 into a large Indian Kashmir and a smaller "Free Kashmir" which is under the effective control of Pakistan, it has a high level of cultural homogeneity based on Muslim religion and a more limited degree of homogeneity based on the Kashmiri language. Kashmiris are divided in their aspirations between advocates of independence and those who wish the whole region to be transferred to Pakistan, whereas India controls most of the territory and will not countenance change, for reasons of security and prestige. The dispute has been so long-running mainly for reasons external to the region, to do with cold war alignments, fears concerning nuclear weapons and the general volatility of India-Pakistan relations.[10]

But the boundaries of contested regions, as we have seen in the Ulster case and as Lustick's theory again suggests, are by no means always purely or mainly a problem of external powers. Punjab is a mixed case – a region with clear boundaries and a common language, it was partitioned in 1947 in the context of Indo-Pakistan confrontation. But the cause of that partition lay primarily in the Hindu-Muslim-Sikh religious divisions inherited from previous history, which had come to assume a new ethnic salience. The boundaries of the Basque region have been more problematic: while their demand in principle is for four provinces from Spain and three from France, in practice the Basque nationalist voice has emanated strongly only from a proportion of the territory within Spain. As with Irish nationalism's claim for the entire "island of Ireland" at the same time as it wanted a near-exclusive Gaelic and Catholic state, and with Ulster Unionism's reluctant pragmatic reduction of its claim from nine counties to six, so there is also a disjunction between the Basque claim for a large cross-border region widely conceived, on the one hand, and its parallel desire for an ethnically-and linguistically-unified region on the other.

Where considerable ethnic intermixing exists within a region its fundamental national identification, or its partition, may be at issue. The interface between Italy, Slovenia and Croatia – the territory known in Italy as Venezia-Giulia and in the former Yugoslavia as the Julian March (Julijska Krajina) – is a case in point. There the rural population extending as far west into Italy as the Isonzo river has been solidly Slav, whereas the towns extending south-eastwards down the Istrian and Dalmatian coastline were until 1945 predominantly Italian. Dante described Pola, now the Croatian resort of Pula at the southern tip of the Istrian peninsula, as "the terminus of Italy".[11] This iconic designation has remained something of an inspiration to ethnic Italians of Istrian background now resident in Trieste or elsewhere in Italy. In Belgium, by contrast, the Fleming and Walloon communities were each able to preserve their own discrete homelands, both urban and rural, through the era of industrial change, as a consequence of which they have since the 1960s been able to impose Dutch and French monolingualism on their respective regions with a manageable level of dispute over borderlines. The exception has been the capital city of Brussels, now a separate bilingual region, where conflict persists over both the relative strength of the two languages in the city and the tightly-drawn boundary of the city-region, which is constrained by the strict monolingualism of the neighbouring regions. What Francophones object to as the Flanders "iron collar" around Brussels is welcomed by the Dutch-speaking Flemings as a necessary barrier against the spreading French "oil-stain".[12] Montreal, like Brussels, is the focus of linguistic and political conflict for its wider region. In the case of Quebec, partition is not appropriate to the facts on the ground, the one potential exception being the tentative proposal in 1971 to create a separate English-speaking metropolitan local authority in the western suburbs of Montreal.[13]

Formal decisions on the boundaries of regions have been taken by various means, ranging from plebiscites, treaties and quasi-legal boundary commissions to governmental *diktats* and armistice lines. In the case of Trieste and Istria, so many different boundaries were proposed or implemented between 1918 and 1954 that the ingenuity of academic mapmakers has been severely taxed.[14]   In 1905 the Indian Viceroy and Conservative politician, Lord Curzon, partitioned the Indian state of Bengal into separate eastern and western states. The main reason given was administrative efficiency, but the explanation varied to some extent according to the audience. In truth Curzon's aim was to lessen the importance of Calcutta, then the national capital and the main centre of Indian nationalism, by halving the size of the city's hinterland and by seeking to counterbalance the Congress Party's strength by creating for the Muslims a majority state in East Bengal. Curzon had some initial difficulty in selling his idea to the Muslim elite, but once he had done so the situation got out of hand. After several years of riots against the Hindu minority in East Bengal, a British Liberal Government dismantled the Bengal partition experiment in 1911 and addressed the Calcutta problem in a different way, by moving the national capital to New Delhi.[15]   In contemporary India it is said that the national government is more likely to concede regional autonomy to areas that are "within the fold of the ethnic democracy" than to peripheral territories where regionalist demands are stronger and possibly separatist in intent.[16]

Boundary commissions tend to be presented as impartial, judicial procedures for resolving disputes in divided regions. The story of the Irish Boundary Commission is well-known, and has been referred to above. Its terms of reference were sufficiently vague to permit the two sides to interpret it to themselves and their followers in the way that each wanted, while the main purpose had been to put the most contentious point at issue on the long finger until such time as the remainder of the settlement was in place. The Indian Boundaries Commission of 1947, though it was established in order to obtain a very quick decision rather than to procrastinate, was no more open in its intent. The recent work of Joya Chatterji has shown, for the case of Bengal, that the British Government's intention was simply to achieve sufficient representative endorsement for the principle of partition, so that it could proceed with the implementation of independence along its pre-determined lines of a two-state solution. The Bengal Legislative Assembly was split into two groups, comprising representatives from individual Hindu-majority districts and Muslim-majority districts respectively, following neither the territorial nor the communal principle. Representatives were asked to vote for or against a partition of Bengal, without knowing which side their district would end up on. Many Bengali Muslims opposed partition because, being in an overall majority, they believed that they would have won power in an undivided Bengal. On the basis of the economic arguments which the Commission was empowered to take into consideration, the Muslim League claimed Calcutta and most of its western hinterland for Pakistan. In the event the Commission drew the partition line about 40 miles east of Calcutta, creating a West Bengal region in India in which 29 % of the population were Muslims, and an East Bengal region in Pakistan which included 29 % Hindus. Disappointments were thus balanced, but the main reason that Bengal did not witness the massive bloodbath which accompanied the Punjab partition in 1947 – in which between 200,000 and half a million died – is said to have been the steadying influence of Gandhi, who opposed the entire partition idea, but who stationed himself deliberately in East Bengal as a hostage for the good behaviour of West Bengal Hindus towards their local Muslims.[17]

As with nations, no region is complete without a recognised metropolis. We have seen the importance of Belfast to the Ulster Protestant cause. The importance of a regional capital is indicated by the problems which arise when a region does not feel confident in its possession of one or is challenged in it. Trieste's famed urban *italianità* was crucial to the decision of the western powers in 1945 to hold the Yugoslav frontier at the city's eastern boundary, rather than thirty miles to the west, along the line of the Isonzo River. It was the realisation during the 1960s that bilingual Montreal – and, following that, monolingual Quebec – might be lost to the French language that caused the Francophone majority in the region to abandon its quietist policy of *la survivance* and embrace the values of urbanism and economic advancement. In Belgium the Flemish movement for a long time drew its strength from its cultural base in Antwerp, but since 1945 it has sought to reverse a century of *francisation* in Brussels which had turned it into a French-speaking capital of a majority Dutch-speaking country. In his attempt to partition Bengal in 1905 Lord Curzon stressed to Muslims that the creation of a separate province of East Bengal would reverse the decline of the city of Dhaka and make it a capital once more.[18] Likewise we have seen that a deliberate intention of Curzon's partition was to weaken the political power of Calcutta, while the more effective Bengal partition of 1947 has indeed weakened the former Indian capital by cutting off much of its demographic and economic hinterland.[19] A weakness of the Basque movement is that whereas Bilbao is the centre of Basque economic power, it lacks the cultural standing of San Sebastian or Pamplona, so that the neutral site of Vitoria had to be adopted as the regional capital.[20] Pakistan, too, has struggled with its capital, moving it in 1959 from Karachi, the Sindhi centre on the coast, more than 700 miles north to Rawalpindi/Islamabad. This "Punjabisation" of the Pakistan state has resulted in the stabilisation of the volatile and partitioned Punjab, at the cost of serious disaffection among the Sindhis and Baluchis of the south.[21] From Belfast to Dhaka and from Montreal to Karachi, regional metropoles can have unifying or destabilising effect on their regions.

As well as international and state actors and the peoples of the regions themselves, important roles may also be played by exiles, refugees and other members of the diaspora. An extreme example is the case of contemporary Kashmir, where very large numbers of Kashmiris live in Britain, Germany and elsewhere. Kashmir has to a considerable extent become a remittance economy (or technically *two* remittance economies), while in Pakistani "Free Kashmir" a diaspora representative, most often from Britain, is a nominated member of the regional assembly. Under an apparently extant decree made in 1858 by the then maharajah, Kashmiris retain citizen rights for at least two generations after emigration.[22] Along similar lines, but perhaps with more optimism than realism, the Ulster-based Sinn Féin leader Gerry Adams has demanded votes in Ireland for Irish emigrants.[23] Refugees, too, can be a powerful force with regard to contested regions. Regions such as Ulster and the Basque country have produced no more than relatively small groups of activists on the run, making some slight impact on elements of public opinion in places such as Dundalk, Glasgow and Bayonne. Large scale migrations can be something different. In India, after the partition of 1947, Congress Party representatives originally elected in eastern Bengal continued to dominate regional politics in West Bengal even after they had lost their constituencies.[24] Pamela Ballinger, in a fascinating anthropological study comparing the ethnic Italians who remained in Yugoslav Istria after the 1940s (*rimasti*) with those who fled to Trieste (*esuli*), has shown the ongoing power of refugee politics, even in a west European context: thirty years after the exodus, refugees hostile to the 1975 Italo-Yugoslav Treaty of Osimo (which confirmed the boundaries and arrangements put in place in 1954) were able to found a new political movement, the *Lista per Trieste*, which won a majority on the city council in the following year. Variously described as "impure boundary transgressors who nonetheless symbolise the nation in exile" and as "the illegitimate children of modernity", refugees have played important roles in many contested regions.[25]

Finally, it remains to be asked what alternative visions of contested regions, what examples of intermixing or diffusion of conflict, exist? In Ulster we find little middle ground in a society where ethnic difference is defined by religious identity. Even as levels of religious observance fall and the number of parents opting for "integrated" schools rises, the overall picture presented by electoral and communal behaviour is of increasing political and social separation for about 80 % of the population.[26] In the Istrian case the ethnic Italians who stayed on now tend to regard their region as mixed Italian-Slav, and their level of intermarriage has been high. The exiles on the other hand foster memories of a lost "Italian" Istria, regarding the stayers – even their own relatives – as "Communists", just as they in turn are regarded as "Fascists".[27] In pre-1947 Punjab the official policy of the ruling Punjabi Unionist Party was indeed unity of the region. It was able to sustain a cross-communal political alliance from the 1920s to the mid-1940s based on agricultural policies and power-sharing, but it then collapsed in the face of the bilateral drive for partition coming from the Congress Party and the Muslim League. In Bengal there was no party-political equivalent of this. But there was "a sense of regional cultural unity [which] did appear to transcend religious divisions", and a minority faction within the Bengali Provincial Muslim League which argued for "a united and sovereign Bengal, independent of both India and Pakistan".[28]

In the case of the Saarland, the French premier Clemenceau rather fancifully claimed at the Versailles Peace Conference in 1919 that the region was not really German, but had merely been "Germanised" over the previous century: a period of French control under a League of Nations mandate, he claimed, would soon reverse this.[29] Lloyd George and Woodrow Wilson were not convinced. We have seen that something like this really did happen in nineteenth-century Brussels, as French replaced the Brabant dialect of Dutch as the main language of the city. Language shift was indeed quite common in the growing urban centres of contested regions in the West during most of the nineteenth century. Where there was no religious barrier it was often accompanied by high levels of intermarriage. Who would have guessed, for instance, that provincial Premier Edmund James Flynn was a French-speaking Québécois?[30] The phenomenon was in most cases (including probably Irish Catholics in most of Quebec, though not in Montreal) a measure of social aspiration. In Trieste, Brussels, Budapest and scores of other cities migrants from the ethnic countryside accepted a shift to the locally-dominant language simply as a feature of urban migration. But the emergence of ethnic political activism and minority nationalist movements – in many cases around 1900, but in the Brussels case half a century later – quite swiftly reversed these trends. In conflicts which were based on a religious division, such as Ulster or (for the most part) Quebec, such shifts occurred only in isolated individual cases.

So contested regions do, in my view, constitute a distinct category. They are defined and their development is determined by a variety of internal and external factors, as we have seen. In some cases attempts – successful and otherwise – have been made to resolve their difficulties by partition of the region. In other cases the contested region has continued its existence under the imposed authority of a sovereign state and/or has remained in what is in effect an insulated condition. Where the neighbours really do not wish to be drawn into the problems of a deeply-divided region, or fear that they themselves will be destabilised if they attempt to do so, it tends to remain insulated. A striking feature of the Ulster case is the way in which the people of Northern Ireland are in a sense bound together by their own division. They are obsessed by it, but these days few outside the region are interested. Their violence has been among the worst in post-war western Europe. But the objective differences between the two communities are very slight. It is a frequently-observed phenomenon that, away from the region, individuals from the two Ulster sides will readily come together, sometimes on the basis of prudent avoidance of their inter-communal differences, but probably more often on the basis of discreet but well-understood interrogations designed to establish their respective affiliations, leading to bantering conversations which often focus on and caricature their ethnic differences. Neutral observers who witness such dialogues – which category includes both British and southern Irish people – are in this way marginalised. People can share and embrace territorially-based identities and memories of their regions, even when those regions are riven by bitter communal division.

Notes

1. See Bill Lancaster, Chapter 2, this book.
2. Jack Common, *Kiddars's Luck* and *The Ampersand* (Newcastle upon Tyne, 1975. 1st edn 1951), p.49.
3. During the winter of 1976–77 Belfast's non-partisan political magazine *Fortnight* changed its sub-title from '*An Independent review for Northern Ireland*' to '*The Northern Irish Fortnight*', but protests led to the editor's resignation and a return to the original masthead.
4. A.C.Hepburn, 'Irish nationalism in Ulster, 1995–1921', in D.George Boyce & Alan O'Day, eds, *The Ulster Crisis, 1885–1921* (London & Basingstoke, 2006), pp.108–09.
5. NI HC Deb. vol.xvi, col.1035 (24 April 1934), cited in A.C.Hepburn, ed., *The Conflict of Nationality in Modern Ireland* (London, 1980), p.165.
6. Ian Lustick, *Unsettled States, Disputed Lands: Britain & Ireland, France & Algeria, Israel and the West Bank* (London, 1993), pp.38–39.
7. G.J.Hand, ed. *Report of the Irish Boundary Commission* (Dublin, 1969).
8. 'Ireland is like a ship on fire. It must either be extinguished or cut adrift'. Cited in O.MacDonagh, *Ireland* (Englewood Cliffs, New Jersey, 1968), p.4.
9. Harold I. Nelson, *Land and Power: British & Allied Policy on Germany's Frontiers, 1916–19*

(London, 1963), p.249.

10. Patricia Ellis & Zafar Khan, 'Partition and Kashmir: Implications for the Region and the Diaspora', in Ian Talbot & Gurharpal Singh, eds, *Region & Partition: Bengal, Punjab and the Partition of the Subcontinent* (Oxford, 1999), pp.267–97.

11. Cited in Pamela Ballinger, *History in Exile: Memory & Identity at the Borders of the Balkans* (Princeton, 2002), p.27.

12. A.C.Hepburn, *Contested Cities in the Modern West* (London & Basingstoke, 2004), pp.128–157.

13. *Ibid.*, p.113.

14. See e.g. Bogdan C.Novak, *Trieste 1941–54: the Ethnic, Political & Ideological Struggle* (Chicago, 1970), pp. 5, 261, 269.

15. Vinod Kumar Saxena, ed., *The Partition of Bengal, 1905–11: Select Documents* (Delhi, 1987), pp.1–32.

16. Gurharpal Singh, 'The Partition of India in a Comparative Perspective: a Long-term View', in Talbot & Singh, *Region & Partition*, p.111.

17. Joya Chatterji, 'The Making of a Borderline: the Radcliffe Award for Bengal', *ibid.*, pp.168–202.

18. Saxena, *Partition of Bengal*, p.7.

19. Although still a very large conurbation, Calcutta was replaced by Bombay in 1991 as India's largest city, for the first time since records were kept in 1872.

20. Daniele Conversi, *The Basques, the Catalans and Spain: Alternative Routes to Nationalist Mobilisation* (London, 1997), p.258.

21. Iftikhar H. Malik, 'Regionalism or Personality Cult?', in Talbot & Singh, *Region & Partition*, p.43.

22. Ellis & Khan, 'Partition and Kashmir', *ibid.*, pp.282–91.

23. *An Phoblacht/Republican News*, 7 Dec.2000.

24. Chatterji, 'Making of a Borderline', in Talbot & Singh, *Region & Partition*, p.189.

25. Ballinger, *History in Exile*, p.45; H.Bhattacharyya, 'Post-Partition refugees and the Communists: a Comparative Study of West Bengal and Tripura', in Talbot & Singh, *Region & Partition*, p.325.

26. Integrated schools in Ulster seek to provide a curriculum which respects and reconciles Nationalist and Unionist positions, and are a small but growing third category in education, distinct from both the Catholic Church-controlled and the Protestant/State sectors.

27. Ballinger, *History in Exile*, pp.10–11.

28. Singh, 'Partition of India', in Talbot & Singh, *Region & Partition*, p.104; Chatterji, 'Making of a Borderline', *ibid.*, p.180.

29. Nelson, *Land and Power*, p.257.

30. Edmund James Flynn (1847–1927) was born on the Gaspé Pensinsula, the son of an Irish fisherman and an ethnic-French mother. He was premier of Quebec, 1896–97.

Chapter Eight

Andreevskoe,
an estate in nineteenth-century Iaroslavl'

David Saunders

I hunted out Andreevskoe because it was the birthplace of the German-Russian revolutionary Heinrich Matthäus Fischer, but after I had been there a non-biographical question occurred to me. The estate is recorded as long ago as 1728. Having survived the revolutions of 1917, it was making use of tractors even before Stalin's 'Great Turn'. When I was there in September 2002 it was still a sort of focus for rural economic activity. What explained its longevity?[1]

The answer is not likely to have lain in the soil, for Andreevskoe is more than two hundred miles north of Moscow in Iaroslavl´, where the land is not, on the whole, conducive to agriculture. Iaroslavl´ straddles three ecological boundaries: coniferous forest to the north, deciduous forest to the south; surplus moisture to the north, moderate moisture to the south; 'moderately mild' temperatures to the west, 'moderately cold' temperatures to the east.[2] From the point of view of tillage, the land in Iaroslavl´ is marginal. Most of the soil is clay. Oats and rye prevail over wheat and barley. Crop yields tend to be low. When the distinguished Russian geographer Veniamin Semenov-Tian-Shanskii used the phrase 'Settled Land: Wood-Based Cultures' to describe this north-eastern quarter of the circular diagram he invented to illustrate Russian settlement patterns and economic activity, he implied that grain hardly figured at all in Iaroslavl´. Modern scholars bring out the relative insignificance of grain in the province by calling the area of which it is a part Russia's 'non-black-soil zone' or 'Central Industrial Region'.[3]

In the late-tsarist period on which this paper will concentrate, Iaroslavl´ suffered additionally from a shortage of labour. Its population was 976,866 in 1858, 1,049,971 in 1885 and 1,071,355 in 1897.[4] Since it occupied about 13,700 square miles, an area which made it 50 per cent bigger than New Hampshire and about a seventh of the size of the entire United Kingdom (though only the forty-fifth-biggest of the fifty provinces of the European part of the Russian Empire),[5] it contained, in 1897, only about 78 people per square mile, a density which is not much more than half that of the least densely populated county in early twenty-first-century England (Northumberland).[6] Although it was by no means the emptiest province in European Russia, most of it lay in the fourth of the seven bands for population density into which the contemporary Scottish observer Sir Donald Mackenzie Wallace divided the country.[7] It might perhaps be argued, in view of the fact that almost all its inhabitants belonged to the peasant estate (some 84.5 per cent in 1858, 88 per cent in 1897)[8], that an unusually large fraction of the local population was available for the demanding task of extracting material advantage out of the soil; but the province's environment does not make it seem likely that agriculture would have flourished in Iaroslavl´ at the end of the nineteenth century even if the entire population had engaged in it. Nor was the population increasing at anything like the rate at which the population of the Russian Empire as a whole was increasing.[9]

It was remarkable, in fact, that the population of Iaroslavl´ was increasing at all, for the inhabitants of the province were famous for leaving it. Often said to be the key feature of Russia's entire historical development,[10] migration had long been central to the history of Iaroslavl´. Daniel Morrison has demonstrated that, in the period 1764-95, the province provided the third-largest proportion of peasant enrolment in the urban classes of the city of Moscow (after the provinces of Moscow and Vladimir).[11] Figures published by V. A. Fedorov imply the absence from home of something like 9 per cent of the entire population of Iaroslavl´ for part or the whole of 1856.[12] A late nineteenth-century Iaroslavl´ statistician calculated that some 14 per cent of the peasant population of the province were away from home in 1888.[13] Because most of these migrants were men, Iaroslavl´ had a higher woman-to-man ratio than any other province of the Russian Empire at the time of the empire-wide census of 1897.[14] Tracy Dennison's recent attempt to question the extent of male migration from an estate in the southern part of the province in the first half of the nineteenth century goes against the grain of a large body of literature.[15] By 1914, women were leaving Iaroslavl´ too.[16] The presence of people from Iaroslavl´ in Moscow and St Petersburg in the later years of the Russian Empire struck contemporaries so forcibly that it generated significant amounts of popular literature.[17]

People left Iaroslavl´ not only because its environment was unpropitious, but also because communication networks made it relatively easy for them to do so. The province was a sort of aquatic junction box. At the point where the river Volga comes closest to Andreevskoe, it is flowing roughly northward. By the time it passes Rybinsk (less than twenty-five miles away as the crow flies), it is flowing south-east. The reason for the change of direction is that, between these two points, the rivers Mologa and the Sheksna flow into the Volga from the north-west. Before the coming of rail, these unheralded rivers were crucial to Russia's internal communications. The Mologa was a key component of the so-called 'Tikhvinskii' navigation system, the Sheksna a key part of the 'Mariinskii'.[18] For the first three-quarters of the nineteenth century, most of St Petersburg's grain made its way up the Volga to Rybinsk on big vessels and then continued its northward journey on smaller vessels up the Sheksna and the Mologa.[19] If supplies could go north, so could people. The serf father of the historical painter Fedor Solntsev, a native of the village of Verkhne-Nikul'skoe just to the north-east of

Andreevskoe, worked as a ticket-seller for the imperial theatres in St Petersburg in the first decades of the nineteenth century whilst returning home each summer to see his wife and family.[20] Later in the century, railways made it even easier for Iaroslavl' people to get around. 1870 saw the opening of both the westward line from Rybinsk to Bologoe and the southern line from the city of Iaroslavl' to Sergiev Posad (and therefore Moscow).[21] Towards the end of the 1870s Heinrich Fischer's father, an estate worker at Andreevskoe, gave his son away to the boy's godfather, who was employed at the time as depot chief at the railway station of Medvedevo (some 125 miles to the west of Andreevskoe). In due course, the godfather moved east to Rybinsk. Thus, by virtue of the railways, the future revolutionary became peripatetic at an even earlier stage in his life than most other Iaroslavl' migrants.[22]

Marginal soil, low population density and relative ease of movement inclined many nineteenth-century inhabitants of Iaroslavl' to think in terms of towns, trade, and non-agricultural forms of employment rather than farming. The name of the province's principal city, Rybinsk, comes from the word for fish and evokes one of the region's oldest non-agricultural occupations. Steamships on the rivers brought only a gradual end to the well-developed local profession of barge-hauling.[23] The region's extensive tracts of water may even have encouraged some of its sons to go to sea, for one of the most famous of all Russian sailors, Admiral Fedor Ushakov (1743-1817), came from the Rybinsk area.[24] The letters that Ivan Aksakov wrote from various parts of the province of Iaroslavl' between 1849 and 1851 drew attention to its merchants.[25] A volume published in 1873 said that 'In respect of trade Rybinsk occupies one of the first places in Russia', that the town's permanent population had grown ten-fold in the course of the nineteenth century, and that its population went up by a further factor of four in the six months of the year when the Volga was free of ice.[26] R. J. Kerner pointed out more than half a century ago that although, at first sight, the heart of Russia appears to be landlocked, it is easy to think of Moscow as a port.[27] Thinking of Rybinsk as a port is even easier. Although the Soviet regime appalled the sensibilities of Rybinsk people when it flooded the land between the rivers Mologa and Sheksna in the 1940s to create a gigantic reservoir, in reality it was only intensifying the reliance on water which people in Iaroslavl' had been manifesting for centuries. Borok, not far north of Andreevskoe, is home today to the institute of the Russian Academy of Sciences which studies the biology of internal waters.

Exploiting the land as opposed to the water of Iaroslavl' became more difficult than it was already after serfdom was abolished in 1861. The St Petersburg

Iaroslavl' after 1870

5mm = 12.5 km

— Administrative boundary / – – – River / ++++ Railway / O Town

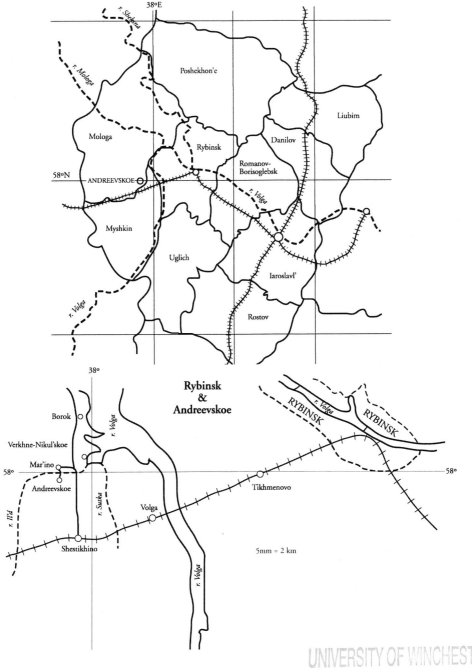

bureaucrats who were charged with working out the terms of abolition expected the non-agricultural nature of the Iaroslavl' economy to work in their favour. One of them recalled that, when the government's 'Editing Commission' summoned gentry deputies from all over Russia in 1859 and 1860. 'We began our consultations with the deputies from Iaroslavl', because it seemed to us that they more than others came close in their thinking to the principles of the legal project drawn up by the Editorial Commission'.[28] In the sense that the deputies of the Iaroslavl' gentry accepted the idea of peasant freedom of movement, St Petersburg was right to think that they were in tune with the idea of ending serfdom. Unfortunately (from St Petersburg's point of view), the Iaroslavl' deputies differed radically from the government in respect of the financial side of abolition. Although they were enthusiastic about ending peasant ascription to the soil, they were not enthusiastic about losing revenue. For reasons that must be obvious by now, most of the province's serfs fulfilled their obligations to their landlords by paying dues rather than working the demesne. Because they could get tickets of leave to work for the imperial theatres in St Petersburg or to fish or haul barges or go to sea, they had many ways of raising cash. As a result, their landlords made good money out of them. Determined to be fully compensated for it, they instructed their deputies to outline a buy-out operation that would embrace 'not only the value of the land which the peasants used under serfdom, but also the capitalization of all the dues which were placed on both the peasants' local and their migrant employment'.[29] To make their case, the deputies had to spell out just how extensive and variegated their peasants' employment opportunities were. In so doing, they produced one of the most vivid descriptions anyone has ever composed of the way in which their province's economy functioned. It concluded that the 'value of [gentry] estates derives from their business benefits ... the size of the peasants' land allocation does not affect their [the peasants'] well-being'.[30] Thus the Iaroslavl' deputies argued that the compensation the local gentry should receive for going along with the abolition of serfdom in their province ought to turn on much more than land; it ought to equal the full extent of the revenue their serfs brought in, above all the revenue they generated from their extensive non-agricultural earnings.

This argument fell on deaf ears. Convinced that the deputies' proposals would have the effect of immiserating the peasants, the government brought serfdom to an end in Iaroslavl' on terms which the local gentry did not consider to be in their best interests.[31] Many of them, as a result, had to sell up. Changes of ownership in Russia's 'Central Industrial Region' played a disproportionately large part in the process which left only about 10 per cent of land in the European part of the empire in noble hands at the outbreak of the First World War.[32]

I return, then, to the question with which I began: why, in view of all the drawbacks to which I have referred, has Andreevskoe had a long history as a centre of rural economic activity?

Ironically, my first answer turns on the estate's location. It was in the south-east corner of the Mologa district. At about 1,950 square miles,[33] this district was almost exactly the same size as the English county of Northumberland. It fell into two halves. The northern half, between the rivers Mologa and Sheksna, was 'nothing but a marsh'.[34] The southern half, on the other hand, offered better prospects for rural economic activity than almost anywhere else in the province of Iaroslavl'. At the end of the nineteenth century official figures recorded that only 35 per cent of the area of the Mologa district was arable,[35] but almost all of it was in the south. Most of the population was in the south as well. Although, at the time of the imperial census of 1897, the Mologa district as a whole contained only just over 60 inhabitants per square mile,[36] Donald Mackenzie Wallace put the southern part in the second rather than the fourth of his bands for population density, a band that represented between 91 and 114 inhabitants per square mile.[37] It is likely, furthermore, that an unusually high proportion of the people who lived in the Andreevskoe area actually made their living from the land (rather than from off-farm activities). At the time of the 1897 census, 84.3 per cent of the inhabitants of the Mologa district, as opposed to only 72.4 per cent of the inhabitants of Iaroslavl' as a whole, found employment in agriculture.[38] Only 12.57 per cent of the population of Mologa migrated for work in 1896-7, whereas 21 per cent of the population of the adjacent district of Rybinsk did so.[39] When Mologa peasants leased additional land at the end of the nineteenth century, they did so not merely to feed themselves but to produce commodities for sale.[40] On the basis of these indicators it seems legitimate to argue that, for a rural district more than two hundred miles north of Moscow, the southern part of Mologa was economically attractive. The local peasant who, in 1881, volunteered 500 rubles to re-gild the iconostasis in the church at Mar'ino (next door to Andreevskoe) may not have been unique in having cash in his pocket.[41]

It is conceivable, furthermore, that the estate of Andreevskoe possessed highly specific geographical advantages. Where exactly its boundaries lay is unclear, but its area in the late 1850s fits neatly into the rectangle formed by the river Il'd in the west and north, the road between Shestikhino and Borok in the east, and the present line of the railway in the south. The fact that the last of its gentry proprietors owned land in Myshkin as well as in Mologa and that her husband owned a brickworks at Shestikhino certainly suggests a southern rather than a northern orientation.[42] Even if these speculations are inaccurate, the estate certainly benefited from proximity to the Volga.

By the standards of some of the estates further north in Mologa, Andreevskoe was relatively small. Just before the abolition of serfdom, it occupied 8,578 acres.[43] Although this was well above the average for the district (which was two thousand acres at the time of the governmental land survey of 1877–78[44]), and although it was a large area by the standards of, for example, the nineteenth-century British aristocracy, it was a manageable holding by the standards of the upper echelons of the Russian aristocracy. 'Large', in Mologa, meant something like the Musin-Pushkins' estate of Borisogleb on the river Mologa, whose area was about 178,000 acres in 1860.[45] It was estates like those of the Musin-Pushkins that made the average size of estates in the Mologa district massively higher than that of estates in any other district of Iaroslavl' province.[46] Really large estates, however, were probably too large to get much attention. Most local gentry seem to have responded to their predominantly intractable environment by adopting a sort of broad-brush approach to the problem of exploiting it. Economic activity at the Musin-Pushkins' Borisogleb, for example, centred on logging.[47] Smaller estates, on the other hand, could inspire things like the near-manic obsession with drainage which the grandfather of the Russian revolutionary Nikolai Morozov displayed at Borok.[48]

If general and particular aspects of its location and size go part of the way towards explaining Andreevskoe's durability, its landlords were important too. Collectively, three of its owners make up my second answer to the question why the estate entered the twentieth century in a sufficiently attractive condition to be thought worthy of preservation and development by the post-1917 authorities. The likelihood that a particular estate would receive the dedicated attention of a series of committed owners was not very great in the Mologa district, for rural gentry were not very numerous there. Outside the town of Mologa, the district contained a mere 118 members of the gentry estate in 1864, 210 in 1895 and 237 in 1897.[49] 'Because of the paucity of nobles, the duties of Marshal [of the nobility] and Chairman [of the district zemstvo] were usually combined in the Mologa district'.[50] In the 1860s, only 26 of the 718 populated points in the district were villages with manor houses (sel'tsa).[51] The reason why Andreevskoe appears not to have received much attention in the eighteenth century was presumably that, at that time, it belonged to the Musin-Pushkins, who as owners of Borisogleb either did not need to develop all their many other holdings in the Mologa district or simply preferred not to develop the finer skills that they would have had to bring into play in order to make the most of what, in their terms, was a small estate in a non-central part of the district.[52]

When, however, Count Aleksei Ivanovich Musin-Pushkin gave Andreevskoe to his daughter Natal'ia on the occasion of her marriage in 1811 to the soldier (later senator) Prince Dmitrii Mikhailovich Volkonskii, things changed. No doubt for a mix of reasons – because he saw the possibilities of the property, because his own family had many associations with the Mologa district, because his wife gave birth to their son Mikhail within a year of their marriage, because his property in Moscow came under threat during the French occupation in 1812, because he welomed the chance to be near his in-laws – Prince Dmitrii put Andreevskoe on its feet. His diary for October and November of 1812 shows him busily planning the house and park, ordering wood, commissioning the carpenter who was to do his building for him and taking advice from the nobleman on the next estate about the sort of instructions he should be giving his serfs.[53] By 1815 he was having one of the serfs paint his portrait.[54] In putting down roots, he set in train a process of development which his heirs were to continue.

His son, Prince Mikhail Dmitrievich Volkonskii, was an improver. No sooner had he inherited Andreevskoe in 1835 than he founded the school at nearby Mar'ino.[55] In 1837 he published an article about the merits of the scythe in which, after calling his Iaroslavl' peasants 'perpetual enemies of innovation' and saying that they had resisted the new tool at first on the grounds that it was just as tiring and slow as the sickle, he described how he had sent two of them to Mitava (Mitau, Jelgava) in the Baltic provinces to learn how to use the new implement under the supervision of a Lutheran pastor of his acquaintance, whereupon they became enthusiastic advocates of it. 'By comparison with the past,' Volkonskii wrote, 'I now have much more straw, which is so necessary for litter'.[56] S. A. Kozlov, the principal student of agricultural innovation in the non-black-soil region of Russia in the later years of serfdom, places M. D. Volkonskii in the circle of Efim Karnovich, founder of the Iaroslavl' Agricultural Society and guide to August von Haxthausen when the German was making his celebrated investigation of the Russian countryside in 1843–44. Kozlov implies that Volkonskii employed a German steward at Andreevskoe and states explicitly that he and Karnovich participated in the Great Exhibition in London in 1851. Volkonskii's distillery at Andreevskoe, meanwhile, bespeaks a certain commercial bent, and the way in which he described the duties of Andreeevskoe peasants in the government survey of gentry estates of 1860 seems to indicate that he had utterly rationalized the way in which he expected them to work his land. (He had divided the entire area of the estate into 228½ plots, assigned 225 to 'active workers' and 3½ to the maintenance of widows and orphans, and let the peasants get on with things). Although an aristocrat of the next generation who can have known him only towards the end of his life depicted him as almost a 'holy fool', the image does not square with what is known about his life as a whole.[57]

At the point serfdom was abolished, Volkonskii seems to have been doing well out of Andreevskoe. He required a male serf who was away from the estate all the year round to pay him the annual sum of thirty rubles, three times as much as the maximum that St Petersburg thought reasonable when it was working out what peasants in Iaroslavl' ought to pay in return for their freedom.[58] After abolition, on the other hand, generating large sums from the land that was left to him did not look as if it was going to be easy. The legal standing of the peasantry had improved and his share of the partitioned estate seems to have been only about 3,680 acres.[59] Although his share of the land was no doubt of the best quality, and although, in area, it was certainly larger than the area that Prince Mikhail had treated as demesne under serfdom,[60] against these considerations had to be set the fact that the estate was now in about twenty small packets, none of them larger than the 570 acres which the Volkonskii family retained at the village of Andreevskoe itself.[61] In view of the changes, Prince Mikhail may not have felt too much regret when he assigned the property to his daughter, Elizaveta Mikhailovna, on the occasion of her marriage to Prince Anatolii Aleksandrovich Kurakin at the end of April 1864.

Andreevskoe turned out, however, still to be in good hands, for the new owner and her husband devoted themselves to it. The incoming Prince Kurakin had no prior local connections, but like the first Volkonskii in 1811 he had grounds for making Andreevskoe his principal rural base. As the younger son of a younger son, he was not in line for the principal Kurakin estate of Nadezhdino in Saratov. Although, in accordance with the Russian principle of partible inheritance, he was to inherit large estates in Orel and Penza,[62] at the time of his marriage his father was still alive and he did not own land at all. By the time his father died, in 1870, he was Marshal of Nobility for the Mologa district, head of the local zemstvo, and a Iaroslavl' dignitary. Scattered data from later years betray a continuing commitment on his part to his home in Iaroslavl'. He flew a flag at Andreevskoe when he was in residence there; he commissioned a major St Petersburg architect,

V. A. Shreter, to design the manager's house for his brickworks at Shestikhino; and he may have taken a lease on the adjacent Azancheev estate of Gorshkovo. It was at Andreevskoe that he entertained the Bishop of Iaroslavl' in 1881, it was at the timber factory there that Heinrich Fischer found work when he made an enforced stay of nearly a year at Andreevskoe in 1895, and it may have been by virtue of a presence there that Kurakin entered himself separately from his wife in A. S. Suvorin's commercial directory *All Russia* in 1899.[63]

Kurakin's wife, meanwhile, worked on adapting Andreevskoe to a world without serfs. She introduced a nine-field crop rotation, applied fertilizer, introduced machines, utilized the latest agronomic techniques, procured a yield of 10:1 on her rye, grew large quantities of clover, participated in all-Russian agricultural shows, and kept a top-quality dairy herd.[64] To judge by the article in the local church newspaper which mentioned a peasant offering 500 rubles to re-gild the iconostasis at Mar'ino, she appears also to have retained close relations with the peasants who had once been her father's serfs, for the article also described a complex but fruitful local crop rotation which had been in place since 1872 'by general agreement of the parishioners' and which, in its emphasis on clover, seems to have had a good deal in common with Princess Kurakina's system.[65] Heinrich Fischer recalled that his father worked at Andreevskoe as 'stockman, miller, forester, enjoying great authority among the peasants as a vet', and that his mother specialized in poultry there; 'Peasants used to come to them for advice from 20 or 30 versts away.'[66] When he returned to the estate in 1895, his mother and a number of his siblings were still there, some of them working, some of them at school. Although, according to memoirs which he published under Stalin, Fischer was not sympathetic either to the 'capitalist' economy of the estate or to the outlook on life of most of the local peasantry, it is nonetheless clear from his description that at the end of the nineteenth century Andreevskoe was a lively place which required labour in a wide range of rural undertakings and procured it, one way or another, from the community which had once provided its serfs.[67] In short, the estate was taking the path of gentle modernization which Daniel Field has discerned in Iaroslavl' as a whole in the decades after the abolition of serfdom.[68]

Prince Anatolii Aleksandrovich and his wife owned Andreevskoe until the Russian revolutions of 1917.[69] Their son Ivan Anatol'evich (1874-1950), a right-winger in national politics, served as Marshal of Nobility for the province of Iaroslavl' between 1906 and 1915. Two of his eight children were born at Andreevskoe, one of whom, long after the revolutions of 1917, became the second wife of a Grand

Duke. Widowed in the revolutionary year, Ivan Anatol'evich was ordained in the Orthodox Church in western Europe at the end of the 1920s and eventually became a bishop. He has not been forgotten by people in the vicinity of Andreevskoe, for the school hall at Mar'ino has pictures of him, his mother, and his mother's father.[70]

Andreevskoe survived into the Soviet period, then, partly because, by comparison with estates in most other parts of the province of Iaroslavl', it was relatively highly favoured from the point of view of geography, and partly because, in the nineteenth and early twentieth centuries, it had committed owners. One of the many striking developments in post-Soviet historiography has been the awakening of significant interest in the gentry side of the way in which estates operated in the tsarist period. In addition to the work we have had for some time on the peasants of individual estates,[71] we are now also beginning to get studies of the manor.[72] Local study, however, is not a very well established principle in the field of Russian history. It was probably more firmly entrenched in late tsarist times than it is today.[73] Charles King, a scholar who specializes on one of the most variegated parts of the world, writes that 'No regional label can stand too much interrogation'.[74] The sweeping 'regional labels' that are usually employed in the study of Russian history are certainly open to this criticism, but before we abandon them we could try refining them.

Notes

1. For my work on Fischer see David Saunders, 'A Russian Bebel Revisited: The Individuality of Heinrich Matthäus Fischer' (1871-1935), *Slavonic and East European Review* lxxxii (2004), pp. 625–54; the details about Andreevskoe in this paragraph come from N. A. Sakharov, *Byloe* (Rybinsk, 2000), pp. 88, 97, 99, 154.
2. See the map in R.E.F. Smith, *Peasant Farming in Muscovy* (Cambridge, 1977), p. 220.
3. For soil types and crops in Iaroslavl' see P. F. Besedkin, *Obzor iaroslavskoi gubernii* (Iaroslavl', 1892–6), i, pp. 12–14, and S. Sh., 'Iaroslavskaia guberniia', *Entsiklopedicheskii slovar'*, ed. I. E. Andreevskii *et al.*, (St Petersburg, 1890-1904), xlia, pp. 821–2, 823–4. Semenov-Tian-Shanskii's diagram is in his *Gorod i derevnia v evropeiskoi Rossii* (St Petersburg, 1910), p. 207. Maps which employ the terms 'Non-Black Soil Center' and 'Central Industrial Region' include Seymour Becker, *Nobility and Privilege in Late Imperial Russia* (DeKalb, ILL, 1985), endpapers, and M.P. Perrie, *The Agrarian Policy of the Russian Socialist-Revolutionary Party from its Origins through the Revolution of 1905–1907* (Cambridge, 1976), p. xii.
4. N. A. Troinitskii, ed., *Pervaia vseobshchaia perepis' naseleniia Rossiiskoi imperii*, 1897g., (St Petersburg, 1899–1905), l, p. iii.
5. S. Sh., 'Iaroslavskaia guberniia', pp. 820, 824; Alison Ewington *et al.*, eds, *The Times Atlas of the World: Family Edition* (London, 1988), pp. 38, 40.
6. Northumberland contains some 300,000 people in c. 1,950 square miles.
7. Sir Donald Mackenzie Wallace, Russia, 2nd edn (London, 1905), pull-out map after i, p. 456.

8. N. M. Zhuravlev, *Putevoditel' po Iaroslavskoi gubernii* (Iaroslavl', 1859), pp. 123–4; Troinitskii, *Pervaia vseobshchaia perepis'*, I, pp. 50–1.

9. The population of the fifty provinces of the European part of the Russian Empire rose by 52.1 per cent between 1863 and 1897 (A. G. Rashin, *Naselenie Rossii za 100 let* [Moscow, 1956], p. 95).

10. Recent literature on the subject includes David Moon, 'Peasant Migration and the Settlement of Russia's Frontiers, 1550–1897', *Historical Journal* xl (1997), pp. 859–93, and M. K. Liubavskii, *Obzor istorii russkoi kolonizatsii s drevneishikh vremen i do XX veka* (Moscow, 1996).

11. Daniel Morison, '*Trading Peasants' and Urbanization in Eighteenth-Century Russia: The Central Industrial Region* (New York and London, 1987), pp. 169, 186.

12. V. A. Fedorov, *Pomeshchich'i krest'iane tsentral'no-promyshlennogo raiona Rossii kontsa XVIII - pervoi poloviny XIX v.* (Moscow, 1974), pp. 298–9.

13. Besedkin, *Obzor*, i, p. 22.

14. P. Bechasnov, 'Kratkii obzor tsifrovykh dannykh,' *Obshchii svod po imperii rezul'tatov razrabotki dannykh pervoi vseobshchei perepisi naseleniia*, ed. N. A. Troinitskii (St Petersburg, 1905), i, p. iv.

15. Tracy K. Dennison, 'Serfdom and Household Structure in Central Russia: Voshchazhnikovo, 1816–1858', *Continuity and Change* xviii (2003), pp. 398–401.

16. Barbara Alpern Engel, *Between the Fields and the City: Women, Work, and Family in Russia, 1861–1914* (Cambridge, 1994), esp. ch. 3.

17. For modern editions of some of this literature see Iaroslav Smirnov, *Zhizn' i prikliucheniia iaroslavtsev v obeikh stolitsakh Rossiiskoi imperii* (Iaroslavl', 2002).

18. On these water systems at the time of their pre-eminence see E. G. Istomina, *Vodnyi transport Rossii v doreformennyi period* (Moscow, 1991), pp. 179-93.

19. A. A. Bakhtiarov, *Briukho Peterburga* (St. Petersburg, 1994 [first published in 1887]), pp. 77–103.

20. F. G. Solntsev, 'Moia zhizn' i khudozhestvenno-arkheologicheskie trudy', *Russkaia starina* xv (1876), pp. 110, 112.

21. V. P. Semenov, ed., Rossiia: *Polnoe geograficheskoe opisanie nashego otechestva* (St Petersburg, 1899–1914), i, p. 201; Inna Simonova, *Fedor Chizhov* (Moscow, 2002), p. 221.

22. Saunders, 'A Russian Bebel Revisited', pp. 631-2.

23. Bakhtiarov, *Briukho*, pp. 82–3.

24. L. M. Marasinova, 'K voprosu o vozrozhdenii russkoi usad'by', *Musiny-Pushkiny v istorii Rossii*, ed. S. O. Shmidt *et al.* (Rybinsk, 1998), p. 350.

25. Ivan Sergeevich Aksakov, *Pis'ma iz provintsii* (Moscow, 1991), pp. 314–17.

26. P. Semenov, *Geografichesko-statisticheskii slovar' rossiiskoi imperii* (St Petersburg, 1863–85), iv, pp. 353, 355.

27. R. J. Kerner, *The Urge to the Sea* (Berkeley and Los Angeles, 1946), pp. 90–1.

28. P. Semenov, *Memuary* (Petrograd and Moscow, 1915–46), iii, p. 308.

29. *Ibid.*, p. 310.

30. A. A. Kornilov, 'Gubernskie komitety po krest'ianskomu delu v 1858–1859 gg.', in his *Ocherki po istorii obshchestvennogo dvizheniia i krest'ianskogo dela v Rossii* (St Petersburg, 1905), p. 244n.

31. P. Semenov, *Memuary*, iii, pp. 311–14.

32. Geroid Tanquary Robinson, *Rural Russia under the Old Regime* (Berkeley and Los Angeles, 1932), p. 270 (10 per cent); A. P. Korelin, *Dvorianstvo v poreformennoi Rossii 1861–194gg.* (Moscow, 1979), p. 56 (disproportionate part).

33. S. Sh., 'Mologa', *Entsiklopedicheskii slovar'*, xixa, p. 640.

34. *Idem*, 'Iaroslavskaia guberniia', p. 823.

35. *Ibid.*

36. Its population was 117,696 (Troinitskii, *Pervaia vseobshchaia perepis'*, l, p. 1).

37. Wallace, *Russia*, pull-out map after i, p. 456.

38. Troinitskii, *Pervaia vseobshchaia perepis'*, l, pp. 140, 142–3.

39. S. Sh., 'Iaroslavskaia guberniia', p. 826.

40. A. M. Anfimov, *Zemel'naia arenda v Rossii v nachale XX veka* (Moscow, 1961), p. 113.

41. *Iaroslavskie eparkhial'nye vedomosti, chast' neoffitsial'naia*, 19 December 1881, p. 418.

42. For the fact that Elizaveta Mikhailovna Kurakina (née Volkonskaia) owned land in Myshkin as well as Mologa see the service record of her husband, Anatolii Aleksandrovich Kurakin, in Rossiiskii goudarstvennyi istoricheskii arkhiv (St Petersburg), f. 1162, op. 6, ed. khr. 272 (I am indebted to Professor Dominic Lieven for this reference). For the brickworks see Sakharov, *Byloe*, p. 42.

43. Anon, *Prilozheniia k trudam redaktsionnykh kommissii, dlia sostavleniia polozhenii o krest'ianakh, vykhodiashchikh iz krepostnoi zavisimosti: svedeniia o pomeshchich'ikh imeniiakh* (St Petersburg,1860), iv, pagination entitled 'Iaroslavskaia guberniia', pp. 18–19.

44. P. A. Zaionchkovskii, *Provedenie v zhizn' krest'ianskoi reformy 1861g.* (Moscow, 1958), p. 443.

45. *Ibid.*, pp. 22–3.

46. *Ibid.*, p. 443.

47. V. P. Semenov, *Rossiia*, i, p. 352.

48. N. A. Morozov, *Povesti moei zhizni* (Moscow, 1962), i, p. 26.

49. P. Semenov, *Geografichesko-statisticheskii slovar'*, iii, p. 299; S. Sh., 'Mologa', 641; Troinitskii, *Pervaia vseobshchaia perepis'*, l, p. 50.

50. Boris Veselovskii, *Istoriia zemstva za sorok let* (St Petersburg, 1909–11), iv, p. 463.

51. P. Semenov, *Geografichesko-statisticheskii slovar'*, iii, p. 299.

52. For a list of the Musin-Pushkins' extensive holdings in Mologa see N. M. Alekseev, 'Musiny-Pushkiny na Mologskoi zemle', *Musiny-Pushkiny*, p. 173.

53. A. G. Tartakovskii, ed., *1812 god ... Voennye dnevniki* (Moscow, 1990), pp. 150–1.

54. *Idem*, 'Portret i ego prototip', *Panorama iskusstv* xiii (1990), pp. 268–9.

55. A. Abrosimova and N. Alekseev, 'Bogatoe nasledie: iz istorii zemli nekouzskoi', *Mologa: Literaturno-istoricheskii sbornik* iv (1999), p. 62.

56. Kniaz' Mikhail Volkonskii, 'O koshenii khleba', *Zemledel'cheskii zhurnal* iv (1837), pp. 65–70.

57. S. A. Kozlov, *Agrarnye traditsii i novatsii v doreformennoi Rossii (tsentral'no-nechernozemnye gubernii)* (Moscow, 2002), pp. 122, 158, 355, 432 n. 344, 448; August von Haxthausen, *Studies on the Interior of Russia*, ed. S. Frederick Starr (Chicago and London, 1972), pp. 37, 62–3; P. Semenov, *Geografichesko-statisticheskii slovar'*, iii, p. 299 (distillery); Anon, *Prilozheniia*, pp. 18–19 (serfs' labor); S. D. Sheremetev, *Memuary* (Moscow, 2001), p. 182 ('holy fool').

58. Anon, *Prilozheniia*, p. 19; P. Semenov, *Memuary*, iii, p. 310.

59. Assuming that Elizaveta Mikhailovna Kurakina's 1,363 *desiatiny* of land in Mologa (RGIA, 1162/6/272) represented the post-abolition area of Andreevskoe.

60. According to Anon, *Prilozheniia*, pp. 318–19, only a little over 2,500 acres of land at Andreevskoe were 'not in peasant use' in 1860.

61. Rybinskii filial, Gosudarstvennyi arkhiv iaroslavskoi oblasti (Rybinsk), f. 207, op. 1, d. 65, folios 5–6 (a list of the lands owned by Elizaveta Mikhailovna Kurakina in the Mologa district in 1883).

62. RGIA, 1162/6/272.

63. Jacques Ferrand, *Les familles princières de l'ancien empire de Russie (en émigration en 1978)* (Montreuil, n. d.), pp. 140–1 (Kurakin's descent); Veselovskii, *Istorii zemstva*, iii, p. 221 (his office-holding); A. Azancheev, 'Davno ... Davno ...', *Mologa: Literaturnyi-istoricheskii sbornik* iii (1997), p. 32 (flag); Sakharov, *Byloe*, p. 85 (manager's house); *Iaroslavskie eparkhial'nye vedomosti, chast' neoffitsial'naia*, 19 December 1881, p. 418 (bishop); G. Fisher, *Podpol'e, ssylka, emigratsiia* (Moscow, 1935), pp. 81–2 (timber factory); *Vsia Rossiia* (St Petersburg, 1899), ii, 'Sel'sko-khoziaistvennyi otdel', col. 411 (separate entry).

64. Sakharov, *Byloe*, p. 42.

65. *Iaroslavskie eparkhial'nye vedomosti, chast' neoffitsial'naia*, 19 December 1881, p. 418.

66. Fisher, *Podpol'e*, p. 7.

67. *Ibid.*, pp. 79, 81–4.

68. Daniel Field, 'Levels and Tendencies of Modernization: A Russian Province, 1870–1905', *Data Modelling: Modelling History*, ed. Leonid Borodkin and Peter Doorn (Moscow, 2000), pp. 255–71.

69. For photographs of their Golden Wedding festivities in April 1914, see *Stolitsa i usad'ba* x (1914), p. 25.

70. The biographical data in this paragraph is from Ferrand, *Les familles princières*, pp. 141–5; I saw the pictures with my own eyes.

71. Perhaps most notably Steven L. Hoch, *Serfdom and Social Control: Petrovskoe, a Village in Tambov* (Chicago and London, 1986).

72. Especially Serge Schmemann's outstanding *Echoes of a Native Land: Two Centuries of a Russian Village* (London, 1997), but for a review article on some of the other literature in this vein see John Randolph, 'The Old Mansion: Revisiting the History of the Russian Country Estate', *Kritika* i (2000), pp. 729–49.

73. For see Viktor Berdinskikh, *Uezdnye istoriki: russkaia provintsial'naia istoriografiia* (Moscow, 2003).

74. Charles King, *The Black Sea: A History* (Oxford, 2004), p. 7.

Part Three

Region and Politics

Chapter Nine

A regional history of modern Europe. Territorial management and the state

Michael Keating

The uses of history

This chapter is written from the perspective of a political scientist with a historical bent and interested in two aspects of the use of history in political analysis, one more analytical and the other more normative. The first concerns the evolution of the state, its critical historical junctures and state traditions. These create what some political scientists call "path dependency", in which policies create institutions as well as the other way round, institutions and policies create constituencies of interest, and institutions outlive the purposes for which they were created, moulding politics over the longer term (Mahoney and Rueschmeyer, 2003). Historical analysis is used to explore these patterns, to explain the present, and to mark the parameters of future change. The second aspect concerns historiography and the way in which the agenda of historical studies changes with current events, and the manner in which historical arguments are used to sustain current political claims. A recurrent theme in debates about changing the political order is the tendency for reformers to look both ways, arguing either that the constitution needs to be changed to meet modern needs, or that it needs rather to be reinterpreted in a historically more authentic manner, reflecting original intentions or time-honoured convention (Tierney, 2004). There may be some conflict between these two uses of history. One is analytical and positivist, assuming that we can, at least generally, know the past. The second takes us into the normative dimension and deeply into matters of interpretation. At the extreme, a post-modern historiography may insist that the past is unknowable and that all is interpretation. Yet, not taken to the extremes of positivism and constructivism, but relying rather on empirically-informed interpretation, both provide ways of understanding regional politics both historically and in the present.

State and regional history

A common feature of the disciplines of history and political science in the modern era has been their focus on the nation-state both as unit of analysis and as the container for social, economic and political processes, movements and actors. A teleological vision of the state as the end-point of development has often confounded the consolidation of the state with the process and condition of modernity itself. History was, for much of the nineteenth and twentieth century, national history, or the story of the interaction of nation-states and national historians have tended to emphasise the exceptionality of their own case. Indeed one might argue that one of the few common elements in national histories is that each of them claimed to be exceptional. Political science and sociology, too, operated largely within national boundaries and was imbued with similar teleological assumptions. Theories of national integration as developed from the mid-twentieth century emphasized the process of functional and normative integration, usually by diffusion from a central point (Shils, 1975; Deutsch, 1966). The national capital gradually extends its influence to the periphery, breaking down previous forms of authority, establishing the uniform bureaucratic state, and incorporating it into the national market. Cultural and normative assimilation follow, as pre-modern norms and structures are broken down, the state language predominates and impersonal bureaucratic and market norms replace particularistic relationships. Durkheim (1964, p.187) had argued in a similar vein, insisting that "we can almost say that a people is as much advanced as territorial divisions are more superficial". In the limiting case, where territories cannot be accommodated, they will secede, so producing "sovereign governments which have no critical regional or community cleavages" (Deutsch, 1966, p.80). So even the existence of territorial cleavages confirms the inevitability of the nation-states. The experience of the First World War and its aftermath is taken to confirm the non-viability of multinational empires with the Habsburg monarchy doomed to extinction because of the nationality question. Generations of international relations specialists, for their part, have been brought up to believe that the Peace of Westphalia of 1648 established the model of sovereign states and state system with which we have been familiar in the twentieth century.

An exception was the work of Stein Rokkan (1980) (Flora, 1999), who studied European space as a whole, pointing to critical historical junctures that shaped the state system as a whole. These left behind, not fully-integrated nation-states, but a complex pattern of cleavages, including the religious one, the industrial one and the territorial, within and across states. Economic, cultural, institutional and political integration did not necessarily coincide in time and place. National integration was rarely complete and territory remained an important factor in many modern political and social systems. Tilly (1975, 1990), in a series of works, showed how states were actually constructed, at first concentrating on military force but in later work including economic factors. Spruyt (1994) also presents the state as historically contingent and capable taking different forms. The result is a differentiated view of different state types in different times and places. Osiander (1994; 2001) has challenged the Westphalian myth, showing how different historical outcomes were possible, and also how these were suppressed by much nineteenth-century historiography, with its determination to celebrate the nation-state. Even these works, however, tend to see territorial politics and regional differentiation as a legacy of incomplete state and nation building rather than a living principle animating politics through to the present.

Regions rediscovered

In recent years a reconsideration of history has been provoked by the changed circumstances of the present. European integration and the complex of processes known as globalisation have forced a rethinking of the nature of the nation-state, its future and thereby its past. The state has undergone a functional transformation, which may not have reduced its importance overall but which has challenged its supposed omnicompetence. Intergovernmentalist analysts of European integration continue to insist that the nation-state is the basis of the European order, merely delegating authority to EU institutions, but their claims look ever more formal. Legal scholars have increasingly accepted that the European Union is a legal order in its own right, sharing sovereignty with member states (MacCormick, 1999). Domestically, states have lost their ability to integrate societies, to manage the economy and to implement their policy preferences. They are forced to share power with other actors in complex networks. State functions have been redistributed at various spatial levels so that, while it retains vital powers, there is no longer a core set of essential competences that define the state – not even control of borders, the currency or defence. Regional and minority nationalist movements have challenged the state's assumption to be the only fount of legitimacy. As it loses its mystique, the state comes under ever greater scrutiny from scholars willing to deconstruct it and relativise it. Increasingly it is seen as a bundle of powers and normative claims, a historically contingent form, belonging to a particular time and place and differing from one instance to another. Scholars show an increased interest in other spatial levels of action, interest articulation and public policy-making and other democratic spaces. For some, this is quite new, a radical shift in authority and power; for others it is merely another stage in the evolution of the territorial state.

Territorial management and the state

An alternative to unidirectional accounts of national integration is to pose the question of territorial integration as a central and continuing task of states. What needs to be explained is not just the formation of the state, or its occasional disintegration, but its continued existence. National unity is not a one-off process after which "normal" politics can take over, but a central part of politics itself. The resurgence of centrifugal tendencies in some western democracies from the 1970s was widely seen by political scientists as a form of pathology in the body politic, a historical reversal of national integration, or as evidence that national integration, in these exceptional cases, must never really have occurred. Nowadays, it is more accepted that such territorial tensions are part of normal politics, more apparent at some times and in some places than others. This in turn leads to a reappraisal of the history of states and a reassessment of the place of territory within it.

The emergence of a recognizably modern politics dates from the late nineteenth century, with industrialisation, the extension of the franchise, mass mobilisation and the penetration of the bureaucratic modern state into society, both sectorally and territorially. This created the cleavages that were to mark the politics of modernity. Modernists generally see these functional cleavages as new and contrast them with the territorial and other divisions of traditional society, acknowledging that in a transition period there would be territorial resistance to modernity. An alternative perspective, however, denies the fundamental conflict between function and territory, arguing that the two are always interconnected and that functional cleavages are themselves shaped and sustained by territory. If we acknowledge that the nation-state is itself a partial territorial framework and not the merely the bearer of universal values, then we can trace the impact of the creation of national markets and cultures on territorial balance.

The late nineteenth century, which saw both the consolidation of the nation-state and the first instance of "globalisation" provides some illustrations. Trading centres that were central in the pre-modern era of maritime trade became peripheral within the state; Brittany is an example. Former peripheries like Glasgow, Liverpool or Marseille became central places in trading empires while the imperial trading cities of Spain declined after 1898. Europe's central trading belt (corresponding largely to Rokkan's shatter-belt between state projects) declined as national markets were created around it, to re-emerge later in the European single market. New industrial and trading centres in Lombardy, Vizcaya, Manchester, Glasgow, the Ruhr valley, eastern France or southern Belgium created disjunctures between economic power and the political dominance of the capital. Industrial class interests were shaped by territory. British industrialists in Glasgow and Manchester were committed to free trade until after the First World War while elsewhere they looked to the national state for protection. The bourgeoisie of Catalonia were cross-pressured, seeking to escape the weight of the agrarian-military-clerical interests in Madrid, but needing the Spanish state to secure their protected markets and keep their unruly proletariat in order. In Italy, a territorial/sectoral alliance developed of northern industrialists with southern landowners; in due course the northern proletariat were given a share of the goods, excluding still the southern peasants (Gramsci, 1978). In Germany, a similar protectionist alliance united the grain producers east of the Elbe and the industrialists of the Ruhr (Conze, 1962). French northern industrialists used protectionism to their advantage, to the detriment of the south (Brunstein, 1988). Aristocratic interests prevented the industrialization of Hungary, in contrast to Bohemia.

Working-class organization was often localist, tied into specific labour markets or cultural norms and resistance and had to adapt itself to local linguistic, ethnic or religious forms. Modernists have tended to argue that class politics characterized the modern industrial state, breaking down particularistic loyalties; but then to adopt a rather different frame of analysis to explain why class solidarity stopped at state borders. The reality is more complex. In many cases, class consciousness combined with loyalty to the nation-state triumphed. In others localist or ethnic identities won out over class or profoundly shaped the form of class politics. In others again, the two principles contended for domination, as in the Basque Country, Flanders or Scotland.

Religious cleavages, the basis of much voting behaviour in the nineteenth century and much of the twentieth, were also territorialized. Germany was divided between Catholics and Protestants. In France, Belgium and to some extent Spain and Italy, Catholicism sought protection in regionalism and locally integrated societies, while lay and anti-clerical forces tended to be republican and centralizing. Fundamentalist Protestantism flourished around the periphery of Scandinavia and Great Britain.

Industrialization and the need for mass literacy have been credited by modernist scholars with the rise of nationalism in Europe, linked inexorably to the creation of the modern state (Gellner, 1983). Critics have persistently objected that this does little credit to the complexity of the phenomenon and, indeed, modernization and the expansion of the state in the nineteenth century elicited a range of responses. There was a widespread phase of territorial mobilization, in the form of minority nationalisms and regionalisms, sometimes interpreted by modernists as the last gasp of the old order as it gave way to the universal norms of the modern state apparatus and market economy. Closer analysis, however, reveals that territorial politics persisted within the nation-state, which adopted a variety of techniques to manage its component territories.

Old forms of management, linking traditional elites to the state centre faded, but were replaced by new ones. Tariff policies were an instrument of territorial brokerage, used to favour certain territorial/sectoral interests and classes across much of Europe. Territorial intermediaries emerged to manage the relations between the state and its localities and regions. Where traditional territorial elites had their roots in and drew legitimacy from local society, the new notables flourished at the interface between local society and the state. Such were the *notables* of Third Republic France, the *notabili* of liberal Italy and the *caciques* of Restoration Spain. Clientelism, often seen as a temporary phenomenon arising where traditional society meets the modern state, survived as a regular mode of territorial management, dispensing both individualistic and collective patronage. Even (or perhaps especially) Napoleonic states had to adapt themselves to territorial diversity by allowing field administrators scope to bend policy to local needs and demands. Scotland was governed in the eighteenth century through an elaborate system in which the "manager" was given freedom in distributing patronage in return for delivering votes to the government in power. After this had collapsed, there was a period of turbulence until the Scottish Office and its minister, established in 1885, gradually took over the role of territorial manager, representing Scotland in London and London in Scotland.

National political parties, especially of the left, were another factor in national integration and homogenisation. Yet often these had to adapt to local conditions, taking over existing networks and norms, so that the appearance of homogeneity in voting was misleading. This was particularly true of conservative and liberal parties, but was also the case in the social democratic camp. By the mid-twentieth century, the received view was that national integration had triumphed, with regional specificities a diminishing legacy.

The politics of regional policy

Unitarist accounts of national development peaked in the early 1970s, on the eve of an explosion of nationalist and regionalist politics that took most observers by surprise. Some resorted again to modernisation theory to explain the resurgence of particularism, arguing that it was the reaction of traditional societies faced with the impact of modernity. This view might have had more credibility were it not invoked in serial manner, with modernity being shifted from the seventeenth century, to the nineteenth and then the mid-twentieth as a permanently available explanation. In fact, a great deal of territorial politics had continued within the framework of apparently unitary states, as works from the 1970s increasingly made clear (Grémion, 1976; Keating, 1975). The new territorial politics from the 1970s thus did not emerge from nowhere, but represented a new phase in the continual play of territorial management and accommodation. One common factor is the crisis of the existing system of territorial representation under the impact of political change and the intervention of the state itself, a process that bears comparison with the territorial explosion of the late nineteenth century.

Following the Second World War, western European states assumed responsibility for national economic management and the insertion of national economies into the new international trading system. Key aims were continued economic growth, low inflation and full employment. Regional policies developed as a complement to this, to ensure even territorial development through diversionary measures such as restrictions on investing in booming areas and grants for investment in poorer regions; expansion and modernization of infrastructure; and the use of public firms to stimulate growth. Policy had complementary economic, social and political goals. Economically, diversionary policy could benefit poor regions, relieve physical and inflationary pressures on booming regions, and help the national economy by bringing into use idle resources. Socially, it represented the territorial expression of national solidarity and the welfare state. Politically, it served to increase support in problem regions both for the state and for ruling parties. Since these goals were mutually supportive, it could be sold as a positive sum game. Over time, policies became more sophisticated, with a refinement of spatial levels and the elaboration of systems of regional planning and urban development to complement diversionary policies. Policy was top-down, managed by central government or (in Germany) with an increasingly centralised bias, and was to a degree depoliticised. As it became more elaborate, however, there was a need for local interlocutors and collaborators, but existing territorial representatives were generally by-passed in favour of new, technical elites. Policy was to be negotiated and applied on the ground through various forms of corporatist machinery bringing together modernizing forces.

This coincided, in some places, with the emergence of new territorial actors, the *forces vives*, challenging the distributive politics of the old notables with a new politics of growth and change. Old local elites could look on complacently, as this manna (as it was described in France) fell upon them without their having to do anything, but the longer-term effect was to undermine their status as territorial brokers in the face of the state. Nor were the effects of centralized regional policy all beneficial. Old systems of production were displaced, cultures threatened and painful adjustments needed, provoking a wave of movements of territorial defence. These often flowed into other movements, of pacifists, cultural activists, minority nationalists or ecologists, to form broader social movements. Territorial management systems were destabilised with the by-passing of the old territorial intermediators, while the regional development machinery encouraged citizens and groups to articulate their demands in a regional framework. This led to a politicisation of the field, with competing views on how regions should be developed and objections to their subordination to national economic strategies. Mixed organs, like the regional development councils in France, Italy, Belgium and the United Kingdom, were torn between their role in delivering central policy in the region, and representing a genuinely regional perspective on development, and were forced forward, towards regional government in the first three cases. The United Kingdom moved back to centralization, although the special arrangements for Scotland and Wales survived and served to shape distinct territorial political arenas until the end of the century.

Regional governments, however, were colonised by the brokers of the old type, albeit sometimes in a modernized form. In France, the Gaullists, previously at loggerheads with the Fourth Republic notables who survived in the localities, themselves established a local presence during the 1960s and 1970s. Indirectly-elected regional councils set up in 1972 gave the management of regional change to them, although central agencies, like the DATAR, kept their autonomy. In turn the opposition Socialists, during their rise in the 1970s, undertook a "march through the institutions", using success at regional level to consolidate their basis and, in the process, converting themselves to the merits of regionalism. Italy's Christian Democrats, having challenged the old Liberal *notabili* in the name of modernization, took over their patronage role and developed it to a new level of efficacy and sophistication. During the 1960s the agencies for regional development, such as the *Cassa per il Mezzogiorno*, were colonized by the party machines, who then took over the regional governments set up in 1970. Left-wing forces did, however, manage to establish themselves in some cities and regions and use them to advance the cause of territorial autonomy of which, on general ideological grounds, they were historically rather suspicious. The gradual process of regionalization in Belgium was managed by the existing political elite, who were its beneficiaries.

Regionalist political movements, often rather heterogeneous, failed to establish a convincing policy synthesis themselves and lost momentum. States seemed to be regaining control of territorial politics, but the victory was only temporary (see below). Spain is something of an exception. The paranoia of the Franco regime about anything regional meant that they did not set up even the technocratic type of regional arrangement found elsewhere (although some modernizing technocrats in the regime were in favour). There was no co-option of regional elites or regionalized system of brokerage. Regionalist and minority nationalist movements thus remained united with other opposition forces, so ensuring that regional devolution would be a priority of the democratic regime after 1978.

The new regionalism

National regional policies were undermined by the economic crises of the 1970s and the end of the assumption that national Keynesianism could guarantee constant growth, which the state could redistribute. With rising unemployment, the positive-sum assumptions of regional policy could no longer be sustained and regions were pitched into more explicit competition. The opening of European and global markets and capital mobility further weakened national diversionary instruments, since investment now had a wide choice of locations. There has been a reappraisal of regional economic growth, with a new paradigm stressing the importance of place in explaining success and failure and the need for endogenous growth strategies (Storper, 1997; Scott, 1998). Territories are no longer considered interchangeable, so that manipulating the grant and tax system, lowering transport costs, or providing infrastructure can not now be used to make any place suitable for more or less any activity. Rather, places are seen as social systems sustaining norms and practices conducive to particular types of activity. Markets and capitalism are not the same everywhere, but vary from one place to another, as does the extent of entrepreneurial activity. Another strand of thinking is territorial competition. In modern conditions of production, comparative advantage, in which all territories find their niche in the division of labour, has given way to competitive advantage, with winners and losers. This thinking has been much criticized as an ideological construction or rationalisation for a policy that allows the state to disengage from its responsibilities for local and regional development (Lovering, 1999). It is certainly true that the political interpretation of the new models of growth has fostered a type of regional neo-mercantilism, in which regional elites can postulate a common territorial interest in beating competitors, allowing them to use territory as the basis for their political appeal.

The context of this inter-regional competition is no longer national but global and European and the European Union has, to some degree, taken over the role of the state in regional policy, using rather similar arguments to those for national regional policy in the 1960s and 1970s, with their mixture of economic, social and political elements. Regions, affected by a range of European policies, have sought ways of influencing the European level, via their national governments, by direct lobbying, or through inter-regional networks.

Economic development is not the only function to have changed its spatial scale. Cultural and linguistic minorities have increasingly territorialized, even in the presence of modern communication technology, since public institutions are needed to sustain the communities concerned. To a degree, social solidarity may have territorialized, in those places with a strong sense of identity, affecting the politics of the welfare state. Territory is becoming more important as a source of political identity. States across Europe have established intermediate, regional or "meso" level governments to manage the process of social and economic change, plan infrastructure and rationalise the welfare state. We are thus seeing the emergence of the regional level as an economic space, a cultural space, a political space, and a set of government institutions (Keating, 1998) although not all of these affect all regions.

The resulting order has often been described as new, a system of "multilevel governance" replacing the old hierarchical and centralized state. Alternately, it is described as a new medievalism, a return to a pre-modern form of overlapping and asymmetrical forms of authority. It is neither, merely the latest manifestation of an enduring reality, that states and supranational authorities govern complex territories, constantly evolving and shifting.

Globalization has been here before, as have complex forms of government and European networks transcending political jurisdictions. Political scientists do not need new paradigms or concepts and have a wealth of comparative material from the past. Territorial management changes its form but never disappears. Rather than a sign of delayed modernity or a transition to a new form of integrated polity, it is part of normal politics. This has all provided a stimulus to the rediscovery of regional histories (Applegate, 1999) and alternative teleologies. I have presented above some ways of challenging the integrationist paradigm with an approach more sensitive to the continual nature of state-building and territorial management. A regional history of Europe would be an altogether more ambitious task, although some work is being undertaken in the Rokkanian tradition. Yet once we challenge the teleology of the consolidated nation-state, it becomes difficult to agree on what an alternative account would look like, what would be its structuring principles. The debate at this point becomes entangled with normative claims, which draw on some of the same historical materials.

The usable past

There is a strong normative bias in national histories across Europe. The statist teleology has both conservative and progressive versions. Spain has a conservative version, in which the state is the repository of Catholic traditionalism, threatened by provincial subversion, but also a liberal and progressive one dating from the nineteenth century and associated the *Institution Libre de Enseñanza* (Fox, 1997). In France, the regions were for a long time presented as hotbeds of counter-revolutionary and clerical reaction against the liberating forces of the Jacobin state. The British Whig historians showing how the incorporation by England of the peripheral territories was unquestioningly progressive had their counterparts in Spain, France, Belgium, Canada and elsewhere (Keating, 2001). John Stuart Mill's (1972) scathing views on non-assimilated European minorities have been widely cited. In more recent times, Ralph Dahrendorf (1995) has written in a similar, if less provocative, vein, while Larry Siedentop (2000) associates regionalism with throwing away civic culture and democratic norms forged in the nation-state.

Yet the transformation and demystification of the state and the linking of regional and sub-state nationalisms to the project of European integration have provoked a new historical revisionism. In the past, minority nationalist historiography was often a mimesis of the statist version, merely substituting the smaller nation for the larger. So the nation, trapped in an artificial union, was suppressed and unable to express itself. There were often myths of primitive independence, taken away in the past. Free from these shackles, the nation could take its place in the family of states. Such was the vision of Sabino Arana (1892), constructed in a brief time at the end of the nineteenth century, when the destiny of a nation seemed to be to have its own state.

More interesting is the rediscovery in present circumstances of older doctrines of shared sovereignty, overlapping authority and negotiated order. Such visions have always been around, especially in small peoples with powerful neighbours like the Catalans or the Finns (Puig, 1998), the Czechs, or Scotland. In the multilevel European political order, in which nobody has absolute sovereignty, this gives some nations and regions a usable past, which national and regional movements can deploy in a strategy to gain autonomy and leverage. Scottish home rulers have recalled that the doctrine of parliamentary sovereignty is unknown in Scots law but that the principle of popular sovereignty is well entrenched (CSA, 1988; MacCormick, 2000). Catalans refer back to their history as a self-governing trading nation within the Kingdom of Aragon, itself embedded in a complex Spanish and European order. Moderate Basque nationalists look to their traditional privileges, the fueros, not as a form of absolute independence, but as original rights which are historically and legally prior to the Spanish constitution. This leads to a pactist and confederal view of the Spanish state and the European Union. In Canada, too, there has been a strong revival of the "two nations" or pactist theory of confederation, presented as historically better-informed and a guide to present practice (McRoberts, 1997; Romney, 1999). This kind of reasoning is not universal or at least is not always extended to constitutional matters. Flemish nationalists and regionalists make much of the glories of Flanders in the golden age, its culture and its economic might, but do not refer much to the constitutional legacy of the Burgundian and Austrian Low Countries, in which rulers had to accommodate local usages and negotiate with the communities. Perhaps it is because the modern Flanders is so different from the historic territories, perhaps because the experience of the centralised Belgian state removed the historic memory. In the former Habsburg domains there is an understandable reluctance to recall the memory of the empire, and highly statist positions have been taken by the political elites, but there is some interest in older forms of complex authority. There is also some recognition that the empire was not necessarily doomed because of the nationalities question, and a renewed interest in those, such as the Austro-Marxists, who sought to convert it into a democratic multinational federation (Nimni, 1999).

There is equally a challenge to the normative teleology of the state, the idea that it is the only possible frame for liberal democracy. Pre-modern forms of negotiated authority have often been associated with reaction, defence of privilege and inequality, their destruction as the precondition of progress. Yet it might equally be argued that no societies were democratic in the middle ages and early modern period, but that more than one form could contain the seeds of democracy. Modernists might decry the Declaration of Arbroath, with its lofty sentiments about limited monarchy and the rights of the Scots, as the concoction of some monks for self-interested barons; but it is surely inconsistent at the same time to see Magna Carta as the fountainhead of English/British liberties. The Basque fueros may have been the product of a deeply unequal society, but this does not mean that they could not be democratized while absolutist polities in France and Spain could. Doctrines of historic rights have usually been scorned by modernists, who argue that the fact that a right pertained to a particular territory in the past is normatively irrelevant to the present. Rights are inherent only in individuals or in groups of individuals democratically agreeing to create a polity. Yet the rights of states themselves to independence and jurisdiction rests less upon a fictive Lockean bargain than upon the fact that they already exist and can trace their legitimacy back in time often deploying nationalist myths. As the state is demystified and placed on the same moral plane as other human collectivities, doctrines of historic rights for stateless nations and regions come back into political discourse (Herrero de Miñon, 1998).

At some point the deconstruction of historical teleologies leads to an intellectual nihilism, or a post-modernist account in which there is no structure, no narrative, no conclusion and no normative implication (Létourneau, 2000). Any myth can be debunked and both nationalist and regional accounts tested to destruction. Once the state is eliminated as the privileged unit of analysis, it is easy to knock down any alternative. Yet we do not have to go all the way down the deconstructionist path or succumb to a regionalist or minority nationalist teleology in the search for alternative structuring principles for historical narrative. Such patent fabrications as the history of Padania (Oneto, 1997) can reasonably be discounted even as other histories are contested. A more promising approach is to consider the history of nations and regions within and across states, not as reified entities, but as constantly in flux, being made and remade in different historical conditions. Nothing is predetermined, neither the state nor its rivals, but theoretically informed interpretation of history is possible. This is the aim of the "new" British or Islands history (Pocock, 1975; Kearney, 1995; Davies, 1999), in turn criticized for not placing the islands in the broader European context (Scott, 2000). Even the unitary history of England has come under challenge (Tomaney, 1999). There are similar projects in other European countries and in Canada (Le Roy Ladurie, 2001; McRoberts, 1997; Morelli, 1995; Romney, 1999; Tusell, 1999; Wils, 1996). We will never again have anything equivalent to the certainties of the school textbooks of another era but social scientists still need, and might even contribute to, the discipline of history.

References

Applegate, C. (1999) 'A Europe of Regions: Reflections on the Historiography of Sub-National Places in Modern Times', *American Historical Review*, 104.4. pp.1157–82.

Arana, S. (1892) 'Vizcaya por su independencia', in Santiago de Pablo, Jose Luis de la Granja and Ludger Mees (eds), *Documentos para la historia del nacionalismo vasco*. Barcelona: Arid.

Brunstein, W. (1988) *The Social Origins of Political Regionalis*. Berkeley: University of California Press.

CSA (1988) Campaign for a Scottish Assembly, 'A Claim of Right for Scotland', in O. Dudley Edwards (ed.), *A Claim of Right for Scotland*. Edinburgh: Polygon.

Conze, W. (1962) 'The German Empire', in *The New Cambridge Modern History*. Vol.XL *Material Progress and World-Wide Problems, 1870–1898*. Cambridge: Cambridge University Press.

Dahrendorf, R. (1995) 'Preserving Prosperity', *New Statesman and Society*, 15/29 December, pp.36–41.

Davies, N. (1999) *The Isles. A History*. London: Macmillan.

Deutsch, K. (1966) *Nationalism and Social Communication. An Inquiry into the Foundations of Nationality*, 2nd edition. Cambridge, Mass: MIT Press.

Durkheim, E. (1964) *The Division of Labour in Society*. New York: Free Press.

Flora, P. (ed.) (1999) *State Formation, Nation-Building and Mass Politics in Europe: The Theory of Stein Rokkan*. Oxford: Oxford University Press.

Fox, I. (1997) *La invención de Espñna. Nacionalismo liberal e identidad nacional*. Madrid: Catédra.

Gellner, E. (1983) *Nations and nationalism*. Oxford: Blackwell.

Grarnsci, A. (1978) 'Operai e contadini', in V. Lo Curto (ed.), *La questione meridionale*, 2nd edition. Florence: G. D'Anna.

Grémion, P. (1976) *Le pouvoir peripherique. Bureaucrates et notables dans le systeme politique français*. Paris: Seuil.

Herrero de Miñon, M. (1998a) *Derechos Históricos y Constituci.ón*. Madrid: Tecnos.

Kearney, H. (1995) *The British Isles. A history of Four Nations*. Cambridge: Cambridge University Press.

Keating, M. (1975) *The Role of the Scottish MP*, PhD thesis. Glasgow College/CNAA.

Keating, M. (1998) *The New Regionalism in Western Europe. Territorial Restructuring and Political Change*. Aldershot: Edward Elgar.

Keating, M. (2001) *Plurinational Democracy. Stateless Nations in a Post-Sovereignty Era*. Oxford: Oxford University Press.

Le Roy Ladurie, E. (2001) *Histoire de France des Régions. La périphérie française des origins à nos jours*. Paris: Seuil.

Létourneau, J. (2000) *Passer à l'avenir. Histoire, mémoire, indentité dans le Québec' d 'aujourd'hui*. Montreal: Boreal.

Lovering, J. (1999) 'Theory Led by Policy: The Inadequacies of the "New Regionalism', *International Journal of Urban and Regional Research*, 23.2, pp.379–95.

MacCormick, N. (1999) *Questioning Sovereignty. Law, State and Nation in the European Commonwealth*. Oxford: Oxford University Press.

MacCormick, N. (2000) 'Is There a Scottish Path to Constitutional Independence?', *Parliamentary Affairs*, 53, pp.721–36.

McRoberts, K. (1997) *Misconceiving Canada. The Struggle for National Unity*. Toronto: Oxford University Press. University Press.

Mahoney, J. & Rueschmeyer, D. (eds) (2003) *Comparative Historical Analysis in the Social Sciences.* Cambridge: Cambridge University Press.

Mill, J.S. (1972) *Utilitarianism, On Liberty and Considerations on Representative Government.* London: Dent

Morelli, A. (1995) 'Introduction', in Ann Morelli (ed.) *Les grands mythes de l'histoire de Belgique, de Flandre et de Wallonie.* Brussels: Vie Ouvrière.

Nimni, E. (1999) 'Nationalist multiculturalism in late imperial Austria as a critique of contemporary liberalism: the case of Bauer and Renner', *Journal of Political Ideologies,* 4.3, pp.289–314.

Oneto, G. (1997) *L 'invenzione della Padania. La rinascità della communitè più antica d'Europa,* Ceresola: Foedus.

Osiander, A. (1994) *The States System of Europe, 1640–1990. Peacekeeping and the Conditions of International Stability.* Oxford: Clarendon.

Osiander, A. (2001) 'Sovereignty, International Relations and the Westphalian Myth' *International Organisations,* 55, pp.251–287.

Pocock, J.G.A. (1975) 'British History: A Plea for a New Subject', *Journal of Modern History,* 47.4, pp.601–28

Puig i Scotoni, P. (1998) *Pensar els camins a la sobirania.* Barcelona: Mediterranea.

Rokkan, S. (1980) 'Territories, Centres, and Peripheries: Toward a Geoethnic-Geoeconomic-Geopolitical model of Differentiation within Western Europe', in J. Gottman (ed.) *Centre and Periphery. Spatial Variations in Politics.* Beverly Hills: Sage.

Romney, P. (1999) Getting it Wrong. *How Canadians Forgot Their Past and Imperilled Confederation.* Toronto: University of Toronto Press.

Scott, A. (1998) *The Regional World.* Oxford: Oxford University Press.

Scott, J. (2000) *England's Troubles. Seventeenth-Century English Political Instability in European Context,* Cambridge: Cambridge University Press.

Shils, E. (1975) *Center and Periphery. Essays in Macrosociology.* Chicago: University of Chicago Press.

Siedentop, L. (2000) *Democracy in Europe.* London: Allen Lane, Penguin.

Spruyt, H. (1994) *The Sovereign State and its Competitors.* Princeton: Princeton University Press.

Storper, M. (1997) *The Regional World. Territorial Development in a Global Economy.* New York and London: Guildford.

Tierney, S. (2004) *Constitutional Law and National Pluralism.* Oxford: Oxford University Press.

Tilly, C. (1975) *The formation of national states in Western Europe.* Princeton: Princeton University Press.

Tilly, C. (1990) *Coercion, Capital and European States,* AD 990–1990. Oxford: Blackwell.

Tomany, J. (1999) 'In Search of English Regionalism: The Case of the North East', *Scottish Affairs,* 28, pp.62–82.

Tusell, J. *(1999) España. Un angustia nacional.* Madrid: Espasa Calpe.

Wils, L. *(1996) Histoire des nations beiges.* Ottignies: Quorum.

Chapter Ten

Bavaria's "German Mission": the CSU and the politics of regional identity, 1949–c.1962

Ian Farr & Graham Ford

Arguably few parts of Europe have such a pronounced sense of their own regional identity and particularity as Bavaria. This sentiment, one stemming in no small measure from the successive efforts of the state bureaucracy since the early nineteenth century to forge a distinct state consciousness (*Staatsbewußtsein*),[1] is reinforced by a conviction, shared by many outside Germany's second most populous state (*Land*), that Bavaria is different, that "in Bavaria the clocks run differently". Despite this, analysis of modern Bavaria *as a region* has, until very recently, been distinctly lacking. In part this can be explained by the almost complete absence in Bavaria of the autonomist, separatist or ethno-nationalist politics that initially did so much to determine, but also in the longer term to disfigure, historical and social-scientific interest in regions and regionalism in the 1970s. One conspicuous casualty of this preoccupation with "unhappy" regions was an appreciation of the relationship between national unity and regional diversity in more decentred nations such as Germany.[2] Sensitivity to this key dimension of the German past had already been blunted by the stigmatisation of the provincial in German national – or Borussian – historiography, which emphasised the erosion of regional identities and regionalist politics in the face of nationalising processes. Where such identities and/or politics survived, they were characterised as "premodern", "backward" and "particularistic", that is, in opposition to the nation and the national.[3] To be sure, historians of Germany are nowadays much more ready than they once were to acknowledge that locality, region and nation, rather than being mutually antagonistic, were reinforcing and interdependent. Inspired by Benedict Anderson's pathbreaking study of the nation as an imagined community, Celia Applegate's work on the German idea of *Heimat* and Alon Confino's on the negotiation between local memory and national memory in Württemberg have pioneered a much more sophisticated and nuanced view of nation-building processes, particularly in the period between German unification and the outbreak of the First World War. Abigail Green has subsequently demonstrated that attempts to foster state loyalty and identity by the medium-sized German states did not lead to a "regional" rejection of the nation-state, but contributed instead to the construction of specific forms of national sentiment after 1871.[4] Indeed, so successful have been such approaches that historians of other countries too have begun to stress the dynamic and sometimes contradictory relationships between region-building and nation-building.[5]

Despite these significant and welcome trends, Bavaria continues to be seen, not so much as an illustration of Germany's diversity, but more as a rather puzzling anomaly. It is certainly not our purpose here to deny what was and remains distinctive about Bavaria. That would be impossible. The critical American decision to re-establish Bavaria – minus the semi-detached Palatinate and, initially, Lindau – as a state in September 1945 ensured that Bavaria was the only German region, with the exception of the city-states of Hamburg and Bremen, which enjoyed an obvious territorial continuity with the pre-Nazi era. In its 1946 constitution it was able, with some legitimacy, to lay claim to a thousand years of unbroken Bavarian history. Like other German states, Bavaria had been reluctant to join the Bismarckian Empire in 1871, but, unlike most of the other larger German territories, it continued to have an uncomfortable relationship with what constituted Germany. This was shown by its disenchantment with, and vain efforts to revise, the centralising tendencies of the Weimar Constitution, its rejection of West Germany's Basic Law in 1949 and its hostility to the Federal Republic's attempts from the late 1960s at a more constructive engagement (*Ostpolitik*) with the German Democratic Republic (GDR). Finally, Bavaria's distinctiveness is most apparent when we survey its current party-political landscape, one dominated by the Christian Social Union (CSU). The CSU is the only surviving regionalist party from West Germany's early postwar history, has been out of office for only three years (1954–57) since 1946, has been the sole party of government since 1966 and has polled more than 50 % of the vote in every Landtag election since 1970. However, the problem we confront is that the political hegemony of the CSU tends to serve as both premise and conclusion. Bavarian exceptionalism explains the CSU, while no further evidence of Bavarian peculiarity is needed other than the CSU and its "particularist" defence of Bavarian regionalist interests in Germany and Europe.[6]

This essay attempts to challenge this teleology by focusing on the way in which the CSU, particularly through its organ, *Bayern-Kurier*, envisioned Bavaria's place in the Germany of the 1950s and early 1960s.[7] Although we now know a great deal about the years between 1945 and 1949, the importance of regional politics in the Western zones of occupation, the revival of federal concepts of German nationhood and the role of Bavaria in the formation of the Federal Republic, it is noticeable, as Thomas Schlemmer and Hans Woller have observed, that research on the years immediately thereafter has tended to gravitate away from the regions and towards national politics.[8] But these were precisely the years when, because of the Nazis' destruction of German popular faith in nationalism, regional politics and identities were most likely to be constitutive of national politics. It was a period when the CSU, having voted "No to the Basic Law", but "Yes to Germany" in 1949, faced two significant and interrelated challenges, both of which required it to construct and articulate a vision of Bavaria's place within the fledgling West German state: the emergence of a rival party claiming to represent the regionalist interest, in the shape of the Bavarian Party (BP); and the need to defend and shape the institutions of federalism as the constitutional practice of the Bonn Republic unfolded.

The licensing of the Bavarian Party in 1948 exposed a conflict within Bavarian regionalist politics over questions of Bavarian statehood (*Eigenstaatlichkeit*) and autonomy (*Eigenständigkeit*).[9] Historically, Bavarians had been divided in their attitudes towards German unification, with the Catholics of "Old Bavaria" displaying much more reluctance to embrace the lesser German (*kleindeutsch*) nation-state than the Protestants, and even Catholics, of the Palatinate, Swabia and Franconia ("New Bavaria"). These different traditions were to be found within the CSU itself, which, from the beginning, was divided into "Bavarian" and "German" wings.[10] Under the leadership of Hans Ehard, it was gradually to reconcile these differences, as we shall see below. The BP, on the other hand, articulated a form of "Bavarian nationalism" that has been variously described as "extreme federalism", "particularism" and even "separatism". Rejecting the Basic Law, the BP initially favoured "an independent, viable Bavarian state within the framework of a German and European community of states", a loose formulation which reflected differences of opinion within the party itself,[11] but which nevertheless resonated with many Bavarian voters during the Federal Republic's early years.

In the 1946 Landtag elections, before the BP was licensed, the CSU had polled 52.3 % of the vote, apparently ensconcing itself as the party of the Bavarian regionalist interest. However, in the 1949 Bundestag elections the CSU's vote fell to 29.2 %, with the BP polling 20.9 %. In the following year's Landtag elections both parties lost votes, the CSU polling 27.4 % to the BP's 17.9 %. But the 1950 results mask the scale of the BP's challenge to the CSU in the two principal "counties" (*Regierungsbezirke*) of Old Bavaria. Here the two parties were running neck-and-neck: in Lower Bavaria the CSU polled 29.8 % of the vote compared to the BP's 27.4 %, while in Upper Bavaria the BP (22 %) came within a whisker of the CSU (22.1 %).[12] While the BP's performances in 1949 and 1950 were not enough to displace the CSU as the principal regionalist party in Bavaria, the splitting of the vote nevertheless transformed Bavarian politics. Tellingly, the CSU actually polled fewer votes than the Social Democrats in 1950, though the vagaries of the electoral system meant that it still emerged as the largest party – by one seat – in the Bavarian Landtag.[13]

Opinion in the CSU, though, was divided on how to deal with the BP. The "Bavarian" wing of the party, with its heartland in Old Bavaria, was broadly sympathetic to the BP and favoured closer cooperation between the two parties, including the prospect of a coalition government in Munich.[14] However, Hans Ehard, the Bavarian Minister-President, feared that association with the BP would do the cause of federalism more harm than good and therefore resisted such pressures.[15] The CSU's "German wing", on the other hand, believed the party was locked in a "life or death struggle"[16] with the BP. In June 1950, the CSU launched a new weekly organ, *Bayern-Kurier*, on the initiative of one of its most committed "German" politicians, the young Franz Josef Strauß.[17] And this paper would be used to intensify the political struggle against the BP. This took various forms, one of which was to expose the BP's vision for Bavaria as insular, while articulating a CSU mission that combined "love of Bavaria" with "loyalty to Germany",[18] thereby locating Bavaria at the heart of the new West German state.

For *Bayern-Kurier*, Bavaria was – historically, politically, culturally and economically – an integral part of Germany. As an electoral appeal to civil and public servants put it in 1950: "There has never yet been a Germany without Bavaria."[19] Yet Bavaria could only have political weight "if it says "yes" to Germany – if it acknowledges the unity of the German tribes (*Stämme*) and territories (*Landschaften*) –, if it is prepared to cede that part of its sovereignty and its law that the Federation needs to look after German interests."[20] Herein lay an acknowledgement that Bavaria was sovereign, but that sovereignty was divisible; that the Federal Republic drew its legitimacy from the regions and that Bavarian interests were in turn enhanced by the Federal Republic.[21] It was this beneficial and interdependent relationship between the Bavarian region and the West German state that was threatened by the BP. Given the vagueness of the BP's constitutional aims, *Bayern-Kurier* did not dwell unduly on the question of separatism, but rather painted the BP as an insular party, more concerned with parochial politics and therefore unable and unwilling to represent and defend Bavaria's interests in Germany and Europe, let alone show solidarity with the rest of the German nation.

This parochialism was articulated forcefully in a bitingly satirical poem that inverted Ernst Moritz Arndt's famous patriotic song "The German's Fatherland" (1813), with its emphasis on German unity, to attack the BP. Directed ostensibly at a BP activist by the name of Mayer, the gist of the poem was clear. "What is Mr Mayer's Fatherland?" it asked. Was it Europe? No, it was smaller than that! Was it the German Reich? No, it was smaller than that! Was it the German state (i.e. the

Bonn Republic)? No, was smaller than that! Was it Bavaria? No, it was smaller than that! Was it the "real" Bavaria (i.e. Old Bavaria)? No, it was smaller than that! "What is Mr Mayer's Fatherland?" "It is the village of Hinterwaldshausen" (i.e. the village at the back of beyond). The penultimate stanza went even further: even Hinterwaldshausen was not "pure", for one of its inhabitants was from Lippe, while another was from Prussia. But did Mr Mayer ask what this meant? No, for he was unconcerned by the threat of Bolshevism or that "Asia's wild hordes" were murdering fellow Germans in the north. For the world might go to wrack and ruin, but Hinterwaldshausen would endure. And with that thought, Mr Mayer sat back and lit his pipe.[22]

Other stories developed this theme, reinforcing the detrimental consequences of the BP's parochialism for both the region and the nation. The Bavarian interest, therefore, was prejudiced by the BP's overblown "white-blue" rhetoric, for it gave other Germans the impression that Bavaria was some sort of "nature reserve" or a "land of yodellers",[23] a situation no doubt exacerbated by the BP's tendency to campaign "in the traditional costume of leather shorts and chamois-beard hats".[24] As Strauß put it following the 1953 Bundestag elections, at which the BP failed to win a single seat: "The disappearance of the Bavarian Party from Bonn is no loss for Bavaria, for exaggerated "folk costume-federalism" (*Trachten-Föderalismus*) has not helped in raising Bavaria's reputation in Bonn."[25] The BP's bombast was therefore contrasted with the CSU's quiet determination to further Bavarian interests, a point Strauß made in a speech several weeks later: "It isn't those who misuse the name of Bavaria most frequently and most loudly for propaganda purposes who do the most for Bavaria, but rather those who take their Bavarian responsibility sincerely and seriously."[26]

Bavarian interests, though, could not be reduced to questions of domestic politics. The division of Germany and Bavaria's geographical location – it bordered both the GDR and Czechoslovakia – meant that the Communist threat loomed large in Bavarian affairs, and the CSU was not afraid to instrumentalise this threat in its battle for political supremacy in the region. In 1950 it raised the issue of "national security" to attack the BP's confederalism: "If any further proof were needed that it is frankly suicidal, when faced by the Soviet bloc, to want to divide West Germany into eleven quite loosely associated states, then developments in Korea have provided it."[27] The CSU, on the other hand, embraced Chancellor Adenauer's policy of Western integration.[28] In so doing, Bavaria was cast in the role of defender of the Christian Occident against the Asiatic East. Strauß, in particular, embodied Bavaria's contribution to the defence of Western civilisation, even before he became Defence Minister in 1956. At the annual Ash Wednesday political rally in Vilshofen, deep in the heart of rural Lower Bavaria – where Strauß first spoke in 1953 – the focal point of his speech was usually on foreign and security policy.[29] While Petra Weber is almost certainly right to argue that the majority of the Bavarian population had little interest in international affairs as such, Strauß's popularity nonetheless points towards a regional pride in a Bavarian politician astride the German and European stage.[30]

The BP's parochialism was not just a threat to Western civilisation, of which Bavaria was an integral part; it was also a rejection of the Bavarians' common destiny with, and attendant responsibilities for, other Germans. This was particularly the case with regard to the millions of expellees and refugees who had sought sanctuary in Bavaria during and after the war and who accounted for about a quarter of the Bavarian population by the early 1950s.[31] The BP was openly hostile to these migrants, adopting such xenophobic slogans as "Bavaria must remain Bavarian" and "Bavaria for the Bavarians".[32] The CSU, on the other hand, became a committed advocate of their cause.[33] This certainly made political sense, for in the 1950 Landtag elections the expellees' own party – the BHE – garnered 12.3 % of the vote. But it also reflected the CSU's understanding of the nation. For the CSU, German identities were rooted in the *Heimat*, so that the essence of the German nation was to be found in the localities and regions. Therefore, as a party representing the Bavarian *Heimat*, the CSU had great sympathy for the expellees' desire to return to their homeland.[34] Yet geo-political realities meant that this was impossible. Instead, the CSU had to reconcile its support for the expellees' lost *Heimat* with the simultaneous need to integrate them into their new Bavarian home. This was achieved most conspicuously among the Sudeten Germans, who accounted for about one tenth of the Bavarian population. In 1954 the Bavarian state became their patron; and Bavarian "tribal" diversity was subsequently redefined to incorporate the Sudeten Germans as Bavaria's "fourth tribe" alongside the Old Bavarians, Franconians and Swabians.[35] When Bavaria's new Minister-President, Alfons Goppel, established his first cabinet in 1962, *Bayern-Kurier* was able to proclaim: "Four tribes in Goppel Cabinet".[36]

During the 1950s, then, *Bayern-Kurier* played an important role in the CSU's struggle for political supremacy against the BP. Integral to this struggle was the construction of a negative mental image of the BP's Bavaria by exposing the hollowness of its "white-blue" rhetoric. Rather than defending Bavarian interests, the BP was portrayed as a party that was willing to turn its back on the German nation, marginalising Bavaria in German and European affairs and making the region vulnerable to the Soviet threat. Under such circumstances, the BP's notion of Bavarian "statehood" was a chimera, with sovereignty an empty shell. It was not enough, however, for the CSU simply to challenge the BP's insularity, important though this was. It had also to develop a coherent and positive vision of Bavaria's place within the West German state, one in which Bavarian statehood would not only be defended, but would actually be enhanced through active participation. The cornerstone of this policy was federalism.

For the CSU, the continuation of Bavarian statehood was dependent on federalism. Any other constitutional system would turn the region into an administrative province of a unitary state. During the late 1940s, though, the party was deeply divided about the nature and extent of Bavaria's federal relationship with a future West German state. Although Hans Ehard was more sympathetic to the Bavarian wing of his party, he nevertheless pursued a policy of flexible engagement in order to realise his federalist objectives.[37] In so doing, Bavaria asserted its role as the leader of the German regions in the shaping of a federal Germany. This was, in Ehard's words, Bavaria's "German mission" (*Aufgabe*).[38] But Ehard was also pragmatic enough to accept the need to compromise with more centrally-minded forces, above all during the deliberations on the West German constitution or Basic Law. Hence, while Bavarian pressure eventually succeeded in institutionalising regional participation in the national legislative process through the establishment of the Bundesrat (Federal Council), the constitution was less federal than Ehard – and the majority of the CSU – would have liked. Indeed, Ehard later referred to the Basic Law's provisions as "unstable federalism" (*labiler Föderalismus*).[39] As a consequence, Bavaria's "German policy" did not change in its essentials after the creation of the Federal Republic in May 1949:[40] Bavaria continued to assert its leadership of the regions as the guardian of the federal principle.

Bavaria's claim to such a role was justified in terms of its territorial continuity and historic statehood. As Hanns Seidel noted in 1955, Bavaria "is probably the only regional state with a genuine and mature state consciousness" and "has a particular mission to perform in the Federal Republic."[41] The other regions, as essentially postwar creations, did not yet possess this consciousness sufficiently, it was argued, and some were even inclined to conceive of themselves as little more than Prussian provinces.[42] For some scholars, Bavaria's trenchant defence of federalism was akin to particularism, namely that the rights of the individual regions were of more importance than rebuilding national unity.[43] Yet this is misleading. While federalist rhetoric was certainly used to defend Bavarian autonomy against centralising tendencies emanating from Bonn, federalism also offered an alternative narrative of German unity and nationhood, one that had allowed for German unity within a framework of territorial and cultural diversity.[44] The Holy Roman Empire, the German Confederation and, to a lesser extent, the Bismarckian Reich were therefore presented as generally positive antecedents, each of which had offered an historically specific federal solution to the problem of German unity. The Weimar Republic, on the other hand, was cast in a negative light, with its weakening of regional autonomy cited as one factor contributing to the Nazi seizure of power. Only once, though, had the Germans completely embraced a unitary state, the Third Reich, with catastrophic consequences for the German nation. Federalism, then, was not the antithesis of German unity, but rather, as history and tradition showed, the constitutional order best suited to German conditions and needs, to reconcile unity with diversity and, in Ehard's words, to ensure "unity" without the need for "uniformity".[45] But the CSU went even further: federalism, the party contended, required individual freedom and democracy, whereas a unitary state always contained the potential for totalitarianism. After all, the Nazis had quickly subverted Weimar's weak regional structure; and this argument was lent added weight by East Germany's abolition of its regions in 1954.[46] In this respect, Bavaria was not simply the guardian of the federal principle: by extension, it was also the guardian of German freedom and democracy.

Given this national responsibility, Bavaria was pivotal in shaping the federal constitutional practice of the West German state, especially in the early 1950s. Although the Basic Law created a federal political system, its parameters were particularly open to interpretation, negotiation and alteration during these years. With Bonn eager to extend its powers from the beginning, the CSU's federal vision was immediately on the defensive. While Bavaria was unable to resist all of these centralising pressures, Ehard was nevertheless instrumental in institutionalising the role of the regions within the West German body politic. As Karl-Ulrich Gelberg has shown, Ehard initially conceived of federalism as regional participation in national politics through the Bundesrat. And he therefore worked to ensure that this chamber established itself as an active and constructive element in the legislative process.[47] He soon came to realise, however, that the Bundesrat alone was insufficient to entrench federalism. Instead, Ehard sought to intensify regional cooperation through bilateral meetings with other Minister-Presidents.[48] But in 1954 he went further: by calling for a Minister-Presidents' conference in Munich, Ehard reasserted Bavaria's leadership of the regions and his determination to deepen federalism through regional cooperation.[49] The subsequent institutionalisation of such conferences and intensification of regional cooperation strengthened the intergovernmental dimension of West German federalism.[50] This opened up an era of state treaties and administrative agreements between the regions – to which Bonn was also often party – that reconciled the national interest without the need for direct federal intervention.[51]

Bavaria's role in the construction of the West German state was not just restricted to Munich, for the CSU was also an influential political force in Bonn.[52] Although the CSU was an independent party, its Bundestag deputies or Landesgruppe nevertheless formed a joint parliamentary grouping (*Fraktionsgemeinschaft*) with the CDU, which meant that its regionalist interests became intertwined with national political responsibilities. Indeed, the CSU provided cabinet ministers in successive West German governments between 1949 and 1969. Recently historians have noted tensions between the CSU in Bonn and the CSU in Munich, not least because of their differing conceptions of federalism.[53] But these tensions were rarely aired in public. Instead, the CSU's parliamentary groups in Bonn and Munich were presented as having different, though complementary, roles.[54] In this respect, the CSU's active involvement in federal politics highlighted Bavaria's symbiotic relationship with the West German state.

The activities of the *Landesgruppe* were therefore motivated, it was suggested, by both a duty to Germany and care for the Bavarian *Heimat*. And in fulfilling the former, the party was enhancing the latter.[55] Particular importance was accorded to cabinet ministers as prominent Bavarians shaping Germany's future, though three dominated: Ludwig Erhard,[56] Fritz Schäffer and Franz Josef Strauß.[57] Along with the imposing figure of Konrad Adenauer these men were presented as the architects of the new German state, and, as such, they were soon inducted into the pantheon of CSU political mythology, their achievements testimony to Bavarian influence on the Federal Republic. This is well illustrated by an electoral appeal in *Bayern-Kurier* during the 1965 Bundestag elections: "Bavaria's contribution to German recovery was decisive. Erhard from Fürth was the creator of the D-Mark and the prosperous economy. Fritz Schäffer from Passau created healthy public finances and made the D-Mark stable. Strauß from Munich took Germany into the atomic age and was the architect of German security."[58]

West German recovery also meant a thriving Bavaria, for as Hermann Höcherl, the chairman of the *Landesgruppe*, explained in 1959: "With its contribution to

German politics, the CSU *Landesgruppe* has also acted in the best interests of Bavaria. It would not have been a Bavarian party if, in its political activities, it had not kept its eye on its *Heimat*. The programme of redevelopment for deprived areas, aid for the border area, the development of existing and new roads, all stem from these endeavours."[59] And such support was important given that Bavaria was one of the weakest regions in the Federal Republic, both structurally and financially, until the late 1960s.[60] As Petra Weber has recently demonstrated, the *Landesgruppe* was therefore able to advance Bavarian interests within the context of West German federal politics. In so doing, it contributed to the modernisation of the regional economy,[61] a process that reinforced and reinvigorated Bavaria's claims to leadership of the regions.

Historically, Bavaria was predominantly an agricultural region, though with islands of advanced industrial development. But during the 1950s Bavaria underwent a process of late industrialisation, characterised by the development of such modern industries as chemicals, electrical engineering, automobile and aircraft production.[62] Although various factors explain this transformation, including considerable financial aid from Bonn, it is also the case that the Bavarian government pursued a policy of regional economic modernisation. As early as 1951, the Minister of Economics, Hanns Seidel, was arguing that Bavaria was no longer an agrarian region, but rather the prototype of an "industrial-agrarian state".[63] And this concept subsequently became a leitmotiv of CSU rhetoric: it conveyed the party's political commitment to industry, agriculture and the *Mittelstand*, while simultaneously articulating Bavaria's growing self-confidence within the West German state.[64] As *Bayern-Kurier* put it in 1962: "Bavaria is a modern region with tradition. In hardly any region have so many initiatives been launched as in Bavaria. Bavaria is not an endearing museum; it has become a model for our times."[65]

Although the extent of this economic transformation should not be exaggerated, Bavaria's industrialisation was nonetheless crucial in infusing the region's statehood with modern legitimacy, further bolstering the CSU's assertion that federalism, far from being antiquated, was in fact a "modern" form of government.[66] The CSU certainly continued to cultivate Bavaria's "centuries-old traditions". But Bavaria was no longer a "backward" region on the margins of the German economy; on the contrary, it was now a site of economic modernity and therefore one of the focuses of West Germany's industrial-technological future. Although North Rhine-Westphalia was a wealthier region during the 1960s, the combination of Bavarian tradition and the Bavarian "economic model" helped Munich rather than

Düsseldorf become West Germany's "secret capital".[67]

Even this necessarily cursory glance at the CSU's politics of Bavarian identity demonstrates the dangers of seeing the CSU's eventual hegemony as the inevitable consequence of Bavarian otherness. Between the late 1940s and early 1960s the politics of Bavarian regionalism was a contested terrain, exemplified by the competition between the CSU and the BP. In the course of that struggle the CSU profited by campaigning around two opposing mental constructs: a Bavaria marginalised in German and European affairs (BP), the other a Bavaria located at the heart of Germany and Europe (CSU). The CSU's conception of Bavaria's "German mission" cannot be dismissed as particularism, let alone separatism. The CSU understood the essence of the nation as residing in the regions and localities; the regions created the nation, and the nation, in turn, enhanced the regions. This was a symbiotic relationship sustained by federalism, a constitutional order that allowed for subsidiarity, which was not simply a division of responsibilities between regions and nation, but a system of mutual support between the two.[68] This insistence on federalism was significant and had its roots in the Bavarian and German past. Bavaria's historic statehood and territorial continuity mattered. With Austria excised from Germany in 1866 and reduced to a rump in 1918, and with Prussia abolished in 1947, Bavaria had a unique opportunity to reshape Germany as a decentred nation rooted in the regions. In this respect, the CSU might bear comparison with the Lliga Regionalista in early twentieth-century Catalonia. Both parties were rooted in distinct regional traditions; and both saw their region as having a "mission" to shape and regenerate their respective nations.[69] Although the CSU attained a "unique" place in the West German party system, its very uniqueness highlights the role of the region in shaping the national. But it is only by paying more attention to the other West German regions, and the diverse regional-national interactions that shaped the Federal Republic that will we discover, in turn, what was truly "unique" about Bavaria.

Notes

1. Werner Blessing, *Staat und Kirche in der Gesellschaft: Institutionelle Autorität und mentaler Wandel* (Göttingen, 1982); Manfred Hanisch, *Für Fürst und Vaterland: Legitimitätsstiftung in Bayern zwischen Revolution 1848 und deutscher Einheit* (Munich, 1991); Karl-Ulrich Gelberg, 'Staatsbewusstsein und Föderalismus in Bayern nach 1945', *Politische Studien* 392 (November/December 2003), pp. 65–78; Thomas Mergel, 'Staatlichkeit und Landesbewußtsein. Politische Symbole und Staatsrepräsentation in Bayern und Nordrhein-Westfalen 1945 bis 1975', *Bayern im Bund. Bd. 3: Politik und Kultur im föderativen Staat 1949 bis 1973*, ed. Thomas Schlemmer and Hans Woller (Munich, 2004), pp. 281–347. For a sensible critique of Bavarian identity, see Ulrike Stoll, 'Bayern – ein Land ohne Identitätsprobleme?', *Geschichte im Westen* 16 (2001), pp. 20–37.

2. Two examples of the preoccupation with 'would-be nations' are Stein Rokkan and Derek Urwin, *Economy, Territory, Identity: Politics of West European Peripheries* (Beverly Hills, 1983) and Rainer Elkar, ed., *Europas unruhige Regionen* (Stuttgart, 1981).

3. For an intelligent discussion of these and related issues, see Celia Applegate, 'A Europe of Regions: Reflections on the Historiography of Sub-National Places in Modern Times', *American Historical Review* 104 (1999), pp. 1157–82. Decisive in encouraging historians to rethink their assumptions was James Sheehan, 'What is German History? Reflections on the Role of the *Nation* in German History and Historiography', *Journal of Modern History* 53 (1981), pp. 1–23.

4. Benedict Anderson, *Imagined Communities: Reflections on the Origin and Spread of Nationalism*, 2nd edn (London and New York, 1991); Celia Applegate, *A Nation of Provincials: The German Idea of Heimat* (Oxford, 1990); Alon Confino, *The Nation as a Local Metaphor: Württemberg, Imperial Germany, and National Memory, 1871–1918* (London, 1997); Abigail Green, *Fatherlands: State-Building and Nationhood in Nineteenth-Century Germany* (Cambridge, 2001). See also James Retallack, ed., *Saxony in German History: Culture, Society, and Politics 1830–1933* (Ann Arbor, 2000).

5. Xosé-Manoel Núñez, 'The Region as *Essence* of the Fatherland: Regionalist Variants of Spanish Nationalism (1840–1936)', *European History Quarterly* 31 (2001), pp. 483–518.

6. The charge of particularism is made by both Christopher Harvie, *The Rise of Regional Europe* (London, 1994), p. 67 and Aline Kuntz, 'The CSU and the Vicissitudes of Modernity: An End to Bavarian Exceptionalism?', *German Politics and Society* 14 (1988), p. 14. See also Peter James, *The Politics of Bavaria – An Exception to the Rule: The Special Position of the Free State of Bavaria in the New Germany* (Aldershot, 1995).

7. The standard work on the CSU remains Alf Mintzel, *Die CSU: Anatomie einer konservativen Partei 1945–1972* (Opladen, 1975). The emphasis here, and in Mintzel's subsequent publications on the CSU, is on the organisational transformation of the party in the 1950s. This also holds true for Konstanze Wolf, *CSU und Bayernpartei: Ein besonderes Konkurrenzverhältnis 1948–1960* (Cologne, 1984).

8. Introduction, *Politik und Kultur*, ed. Schlemmer and Woller, p. 2. On the years 1945–49, see Peter Kock, *Bayerns Weg in die Bundesrepublik* (Stuttgart, 1983); D.R. Dorondo, *Bavaria and German Federalism: Reich to Republic, 1918–33, 1945–49* (Basingstoke, 1992); Thomas Nipperdey, 'Der Föderalismus in der deutschen Geschichte', *Nachdenken über die deutsche Geschichte*, ed. Thomas Nipperdey (Munich, 1986), pp. 96ff.

9. Wolf, *CSU und Bayernpartei*, p. 244.

10. Ibid., pp. 11–12; 'Interview mit Landtagspräsident a.D. Dr. Franz Heubl', *Geschichte einer Volkspartei: 50 Jahre CSU 1945–1995*, ed. Burkhard Haneke (Grünwald, 1995), p. 543.

11. Arnold Bauer, 'Die Bayernpartei als föderalistische Landespartei', *Parteien in der Bundesrepublik* (Stuttgart and Düsseldorf, 1955), pp. 468–82, esp. pp. 471–5; Ossip Flechtheim, *Dokumente zur parteipolitischen Entwicklung in Deutschland seit 1945. Bd. 2/I: Programmatik der deutschen Parteien* (Berlin, 1963), p. 238; Ilse Unger, *Die Bayernpartei: Geschichte und Struktur 1945–1957* (Stuttgart, 1979), pp. 142–6.

12. Alf Mintzel, 'Bayern und die CSU. Regionale politische Traditionen und Aufstieg zur dominierenden Kraft', *Geschichte einer Volkspartei*, ed. Haneke, table 1, p. 221.

13. Wolf, *CSU und Bayernpartei*, p. 13.

14. Unger, *Die Bayernpartei*, pp. 158–9, 161–3.

15. *Bayern-Kurier*, 30 June 1951.

16. Minutes of the CDU/CSU *Bundestagsfraktion*, 1 September 1949, quoted in Edgar Wolfrum, 'Geschichtspolitik in Bayern. Traditionsvermittlung, Vergangenheitsbearbeitung und populäres

Geschichtsbewußtsein nach 1945', *Politik und Kultur*, ed. Schlemmer and Woller, p. 357.

17. Wolf, *CSU und Bayernpartei*, p. 17; Mintzel, *Die CSU*, p. 165.

18. *Bayern-Kurier*, 3 June 1950.

19. *Bayern-Kurier*, 18 November 1950.

20. *Bayern-Kurier*, 3 June 1950.

21. More generally, see Núñez, 'The Region as *Essence* of the Fatherland', p. 486.

22. *Bayern-Kurier*, 10 June 1950.

23. *Bayern-Kurier*, 25 November 1950; *Bayern-Kurier*, 14 November 1953; *Bayern-Kurier*, 21 August 1954.

24. U.W. Kitzinger, *German Electoral Politics: A Study of the 1957 Campaign* (Oxford, 1960), p. 42

25. *Bayern-Kurier*, 23 January 1954.

26. *Bayern-Kurier*, 6 March 1954.

27. *Bayern-Kurier*, 11 November 1950.

28. *Bayern-Kurier*, 27 November 1954.

29. *Bayern-Kurier*, 24 February 1955; *Bayern-Kurier*, 5 March 1960; *Bayern-Kurier*, 18 February 1961; *Bayern-Kurier*, 10 March 1962.

30. Petra Weber, 'Föderalismus und Lobbyismus. Die CSU-Landesgruppe zwischen Bundes- und Landespolitik 1949 bis 1969', *Politik und Kultur*, ed. Schlemmer and Woller, pp. 115–16.

31. *Bayern-Kurier*, 25 September 1954.

32. Bauer, 'Die Bayernpartei', p. 472; Gelberg, 'Staatsbewusstsein und Föderalismus', p. 74.

33. *Bayern-Kurier*, 5 September 1953.

34. *Bayern-Kurier*, 29 July 1950; *Bayern-Kurier*, 5 September 1953.

35. *Bayern-Kurier*, 10 June 1961; Hans Schütz, 'Die Eingliederung der Vertriebenen in Bayern', *Bayern-Deutschland-Europa: Festschrift für Alfons Goppel*, ed. Ludwig Huber (Passau, 1975), pp. 72-3.

36. *Bayern-Kurier*, 22 December 1962.

37. Ehard's federalist policies are detailed in Karl-Ulrich Gelberg, *Hans Ehard: Die föderalistische Politik des bayerischen Ministerpräsidenten 1946–1954* (Düsseldorf, 1992). More concisely, see Karl-Ulrich Gelberg,'Vom Kriegsende bis zum Ausgang der Ära Goppel (1945–1978)', *Handbuch der bayerischen Geschichte. Bd. IV: Das Neue Bayern: Von 1800 bis zur Gegenwart. Erster Teilband: Staat und Politik*, ed. Alois Schmid 2nd edn (Munich, 2003), pp. 684–701.

38. Gelberg, *Hans Ehard*, p. 23 incl. n. 83.

39. *Bayern-Kurier*, 17 January 1953.

40. Gelberg, *Hans Ehard*, p. 274.

41. *Bayern-Kurier*, 29 January 1955.

42. *Bayern-Kurier*, 2 August 1958; Gelberg, *Hans Ehard*, pp. 23, 371.

43. Kuntz, 'The CSU and the Vicissitudes of Modernity', p. 14.

44. For further discussion, see Nipperdey, 'Der Föderalismus'; Helmut Berding, 'Staatliche Identität, nationale Integration und politischer Regionalismus', *Blätter für deutsche Landesgeschichte* 121. (1985), p. 390; Introduction: German Federalism in Historical Perspective, *German Federalism: Past, Present, Future*, ed. Maiken Umbach (Basingstoke, 2002), pp. 4–7.

45. *Bayern-Kurier*, 12 July 1952; *Bayern-Kurier*, 31 March 1955; *Bayern-Kurier*, 4 June 1955; *Bayern-Kurier*, 11 June 1955; *Bayern-Kurier*, 23 January 1960.

46. *Bayern-Kurier*, 5 September 1953; *Bayern-Kurier*, 1 March 1958; *Bayern-Kurier*, 6 June 1963.

47. Gelberg, 'Vom Kriegsende', pp. 807–9.

48. Gelberg, *Hans Ehard*, pp. 486–89.

49. *Bayern-Kurier*, 6 February 1954; *Bayern-Kurier*, 13 February 1954; Gelberg, *Hans Ehard*, pp. 489–504.

50. *Ibid.*, p. 504.

51. *Bayern-Kurier*, 25 June 1960; Gelberg, *Hans Ehard*, p. 504; Rudolf Morsey, 'Das föderalistische Konzept Hans Ehard', *Zeitschrift für bayerische Landesgeschichte* 56 (1993), p. 774.

52. 'Interview mit Landtagspräsident a.D. Dr. Franz Heubl', p. 552.

53. Weber, 'Föderalismus und Lobbyismus', p. 57; Gelberg, 'Vom Kriegsende', p. 701.

54. Weber, 'Föderalismus und Lobbyismus', pp. 61, 113.

55. *Bayern-Kurier*, 19 September 1959.

56. Erhard was actually a member of the CDU, but he was a Bavarian by birth and had served in the Bavarian cabinet in 1945–46.

57. *Bayern-Kurier*, 2 September 1950; *Bayern-Kurier*, 6 March 1954.

58. *Bayern-Kurier*, 4 September 1965.

59. *Bayern-Kurier*, 19 September 1959.

60. Weber, 'Föderalismus und Lobbyismus', p. 113.

61. *Ibid.*, passim. For a recent discussion of the CSU's role in Bavaria's economic modernisation, see Mark S. Milosch, *Modernizing Bavaria: The Politics of Franz Josef Strauß and the CSU, 1949–1969* (New York and Oxford, 2006).

62. Gelberg, 'Vom Kriegsende', p. 811.

63. *Bayern-Kurier*, 15 December 1951.

64. *Bayern-Kurier*, 1 March 1958; *Bayern-Kurier*, 25 June 1960; *Bayern-Kurier*, 17 November 1962. For the decline in Bavarians' 'inferiority complex' during the 1950s, see Mintzel, 'Bayern und die CSU', pp. 235–6.

65. *Bayern-Kurier*, 17 November 1962.

66. *Bayern-Kurier*, 1 March 1958; *Bayern-Kurier*, 14 February 1959; *Bayern-Kurier*, 10 August 1963.

67. *The Times*, 19 September 1963; Hermann Bössenecker, *Bayern, Bosse und Bilanzen: Hinter den Kulissen der weiß-blauen Wirtschaft* (Munich, 1972), p. 12.

68. *Bayern-Kurier*, 12 July 1952; *Bayern-Kurier*, 3 September 1955; *Bayern-Kurier*, 5 January 1962.

69. Charles E. Ehrlich, '*Per Catalunya i l'Espanya Gran*: Catalan Regionalism on the Offensive, 1911–19', *European History Quarterly* 28 (1998), pp. 189–217.

Chapter Eleven

Italianità and city patriotism in the states of Florence and Milan at the turn of the fourteenth century

Patrick Gilli

The slogan "Italy for the Italians, Gaul for the Gaulians" was written and stated by Enea Silvio Piccolomini, the humanist from Sienna who became Pope Pius II in 1458.[1] There can be no doubt that the words lead us to suppose a strong desire for political independence in the peninsula in the middle of the fifteenth century. However, there was no question of a unified Italy at this period. So, what can be the meaning of a call for territorial integrity which was not at the same time a demand for state sovereignty? To be more exact, the Italy of the fourteenth and fifteenth centuries was to witness the emergence of powerful regional states boasting government bureaucracies, ambassadors, and other symbols of state apparatus. The question which is raised is the following: did these regional states lead to "national" identities which would follow the outline of the territories which they controlled? In other words, did the inhabitants of Italy consider themselves Italian (if indeed it can be said that a feeling of Italian identity had appeared at all at the end of the Middle Ages, which would be the first point to establish) rather than Florentine, Milanese or Venetian?

Even so, the question needs to be made more precise. The appearance of the regional states took place to the detriment of smaller and weaker structures, the communes, which tended to function as isolated political units despite general loyalties to supra-national institutions, such as the Empire for the Ghibelline cities, and the Church for the Guelf cities. These cities defended their territory jealously. If we remember the military difficulties faced by the Florentines in taking control of Pisa or Volterra as late as the fifteenth century it is easy to understand that regional political unification was no easy matter. Italian scholars and writers of the period lived with these overlapping identities (city, regional and Italian), and endured their contradictions. Employed in the princely courts, they had to praise the policies of their protector or of the state at the same time as the ancient classics were being rediscovered with their reminders of the grandeur of Roman Italy as a whole.

Indeed, there was an awareness of Italian feeling separate from questions of territorial unity.[2] In the fourteenth century, praise of Italy and of its inhabitants is to be found both in the literary tradition of Dante and of Petrarch, as well as in political ideas such as Cola di Rienzo.[3] But during the trecento, Italian consciousness was an expanded form of Roman awareness.[4] In this context, we can recall the strident calls from the Romans, confronted in the 1378 Papal conclave by the menace of the election of a French pope which was later to lead to the great schism: "We want a Roman or an Italian Pope". This was clearly the (spontaneous?) expression of a Roman awareness expanded to the whole peninsula.[5] Just as significant is the "domestic" representation of Italy by Benvenuto d'Imola (c.1375), one of the most famous commentators of Dante, as the most beautiful house in the world of which Rome is the "arx" and the head, Tuscany, the "camera", Lombardy, the well filled "sala", Apulia, the "stable", etc.[6] Nevertheless, this Roman awareness, which pushed Italian awareness to its limits, was no longer accepted in the large cities. Giovanni Villani made fun of the naivety of Cola di Rienzo and the lack of realism of his plan to revive the Senate. "Volea riformate tutta Italia all'ubedienza di Roma almodo antico; la detta impresa del tribuno era un opera fantastica e de poco durare".[7] Thus, in the middle of the fourteenth century, when the leading cities were starting to conquer the smaller cities which were subjected to their "dominium", the idea of Rome as a support for Italian consciousness became the object of criticism.

I would like to discuss the fluctuations of this feeling of Italian consciousness from the end of the fourteenth century to the middle of the fifteenth. The period under consideration is marked by the conflict between the regional imperialisms, particularly those of Florence and Milan, which had been able, hitherto, to develop without coming into conflict, but which were subsequently obliged to fight in order to stabilise their possessions. In the decades of crisis at the end of the fourteenth century, when there was continual conflict between Florence and Milan, the propaganda arguments of both sides reveal an extreme sensitivity to the question of Italian identity. Later, as the political situation calmed down, the early fifteenth century seemed ready for the beginning of a regional, rather than Italian, identity. These efforts to sow the seeds of a regional patriotism in Tuscany (the case of Lombardy, in this respect, was different), and their failure, will be discussed below.

Italian consciousness during the establishment of the regional states.

The praise of Latin unity in the propaganda of the Visconti wars (1370–1402)

In the bitter struggle between Giangaleazzo Visconti, Duke of Milan, and the government of Florence towards the end of the fourteenth century, political propaganda was a weapon used without restraint.[8] Among the arguments put forward by the poets of the Milanese court was the possibility of Giangaleazzo Visconti acceding to the crown of Italy, as in the poem by Saviozzi di Sienna which states that the whole of Italy called him "padre" and hoped "incorare le tue benigne e precioze chiome".[9] Nevertheless, the idea of a royal coronation seemed just as likely to the Florentine enemies of the Visconti whose poets described the possibility as a disaster for Italy.[10] We can quote an anomynous poet from Arezzo who wrote: "E un signor avra Italia bella/che tanto e stata vedovella./De conte, duca e poi sara reale/un che é tiranno nella gran pianura".[11] The theme of unifying tyranny on which the Florentines based their counter propaganda shows that feelings of Italian consciousness were less important than that of liberty and that the nature of the political domination (in the event the republic as opposed to the tyranny/monarchy) is more important than the "nationality" of the leader.

On the other hand, the Milanese played the card of antiquity to show that the unity of the Italian peoples was worth a special effort. It was not for nothing that the humanist Antonio Loschi, then in the service of the Milanese government, recalled in one of his poems sent to Francesco Novello da Carrara, Lord of Padua, and one of the military leaders of the Visconti army fighting against Florence that the aim of the war was nothing less than the reconquest of Latin unity: "Onward, captains of the Duke, give the Florentines no rest. Fall on them like bolts of lightning. God wants the security of Italy and the peace which all latins desire".[12] It is also striking to note that the bulk of the works and the poems of this humanist concerning the affairs of the Visconti present the Visconti wars as being for Italy as opposed to Lombardy.[13] Thus, the defence of the peninsula remains a rhetorical reference (instead of being a political objective, whereas it is "only" a question of regional battles between two "imperialisms" for a local hegemony).[14] Even so, the Milanese make use of the pan-Italian theme, and draw all the possible consequences.

Consequently, they criticise Florence for calling upon foreigners, in this case the French, to help in their defence and running the risk of letting the wolf into the Italian fold.[15] In this context we can quote the remarkable letter of the Milanese anbassadors to the government of Venice:

> *Firenze contro ai costumi degli antichi, ha dato opera di far passare in Italia, Francesi e Tedeschi, nazione strane e barbare e inimiche del nome italiano, per inducere sopra le teste degl'Italiani coloro i quali la natura coll'opposizion delle Alpi, gli ha eschiusi dall'Italia. Ed e tanta la cecita del loro consiglio che non si intendono, se i Francesi o i Tedeschi si conducono in ytalia essere la commune ruina di tutti gl'Italiani, e non meno tornare sopra i loro capi che sopra le teste degli altri.*[16]

The importance given to the contrast between those from either side of the Alps and the implication that the Alps are a natural frontier are both arguments used to justify the claim that the Italians should not "wash their dirty linen in public".

Two comments can be made regarding this text: firstly, considering the Alps as a natural frontier was not an obvious point. We only need to recall the existence of Savoy, astride the alpine barrier, to be surprised by this argument (leaving aside Montferrat and the Duchy of Saluces, both feudal subjects of the French crown for at least part of the fifteenth century). Culturally and linguistically these regions were not always considered by the Italians themselves as being fully Italian. This is what Dante said in *De Vulgari Eloquentia*:

> *Consequently, [...] I say that these cities of Trente, Turin and also Alexandria are located so close to the borders of Italy that they cannot have a pure language...If our only game is the pure Italian we will not find its tracks in these areas.*[17]

Secondly, it is obvious that the advisors of the Duke, who are also the propagandists of his policies, base their arguments on the defence of an Italian consciousness which is above the level of the state. There is no question of praising a possible Lombard patriotism as opposed to a patriotism from Florence. The argument concerns the entire peninsula. Obviously, the Milanese would not run the risk of glorifying Lombardy in a letter to the Venetians aimed at obtaining their favourable neutrality. But even in the purely internal documents there is no sign of an attempt to glorify the region (by "region" is understood the political territory subject to the power of a single person, the Duke).

In 1397, in the same circumstances of diplomatic tension, Antonio Loschi became Chancellor of Milan and also wrote his "Invectiva in Florentinos". The text has been preserved in the reply given by the Chancellor of Florence, Coluccio Salutati, who quoted the arguments of the Chancellor of Milan point by point in order to refute them.[18] In his attack, Loschi had accused Florence of destroying the fatherland and of troubling the peace of Italy, to which Salutati replied by saying that it was necessary to define the word "fatherland":

> *What does devastating the fatherland mean other than ruining it? If, by fatherland, you mean ours (i.e. Florence), then you must certainly hope for it, but there is nothing to regret. If you mean Liguria, Flaminia and Venetia, which are oppressed by the yoke of your master, then please be sad, but don't blame him, and we wish you and your friends, destroyers of the fatherland, good fortune. But do not be sorry for the rest of Italy.*[19]

There is here a distinction between the Italian homeland, implied by the administrative names of the regions of Roman Italy of antiquity, and the "little" local or regional homeland, which is only a sub-unit of the former zone.

Loschi had also made fun of the Florentines who claimed to be the worthy heirs of antique Rome (*vastatores patriae et quietis Italiae turbatores*).[20] In reply, the Chancellor of Florence, going back to the ancient origins of the city, did his utmost to find its Roman ancestors showing that the city was a Roman construction which was shown by several monuments.[21] In this way, the Florentines, by the intervention of their Chancellor, also claimed their place in the joint Roman fatherland.[22] There is nothing to be seen, in the closing years of the fourteenth century, in the form of local feeling which would reduce the principal pride of being Italian, that is to say, a descendant of the Romans. Not, of course, that there is a lack of glorification of their city amongst the scholars and writers, but rather that the pride in this citizenship is associated to the feeling of having a shared antiquity, ("contro ai costumi degli antichi" was the expression used in the the letter of the Milanese quoted above) which seems more important than any localism.[23]

The feeling of Tuscan unity?

Nevertheless, in this reply of the old Chancellor of Florence there is a less well-known passage concerning the relations between leading cities and dominated cities which makes it possible to throw some light on the links between local and regional identity. The Chancellor of Milan criticised Florence for enslaving the cities which had fallen under its domination and for having replaced a local tyranny by an even greater oppression. Salutati replied in terms which are useful for our purpose.

> So the subjects which our city has organised, structured and torn from the hands of tyrants are oppressed by tyranny and deprived of their dignity ancient times? You believe that part of the people of Florence which is outside the city walls and which inhabits the rural areas and the towns and whose liberty you cannot imagine would rather, instead of being our subjects be subject to your master? What does being Florentine mean, if it is not being a Roman citizen, and so free and not a slave?[24]

So the subjects of the contado, which included prestigious cities like Arezzo, annexed in 1384, (not to speak of what was to be the symbol of the imperialism of Florence, the conquest of Pisa in 1406, just before the text of Salutati but which the leaders of Florence were already thinking about when the reply to Loschi was written) were supposed to feel Florentine first of all. This was an interesting comment which implies that the ruling elite thought the conquest of the outlying regions should be accompanied by a "policy of cultural integration".[25] Unfortunately, we can find no trace of this in practice since the citizenship of Florence remained a rare privilege, and the feeling of local attachment remained strong.[26] So we come back to the point of departure. The pride in being Florentine remained, for Salutati, a form of pride derived from the pride of being Italian and of being Roman.

Tentative efforts to establish a regional patriotism

The Florentine difficulties

The situation was to change somewhat in the early part of the fifteenth century, when Leonardo Bruni became Chancellor.[27] With him, Florence claimed a status of ideological independence and the pride of being Florentine replaced the glory of the Roman inheritance.[28] Besides, Bruni, in contrast to his master, Salutati, avoided stressing the liberties of Rome in his historical writings, preferring those of Florence. Several elements indicate this new direction. From his appointment as Chancellor to one of the most prestigious posts of the republic, Bruni made himself known as a zealot for city (he was in fact from Arezzo, the nursery of "Florentine" intellectuals), where he was to spend most of his career, by publishing a book in praise of Florence which was to become a classic throughout the fifteenth century – the *Laudatio Florentiae Urbis* (1404–1405).[29] Without going into the book in detail, we will simply note that one of its most important objectives was to break with the Roman tradition of the city, or, more exactly, to state that Rome was dead but that its spirit lived on on the banks of the Arno. It was no longer a question of filiation, but rather one of substitution.[30] The humanists from Milan, led by Pier Candido Decembrio in his *De Laudibus Mediolanensium Urbis Panegyricus* of 1435–36 as well as Lorenzo Valla (who can rightly be considered as a Pro-Visconti on this question: he had stayed in Lombardy on several occasions and was a member of the literary circle of Milan) were angry to see Bruni proclaim the death of Rome so as to be able to claim the inheritance. Valla, in a letter of 1436 sent to Decembrio, made exactly this point: "He (Bruni) wants Florence to be the heir of the empire of the people of Rome, as if Rome were dead, and Florence to be born from the best of the Romans."[31]

What interests us in this polemic is above all the attempt by Bruni to set up a Florentine identity which would thenceforth be cut off from the real geographic Rome and find its roots in a genetic or rather spiritual link and absorb the essential part of the heritage of antiquity. Are we not to see here the seeds of a patriotism entrenched in the land which is Tuscan before being Italian?[32] The Etruscan world was a prefiguration of the Florentine state, and Florence itself was born as a mixture of the two most famous Italian people, as Bruni wrote in his *Oratio in funere Johannis Strozzi* (Autumn 1427–May 1428).[33] In the *Laudatio*, Bruni, breaking with all traditions, was happy to state that in future any Italian would have a double patriotic dependence." Everybody throughout Italy has a dual homeland: privately, the homeland of each one of us and publicly, the City of Florence."[34] Florence, *altera Roma*!

In his *History of the Florentine People*, started in 1416, (note "of the Florentine people" and not "of Florence"; stressing the idea of "populus" is designed to indicate an equal status to the "populus romanus") he wrote, as a vigorous defender of his city and against the centralising monopoly of Rome:

> *Just as great trees can prevent young plants from growing taller, so the powerful city of Rome, crushing its neighbours by its grandeur, could not accept that any Italian city should grow more than she did.*[35]

We are now far from the claim of filial descent from Rome where Florence was but one of the offspring. If factual proof for this political point of view were required, we only need to recall that in March 1434, the Pope Eugene IV consecrated the *Duomo* of Florence, whose dome had just been completed by Brunelleschi a few weeks before. The significance of this new construction was given to us by the architect and humanist, Leon Battista Alberti, who was present at the ceremony: "(The dome) was such a massive structure, stood above the sky and was wide enough to cover *all the Tuscan people* (our italics) with its shadow."[36] It was no longer a monument to the glory of a city like the belfry of Giotto, but a symbol for the wider horizons of Florence. Could there be a better definition of Florentine annexationism in the fifteenth century?

The same Leonardo Bruni, when he was pontifical secretary, had gone very far in his determination to integrate the subject territories legally. As was often the case with the humanists, political opinions were stated after an examination of antique sources. In the case which interests us, it concerns a discussion on the meaning of *civitas* and *urbs* in a letter of February 1409 to his friend Niccolo Niccoli. *Civitas*, he says, defines the whole of the jurisdiction of a city, and not simply the urban area, so that an *urbs* can be quite limited but the *civitas* can be very extended.[37] From this legal doctrine Bruni rejected the usual distinction between city and *contado*, arguing that there was no contradiction between them.

In addition, the argument proves that for the ancients, the distinction was between citizens and foreigners and not, as we believe today, even if we do so through our incompetence, (in our degraded era our incompetence leads not only to a confusion regarding things but even of words) between citizens and inhabitants of the contado.[38]

Why struggle with words unless it is to prove that the inhabitants of the regions conquered by Florence (the *comitatini* according to Bruni) are well and truly an integral part of the Florentine citizenship? Lacking a Florentine identity in the wider sense, Bruni works towards a legal unification of the conquered regions to the city, making a clear break with previous medieval tradition and enlarging the frontiers of a city to those of a state.

A major doubt remains. Was this "Florentine consciousness" shared by those of non-Florentine origin? In other words, did the feeling of belonging to a Florentine fatherland spread in Tuscany in the early fifteenth century? It is almost impossible to reply to this question.[39] Nevertheless, it can be noted that certain non-Florentine intellectuals tended to accept this domination. This was notably the case of Antonio Ivani da Sarazana, typical of the humanists looking for a prestigious position in the major princely courts of the fifteenth century. While waiting for a post worthy of him, he was notary and Chancellor of Volterra, between 1466 and 1471, just before the ferocious suppression of the Volterran revolt by Lorenzo the Magnificent.[40] Immediately before the city was subdued he wrote a letter to his friend Sebastiano Borselli, who had stayed in the city, to comfort him. The following passage is worth noting:

If besides, you consider the whole political situation in Italy, you will see that a large number of towns and cities are governed by the judgement of certain people. Indeed, we must not consider it unworthy to be governed justly and usefully by the best princes.[41]

The recognition of princely regimes, here specifically the domination of Lorenzo the Magnificent, is based on the criticism of municipal government. But the evaluation is limited to the political principles of efficiency and justice. Once again, there is no trace of the emotion and the glorification of a regional imperialism which would lead to a local patriotism.[42]

The obstacles facing a Lombard patriotism

Similarly, the Milanese were not in a position to put forward a patriotic structure. They were faced by a dual difficulty. If they were to develop a local patriotism, they would have to create a pride based on a territory with well defined frontiers and, at the same time, benefit from a political regime legitimately established on that territory. However, the power of the Visconti, albeit strengthened by the grant of the title of Duke from Emperor Wenceslas in 1395, theoretically remained that of imperial representative in Milan. Even if the legal experts confirmed that this title now gave as much power in the territories concerned as the Emperor himself, it was nonetheless true that this power could not exceed that of the Emperor.[43] In addition the Emperor had a strictly reduced imperial power over the Lombard cities, defined constitutionally by the Peace of Constance in 1183 and signed by Frederic Barberousse and the Lombard League. Successive emperors had had to respect this situation. Some Lombard legal experts of the fifteenth century quoted this fundamental document to point out that the Visconti did not have the power to manipulate the rights of the cities as they wanted.[44] Over and above the delicate procedures by which the Visconti, Giangaleazzo first of all, were able to impose their control over the subject cities (in particular, by means of the nomination of first magistrates, the imposition of taxes or the control of episcopal nominations) it remains noteworthy Lombardy, despite being a unified territory, did not have a common feeling of unity.[45] This remained excluded as long as the cities, basing themselves on the rigid constitutional principles of the Peace of Constance, imposed their constraints. A citizen of Lodi, to reemploy an example used by a fifteenth century lawyer, could quite easily be under the authority of a magistrate nominated by the Visconti, even though the city of Lodi was fully able to defend its *jurisdictio* against the pressure of the lords of Milan and their representatives.

The various efforts of the Visconti to obtain the royal title by re-establishing the entity the *regnum Italiae or Lombardiae* as prior to the Peace of Constance could also be interpreted in this context as a way out of the constitutional paradox. This entity would be all the easier to present as a unified structure. It is not by chance that the politico-historical plan of the Sforza, the successors of the Visconti, was specifically aimed at restoring the former splendour of the Lombards, the founders of the *regnum Italiae*,[46] and at presenting the Visconti as their descendants. The Visconti themselves did not involve themselves in this kind of historical propaganda. Nevertheless, some of their most faithful supporters set out on a path not unlike that undertaken by Bruni in Florence. This was the case of the Augustinian friar, Andreas Biglia, a humanist and a historian who wrote a history of Milan under the Visconti.[47] In 1429 he pronounced the speech in memory of Giangaleazzo (who died in 1402), in which he defined what had been the function of the Duchy of Milan since the death of Giangaleazzo. Why, he wondered, should we love the house of the Visconti? He put forward several reasons. The first was:

> When before, in Italy, there were almost more kingdoms than cities and there was no space for liberty or dignity, it was they (the Visconti) who brought law and authority to this province. The result was that once the upstarts, or rather the brigands, were chased out or brought under control all the power was in the same hands.[48]

The construction of the regional Lombard state was here being highly praised as a source of order and justice, and, in particular, the annexationist policies of Milan were said to find their legitimacy in their ability to restore dignity and common liberties to all who were under their authority. Without going as far as Bruni, Biglia advanced the daring hypothesis of a unity of conquered territories by likening jurisdictional areas (*regna and oppida*) to simple dens of thieves which Giangaleazzo had eliminated. The second reason given for justifying the Visconti policy was the role of defender of Italy against invasions coming from across the Alps. "In my opinion, our foreign enemies would never have failed to invade Italy if this province had not had a single and powerful leader."[49] The argument this time is politico-military, but the author bases it on the idea of province blocking an indomitable extra-Italian otherness. In other words, Biglia glorifies the political unity of Lombardy without going as far as positing a Lombard patriotism. Italy remains for him an unavoidable geographic and emotional entity.

This incapacity to give rise to a patriotic feeling based on either a precise and defined political area or dynastic loyalty is all the more surprising in view of the period under consideration. The end of the fourteenth century and the beginning of the fifteenth was favourable to the emergence of such an awareness. The endless struggles between regional powers (Milan against Venice, Venice against Genoa, Milan against Florence) or the rivalries of foreign dynasties (Angevins against the Aragonese for the kingdom of Naples) could have destroyed any reference to a common Italy. This did not happen, despite feeble efforts like that of Bruni which remained too ideological or polemical to attract a following, especially, and this is the main point, since the political practices of the leaders adapted very well to intra-regional disagreements provided domination (dynastic or "republican") was respected. The second half of the fifteenth century, entirely characterised by a policy of (an unstable) balance of power between the regional powers was to see the return of a reinvigorated Rome (and papacy) as a rallying point of humanistic culture. Significantly, Flavio Biondi published his *Roma Instaurata* (1446) followed shortly by his *Italia Illustrata* (1453) which were presented as two aspects of the same glory.[50] At a deeper level, the complete diplomatic interaction of the leading Italian courts in the second half of the fifteenth century who shared (at least in principle) the same objective of keeping the foreigners, the French and the Germans, out of the peninsula contributed to giving a feeling of political unity to Italy *ante litteram*: a political cultural unity which was not to moulded into the form of a single state.[51] This contradiction between separated state apparatuses and an "Italian" cultural awareness (this awareness was at least shared by the humanistic *sodalitas* which is the only one we can examine) was certainly one of the weaknesses of the peninsula. It made Italy weaker still in the face of its powerful neighbouring monarchies who saw the peninsula as an area ripe for conquest.

Notes

1. See, for example, the letter of the Milanese ambassador, Otto di Caretto Francesco Sporza which reports that this statement was the political principle of Pius II (text in J. Combet *Louis XI et le Saint Siège*, Paris, 1903, p.221). Also see our article, 'Eléments pour une histoire de la gallophobie italienne à la Renaissance Pie II et la nation française', *M.E.F.R.M.*, 106, 1994, pp.275–311, and P. Gilli, *Au miroir de l'humanisme. Les représentations de la France dans la culture savante italienne à la fin du Moyen Age* (c.1360–1490), Rome, 1997.

2. For variations of this feeling during the late Middle Ages, see voir G. Galasso, *L'Italia come problema storiografico*, Turin, 1992, (réédition de l'introduction de l'A. à la *Storia d'Italia*, U.T.E.T., Turin, 1981), pp.49–53, about the use of *italicus* or *italiensis*. For Italian consciousness at a later period see, A. Tenenti, 'Profili e limiti delle realtà nazionali in Italia fra Quattrocento e Seicento', in *Id., Stato : un'idea, una logica*, Bologne, 1987, and Diana Webb, 'Italians and Others: Some Quattrocento Views of Nationality and the Church', in *Religion and National Identity. Papers read at the Nineteenth summer Meeting and the Twentieth winter Meeting of the Ecclesiastical History Society*, Stuart Mews ed., Oxford, 1982, pp.243–260, and P. Gilli, « L'impossible capitale ou la souveraineté inachevée : Florence, Milan et leurs territoires (fin XIVe–XVe s.) », dans *Les villes capitales au Moyen Âge, colloque d'Istanbul, juin 2005, actes du XXXVIe congrès de la SHMESP*, Paris, Presses de la Sorbonne, 2006, pp.75–95.

3. On Dante's references to Italy, see A. Cecilia et F. Brancucci, *Enciclopedia dantesca*, III, Rome, 1971, *s.v.* 'Italia'. On the cultural nationalism of Petrarch, apart from the *canzone* 'Italia Mia', see his last ideological battle against the French cistercian monk, Jean de Hesdin, *Invectiva contra eum qui maledixit Italiae*, de 1373 (on the topic, see P.G. Ricci, 'La cronologia dell'ultimo certamen petrarchesco', *Studi petrarcheci*, IV, 1951, pp.47–57); a French edition of that *certamen* is now available : Pétrarque, *Invectives*, Grenoble, 2003, translated by Rebecca Lenoir. For Cola di Rienzo's political image of Italy, see E. Rota, *Genesi storica dell'idea italiana, II*, Milan, 1948, pp.1–24. It should be remembered that one of the first actions of Cola, as tribune, was to grant Roman citizenship to all Italians. On that character, see A. Collins, *Greater than Emperor: Cola di Rienzo and the world of Fourteenth-Century Rome*, Ann Arbor, 2002.

4. All the same, the glorification of this Roman consciousness in the *Trecento* was partly in contradiction with the cultural tradition of the duecento which, against a background of

expanding communal cities opposed to any superior powers, be they imperial or ecclesiastical, was anchored in the demand for liberty, *i.e.* autonomy. The extreme form of this demand was the publication of the communal statutes which claimed with mixed success precedence over Roman law. The rejection was such that one can speak of the 13th century as the century without Rome (G. Toffanin, *Il secolo senza Roma. Il Rinascimento del secolo XIII*, Bologne, 1942).

5. Noël Valois, *La France et le grand schisme d'Occident*, I, Paris, 1896, pp.46–47. It should be remembered that several canonists and theologians from Avignon had revived in the fourteenth century the doctrine 'Ubi papa, ibi Roma', which was likely to weaken the 'historical' Rome: J. Gaudemet, 'Ubi papa, ibi Roma?', in *Roma fuori di Roma: Istituzione e immagini, Rome, Università degli studi 'La Sapienza'*, Rome, 1985, pp.69–80.

6. Benvenuto de Imola, *Comentum super D. Aligherii Comoediam*, éd. G. F. Lacaita, Florence, 1887, III, pp.184–85, quoted by r L. Cracco et G. Cracco, *op. cit.*, p.44.

7. Giovanni Villani, *Nuova Cronaca*, ed. G. Porta, Padova, 1990, XII, 90.

8. On this theme, apart from the essential Hans Baron, *The Crisis of Early Italian Renaissance. Civic Humanism and Republican Liberty in an Age of Classicism and Tyranny*, Princeton, 1959, see also A. Medin, 'I Visconti nella poesia contemporanea', *A. S. L.*, 18, 1891, pp.733–795.On the propaganda battles during the Visconti wars, see A. Lanza, *Firenze contro Milano. Gli intelletuali fiorentini nelle guerre contro i Visconti (1390–1440)*, Rome, 1991.

9. Nevertheless, it should be remembered that the title 'kingdom of Italy' was still understood in a traditional and historical sense to be that of the the kingdom of Italy of the Lombards, i.e. the padan Italy, Lombardy without Venetia. The Visconti, and later the Sforza, preferred the regnum Lombardiae to the regnum Italiae. At one time, Galeazzo Sforza, successor to Francesco Sforza, even suggested establishing a kingdom of Milan before accepting the idea of a kingdom of Lombardy. See D.M. Bueno de Mesquita, 'The Sforza Prince and his State' in *Florence and Italy. Renaissance Studies in Honour of Nicolai Rubinstein*, Denley Peter et Elam Caroline éds., Londres, 1988., p.168, n.32. *Rime di Cino di Pistoia e d'altri del sec. XIV*, G. Carducci ed., Florence, 1862, p. 590.

10. On Florentine concerns about the accession to royal status, see Cipolla, *Storia delle signorie italiane dal 1313 al 1530, Milan*, 1881, p.203.

11. Text of this anonymous poet from Arezzo edited in *Miscellanea francescana*, II, p.4, quoted by A. Medin, *op. cit.*, p.765.

12. On the details concerning the events and the composition of this poem, see V. Zaccharia, 'Le epistole e i carmi di Antonio Loschi durante il cancelleriato visconteo (con tredici inediti)', *Atti del Accademia nazionale dei Lincei*, série VIII, vol. XVIII, 1975, pp. 379–80. The letter was written between 1387 and 1392. Latin text in G. Da Schio, *Sulla vita e sugli scritti di Antonio Loschi*, Padova, 1858, p.65.

13. For the texts concerning Giangaleazzo, see V. Zaccharia, *op. cit.*, pp. 411–443.

14. On the imperialist aspects of the Florentine action in Tuscany, see R. Fubini, 'Classe dirigente ed esercizio della diplomazia nella Firenze quattrocentesca. Rapprezentanza esterna e identità cittadina nella crisi della tradizione comunale', in *I ceti dirigenti nella Toscana del Quattrocento*, Florence, 1983, p.147 sq., et W.J. Connell, 'The Commissioneer and the Florentine territorial state', *Ricerche Storiche*, 18, 1988, pp. 591–617. Those two papers show how deep was the imperialist process in Florence in the fourteenth-century, actually stronger than that of Milan, at least from 1384 and the acquisition of Arezzo.

15. It concerns the military alliance formed between Florence and France. On the same series of events, L. Mirot, *La politique française en Italie de 1380 à 1422, I, les préliminaires de l'alliance florentine*, Paris, 1934.

16. Florence, with the contempt of the habits of the Ancients got busy to make pass to Italy the French and Germans, foreign and cruel nations and enemies of the Italian name, to make carry on the head of the Italians all those which nature, by the opposition of the Alps, had excluded from Italy. And the blindness of their opinion is such as they do not understand only if the French and the Germans come to Italy, that will be the common ruin of all the Italians and that will weigh not less on their head that on that of the others", in G. Romano, 'Giangaleazzo Visconti e gli eredi di Bernabo', *Archivio storico lombardo*, 1891, p.76.

17. Dante, *De l'éloquence en langue vulgaire*, I, XV, 8, in Dante, *Oeuvres complètes*, trad. A. Pézard, Paris, 1965, p.584–85. This assessment should be compared with the poem *Italia mia* by Petrarch dealing with the *schermo* of the Alps which separates Italy from the Teuton terror.

18. Complete version of the *Invectiva in Florentinos* in D. Moreni, Florence, 1826.

19. I used the partial edition of Eugenio Garin in *Prosatori latini del Quattrocento*, Milan, 1952, p.12, which dates the *Invectiva* of Loschi at 1399 and the reply of Salutati at 1403 : 'Quid enim aliud est vastare patriam quam patriam exhaurire, ut, si de patria nostra sentias, optandum hoc esse tibi deceat, non dolendum? Si vero de Liguria, Flaminia Venetiaque, domini tui pressis iugo, forsan intelligis, doleas, obsecro, non reprehendas, optaque tibi tuisque partibus hostium patriae vastatores, nec reliquam ex hoc deplores Italiam.'

20. *Prosatori, op. cit.*, p.8.

21. *Ibid.*, p.20.

22. On the role of the Chancellor in the political life of Florence, and especially in Coluccio Salutati, see R. Witt, *Coluccio Salutati and his Public Letters*, Genève, 1976, et *Id., Hercules at the Crossroad. The Life, Works and Thought of Coluccio Salutati*, Durham, North Carolina, 1983.

23. For Florence, the chronical of Villani is a hymn to the greatness of the city; nevertheless for a more moderate reassessment of the chronical of Villani (and of its continuation by his brother Matteo) see Marvin B. Becker, 'Towards a Renaissance Historiography in Florence', in *Renaissance Studies in Honor of Hans Baron*, Florence, 1971, pp.141–173, which shows how faith in the permanent values of the city was gradually destroyed.

24. *Prosatori, op. cit.*, pp.30–31: 'Tyrannide ne suffocantur aut dignitate pristina spoliati sunt Florentinorum subditi, quos vel urbs nostra constituit atque fecit, vel de tyranorum manibus eruit aut recepit?'.

25. Julius Kirshner, 'Civitas sibi faciat civem': Bartolus of Sassoferrato's Doctrine of the making of a citizen', *Speculum*, 48, 1973, pp.694–713, and Id., 'Ars imitatur naturam. A Consilium of Baldus on Naturalization in Florence', *Viator*, 5, 1974, pp.289–331 These articles show the difficulties faced by someone of non-Florentine origin in obtaining legal and political integration in Florence, obsessed by family roots. Many decades after, francesco Vettori, fried of Machiavelli, was also to say that Florence managed its *contado* in a tyrannical manner (see C.C. Bayley, *War and Society in Renaissance Florence*, Toronto, 1961, p.277). As to the idea of 'municipe' used by Salutati, it must be taken in its antique sense: a city under Rome's power and without the right to citizenship. In most cases, the citizens of cities conquered by Florence who wanted to emigrate to the capital paid taxes to it for twenty years and had to spend thirty years there before becoming electors.

26. Throughout the *Trecento*, many Tuscan authors criticised the anexationist policies of Florence. See particularly the examples given by F. Tateo, 'I Toscani e gli altri', in *La Toscana nel secolo XIV. Caratteri de une civiltà regionale*, S. Gensini ed., Pise, 1988, pp.11–14. See also Marco Tangheroni, « Il secolo XIV », in Gabriela Garzella ed., Etruria, *Tuscia, Toscana. L'identità di una regione attraverso i secoli. II (secoli IV–XIV)*, Pisa, 1998, pp.121–132.

27. On this personality, one of the most important humanists of the fifteenth century, to whom H. Baron has already drawn our attention on several occasions, see *Leonardo Bruni cancelliere della*

Republica di Firenze, Convegno di Studi (Firenze, 27–29 Ottobre 1987), Paolo Viti éd., Florence, 1990.

28. This is what Anna Maria Cabrini notes in 'Le Historiae del Bruni: risultati e ipotesi di una ricerca sulle fonti', in *Leonardo Bruni cancelliere della Republica di Firenze, op. cit.* p.298.

29. See the recent articles by H Goldbrunner, 'Laudatio urbis: Zu neuren Untersuchungen über das humanistische Städtelob', *Quellen und Forschungen aus Italienischen Archiven und Bibliotheken*, 63, 1983, pp.313–328, and A. Santosuosso, 'Leonardo Bruni Revisited: A Reassessment of Hans Baron's Thesis on the Influence of the Classics in the Laudatio Florentine Urbis', in *Aspects of Late Medieval Government and Society. Essays Presented to J.R. Lander*, J.G. Rowe éd., Toronto-Buffalo-Londres, 1986, pp.25–51, and more recently, R. Fubini, '*La Laudatio Florentiae urbis* di Leonardo Bruni: immagine reale o programma politico?', in *Imago urbis. L'immagine della città nella storia d'Italia*, F. Bocchi and R. Smurra ed., Rome, 2003, pp.285–296.

30. See the comments of Hans Baron, H. Baron, 'The Changed Perspective of the Past in Bruni's Histories of The Florentine People' in *Id., In Search of Florentine civic Humanism*, I, Princeton, 1988, p.51, which discusses the copernician revolution of Bruni: the world stops revolving around Rome.

31. *Laurenti Valle Epistole*, Ottavio Besomi et Mariangela Religiosi éds., Padoue, 1984, p.161: 'Vult Florentiam esse heredem imperii populi romani, quasi ipsa Roma extincta sit, eademque progenitam ab optimis (p.162) illis Romanis, tanquam posteriores Romani non ab illis priscis originem ducant;'. Written in 1404–1405, the *Laudatio* got a new celebrity in 1435–1436, when the council of Basle was supposed to leave the imperial city; several Italian towns proposed themselves to welcome the Fathers, and tried to attract them through a campaign ; those *Panegyrici* were part of this strategy.

32. In addition, it is noteworthy that Bruni was also one of the first humanists to be interested in the Etruscan remains in Tuscany; a glorious period when the small cities of Etruria had not waited for the extension of Roman civilisation to flourish. On the 'Etruscan revival', see G. Cipriani, *Il mito etrusco nel Rinascimento fiorentino*, Florence, 1980.

33. Leonardo Bruni, *Opere letterarie e politiche*, Paolo Viti ed., Torino, 1996, p.714 : 'Natus est [Nanni Strozzi] enim in civitate amplissima atque maxima, lati dominii, summe auctoritatis, Etruscorum quidem civitatem sine controversia omnium principe, Italicarum vero nulli neque genere neque opibus neque magnitudine cuiquam secunda; ad cuius originem civitatis due nobilissime et potentissime totius Italiae gentes coierunt: Tusci veteres Italie dominatores, et Romani, qui terrarum omnium virtute sibi et armis imperium peperunt'.

34. L. Bruni, *Laudatio Florentinae urbis*, éditée par H. Baron, *Humanistic and Political Literature in Florence and Venice at the beginning of the Quattrocento*, Cambridge (Mass.), 1955, p.251 : 'Nec ullus est iam in universa Italia qui non duplicem patriam se habere arbitretur: privatim propriam unusquisque suam, publice, autem Florentiam urbem'. The idea of a double homeland goes back to the Justinian Digest where it is stated that any subject of the empire had two homelands, his city of origin (*propria communis*) and Rome (*communis patria*). Bruni made full use of the Roman legal tradition to the advantage of Florence.

35. Leonardo Bruni, *History of the Florentine People*, James Hankins ed., Harvard, 2001, p.16: 'Ut enim ingentes arbores novellis plantis iuxta surgentibus officere solent nec ut altius crescant permittere, sic romanae urbis civitatem maiorem in modum crescere patiebatur'.

36. Leon Battista Alberti, *De la peinture*, trad. J.L. Schefer, Paris, 1993, p.69.

37. Leonardo Bruni, *Epistolario*, L. Mehus ed., Florence, 1746, I, p.78 : 'licet urbs ipsa parva fuerit, civitas nichilominus maxima et amplissima fuisse potuerit', quoted by R. Fubini, 'La rivendicazione di Firenze della sovranità statale e il contributo delle 'Historiae' di Leonardo Bruni',

in *Leonardo Bruni cancelliere della repubblica di Firenze. Convegno di Studi (Firenze, 27–29 ottobre 1987)*, Florence, 1990, pp.51–52.

38. *Ibid.* :'Probat insuper ratio, quod apud veteres distinctio sit inter cives et peregrinos, non, ut hodie facimus, ineptissime quidem sed tamen facimus (imperitia enim non solum rerum, sed etiam verborum omnia in hac temporum faece confundit) inter cives et comitatinos'. For the legal discussion see the comments of R. Fubini, quoted above.

39. Probably, for the Tuscans of the *contado* of Florence, the feeling of belonging to a homeland was hardly to be distinguished from questions of taxation. It should however be pointed out that the state of Florence was the best run of all the Italian states of the time, and wasn't destroyed 'in a night' like the Visconti'Empire in 1402 and 1447. L. Martines, 'Firenze e Milano nel Quattrocento. IL ruolo dei giuristi', in G. Chittolini ed., *La crisi degli ordinamenti comunali e le origini dello stato del Rinascimento*, Bologne, 1979, p.218 sq ; and above all, S.K. Cohn, *Creating the Florentine State: Peasants and Rebellion*, 1348–1434, Cambridge, 1999, on the resistance to the Florentine conquest and domination. See also Patrick Gilli, 'L'impossible capitale ou la souveraineté inachevée: Florence, Milan et leurs territoires (fin XIVe–XVe siècle)', dans *Les villes capitales au Moyen Âge, XXXVIe Congrès de la SHMESP, Istanbul, 1er-6 juin 2005)*, Publications de la Sorbonne, 2006, pp. 75–95.

40. Some years ago, Riccardo Fubini drew attention to this personality (whose collected letters exceed 700 in number, but who is best known for his *Historia de Volterrana Calamitate*) in 'Antonio Ivani Sarzana: un teorizzatore del declino delle autonomie comunali', in *Egemonia fiorentina ed autonomie locali nella Toscana nord-orientale...*, Pistoia, 1978, pp.113–174. On this episode, see E. Fiumi, L'impresa di Lorenzo de' Medici contro Volterra (1472), Florence, 1948.

41. Quoted by Riccardo Fubini, 'Antonio...', p.113 : 'Si recte praeterea considerabitis universum Italiae statum, intelligetis urbium et oppidorum ingentem numerum gubernari arbitrio paucorum. Non enim videtur indignum quam a clarissimis principatibus aeque utiliterque reguntur'.

42. But note the comment of Ivani: 'Esse enim aliquid ac esse potestis [the inhabitants of Volterra] colendo populum Florentinum. Illarum [sc. Tuscan towns dominated by Florence] vero plures ad nihilum sunt redactae' (in R. Fubini, *op. cit.*, p.157).

43. See the *consilium* de Baldus, (*Consilia*, Venice, 1580), quoted by J.W. Black, 'The limits of Ducal Authority: A Fifteenth-Century Treatise on the Visconti and their Subject Cities', in *Florence and Italy. Renaissance Studies in Honour of Nicolai Rubinstein*, P. Denley et C. Elam eds., London, 1988, p. 150.

44. J.W. Black, *op. cit.*, p.153; see nevertheless the contrary opinion of G. Barni, 'La formazione interna dello stato visconteo', *Archivio storico lombardo*, I–IV, 1941, pp.48–51.

45. On this last point see L Prodoscimi, who underlines the period of the great schism and crisis in the establishment of ducal control over ecclesiastical nominations in Lombardy by means od the 'placet' of the duke 'Chiesa e istituzioni ecclesiastiche a Milano di fronte alla formazione dello stato territoriale', in *Id., Problemi di storia religiosa lombarda*, Milan, 1969, pp.92–95; more recently M Ansalmi, 'La provvista dei benefici (1450–1466). Strumenti e limiti dell'intervento ducale', in *Gli Sforza, la chiesa lombarda, la corte di Roma*, G. Chittolini ed., Milan, 1989, pp.1–88, who shows the permanent search for an agreement by the Sforza with the pope for a sort of beneficial concordat.

46. The Visconti did not order this historical work which praised the antique kingdom of Italy. The work was undertaken by the Sforza, especially at the time of More who asked Giorgio Merulla to write a history of the Visconti which would have this family shown as descendants of the Lombards and call for the creation of vast monarchy in the region : G. Merula, *Historia Vicecomitum*, col 65, : 'Liber V. Reperitur Vicecomitum origo Vicecomitum gentem a regibus

Longobardorum prognatam satis constat.', in J. Graevius, *Thesaurus Antiquitatum et Historiarum Italiae*, t.III, part.I, Lugduni Batavorum, 1704. On that book, see Gary Ianziti, *Humanistic Historiography under the Sforzas. Politics and in Fifteenth-Century Milan*, Oxford, 1988.

47. E. Cochrane, *Historians and Historiography in the Italian Renaissance*, Chicago, 1981, p.111.

48. G. Romano, 'Un giudizio di A. Biglia sulla funzione dei Visconti e del ducato di Milano', *Bollettino della società pavese di storia patria*, XV, 1915, p.140 : 'quum antea Italia plura paene regna haberet quam oppida neque libertati aut dignitati locus esset, hi primum in hanc provinciam cuiusdam auctoritatis nomen aut ius intulere. Unde factum est ut, dissipatis ac sublatis regulis, aut, si verius dicendum est, latronibus, universa res in unam dominationem concesserit.' Note that the identification of local tyrants with buglars is a biblical theme (*Book of Kings*, 4, 24, 2).

49. *Ibid.*: 'Atque ut sententiam meam proferam, numquam deerunt peregrini hostes qui Italiam invadant, si non haec provincia unum atque eundem potentem ducem habuerit'.

50. See the contribution of V. De Caprio, 'Illuc hanc urbem Romanam esse ubi curia sit', in *Letteratura italiana, Storia e geografia, II, l'età moderna*, I, Torino, 1988, pp.335- sq.

51. Paolo Margaroli, 'L'Italia come percezione di uno spazio politico unitario negli anni cinquanta del XV secolo', *Nuova rivista storica*, LXXIV, 1990, pp.517–536. The author does not fail to show how much the theme of excluding the foreigners from Italy plays a federating role in the foreign policies of the peninsula; but it also shows the contradictions in this refusal of foreign intervention, as in the letter of the Doge of Venice to the ambassador of Francesco Sforza at Venice where the Doge says, regarding the refusal of Genoa to ally with France in 1458 that an agreement with the King of France is better than an agreement between Genoa and the King of Naples : 'Non voressemo che Gienova havesse preso altro partito, si pur quando dovendolo pigliare nuy stimemo che questo del re di Francia sia lo manco reo ch'el habia possuto pigliare per li fatti nostri d'Ytalia' (p.534). This is also what Vincent Ilardi has shown concerning a later period : 'Italianità among some Italian intellectuals in the Early sixteenth Century', *Traditio*, XI, 1956, pp.339–367.

Part Four

Region and City

Chapter Twelve

The City of London and the British regions: from medieval to modern[1]

Ranald Michie

Introduction

A cuckoo in the nest or the jewel in the crown? These two expressions neatly express the highly divergent views on the economic relationship between the City of London and the regions of Britain. From the perspective of many the City of London is not a British financial centre. Though physically located within Britain, the activities of the City of London were driven by international flows of credit and capital. These made it unresponsive to the needs of the rest of Britain.[2] The influential commentator, Anthony Sampson, summed up this view when he concluded that the City was "...more like an offshore island than part of the United Kingdom."[3] Such a view of the City of London was not confined to the late twentieth century for it was extended back in time. The City of London was seen to have always had a strong international orientation, particularly towards the Empire, and became increasingly remote from the rest of the British economy. Over time a process was at work in which the autonomous regional financial markets within Britain lost their distinct identity, being absorbed into an integrated national market within which the City of London was the dominant element. As the City of London served global financial markets Britain's own economic self-interest was sacrificed as a consequence.[4]

Conversely, there are those that argue that London was the engine of growth for the British economy and that the country's economic performance was dependent upon the international success of the City of London. A recent report commissioned by the Corporation of London concluded that "...London's success has contributed to continued development, and stimulated growth, throughout the rest of the country."[5] By then London was closely identified with the financial sector. An investigation commissioned by the British government had identified the City of London as one of the foremost financial clusters in the world and thus one of the most competitive.[6] It was estimated that those employed in the City of London, though only 1.25 % of the UK labour force in 2001, generated 3.5 % of Gross Domestic Product, and did so by exporting at least half the services they provided.[7] This more positive judgement on the City of London's contribution to the British economy has also been extended back in time. For the early modern period a positive relationship has been suggested,[8] while those investigating the British economy's performance over the nineteenth and twentieth centuries have recently concluded that the City of London did meet the financial needs of businesses located in the regions, despite the views of contemporaries.[9] However, what has not been investigated is the continuous long-term relationship between the City of London and the British regions.

Medieval, 1000–1500

Financial activities were already of growing importance in London in the Middle Ages. Not only was it necessary to finance London's own trading relations at home and abroad but London was also the seat of government and home to many of the aristocracy, and their needs had to be met.[10] Even in the medieval period London also provided financial services for the country as a whole and, over time, these reached more and more remote corners of the Kingdom, became more varied in what was provided, and intensified in terms of the degree of contact. The prime function that the City of London provided for the medieval English economy was the finance of international trade. Medieval London acted as the interface between all of England and the world economy in terms of financial flows. Without the services provided by the largely foreign merchant bankers in London England's international trade would have had to be conducted on the basis of payments in gold and silver. As these were in limited supply the result would have been to greatly reduce the amount of foreign trade taking place, with serious consequences for the development of the English economy. Furthermore, with their experience in international commerce and the access they had to funds, London merchants were also ideally placed to undertake the finance of domestic trade. By the thirteenth century London merchants had established a leading, though not dominant role in the finance of inland trade, and this grew in reach and extent over the fourteenth and fifteenth centuries. Nevertheless, important as these London activities were most of the medieval economy's financial requirements were conducted locally.[11]

Early modern, 1500–1750

During the early modern period financial activities became more important within the City of London.[12] A prime focus remained the needs of London's own large, expanding and wealthy population. These were not only London's permanent residents but also the wealthy aristocrats from throughout England who now had their own houses in London. The City also continued to provide the government with funds when it needed to borrow, especially because of the endless wars. However, a presence in London was required for any person wishing to utilise either the banking facilities it provided or the market in securities it offered. The direct finance of economic activity remained a primarily local affair with the City's role remaining confined to London, government and trade.[13] As London continued to dominate English exports and imports throughout this period, the financing of this trade was virtually monopolised by merchant bankers located in the City of London. Thus the City continued to act as the interface between England and the wider world in terms of financial transactions. In addition to that international role the City of London came to dominate the finance of internal trade in this period. From the fifteenth century onwards the inland bill of exchange became the means through which the inter-regional movement of goods within Britain was financed and this was organised from London. By the seventeenth century the City was at the centre of a dense network of financial connections while the London money market exerted a dominant influence over the British economy by the beginning of the eighteenth century. This ensured that abundant and cheap credit was provided for internal trade and that remunerative outlets were provided for idle funds. In turn this contributed to both the ongoing process of specialisation within Britain and the mobilisation of savings for productive use, so making an important contribution to nationwide economic growth. However, much was also lent to the government whose needs were driven by military not civil requirements.[14]

Industrial Revolution, 1750–1850

Despite the economic vitality of the regions during the Industrial Revolution London continued to grow both in absolute terms and relative to the rest of the country.[15] The City continued to focus ever more on financial activities in response to growing demands within London. The growing habit of even the lesser gentry having homes in London, or visiting it regularly for prolonged stays, meant that the City's financial services were used extensively by those from elsewhere in Britain. With gradual improvements in transport and communications it became easier to visit London or to do business there by post, so that City bankers and stockbrokers increasingly established contacts farther and farther from London. It was only in London that were to be found many specialised financial services.[16] The strong connections between London and the regions that existed during the Industrial Revolution is most clearly seen in the development of the well-organised correspondent system within banking. Banks in the City of London built up a strong network of links to individual banks and bankers located throughout Britain, and through these connections flowed either money or bills of exchange. Those banks located in areas where surplus funds built up, such as in rural areas once the harvest had been sold, sent money to their London correspondent, who paid them interest on the deposit. Conversely, those banks located in expanding industrial areas faced an excessive demand for credit and so sold the bills of exchange, which represented the loans they had made, to their City correspondent. These deposits and bills were then matched within the London money market.[17]

Though banking provision became increasingly widespread in Britain during the eighteenth century the resulting provision of credit was mobilised and directed from the City of London.[18] However, this did not mean that the City of London was instrumental in financing the development of the British economy during the Industrial Revolution. As in the past most financial arrangements remained local and even personal. Even the provision of major infrastructure projects like canals in the late eighteenth century or railways in the 1840s drew heavily on local sources of finance. Housing, for example, was undertaken using local savings organised on a local basis. Instead, the City of London's principal focus remained the finance of trade, both internal and external, and raising finance for the government, especially during times of war.[19]

Financial integration, 1850–1914

Between 1850 and 1914 financial services grew in importance not only in London but in every region. This was in response to rising incomes and growing wealth. It was in this period that provincial centres such as Manchester and Liverpool acquired significant financial sectors as they now possessed a sufficient number of wealthy individuals so as to justify the provision of the specialist financial services (see table 1). In 1800 stockbrokers, for example, were to be found only in London but by 1900 they were operating in numerous towns throughout the British Isles, while all the major cities had their own stock exchange.

Table 1. Regional employment in financial services: share of total employment in each region, 1851–1971[20]

Region	1851	1881	1911	1951	1971
London	0.11%	0.63%	2.1%	5.0%	9.3%
South	0.06%	0.33%	1.4%	1.5%	3.4%
Midlands	0.05%	0.27%	1.0%	1.1%	2.5%
North	0.05%	0.36%	1.2%	1.5%	2.9%
Wales	0.04%	0.27%	1.0%	1.3%	2.4%
Scotland	0.05%	0.42%	1.1%	1.5%	2.9%
Britain	0.06%	0.38%	1.3%	2.0%	4.0%

The result appears to suggest a dispersal of financial activities with London losing its domination. Certainly London's relative share of national employment in financial services appears static between 1851 and 1911 while that of the rest of the South of England declines (See table 2).

Table 2. Regional employment in financial services: share of each region in the national total, 1851–1971

Region	1851	1881	1911	1951	1971
London	21.4%	24.1%	22.9%	39.6%	39.8%
South	29.0%	20.1%	24.3%	19.2%	21.8%
Midlands	14.7%	10.4%	11.0%	9.7%	10.5%
North	19.9%	28.0%	27.9%	20.9%	18.6%
Wales	3.9%	3.6%	4.4%	3.1%	2.7%
Scotland	11.2%	13.7%	9.4%	7.5%	6.6%
Britain(total)	5,694	48,444	242,456	435,121	952,170

However, this dispersal was only taking place where there was a need to locate financial services close to the customer as was the case with retail banking and broking. That did not mean that the City of London was losing its position as the dominant financial centre of Britain. In insurance, though provincial insurance companies were large and active, from the late nineteenth century onwards a succession of mergers gave London based companies an increasing dominance.[21] In banking those banks based in the City took increasing control over the entire system, replacing the informal correspondent links with formal networks of branches. A succession of mergers from the 1890s onwards, and the switch of head offices from Birmingham to London by Lloyds Bank and the Midland Bank in the 1880s, led to the creation of a small number of banks controlled from the City but with branches spread throughout the country.[22]

Increasingly the City of London played a growing role in the mobilisation and direction of investment within Britain. Not only did the railways look to the City for capital but so did all the larger regional companies. However, in the City these domestic demands for capital had to compete with others coming from abroad such as foreign railways and overseas mining. Half of all securities listed on the London Stock Exchange in 1913 were foreign.[23] It was this diversion of such a large proportion of Britain's wealth abroad, and the consequences it was believed to have had for the British economy, that has attracted the unfavourable views on the City of London. However, detailed investigations of the connections between the City and the British economy have revealed strong and flexible links.[24] What emerges is how wide-ranging and sophisticated was the London capital market in London at that time. In addition, the continuing vitality of regional capital markets within Britain ensured that much of the finance of business was still conducted on a local or even personal basis, and never reached London.[25] Though it might appear that the growing centralisation of the British capital market in the City of London between 1850 and 1914 diverted funds overseas that would once have been invested in the regions, this does not appear to have been the case. Foreign investment was largely funded out of the money previously directed towards the government which had spent it on war. If the government had chosen to borrow between 1815 and 1914 as in the past the National Debt would have grown by £5.2 billion. That was sufficient to fund completely both the capital costs of the British railway system (£1.3 billion by 1914) and the entire outflow of funds abroad (£ 4.1 billion by 1914).[26]

Economic nationalism, 1914–1939

The First World War ushered in a new era for the City of London because it transformed the open, liberal and relatively stable world economy within which it operated. In its place came one in which government controls and regulations were much more prominent and political, economic, financial and monetary instability was much more prevalent. One consequence of this was to lessen the international orientation of the City of London and emphasise instead its position as a British financial centre. As London and the South-East remained relatively prosperous in the 1920s and 1930s this was where the growth in demand for financial services was to be found. At the same time continuing improvements in transport and telecommunications meant that it was increasingly possible to supply a financial service on a nationwide basis from a City office. The result was both the extension of City based financial services to more and more distant parts of the country and a slow migration of financial services to London from other parts of the country.[27] This increased engagement with the British economy between the wars was reflected in the balance between domestic and foreign business in the City of London. In the London money market domestic business now dominated, especially short-term government borrowing.[28] A similar pattern was observable in the London capital market with many City merchant banks turning to domestic finance, especially in the face of competition from New York for international business. Issues of domestic securities in London rose from 18 % of the total in 1913 to 82 % between 1934 and 1938.

Between the wars the City became the place where British business, wherever located, increasingly obtained the finance it required as that gave it access to the national pool of savings.[29] Despite this domestic orientation there was a common view that the City of London remained detached from the rest of the British economy.[30] To contemporaries it appeared that the City was gaining at the expense of regional financial centres when the reality was that all were suffering in different ways from worldwide economic problems, especially in the 1930s. This belief was to have serious consequences for the City after the Second World War.[31]

Government control, 1939–1979

During the Second World War aerial bombardment destroyed around one third of the built-up area of the City and forced the dispersal of much of the business that was conducted there. When the war was over there was no desire by the government to see the City physically restored as it was vulnerable to bombing, while many were convinced that London's growth had been achieved at the expense of other parts of Britain. The planning controls that came in with the Second World War thus coincided with a post-war policy that sought, deliberately, to prevent the further growth of London, including the City.[32] Until the late 1970s deliberate attempts were made by the government to restrict building in the City of London.[33] However, as the City was located within the most prosperous part of the country and the government's own monetary and financial requirements were huge, financial services still clustered there.[34] Financial services grew in importance within London and its share of the national total remained in 1971 at the one-third achieved by 1951 (see tables 1 and 2). Nevertheless, there was a steady departure of those financial activities in the City that did not require a physical location near each other or the markets. The South-West was a favoured locations for insurance companies. There was also a general move to relocate back office staff out of scarce and expensive City locations but still within easy reach.[35] Generally, the immediate post-war years found the City of London greatly circumscribed by the continuation of government controls, which limited its external operations and forced it to focus on domestic opportunities.[36] Though the degree of control exerted by the government was gradually lessened in the 1950s the pace of liberalisation was a slow one.[37]

From the late 1950s onwards the international position of the City of London began to change because of developments abroad. Restrictions imposed by the government of the United States drove business to London because of ties of language, law and convenience. As a result the City became increasingly popular with foreign banks and brokerage houses. These foreign banks and brokers conducted their business in US dollars on behalf of non-British clients, creating in the City of London a dollar based financial centre during the 1960s and 1970s. However, the City did not stop being a British financial centre at this time. The major players in the City remained the British commercial and investment banks, along with the London Stock Exchange, and their focus remained overwhelmingly domestic. What was happening was a simultaneous external and internal attack on the British element in the City at this time. The external attack was driven by the foreign banks and brokers that rapidly multiplied in the 1960s and 1970s. It was they that dominated the City's international business. At the same time there was a regional attack on the City, which came both from provincial stock exchanges and the building societies. The competition faced by the London Stock Exchange from its provincial counterparts was resolved through a merger of them all in 1973. However, the competition from the regionally based building societies remained. Through their rapidly expanding branch networks and their low cost office operations, these building societies were taking both saving and lending business from the City based national banks.[38]

Liberalisation, regulation and globalisation: 1979 onwards

With the abolition of exchange controls in 1979 the separation between the internal and external components of the British financial system came to an abrupt end. The removal of these controls seemed to act as a catalyst for wholesale change, which was already underway because of the growing competitive pressures faced by the British firms in the City. With the ending of exchange controls not only did the City become an even more attractive base from which to conduct an international business but the foreign banks and brokers located there could now compete for domestic business on the same terms as their established British rivals. Conversely, British banks and brokers could now expand abroad, whether in terms of their own business or the investments they handled. There was a radical re-ordering of the hierarchy within the City as many of the leading British commercial and investment banks were taken over by foreign firms or were challenged by new domestic competitors, such as the merged Halifax Building Society and the Bank of Scotland (HBOS).[39] The very success of the City as a global financial centre also accelerated the exodus of those domestic activities that could not afford the high rents and salaries that went with a City location. The result was that the City of London focussed ever more on the most specialist branches of financial activity, and especially those that necessitated a location closer to each other and the markets. Whereas only 32 % of those employed in banking in Britain in 2002 were to be found in London, the proportion rose to 62 % when it came to securities broking and fund management[40] (See Table 3).

Table 3. Financial employment in the City of London, 1995/2001[41]

Category	Number in 1995	Number in 2001	Percentage Change
Domestic Banking	26,900	15,000	-44%
International Banking	16,100	23,000	+43%
Domestic Securities Trading	14,400	15,000	+4%
International Securities Trading	13,500	36,000	+167%

Though many have suggested that the result for the City of London was that it became hi-jacked by external interests and so neglected domestic finance, especially the needs of those distant from London, investigations reveal, instead, a close and continuing link between the City and British business. Foreign owned banks and brokers, for example, were heavily involved in domestic financial activities whether it involved operations on behalf of the government or business, such as raising loans, structuring corporate finance, dealing in money and securities or managing funds.[42] What was taking place in the wake of the ending of exchange controls not only in Britain but generally was a globalisation of financial activity. The nationality of the bank or broker mattered much less to the client than the service it provided. Within this process the City of London gave Britain a major competitive advantage because it possessed not only the deepest and broadest financial markets but also a depth and range of financial expertise virtually unrivalled in the world, and certainly in Europe. What the City could offer as a financial centre was unique not only within Britain but in the world and thus it alone was able to respond to the growing opportunities that existed for international financial services by the late twentieth century.[43]

In contrast to the interwar and immediate post-war years, the growth of the City of London, from the 1960s onwards, was not achieved at the expense of other financial centres in Britain. Instead it was achieved through its ability to meet the need for specialist financial services in an increasingly integrated global economy. Though the City's success skewed the nature of Britain's financial sector, and made Britain dependent upon the performance of the global economy, it also produced positive benefits for the British economy, including areas far distant from London.

This contribution came through the demands generated by the businesses located in the City and those who worked there as well as the taxes paid there, which were spent nationally.[44] Nevertheless, the outcome was that the financial services sector in Britain was heavily dominated by London and its surrounding areas (See Table 4).

Table 4. UK financial services: regional share by value added, 2000[45]

Region	Share of total value added in each region	Share of value added in the UK
London	11.2 %	32.7%
South	16.0%	32.3%
Midlands	7.0%	9.3%
North	11.7%	15.2%
Scotland	4.7%	6.9%
Wales	3.4%	2.4%
Northern Ireland	3.0%	1.2%

In the wake of this regional distribution of the financial services sector came disparities in regional prosperity because of the ability of the financial sector to generate a large amount of well-paid employment. Thus the widespread tendency to see a connection between the clustering of financial activity in the City of London and the prosperity of that region compared to others in Britain is valid. However, the explanation for those disparities was not to be found in any failure by the City of London to finance economic activity in the regions or a preference for overseas investment. Rather it was due to the fact that the City of London was able to provide the world with a service that was in increasing demand and could not be easily replicated anywhere else in the world. As Hamnett rather reluctantly concluded in a recent study of London, "The conclusion seems to be that there are very few, if any, economic safe havens in the modern world, but that it is better to be over-reliant on the growth sectors than the declining sectors".[46] As with cotton textiles in Lancashire, woollen textiles in Yorkshire, pottery in Staffordshire or shipbuilding in the North East the City of London could offer a speciality that, for a time at least, could not be matched and so prospered as a result.

Conclusion

Over the centuries the City of London exerted a growing control over the British financial system with its reach both broadening and deepening over time. Nevertheless, a large part of the financial system remained outside the orbit of the City of London, especially the finance required to undertake most branches of economic activity such as agriculture, mining, manufacturing, construction and housing. Instead, the City's role was confined to the finance of trade, the finance of government, and providing the financial services required by the very wealthy. There was not a radical change in this position before the First World War, despite the transformation of transport and communications and the pervasive role played by City based banks, insurance companies and other financial intermediaries. The very vitality of regional financial centres, because of widespread economic success, kept the City at bay. It was the collapse of much of the City's international activities from 1914 onwards, and the economic depression suffered by regional economies dependent upon global markets, that transformed the position of the City of London within Britain, These events, along with the growing power of central government, simultaneously undermined regional financial centres while boosting the City's domestic involvement.

By the 1950s the City of London had become domestically focussed, hemmed in as it was by exchange and trade controls. This was despite policies that tried to force a re-location of financial activity to the regions. Within government policy there was a conflict between polices that promoted dispersal and centralisation, and the latter emerged as the clear winner. However, this was to change yet again when the City re-emerged from the 1960s as a global financial centre due to events in other parts of the world. One consequence of that globalisation was the further spread of City activities to the regions, in search of cheaper office space and clerical support. Despite this global role the City of London remained a British financial centre though much of its activities no longer took place in the City, or even London, or were conducted by British firms or British staff. Instead, there had been a merging of regional, national, European and global so that financial services were increasingly provided by firms focussed on meeting the needs of their customers whether this involved retail operations in every town or international operations in wholesale money markets.

The relationship between the City of London and the regions was thus an evolving one and one prone to discontinuities through wars, revolutions in communications, and changes in government policies. The relationship was also a two-way one. The regions gained enormously through the role played by the City as an inter-regional and international interface and the employment and mobilisation of savings and investment. The regions also gained where they could undercut City activities on cost or profit from the restrictions placed on City institutions and markets. Conversely, the regions lost when their financial activities proved uncompetitive with those in the City or when regional savings sought more attractive openings elsewhere as they had no monopoly over finance.

Notes

1. This chapter draws heavily from previous publications. The most relevant are as follows: *The City of London: Continuity and Change since 1850* (London, 1992); " London and the Process of Economic Growth since 1750", *The London Journal*, 22 (1997); "Friend or Foe: Information Technology and the London Stock Exchange since 1750", *Journal of Historical Geography*, 23 (1997); *The London Stock Exchange: A History* (Oxford 1999); "The Changing Relationship between the City of London and the British Government in the Twentieth Century" in R.C.Michie and P A Williamson (eds), *The British Government and the City of London in the Twentieth Century* (Cambridge, 2004).

2. See R. Roberts and D. Kynaston, *City State ; How the markets came to rule our world* (London, 2001).

3. Anthony Sampson, *Who Runs this Place? : The anatomy of Britain in the 21st century* (London, 2004) pp. 242, 252.

4. See, especially, P.J. Cain and A.G. Hopkins, *British Imperialism* 2 volumes (London, 1993), B. Robson "Coming full circle: London versus the rest, 1890–1980" in G. Gordon (ed.), *Regional Cities in the UK, 1890–1980* (London, 1986).

5. Oxford Economic Forecasting, *London's Linkages with the Rest of the UK* (London 2003), Foreword by Michael Snyder.

6. M.E. Porter and C.H.M. Ketels, *UK Competitiveness: Moving to the Next Stage* (DTI Economics Paper No.3, May 2003) pp. 22, 40.

7. Lombard Street Research, *Growth Prospects of City Industries* (London, 2003) p. 20.

8. E.A Wrigley, "A Simple Model of London's Importance in Changing English Society and Economy, 1650–1750", *Past and Present*, 37 (1967).

9. F. Capie and M. Collins, *Have the Banks Failed British Industry?* (London, 1992).

10. D. Keene, "Medieval London and its Region", *London Journal*, 14 (1989) pp. 99–101, 103–6.

11. For the medieval period see C.M. Barron, *London in the Later Middle Ages: Government and People, 1200 –1500* (Oxford, 2004) pp. 10–16, 45–6, 62–3, 76–117; Center for Medieval and Renaissance Studies (eds), *The Dawn of Modern Banking* (Los Angles, 1979) – Blonquist, Prestwich, Bergier, Riu, Munro.

12. Sir Peter Hall, *Cities in Civilization: Culture, innovation, and urban order* (London, 1998) pp. 116–121; J. Alexander, "The Economic Structure of the City of London at the end of the seventeenth century", *Urban History Yearbook*, 1989.

13. B.G. Carruthers, *City of Capital: Politics and Markets in the English Financial Revolution* (Princeton, 1999) pp. 64–5; D.C. Coleman, "London Scriveners and the Estate Market in the late 17th Century", *Economic History Review*, 4 (1951/2) p. 230.

14. E. Kerridge, *Trade and Banking in early Modern England* (Manchester, 1988) pp. 47–84, C. Goodhart, "Monetary Policy and Debt Management in the United Kingdom: some historical viewpoints" in K.A. Chrystal (ed.), *Government Debt Structure and Monetary Conditions* (Bank of England, 1999) annex 2.

15. J. Langton, "The Industrial revolution and the regional geography of England". *Transactions: Institute of British Geographers*, 9 (1984) pp. 162–3, 511; D. Gregory, "The production of regions in England's Industrial Revolution", *Journal of Historical Geography*, 14 (1988) pp. 55–6, 173, D. Barnett, *London, Hub of the Industrial Revolution: A revisionary history, 1775–1825* (London, 1998) pp. 13–17, 32–9.

16. L.D. Schwartz, *London in the Age of Industrialisation: Entrepreneurs, labour force and living Conditions, 1700 –1850* (Cambridge, 1992) pp. 14, 154, 233, 261.

17. I.S. Black, "The London Agency System in English Banking, 1780–1825", *The London Journal*, 21 (1996) pp. 112, 127; I.S. Black, "Geography, political economy and the circulation of finance capital in early industrial England", J. Historical Geog. 15 (1989) p. 381; I.S. Black, "Money, Information and Space: Banking in early nineteenth century England and Wales", *J. Historical Geography*, 21 (1995) pp. 403, 410.

18. S. Shapiro, *Capital and the Cotton Industry in the Industrial Revolution* (Ithaca, N.Y., 1967) pp. 60–1, 84–99, 152–5.

19. Barnett, *London*, pp. 127–132; M. Ball and D Sunderland, *An Economic History of London, 1800 –1914* (London, 2001) p.42, S Chapman, *Merchant Enterprise in Britain: From the Industrial Revolution to World War 1* (Cambridge, 1992) pp. 30, 76, 83, 181–2.

20. The data for tables 1 and 2 is taken from C. H. Lee, *British Regional Employment statistics, 1841–1971* (Cambridge, 1979). The years 1851 and 1881 are drawn from the A series of tables and 1911, 1951 and 1971 from the B series. Unfortunately, both series significantly undercount employment in financial services. Financial occupations are allocated to other categories, such as accountants to professional and scientific services or simply not classified as with stockbrokers. Thus the statistics on financial services are largely confined to banking and insurance and thus omit those in the City of London with more diverse employment. (Commercial occupations in the City do even worse as dealers, merchants, and the like are allocated to such sectors as food, drink and tobacco, textiles, or metal goods. The category of Distributive Trades is largely retail in composition as it ignores those in wholesale occupations.) London includes Middlesex throughout. The South excludes London and Middlesex. As the data comes from the census returns, which is based on place of residence not work, the large numbers commuting into London are not counted among its numbers. Finally, employment data will not capture the higher value added from financial employment in the London compared to those in the regions, as is revealed by the relative wealth of City bankers and brokers. Thus the tables give no more than an indication of the regional distribution of financial services, and will undercount the relative importance of the City of London.

21. H.A.L. Cockerell & E. Green, *The British Insurance Business 1547–1970* (London, 1976) pp. 25, 29, 62.

22. E.W. Nevin & E.W. Davies, *The London Clearing Banks* (London, 1970) pp. 81, 105.

23. Michie, *London Stock Exchange*, p. 88 and Michie, *City of London*, pp. 72, 74.

24. K. Watson, "Banks and Industrial Finance; The experience of brewers, 1880–1913" *Economic History Review*, 49 (1996); F. Capie and M. Collins, *Have the banks failed British industry? An historical survey of bank/industry relations in Britain,1870–1990* (London, 1992).

25. T.Suzuki, *Japanese Government Loan Issues in the London Capital Market 1870–1913* (London, 1994).

26. Michie, *London Stock Exchange* pp. 88–9; Goodhart, *Monetary Policy*, annex 2.

27. S.E. Thomas, *British Banks and the Finance of Industry* (London, 1931) p. 258; R.J. Truptil, *British Banks and the London Money Market* (London, 1936) pp. 136, 167, 176, 187, 199, 287; A.T.K. Grant, *A Study of the Capital Market in Post-war Britain* (London, 1937) p. 223; S. Diaper, 'Merchant Banking in the Inter-war Period: The Case of Kleinwort, Sons & Co.' *Business History*, 28 (1986) pp.56, 59–60, 64, 73–4.

28. R. Roberts, "The City of London as a financial centre in the era of Depression, the Second World War and post-war official controls" in A. Gorst, L. Johnman and W.S. Lucas (eds), *Contemporary British History*, 1931–61 (London, 1991) p. 68.

29. R.C. Michie, "The London Stock Exchange and the British Economy, 1870–1939" in Y.Cassis (ed.), *Capitalism in a Mature Economy* (London, 1989); R.C.Michie, "The London and provincial stock exchanges, 1799–1973" in D.H.Aldcroft and A.Slaven (eds), *Enterprise and Management* (Aldershot, 1995); C. Trebilcock, "Phoenix : Financial services, insurance and economic revival between the wars" in P.Clark and C.Trebilcock (eds), *Understanding Decline* (Cambridge, 1997).

30. J.R. Jarvie, *The Old Lady Unveiled : A criticism and an explanation of the Bank of England* (London, 1933) pp. 44–5.

31. S.V. Pearson, *London's Overgrowth and the causes of Swollen Towns* (London, 1939).

32. D.L. Foley, *Controlling London's Growth: Planning the Great Wen*, 1940–60 (Berkeley, California, 1963) pp. 18, 24.

33. P. Cowan *et al.*, *The Office: A Facet of Urban Growth* (London, 1969) pp. 132, 148–9, 162, 166, 265.

34. Hall, *Cities in Civilization*, pp. 899, 923.

35. Michie, *City of London*, p. 170.

36. J. Fforde, *The Bank of England and Public Policy, 1941–1958* (Cambridge, 1992) pp. 695–7; Roberts, "The City of London", pp. 69–72. See J.H.Dunning and E.V.Morgan, *An Economic study of the City of London* (London, 1971).

37. P. Einzig, *A Textbook on Foreign Exchange* (London, 1966) p. 17.

38. C.R. Shenk, "The origins of the Eurodollar market in London, 1955 – 1963" *Explorations in Economic History*, 35 (1998); R. Fry (ed.), *A Banker's World: The revival of the City, 1957–1970* (London, 1970).

39. Michie, p. 93.

40. London School of Economics, London's place in the UK economy 2003 (London, 2003) p. 61.

41. Lombard Street Research, *Growth Prospects of City Industries* (London 2003) p. 47.

42. See N.Dimsdale and M.Prevezer (eds) *Capital Markets and Corporate Governance* (Oxford, 1994).

43. City Research Project, *London's Contribution to the UK Economy: Special Report* (London, 1993) p. 12.

44. See H.M.Treasury, *The Location of Financial Activity and the Euro* (London, 2003).

45. Oxford Economic Forecasting, *London's Linkages with the Rest of the UK* (London, 2004), Table 5.1.

46. C. Hamnett, *Unequal City: London in the Global Economy* (London, 2003) p. 47.

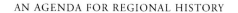

Chapter Thirteen

A city apart: Liverpool, Merseyside and the North West region

John Belchem

In chronicling popular music from the Cavern to the Coral, Paul Du Noyer celebrates Liverpool as *Wondrous Place*, the title of a minor US hit, covered by Ron Wycherley, a Teddy boy tugboat worker from the Dingle, better known as Billy Fury. An important figure in the immediate pre-history of the Beatles, Fury exemplified the trans-Atlantic and other cosmopolitan influences which had long flourished in the great western seaport, home base of the slick "Cunard Yanks".[1] "To be in Liverpool, especially near the docks, is to realise", a journalist wrote in the 1880s, "how closely we are connected with the Americans, and how near we are to America itself. The names of the streets are full of reminders; the speech to which we listen, the names on the signboards, all combine to make us think of our neighbours on the other side of the way."[2] Indeed, in its abbreviated history, multi-ethnic demographic profile and cityscape appearance, late Victorian Liverpool invited comparison with developments across the pond, having risen from obscurity to become, as the International Exhibition of Navigation, Commerce and Industry in 1886 attested, "a wonder of the world. It is the New York of Europe, a world-city rather than merely British provincial".[3] A leading world port, the least "English" of the great provincial Victorian cities (hence perhaps its exclusion from Asa Briggs' selection), Liverpool stands apart from the narrative frameworks and paradigms of national history. While it can be incorporated into international comparative socio-economic and demographic analysis of port cities with dependent labour markets, long distance in-migration and exposure to infectious disease,[4] Liverpool's distinctive cultural character is best captured through more specific comparison with other "edge" cities, de-centred major ports like Naples and Marseille with similar "second city" pretensions and picaresque reputations. Du Noyer describes Liverpool as "a sort of sunless Marseille", defiantly non-provincial, the capital of itself:

> *It's deeply insular, yet essentially outward-looking: it faces the sea but has its back turned on England. There were local men for whom Sierra Leone was a fact but London only a rumour. They knew every dive in Buenos Aires, but had no idea of the Cotswolds. And Liverpudlians speak with merry contempt for their Lancashire neighbours, displaying all the high indifference of a New Yorker for Kansas.*[5]

The proverbial exception in national historiography, Liverpool, then, is no less out of place within a regional framework. In the north of England but not of it, Liverpool was (and has continued to be) highly distinctive, differing sharply in socio-economic structure, cultural image and expression, political affiliation, health, diet and speech from the adjacent "woollyback" industrial districts:

Woollybacks come from Woollydom, in the North of England… a land of cobbled streets, mills, pits and flat caps, where men are fed on pie and mushy peas, black-pudding and tripe; a land where men prize their pigeons, worship their whippets and fondle their ferrets; a land where men are bred not merely born. Wackers are the inhabitants of the city of Liverpool – famed for their humour, football, dockers and judies. Wackers eat scouse and wet nellies. Wackers and Woollybacks are tough yet warm breeds. Although both are Northerners, they are different in many ways; culture and traditions and even language divides them.[6]

In caricature, stereotype, soap opera and scholarship, Liverpool stands apart in images, representations and understandings of the north. Situated on the right side of the Runcorn Bridge, Liverpool is undoubtedly in the "near north". Viewed along a different cultural axis, it is the western gateway to the northern way, the trans-Pennine urban corridor leading from celtic mysticism, a Liverpudlian speciality, to eastern Anglo-Saxon rationality.[7] Although by no means excluded from Dave Russell's recent scholarly investigation into northern England and the national imagination, Liverpool seems far distant from its "Lowryscape" images, from the bracing moors, plain-speaking, commonsensical down to earth folk and hard honest graft always to be found when "looking north".[8] Closer to home, Liverpool sits no less awkwardly within the ill-defined sub-region of Merseyside, a geo-political construction far from coterminous with the city's hinterland which extends over cultural and natural boundaries to include much of North Wales. In its brief existence as an English metropolitan county council – not a happy period in Liverpool's recent history – Merseyside was ridden with cross river and cross-county tensions while excluding from its boundaries genuine scousers (as wackers have come to be called) rehoused in overspill towns like Runcorn and Skelmersdale.[9]

A kind of "city state" in its Victorian heyday – Roscoe's "Florence of the north" – Liverpool defined itself against grimy industrial Manchester and in rivalry with commercial metropolitan London. The "second city of empire", Liverpool transcended the national urban hierarchy, but having risen so high, it had further to fall. Seen in historical perspective, the failure to incorporate contiguous Bootle in the early years of the twentieth century, the end of plans for a "Greater Liverpool", marked the symbolic beginning of decline, allowing Glasgow to assume the mantle of "second metropolis".[10] The Edwardian years, however, were a glorious climacteric, with civic celebrations to mark the dual success of Liverpool in the League and Everton in the F.A. cup in 1906; the "historical pageant" in 1907 to commemorate the 700th anniversary of the granting of letters patent to the borough; and iconic transformation of the Pier Head with the construction of the "three graces", the Mersey Docks and Harbour Building (1907), the Royal Liver Building (1911) and the Cunard Building (1913), the photogenic sea-facing skyline by which Liverpool remains instantly recognizable and has recently acquired UNESCO World Heritage site inscription. After the First World War, Liverpool's fortunes tumbled. A major export port, it was hit disproportionately hard by world-wide depression as trade declined more rapidly than production. Throughout the 1930s the local unemployment rate remained resolutely above 18 %, double the national average.[11] Even so, Merseyside was not designated as a depressed area in the legislation of 1934. Liverpool found itself disabled within interwar discourse of unemployment and economic policy. Priority was accorded to the problems of the industrial north and other distressed manufacturing areas, while efforts to regain comparative advantage as the world's clearing house were exclusively centred on the city of London. Having to come to terms with its distinctive and accentuated structural problems, Liverpool of the depression made itself heard through humour. When asked why Merseyside produced so many comedians, Arthur Askey famously replied: "You've got to be a comic to live in Liverpool."[12] Thereafter with the collapse of the colonial economic system and global restructuring, Liverpool's descent appeared unstoppable, accentuated by the propensity of industrial combines, attracted by the post second world war exercise in economic diversification, to close their new Merseyside plants once development aid and other short-term advantages were exhausted. Here, of course, Merseyside militancy – a myth in the making – helped to justify a board-room decision taken far away from Liverpool.[13] Political concern shifted from regional development to urban regeneration as Liverpool, once the great "beat city" of the 1960s, transmogrified into the "beaten city" of the Thatcherite decades, the "shock city" of post-industrial Britain – a "showcase" of everything that has gone wrong in Britain's major cities'.[14] Test-bed and laboratory for a series of ill-fated social inclusion experiments, Liverpool and its immediate environs, the nebulous "sub-region" of Merseyside, qualified by seemingly irreversible descent for European Union Objective One funding in 1993, the level of GDP per head having fallen to only 73 % of the European Union average.

Liverpool, then, would seem a city part, out of place in a volume on regions and regionalism in history. Studies of its remarkable rise and fall have tended either to apply supra-national models, as in sociological deployment of globalisation theory to explain the collapse "from world city to pariah city"[15] or to insist (sometimes with defiant Merseypride or by what journalists have misinterpreted as mawkish self-pity) on its urban exceptionalism.[16] To the consternation of those unfamiliar with the "wondrous place", Liverpool is currently on the up, boosted by the award of Capital of Culture and UNESCO World Heritage status, factors which should help to sustain its belated urban renaissance. A comparative latecomer to regeneration through conservation, cultural tourism and civic boosterism, Liverpool is being re-badged as Liver-"cool", the trendiest of northern cities.[17]

These introductory observations prompt a number of questions. Did regional factors play any role in Liverpool's rise and fall? Will its current renaissance as creative and cultural city of consumption have any regional impact? Will 2008 see Liverpool acting as a "capital" of culture for the benefit of its sub-region and beyond, or will it be merely a "city" of culture with the benefits (cosmetic and otherwise) largely restricted to those who can afford and adjust to living in its "heritage" city centre?

Regional factors were important in the early stages of Liverpool's tardy rise from insignificance but were soon outweighed by global considerations. The narrative structure of Ramsay Muir's history, written to commemorate the 700th anniversary in 1907, divided Liverpool's past into two phases: the gradual removal of natural and other obstacles to its development within the region; and its subsequent exponential growth into a great world port with a dock system, seven and a quarter miles long, "the most stupendous work of its kind that the will and power of man have ever created", quite without rival "anywhere in the world". Throughout "long centuries of small things" Liverpool had been "nullified" by "a combination of adverse circumstances": "a poor and thinly peopled surrounding country; isolation; great physical obstacles to inland communication; a lack of natural waterways; a successful rival long established and close at hand."[18] While Chester silted, Liverpool benefited from regional infra-structural development in waterways, canals and turnpikes, to become "the supreme transportation node of the North West", prompting an "industrial efflorescence" which was however, as Langton noted, "as brief as it was spectacular".[19] Instead of exploiting such regional industrial dominance, Liverpool sought wider comparative advantage, identifying its prosperity with commerce not manufacture. Led by the enterprise, vision and commercial acumen of its corporate body, sponsors of the innovatory wet-docks system, Liverpool quickly surpassed all other Atlantic ports, becoming in the process the slaving capital of the world. Keen to maximise returns on the "town dues" and the corporate estate, the council continued to improve and enlarge the dock system, assuring Liverpool's supremacy as the great emporium of British commerce.[20] Lucrative dock development was accompanied by de-industrialization: waterfront craft industry was driven far away, to be followed by heavy industry as Liverpool chose not to exploit its regional near monopoly hold of raw materials, particularly coal, from the "inner ring" of its hinterland. A great seaport and commercial centre, the would-be "modern Tyre", Liverpool underwent exponential growth from the central waterfront, attracting long-distance migrants, primarily the Irish, but also significant numbers of Welsh and Scots, expanding outwards in a cultural vacuum to urbanise an area largely without previous geographical and occupational identities.[21] Beneath the skilled city trades and the booming commercial services sector, the casualism of the docks facilitated ready ease of entry. Here indeed the swelling numbers of long-distance migrants (most pressing, of course, at the time of the Irish famine) may have exercised a "crowding out" effect, limiting the extent of in-migration by poor labourers in agricultural areas adjacent to Liverpool. Then there were the unsettled transient poor, caught in a "curious middle place". Disoriented by lack of funds for further travel, poor Irish migrants, Jews and other "moving Europeans" found themselves unexpectedly stuck in Liverpool, the human entrepôt for trans-continental emigration, linking the old world and the new.[22]

All this was very different from the pattern of growth in northern industrial cities. These industrial conurbations grew out of conglomerations of small towns and villages, augmented by short-distance rural in-migration which tended to reinforce their culture, character, status (and speech patterns) as regional centres. The urban speech of Manchester-Salford and Leeds-Bradford differed from that of the surrounding countryside, but it remained speech of the same kind. By contrast, long distance in-migration transformed Liverpool, setting it apart from its environs: through Celtic and other inputs, scouse was to evolve as a new and different language and culture, alien to the inhabitants of surrounding parts of Lancashire and Cheshire.[23] In the absence of surrounding (and/or single industry) out-townships, Liverpool lacked the autochthonous cultural legacies and "structural" foundations upon which northern industrial dialect was readily constructed. The obscure Dicky Sam apart, there was no Liverpudlian equivalent of such long-established identity figures and subsequent dialect heroes as Tim Bobbin, the Lancashire weaver, or Bob Cranky, the Geordie pitman. In the absence of "indigenous heritage", Liverpool became "the creation of its immigrants".[24] Its distinctive scouse accent – by general consent "a mixture of Welsh, Irish and catarrh"[25] – owed much to the multi-ethnic, mainly Celtic inflow.

In the competing and conflicting inflexions of celticism in Liverpool, Scots and Welsh in-migrants – generally of a higher socio-economic status than the locally born – await full scholarly investigation (as does the Liverpool Manx community).[26] Attention has focussed on the Liverpool Irish, irremovably located at the bottom of the social, occupational and residential hierarchy, a kind of under-class, as it were, unable, unwilling or unsuited to take advantage of opportunities elsewhere in Britain or the new world. It is "Irishness" of this order – immobile, inadequate and irresponsible – that has purportedly set Liverpool and its notorious social problems part. With characteristic inverted pride, Liverpudlians have chosen to adopt not to contest this crude stereotype. The unadulterated image of the lowly Irish "slummy", reckless and feckless, has been adopted as the foundation character in recent writings in popular history and working-class autobiography, a symbolic figure of inverse snobbery and pride in the evolution of the true Scottie Road scouser.[27]

Beyond the "inland" Irish Sea, Liverpool's private Celtic empire, the great seaport looked to the oceans, adding an external dimension to the city's cultural life and its migrant mix. The "community" mentality of the Liverpool-Irish Scottie-Road "slummy" co-existed with a broader culture, a seafaring cosmopolitanism (still celebrated in Liverpool 8 bohemianism) which made Liverpool particularly receptive to (unEnglish) foreign ideas (syndicalism, for example) and to American popular music.[28] Cosmopolitanism – "the world in one city" to cite the strapline of the successful Capital of Culture bid – has always been a point of Merseypride, a means of eradicating the stigma of the slave trade and of raising Liverpool above mere provincialism. Significant numbers of Kru, Lascar, Chinese and other sea-faring communities within and beyond the "black Atlantic" were drawn to the port by the opening up of new markets and routes after abolition of the slave trade.[29] "Unlike the dwellers in most English towns", the *Liverpool Critic* observed in 1877:

> *...all of us in Liverpool are, to a great extent, citizens of the world, for everything around us tells us of far-off countries and foreign ways, and in our midst are constantly natives of so many distant lands that we insensibly imbibe and learn to practice(sic) peculiarities not British.*[30]

In an effort to draw attention away from sectarian strife, the *Liverpool Catholic Herald* celebrated the multi-cultural components of Edwardian Liverpool: "the great seaport contains within its area a mixture of races the like of which no other industrial community in the North of England can furnish".[31] However, this precocious multi-cultural demographic profile (a pattern not found in other British cities until the later twentieth century) was not to benefit Liverpool's "proto-typical" pattern of race relations. Identification with non-white groups was transient, restricted to a specific period of cultural hybridity and fusion in the city's "diaspora space".[32] A cultural intersection on the geographical margin, Liverpool is thus a critical site for investigation not only of regional, national and ethnic identities – northern, English, British and Celtic – but also of whiteness and racial constructions.

A favourite port of call for African-American seamen where they enjoyed, Herman Melville recorded, "unwonted immunities", waterfront Liverpool catered (as Dickens discovered) for a vast floating, migrant and casual population.[33] Merging imperceptibly into the Irish "north end", it differed markedly different from other British urban settings, more akin to Five Points, New York (also visited by Dickens), with its "syncretic" fusion between Irish and black culture.[34] Among the more notorious parts of the north end was "Blackman's Alley", the polite sobriquet for the network of streets and brothels where migrant Irish women, in the absence of factory or other regular employment, secured a niche market in the sex industry, servicing "black" sailors ("dark Jack" to use Dickens' terminology), the "numerous negroes always present in Liverpool as ships' cooks, stewards, seamen and labourers."[35] By the beginning of the twentieth century, however, the north end had become no-go territory for blacks. Henceforth, it was the segregated "locale" of the Liverpool-Irish.

This major transformation has not featured in Liverpool's rich but flawed demographic history. Census statistics have been deployed as "hard" evidence for a positivist case study in the paradigmatic "urban transition", placing Liverpool ahead of other cities in its "modern" spatial segregation in which distinct areas took their character and identity from the socio-economic status of the residents with subsidiary variables such as position in the family life cycle, and ethno-sectarian affiliation.[36] Studies of sectarian violence have highlighted disputed borders between "green" and "orange",[37] but the inviolable boundary which kept "black" distant and apart awaits investigation. Obscured from the census, "China town", "dark town" and "other alien quarters" were all located at some distance from the epicentre of Edwardian Irish Liverpool.[38] "Negroes, Chinese, Mulattoes, Filipinos, almost every nationality under the sun" were to be found in the south end, but they seldom ventured into the north end.[39] "Blacks" lived apart (for their own protection) in Toxteth, the "New Harlem of Liverpool".[40]

While the new spatial geography confirmed the Irish as white, it also facilitated their assertion of ethnic difference. The Liverpool-Irish became white and green simultaneously as it were. Reinforced by electoral geography (the Scotland Division was to be T.P. O'Connor's parliamentary fiefdom for over four decades, complemented by the American style machine politics of local Irish nationalist councillors)[41] and by the pattern of Catholic church-building and infrastructural provision, the north end became almost exclusively Irish and Catholic, giving spatial meaning and protection to the hyphenated identity of the Liverpool-Irish. Where working-class Catholics elsewhere in the north-west were drawn either to the national Labour Party or to the regionally-based Catholic Federation,[42] the Liverpool-Irish remained firmly committed to the local Irish nationalist political machine. Having passed into the hands of second generation (i.e. Liverpool-born) Irish, this unique cross-class formation displayed less interest in the fate of Ireland than in the immediate needs of the local Catholic community in housing, employment and education. Efforts to implant a strictly Gaelic "Irish-Irish" culture failed to resonate. Although "apart" in the north end, the Liverpool-Irish had no desire for such cultural withdrawal and autarky. Perfecting their talents in "popular" sports and entertainment through parish leagues within their own "colony", they took delight in beating the British in open city and county-wide competition at their own games – while hurling tournaments had to be postponed or abandoned for lack of teams, referees and spectators, the Liverpool-Irish delighted in the soccer triumphs of the Old Xaverians, not least in defeating the Liverpool Casuals before a crowd of 5,000 at Goodison Park to secure the Lancashire Amateur League in 1903.[43] While built upon primary loyalties, sport led to engagement with wider urban and regional affiliations, such as the involvement of the Catholic Institute in the Merseyside League, an early use of the cross-river term. The pattern of support for the two professional football teams developed a logic of its own, apparently irreducible to ethno-sectarianism, producing an overarching loyalty to the city, although the *Liverpool Catholic Herald* could not conceal its delight when Everton defeated Liverpool 5-0 in October 1914.[44]

While the Liverpool-Irish were to enrich and all but appropriate "white" scouse "Scottie Road" culture (just as they were to capture the local Labour party after the Irish settlement) Liverpool blacks remained apart. Classified as aliens, although often subjects of British colonies, they suffered institutionalised racism (augmented by the notorious Elder Dempster agreements) in inter-war employment practices in the merchant marine.[45] Concentrated (if not marooned) in parts of Toxteth, they lacked the public funds, assistance and multi-cultural pieties that were later to be made available to post Second World War immigrants from the new commonwealth. So far from a register of integration, inter-marriage was condemned as miscegenation, the "social problem" which, having preoccupied inter-war academics and eugenicists, continued to compound what the Gifford Inquiry described as Liverpool's "uniquely horrific" racism.[46] Without a place in mainstream narratives, they are now claiming a specific identity as Liverpool-born blacks, an hyphenated affiliation which reflects no credit on Liverpudlian exceptionalism.

The Toxteth riots of 1981, an indictment of exclusion, deprivation and discrimination, brought Liverpool to the forefront of political attention, hastening the policy shift from regional development to urban regeneration (already embraced by Merseyside County Council in its Stage One Report of 1975, probably the first British planning document to employ the concept).[47] Whether implemented through deregulation and the private sector, or by quangos or direct central government intervention, Thatcherite regeneration initiatives were conducted at the expense of local government. A kind of experimental test-bed, Liverpool had one of the first Enterprise Zones (in Speke in 1981), the first Task Force (the Merseyside Task Force), one of the first City Action Teams (in Granby and Toxteth), one of the two first-generation Urban Development Corporations (the Merseyside Development Corporation, 1981-98), and the first National Garden Festival Site (1984). In the midst of these initiatives, Merseyside County Council, the city-regional tier of government, was abolished in 1986. Once Militant captured control of the moribund Labour party machine, the Catholic caucus having been undermined by slum clearance and relocation to outer Merseyside and beyond, the City Council restricted its regeneration strategy to the renovation and rebuilding of certain parts of the municipal housing stock. The rigid socialism of Militant eschewed any civic boosterism and allowed no concessions to the associational endeavours and representational needs of black, gender, special interest and minority groups. Regeneration was a pious and cruel irony throughout the 1980s as employment and population fell by 23 and 12 % respectively. Seemingly irreversible economic and demographic decline spiralled Liverpool down into European Union Objective One status in 1993, the first major conurbation in an old industrial region to be so defined.[48]

In recent years, the trend seems to have been reversed, encouraged by new mechanisms of partnership and a new dispensation (and modernised) structure of local government in the city, now under the control of Liberal Democrats "almost more 'New Labour' than 'New Labour' itself."[49] The most striking feature is the promotion of "urban living": the stunning conversion of warehouses, lofts and old office buildings has seen the population of the city centre itself increase some fourfold in the 1990s, providing bijou accommodation for affluent young professionals, miles away in every sense from the deprived outer estates. Helen Walsh, the latest literary voice to uphold the L8 bohemian tradition, has written disapprovingly of the new-look city centre and its pretensions:

> *There are new bars, coffee shops and restaurants cropping up all over the place. I don't like it. The city is starting to take on the guise of a salesman who lacks faith in what he is selling. Artificial. Insincere. A barrage of plush eateries bought by drug money and pseudo gangsters who lack the erudition to pull it off.*[50]

Although a group of sacked dockers cannily decided to pool their severance pay to invest in a city centre bar, planners have questioned whether a renaissance built on leisure and entertainment can be sustained. While the average household income in Liverpool is just 79% of the national figure, Liverpool will need to attract shoppers and tourists from the wider region and beyond to succeed as city of consumption. Clearly, Liverpool has to get things right by 2008: it must serve as a genuine "capital" of culture (and consumption) for the north west region and beyond, but it runs the risk of being merely a "city" (centre) of culture of little resonance and relevance to most of Merseyside. The "world in one city" proffers an empowering social imaginary of a city that through partnership forms of governance has overcome political and social conflict and found social harmony in diversity. However, other social meanings and realities suggest that celebration of diversity might well accentuate intra-regional, ethnic and socio-economic inequalities.

It is much to be hoped that this latest "renaissance" will prove more enduring, inclusive and empowering than previous attempts to revise Liverpool's image and fortunes. When public opinion hardened against the slave trade, Liverpool tried to rehabilitate itself through renewed emphasis on cultural capital, undergoing a second stage of the "urban renaissance" which had earlier established the infrastructures and organizations of polite society throughout eighteenth century Britain.[51] Deeply imbued with classical references and legitimacy, the new "Liverpolis", dedicated to commerce, culture and civilisation, sought to underpin the superiority of Liverpool gentlemen (merchants and scholars in the Roscoe mould) over Manchester men. Despite ongoing civic improvement and pioneer exercises in public health reform, Liverpool, the "black spot on the Mersey", failed to sustain Roscoe's vision.[52] Mercenary attitudes prevailed, a culture of capital oblivious of higher things: indeed, mercantile support for the Confederate South suggested that little had changed since the philistine commercialism of the slave trade. The culture of civilized commerce, Ramsay Muir rued, remained restricted to a Liberal minority, a socially exclusive (predominantly Unitarian) elite – an aristocracy of wealth and letters, as Hazlitt had initially designated them – lacking in political influence and popular resonance. Their heritage awareness, as evinced in Philip Rathbone's call for recognition of "the political value of art to municipal life", went unheeded:

> It is for us, with our vast population, our enormous wealth (as a town) but without either politics or philosophy, that the world will care to preserve, to decide whether we will take advantage of our almost unequalled opportunities for the cultivation of Art, or whether we shall be content to rot away, as Carthage, Antioch and Tyre have rotted away, leaving not a trace to show here a population of more than half a million souls once lived, loved, felt and thought. Surely the home of Roscoe is worthy of a better fate?[53]

Even so, Muir was able to close his 700th anniversary history in optimistic mood as Edwardian Liverpool at last recognised and invested in its "civic obligations":

> The city which, at the opening of a new age, is simultaneously engaged in erecting a great cathedral and a great university, is surely no mean city. It is building for itself twin citadels of the ideal, a citadel of faith and a citadel of knowledge; and from the hill which once looked down on an obscure hamlet, and which later saw ships begin to crowd the river, and streets to spread over the fields, their towers will look across the ship-thronged estuary, monuments of a new and more generous aspiration.[54]

Muir's confidence was of course disastrously misplaced, but as the city celebrates its 800th anniversary, there is surely a need for commensurate idealism, vision and commitment In the absence of any major millennium memorial, and with the subsequent abandoning of plans for tramways, a "fourth grace" and other *grands projets*, prospects are not promising, however welcome the cosmetic café-bar make-over of the city centre as it prepares to become European capital of culture.

Notes

1. Paul Du Noyer, *Liverpool: Wondrous Place. Music from the Cavern to the Coral* (London, 2002).
2. 'Our Towns and Their Trades: no. xii –Liverpool', undated cutting, c.1887 in Newspaper Cuttings, 1886–1920, Liverpool Record Office.
3. 'Liverpool: Port, Docks and City', *Illustrated London News*, 15 May 1886.

4. W.R. Lee, 'The socio-economic and demographic characteristics of port cities: a typology for comparative analysis?', *Urban History*, 25 (1998), pp.147–72.
5. Du Noyer, *Wondrous Place*, p.5.
6. Anthony Griffiths, *Scouse Wars* (Liverpool, 1992), p.6.
7. Stephen Caunce, 'Urban systems, identity and development in Lancashire and Yorkshire: a complex question', in Neville Kirk (ed.), *Northern Identities: Historical Interpretations of "the North" and "Northernness"* (Aldershot, 2000), pp. 47–70.
8. Dave Russell, *Looking North: Northern England and the national imagination* (Manchester, 2004).
9. Peter Batey, 'Merseyside', in P. Roberts, K. Thomas and G. Williams (eds), *Metropolitan planning in Britain: a comparative study* (London, 1999), pp.97–111.
10. Matthew Vickers, 'Civic Image and Civic patriotism in Liverpool 1880–1914', unpublished D.Phil. thesis, University of Oxford, 2000, ch.8.
11. S. Davies, P. Gill, L. Grant, M. Nightingale, R. Noon and A. Shallice, *Genuinely Seeking Work: mass unemployment on Merseyside in the 1930s* (Birkenhead, 1992).
12. Quoted in Frank Shaw, *My Liverpool* (Parkgate, 1971: rpt, 1988), p.25.
13. Merseyside Socialist Research Group, *Merseyside in Crisis* (n.p.,1980).
14. *Daily Mirror*, 11 Oct. 1982.
15. Stuart Wilks-Heeg, 'From World City to Pariah City? Liverpool and the Global Economy, 1850–2000', in R. Munck (ed.), *Reinventing the City? Liverpool in Contemporary Perspective* (Liverpool, 2003), pp.36–52.
16. John Belchem, 'Liverpool's story is the world's glory' in his *Merseypride: Essays in Liverpool Exceptionalism* (Liverpool, 2000), pp.3–30.
17. Hence the need for a new edition of my *Merseypride*, published in 2006 with a new introduction, 'The new "Livercool"'.
18. Ramsay Muir, *A History of Liverpool* (London, 1907). In these respects, Muir has stood the test of time, as noted in the new history, commissioned by the City Council and the University of Liverpool for the 800th anniversary in 2007, see John Belchem (ed.), *Liverpool 800: culture, character and history* (Liverpool, 2006), p.11: "As contributors to this volume demonstrate, new sources, perspectives and techniques, such as highly sophisticated computer-aided multi-source record linkage, have enabled historians to broaden our understanding of the social and cultural structure of early Liverpool, but these new approaches have modified and enriched, not undermined, the narrative structure of Muir's 'story of Liverpool'".
19. J. Langton, 'Liverpool and its Hinterland in the Late Eighteenth-Century', in B.L. Anderson and P.M.L. Stoney (eds), *Commerce, Industry and Transport: Studies in Economic Change on Merseyside* (Liverpool, 1983), pp. 1–25.
20. Michael Power, 'Councillors and Commerce in Liverpool, 1650–1750', *Urban History*, 24 (1997), pp.301–23, and 'Politics and Progress in Liverpool, 1660–1740', *Northern History*, 35 (1999), pp.119–38. Jane Longmore, 'Liverpool Corporation as landowners and dock builders, 1709–1835', in C.W. Chalkin and J.R. Wordie (eds), *Town and Countryside: The English Landowner in the National Economy, 1660–1860* (London, 1989), pp.116–46.
21. W. Smith 'Merseyside and the Merseyside District' in *idem* (ed.), *A Scientific Survey of Merseyside* (Liverpool, 1953), pp.1–2.
22. Linda Grant, *Still Here* (London, 2002).
23. G.O. Knowles, 'Scouse: the Urban Dialect of Liverpool', unpublished PhD thesis, University of Leeds, 1973.
24. Du Noyer, *Wondrous Place*, p.53.
25. John Kerrigan, 'Introduction', in P. Robinson (ed.), *Liverpool Accents: Seven Poets and a City*

(Liverpool, 1996), p.2. See also, Belchem, '"An accent exceedingly rare": Scouse and the inflexion of class', in *Merseypride*, pp.31–64.

26. For useful 'contribution' histories, see D.Ben Rees, *The Welsh of Merseyside* (Liverpool, 1997) and Alasdair Munro and Duncan Sim, *The Merseyside Scots: A Study of an Expatriate Community* (Birkenhead, 2001).

27. The great north end thoroughfare of the Liverpool-Irish, Scotland Road has established itself as the 'hallowed patch' of Liverpool's heritage and identity, aided by the presence of a local writers' workshop. According to the blurb on Terry Cooke', Scotland Road: "The Old Neighbourhood" (Birkenhead, 1987) 'it epitomised Liverpool and that special Liverpool spirit that could survive any disaster and then recount the event with typical Scouse humour'. For full-scale reassessment of the Liverpool-Irish, see John Belchem, *Irish Catholic and Scouse: the history of the Liverpool Irish*, Liverpool, 2007.

28. John Cornelius, *Liverpool 8* (Liverpool, 2001).

29. The Kru have attracted most attention, see Diane Frost, *Work and Community among West African Migrant Workers since the nineteenth century* (Liverpool, 1999). Maria Lin Wong, *Chinese Liverpudlians* (Birkenhead, 1989) provides an introduction to the history of the Chinese in Liverpool.

30. 'Americans in Liverpool', *Liverpool Critic*, 13 Jan. 1877.

31. 'Liverpool Results', *Liverpool Catholic Herald*, 22 Jan.1910.

32. For notions of 'space time', including 'diaspora space' see Mark Boyle, 'Towards a (Re)theorisation of the Historical Geography of Nationalism in Diasporas: The Irish Diaspora as an Exemplar', *International Journal of Population Geography*, vii (2001), pp.429–46. See also John Belchem and Donald M. MacRaild, 'Cosmopolitan Liverpool', in Belchem (ed.), *Liverpool 800*, pp.311–92.

33. Herman Melville, *Redburn* (1849; Penguin edn, 1976), p.277. Charles Dickens, *The Uncommercial Traveller*, (final edition, 1869) ch.5.

34. Tyler Anbinder, *Five Points* (New York, 2001). For Dickens' descriptions of Irish and black liaisons in Five Points, see Graham Hodges, '"Desirable Companions and Lovers": Irish and African Americans in the Sixth Ward, 1830–1870', in R.H. Bayor and T.J. Meagher, *The New York Irish* (Baltimore, 1996), pp.107–24.

35. F.W. Lowndes, *The Extension of the Contagious Diseases Acts to Liverpool and other seaports practically considered* (Liverpool, 1876), p.31, and *idem, Prostitution and Venereal Diseases in Liverpool* (London, 1886), pp.3–4.

36. For a critique of the pioneer studies by Richard Lawton and Colin Pooley, see Richard Dennis, *English Industrial Cities of the Nineteenth Century* (Cambridge, 1984), pp.4, 205–65. See also J.D. Papworth, 'The Irish in Liverpool 1835–71: Segregation and Dispersal' (unpublished Ph.D. thesis, University of Liverpool, 1982).

37. Frank Neal, *Sectarian Violence: The Liverpool Experience 1819–1914* (Manchester, 1988).

38. 'Liverpool's Coloured Colonies', *Liverpool Echo*, 6 June 1919. John Belchem, 'Whiteness and the Liverpool-Irish', *Journal of British Studies*, 44 (2005), pp.146–52.

39. Pat O'Mara, *The Autobiography of a Liverpool Irish Slummy* (London, 1934), p.11.

40. Ali Rattansi, 'Race, class and the state: from Marxism to "post-modernism"', *Labour History Review*, 60 (1995), pp.23–36.

41. Sam Davies, '"A Stormy political Career": P.J. Kelly and Irish Nationalist and Labour Politics in Liverpool, 1891–1936', *Transactions of the Historic Society of Lancashire and Cheshire*, cxlviii (1999) pp.147–89

42. P. Doyle, 'The Catholic Federation, 1906–1929', in W.J. Sheils and D.Wood (eds), *Studies in*

Church History, 23: Voluntary Religion (Oxford, 1986), pp. 461–76. For a typical example of the Liverpool-Irish rejection and condemnation of the Federation, see 'The Catholic Federation and Its Mischievous Meddling in Political Affairs', *Liverpool Catholic Herald*, 22 Jan.1910. Restricted to Manchester and Salford, the epicentre of the Federation, Steven Fielding *Class and Ethnicity: Irish Catholics in England, 1880–1939* (Buckingham, 1993) dismisses Liverpool as a sectarian redoubt 'marginal to the cultural and political life of the nation', p.5.

43. *Liverpool Catholic Herald*, 1 and 22 May, 18 Sept, 16 Oct. 1903 and 22 Jan. 1904. See also Anon., *The Liverpool Irishman, or Annals of the Irish Colony in Liverpool* (Liverpool, 1909).

44. *Liverpool Catholic Herald* 18 Oct. 1913 and 10 Oct. 1914. On the surprising absence of sectarianism in football allegiance, see Tony Mason, 'The Blues and the Reds: a history of the Liverpool and Everton Football Clubs', *Transactions of the Historic Society of Lancashire and Cheshire*, 134 (1985), and Vickers, 'Civic Image', ch.10.

45. Laura Tabili, '*We ask for British Justice': workers and racial difference in late imperial Britain* (Ithaca, 1994), pp. 68–77.

46. D. Carradog Jones, *Social Survey of Merseyside* (3 vols: Liverpool, 1934), i, pp.74–5, 205–6, ii, p.102, and iii, pp. 515–46. M.E. Fletcher, *Report on an Investigation into the Colour Problem in Liverpool and other Ports* (Liverpool, 1930). Lord Gifford, Wally Brown and Ruth Bundey, *Loosen the Shackles. First Report of the Liverpool 8 Inquiry into Race Relations in Liverpool* (London 1989). M. Connolly, K. Roberts, G. Ben-Tovim and P. Torkington, *Black Youth in Liverpool* (Voorthuizen, 1992). W. Ackah and M. Christian (eds), *Black Organisation and identity in Liverpool: a local, national and global perspective* (Liverpool, 1997). For important new historical perspectives, see Mark Christian, 'Black struggle for Historical Recognition in Liverpool', *North West Labour History*, 20 (1995–96), pp.58–66; Marika Sherwood, *Pastor Daniels Ekarte and the African Churches Mission Liverpool 1931–1964* (London, 1994); and Diane Frost, 'Ambiguous Identities: constructing and de-constructing black and white "scouse" identity in twentieth-century Liverpool' in Kirk (ed.), *Northern Identities*, pp.195–217; and from a social anthropological perspective, see Jacqueline Nassy Brown, *Dropping Anchor, Setting Sail: Geographies of Race in Black Liverpool* (Princeton, 2005).

47. Batey, 'Merseyside', p.100.

48. Richard Meegan, 'Urban Regeneration, Politics and Social Cohesion: The Liverpool Case', in Munck (ed.), *Reinventing the City?*, pp.53–79.

49. *Ibid.*, p.65.

50. Helen Walsh, *Brass* (Edinburgh, 2004), p.70.

51. Jon Stobart, 'Culture versus commerce: societies and spaces for elites in eighteenth-century Liverpool', *Journal of Historical Geography*, 28 (2002), pp.471–85. For contemporaneous changes in public political language, see Joshua Civin, 'Slaves, sati and sugar: constructing imperial identity through Liverpool petition struggles', in J. Hoppit (ed.), *Parliaments, nations and identities in Britain and Ireland, 1660–1850* (Manchester, 2003) pp.187–205, and Rosemary Sweet, 'Freemen and Independence in English Borough Politics, c.1770–1830', *Past and Present*, 161 (1998), pp.84–115.

52. Cited in P.J. Waller, *Democracy and sectarianism: a political and social history of Liverpool 1868–1939* (Liverpool, 1981), p.13.

53. P.H. Rathbone, *The Political Value of Art to Municipal Life* (Liverpool, 1875), p. 45.

54. Muir, *History*, p.340. His study of central Liverpool, however, regretted the lack of 'a civic opera-house, such as every continental city of any importance'.

Chapter Fourteen

City, region, state and nation:
Berlin as a political capital,
1880–1920[1]

Alastair Thompson

A guide to Berlin and its surroundings published in 1914 offered contemporaries a new aerial perspective of the landmarks of the region that were etched on the public mind. The guide accompanied the Zeppelin tour as it took-off from Potsdam and flew over the Hohenzollern palaces of Sanssouci and the Neues Palais, the latter much to the Empress's disgust. Crossing the waters and villas of Wannsee the airship reached Berlin itself, flying over the cathedral and royal palace, and along the parade street Unter den Linden to the Brandenburg Gate and the Königsplatz, with its victory column, national monument and Reichstag, the imperial parliament. Heading west beyond the city's boundaries the Zeppelin tourists could look down on the Kaiser Wilhelm Memorial Church, Charlottenburg Technical University and the prosperous residences in Grünewald and Zehlendorf before returning to Potsdam. Apart from the royal buildings the main theme was unmistakable: the triumph of technology and urban prosperity. Travellers' attention was drawn to the new 'palaces' of Berlin: grand hotels like the Adlon and Königshof; vast department stores such as Wertheim or the Kaufhaus des Westens; opulent beer and wine houses and museums on an unprecedented scale.[2]

This was an unmistakably new world. Even the representational buildings had mostly been completed after 1890; Wallot's Reichstag building opened in 1894, Raschdorff's bombastic cathedral to a more critical reception in 1903.[3] The airship, like many middle-class Berliners, had avoided the 'other Berlin', the sea of factories and tenements in the north and east of the city.[4] Nor, unlike Theodor Fontane in the decade before and after German Unification, did it wander through the established towns and rural districts of the Mark of Brandenburg. When the Zeppelin flew over the Brandenburg countryside it was to view a further display of modern technology, the Johannistal airfield. To many contemporary Germans Berlin, striving to fulfil its new role of imperial capital and metropolis, Reichshauptstadt and Weltstadt, and rural Brandenburg were worlds apart, despite their geographic proximity.

This disparity even found an ironic reflection in the Märkisches Museum, which moved into its own building after several decades in 1908. The red brickwork and echoes of church architecture may have reminded visitors of provincial Brandenburg. But this was a provincial museum which had little to do with province, and much to do with the growth of Berlin as an urban centre. It was incontrovertibly a project of the Berlin bourgeoisie that provided the associational framework, financed the new building, and donated the great majority of the exhibits.[5] And the more these concerned the nineteenth and twentieth centuries, the more they reflected Berlin, not the surrounding region. And if parts of the collection failed to stimulate the metropolitan press, it was not because of a neglect of Brandenburg, but because the museum did not draw on exhibits across the world unlike other Berlin museums.[6] The cultural critic Oswald Spengler was hardly an impartial observer of the German capital. However, it was hardly just inveterate Berlin-haters who shared Spengler's comment that 'today a Brandenburg peasant is closer to a Sicilian peasant than he is to a Berliner'.[7]

The alienation of Berlin and its provincial surroundings was vehemently felt in both imperial and Weimar Germany. This chapter will examine three aspects of these strained relations. The first is the role of the press as an active participant in debates between Berlin and province. The second focus is on the intensely political character of this divide, powerfully reflected in the rivalry between the Conservative Prussian state and Berlin municipal left liberalism. The third theme to be considered is whether these media and political battles overstated the division between Berlin and its provincial surroundings.

Superficially the history of the press might be taken as an example of Berlin as 'an overestimated metropolis'.[8] Certainly the German press was less concentrated in the capital than its British and French counterparts. Within political Catholicism the Berlin-based *Germania* compared unfavourably with the *Kölnische Volkszeitung*. The major National Liberal newspapers were published outside Berlin. The *Kölnische Zeitung and Münchner Neueste Nachrichten* were more important and influential than the *National-Zeitung and Deutsche Zeitung*, Berlin-based dailies with grand-sounding titles, but small circulations and recurrent financial losses. Although Berlin had established itself as the most important German stock-exchange, the leading financial paper was still the *Frankfurter Zeitunng* rather than the two Berlin-based financial dailies. The leading satirical journal at the turn of the century, *Simplicissimus*, was published in Munich. Germany did not have a national daily press, and most Germans' impressions of the political, economic and social life of the capital continued to be mediated through regional and local newspapers. But it is important to recognise that these increasingly represented local variations on national themes; regional or local responses to national debates centred in Berlin. Be it in print or through the telegraph or telephone wires, an ever expanding volume of images and information flowed out of the German capital.

The role of individual journalists, be they well-connected Berlin political correspondents such as the *Kölnische Zeitung's* Arthur Huhn and August Stern of the *Frankfurter Zeitung*, or feullitonists like Alfred Kerr, paled in comparison to the vast volume of news agency reports and party-political correspondences. Even the majority of political newspapers were maintained in order to play a role in national political debate. The large majority of right-wing newspapers published in Berlin, be they the high Conservative *Die Kreuzzeitung*, the Free Conservative/heavy industry *Die Post*, the orthodox Protestant *Reichsbote*, the radical nationalist *Tägliche Rundschau*, the anti-Semitic *Staatsbürger Zeitung* or the governmental *Norddeutsche Allgemeine Zeitung* were barely bought by Berliners and commercially unviable. The same was true of the *Freisinnige Zeitung*, the newspaper controlled by the left liberal leader Eugen Richter. Their purpose was to articulate a political position, to have articles reprinted or echoed in those provincial and local newspapers that shared their political sympathies, and debated in others that did not. As will be examined below, German Agrarians were amongst the most vehement critics of Berlin, 'this monstrous, Americanised capital that destroys much and creates very little'.[9] However, the history of the Agrarian League is telling evidence of the importance of Berlin as the centre of national and Prussian politics. Though its leaders and around 300,000 members in the years before 1914 were drawn from the provinces, the League was founded in a Berlin meeting and continued to assemble each February in the capital. Besides these demonstrations of strength in the *Zirkus Busch* the League's organisational headquarters and daily newspaper, the *Deutsche Tageszeitung*, were both based in Berlin.

In reporting, and seeking to influence politics, newspapers familiarised Germans with Berlin and mobilised interest in events in the capital. This was supplemented by direct visual images of the city. Berlin was an increasingly visited city before the First World War. The city's hotels and lodging-houses registered one million annual overnight stays by 1906.[10] Although the city was not yet the international tourist attraction of the Golden Twenties, it could hardly be said, as Kaiser Wilhelm II asserted to Chancellor Caprivi in 1892 when dismissing Berlin's aspirations to hold the World Fair, that the city had nothing to attract the visitor.[11] Nevertheless, it was the press more than first-hand experience that ensured increasingly widespread familiarity with Berlin landmarks. The introduction of the rotation press and new type-setting machinery in the 1890s enabled newspapers to reprint illustrations, especially photographs, cheaply and on a massive scale. As its circulation of 500,000 copies in 1900 and a million by 1914 indicated, the *Berliner Illustrierte Zeitung* was bought by many Germans outside Berlin. Its rival photo-journal, Scherl's *Die Woche*, also had a national circulation.[12]

Even Germans who did not buy photo-journals encountered photographs of Berlin in the illustrated supplements included in provincial newspapers.

As historians have recognised, newspapers were important reflections of the everyday life of Berlin and its inhabitants. The pace of Berlin life was reflected in editions at almost all hours of the day, and the *BZ am Mittag's* claim to be the world's fastest newspaper. Newspapers were companions or guides as Berliners increasingly commuted, shopped, reposed in cafés, or attended sporting and cultural events.[13] However, it was Berlin's role within the nation, or in relation to the provinces or the state authorities which were major points of dispute in the press. That most Berliners wanted political argument as well as information and entertainment from newspapers was reflected in the success of the Ullstein and Mosse publishing houses. Whether the Ullsteins' populist *Berliner Morgenpost, BZ am Mittag,* and *Welt am Mittag,* which subsidised the high-brow *Vossische Zeitung,* or *Mosse's Berliner Tageblatt* and *Berliner Volkszeitung,* the papers read by most Berliners conveyed liberal-democratic opposition to the Conservative state establishment as well as information and entertainment. August Scherl's *Berliner Lokal-Anzeiger* certainly sought to provide the latter. But unwilling to offend either Prussian Conservatism or Berlin local pride it remained equivocal about the relative merits of Berlin and the provinces. From being the most widely-read Berlin daily in the 1880s, the *Lokal-Anzeiger's* sales of over 200,000 fell far behind the 400,000 circulation attained by the *Morgenpost* in 1914. By contrast, the *Berliner Tageblatt,* under Theodor Wolff's editorship perhaps the best-written and the most sustained critique of Prussian Conservatism, rapidly gained readers in and outside Berlin, reaching 270,000 subscribers in 1914.

Struggle as they might to gain an economic foothold in Berlin, the right-wing press maintained an insistent criticism of what they claimed represented the abnegation of true German values. Indeed the success of Jewish liberal press barons only sharpened hostility to the capital. The right saw no merit in what might be seen as an archetypal Berlin success story, the life and career of Rudolf Mosse, a self-made immigrant from the east, quick to seize the economic opportunities of press advertising and then to develop his own newspaper empire. For Conservatives and anti-Semites it was a world turned upside down when a left-wing Jewish upstart could buy up a noble estate, have his family depicted in classical pose by the court painter Anton von Werner, and acquire a palatial Berlin residence whose scale challenged the royal palace.

Right-wing papers supported Conservatives in the Prussian state parliament when they condemned the debauched nightlife and 'excesses of automobilism' evident in Berlin.[14] The German capital, the Conservative grandee Count Mirbach-Sorquitten emphasised to his fellow Protectionists and Agrarians in the assembly of tax and economic reformers, was a place of unparalleled criminality whose youth was infected by 'materialism, moral degeneracy and wildness'.[15] Right-wing newspapers criticised what they claimed was an excessive and undeserved 'favouring of Berlin', with the Prussian state providing higher education, museums and theatres in the capital. Numerous civil servants and soldiers boosted the capital's purchasing power. While provincial towns were asked to contribute to the cost of rail improvements, Berlin was provided with the best stations and connections without charge.[16] The Agrarian *Deutsche Tageszeitung* was outraged at 'the urgings of Asphalt Liberals for yet more privileges for cities' while a Conservative daily from the eastern province of Pomerania denounced Berlin as a 'town afraid of paying taxes'.[17]

That it became the capital of a parliamentary republic after November 1918 further intensified right-wing press criticism of revolutionary Berlin. Kurt Tucholsky highlighted the right-wing press in furthering provincial alienation from Berlin during the 1920s.[18] However Berlin as a 'Moloch' or 'ville des parvenus'; a dangerous challenge to established order or prime example of 'modern ugliness' and restless, rootless big city life were well-established images in the decades before 1914. And it was through the press rather than the 1910 book by cultural critic Kurt Scheffler or the sociological investigations of Georg Simmel often cited by historians that most contemporaries encountered this debate.

However, pre-war press images of Berlin for the most part shared neither the left-wing pessimism displayed by Tucholsky in the 1920s, nor the consistent hostility of the right. The spirited characters depicted by the popular caricaturist Heinrich Zille in newspapers and books from 1904 certainly alluded to social problems such as poor housing, but reflected a far more sympathetic view of Berliners than the Conservative and Agrarian press. The economic boom years of 1896 to 1913 formed the peak of relative prosperity in the city. Peter Behrens' AEG Turbine Halls represented the economic power of Berlin as well as an aesthetically pleasing switch from the bombastic architecture of the cathedral and *Siegesallee* to functional elegance.[19]

For anti-Conservatives Berlin was a symbol of progress and prosperity.[20] It was not Berlin that was unworthy of the nation, but provincial Agrarians who were unworthy of Berlin. Olaf Gulbransson's Simplicissimus front-cover in February 1909, 'the Agrarian in Berlin', depicted two cavorting, iron-cross-wearing pigs despoiling a rose garden.[21] The annual Agrarian gatherings in the *Zirkus Busch* were derided for bringing the stench of the sty to the city; the dragooning of dependent estate employees contrasted to Berlin citizens moving as free individuals moving across the city by modern transport. In agreeing with Heinz Potthoff, the left liberal Reichstag deputy for Waldeck-Pyrmont, that it was visitors more than the millions of hard-working Berliners that kept the capital's prostitutes busy, the *Berliner Volkszeitung* was quick to point to the Agrarian week as prime proof of this.[22]

Though admitting that property crime was higher in Berlin than in rural Prussia, left-wing newspapers challenged Conservative claims that Berlin was a city of violence and youth disorder. One in thirty Germans lived in Berlin, but according to the 1905 crime statistics the capital accounted for only four of 271 murder and manslaughter convictions, a ratio of one in 68. Berlin was also underrepresented for offences of dangerous wounding, one in forty five, and sex crimes, one in forty one. Moreover, violent offenders were less likely to be youths in Berlin than elsewhere.[23] The right-wing notion that capital was the 'Wasserkopf' of the monarchy, a bloated burden on the state was scornfully rejected by the bulk of the Berlin press.[24] Repeated criticisms of Berlin by conservative parliamentarians in the Prussian House of Lords and House of Deputies were met with widespread press contempt towards 'Junkers on the warpath'. Dismissing claims that the city could not be trusted the *Berliner Tageblatt* noted that 'it is a oft-observed occurrence that enraged Agrarians of Herr von Pappenheim's sort become red when even the name of Berlin is mentioned'.[25]

Far from being pampered by the Prussian state, non-Conservative newspapers alleged that it was Berlin that was being cheated and exploited. As the *Berliner Volkszeitung* put it in 1914: '*Berlin has to he kept down*: that has been the recipe of the Prussian reactionaries ever since Bismarck's notoriously hate-filled speech'.[26] The fate of the woods surrounding Berlin was a major issue that for many exemplified the attitude of the Prussian state. The Prussian forestry administration was happy to bolster state finances by selling woodland for exclusive villa developments in the Grünewald and Dahlem to the west of Berlin. 'How the Grünewald is being butchered: Environmental Protection Prussian-style' ran the headline of the *Berliner Volkszeitung*.[27] It is the 'hatred of rural backwaters against the city', the *Berliner Tageblatt* declared, 'that dictates the wood-destroying tactics' of the reactionary Prussian state administration.[28] It was not only angry Berliners that shared this scorn. Denial of popular access to woodland raised hackles for rural Germans as well as city-dwellers. And what was in effect participation in land speculation made the words of senior Prussian officials criticising moral values in the city appear hollow and hypocritical.

The message that Berlin represented progress struggling against the constraints and self-interest of the Conservative state and provincial authorities was conveyed across the nation and beyond. As a Viennese liberal daily commented on the opening of the new Berlin municipal office building, the *Stadthaus*, in October 1911, it should 'not be forgotten for a moment how difficult it is for Berlin to push through its just demands against a system of government that rests on East Elbian foundations, and is accustomed to bringing only a very modest amount of good-will towards a Reich capital that has never been Conservative'.[29]

Indeed, the weakness of Conservative support meant left-right differences about Berlin did not generally take the form of direct electoral battles within the city. After Adolf Stöcker and the Berlin movement's failed attempt to use anti-Semitism and economic downturns in the late 1870s and 1880s to break the Progressives' control of the town-hall, Berlin elections were dominated by socialists and left liberals. The Social Democrats built up unassailable majorities in five of Berlin's six Reichstag seats, and narrowly failed to overturn the left liberals in the prosperous and less-populated inner-city ward of Berlin I. After the November 1913 municipal elections the SPD held 45 Berlin council seats, taking all but one of the third class seats in which some 90%, of Berlin voters were placed.[30] Some proletarian districts apart, left liberals of various shades dominated the first and second class contests in which the wealthiest electors voted thus securing a comfortable majority in the council chamber. The left liberals also profited from another form of three class election used for the Prussian state elections taking districts which the SPD won easily under the equal, secret and direct Reichstag franchise.[31]

Although disagreeing sharply on several issues, both Social Democrats and left liberals took an essentially positive view of Berlin. The SPD Berlin daily *Vorwärts* was as insistent as left liberal newspapers in calling for the establishment of a Greater Berlin municipality, and for the woodlands to be taken into city ownership and kept open to the public.[32] Rather than directly competing political parties, it was the strained relationship between the municipal government and the Prussian state authorities which was the most important and protracted reflection of the right/left political divide between over Berlin during the imperial period. To many the requirement that Berlin's mayor should wait in the open at the Brandenburg Gate to receive the carriages of state visitors symbolised the unworthy submission the Prussian sate and monarch expected from the city. *Simplicissimus* described Martin Kirschner as a 'porter at the Brandenburg Gate, and Oberbürgermeister in his spare time'. How long, left-wing newspapers asked, before a visiting foreign prince mistook the mayor for a household servant and slipped him a small tip?[33] However, Prussian state restrictions on Berlin went far beyond the symbolic and ceremonial. In contrast to other cities, ministers refused to allow Berlin to incorporate surrounding districts which were essentially economically part of the city. By 1910 two million Germans lived within the Berlin city boundaries, but the urban conglomeration of Greater Berlin held almost twice this number. Even amongst Berlin municipal employees, one third resided outside the city by early 1914.[34] The Prussian state retained extensive supervisory powers over municipal government. The individuals councillors elected as mayors, members of the council executive (Magistrat), and of local school and health boards required state approval to take up their positions. As elsewhere, Prussia excluded Social Democrats from such posts. But in Berlin Wilhelm II was even reluctant to confirm left liberals. He approved the city council's re-election of Max von Forckenbeck in 1890 and election of Martin Kirschner in 1899 only after substantial delay. Wilhelm also blocked for years the city's proposed portal to Friedrichshain cemetery which contained the graves of the revolutionary democrats who had fallen in Berlin in March 1848.

State hostility to Berlin was evident in the Prussian government's response to a court verdict on church building costs in 1892.[35] On the basis of a consistory ordinance from 1573, the court required the Berlin municipal government to finance new Protestant church buildings. Given Berlin's burgeoning population, this represented potentially a major financial burden, as well as an injustice to Catholic, Jewish, and non-church attending Berlin taxpayers. While Conservative members of the Prussian House of Deputies gloated at Berlin's plight, the Prussian government offered to legislate only if the city compensated Protestant parishes for giving up their rights. The city refused the offer and, when Berlin's subsequent legal victories were confirmed by a decision of the Reich court on 13 June 1904, the city had the verdict published in celebration of a triumph over Conservative reaction in Prussia.

State authoritarianism was personified in the figure of the Berlin Police President. The city's head of police was a Prussian state official neither appointed by, nor responsible to the city council. His powers over building and traffic regulations intervened substantially in the everyday lives of Berliners. Press and politicians repeatedly complained of police cordoning off parts of the city and unnecessarily disrupting citizens' lives. Relations between the Berlin police and citizens was never easy, but antipathy reached a new height during the confrontational period in office of Traugott von Jagow, Berlin Police President from November 1909 until promoted to be Regierungs-Präsident in Silesia, away from immediate firing line of the Berlin press, in 1916. Jagow, a Conservative from a landed Brandenburg family, intended to project and reinforce state authority on a recalcitrant population. He was barely more acceptable to Berliners on the eve of the First World War than when he returned briefly as interior minister of the Kapp Putsch in 1920.[36] It was not only the Socialist press that celebrated when protesters against the Prussian three class franchise outwitted von Jagow's threat to use force against demonstrators in February 1910. The demonstrators gathered in Treptow Park while the Jagow's men, misled by false information fed to police informers, waited for them in the Tiergarten. And newspapers contrasted the orderly conduct of Berlin demonstrators with examples of police excesses. Jagow's petty authoritarianism in banning political adverts from Berlin taxis during the 1912 Reichstag elections was countered by mounting posters on hired furniture vans and driving them round the city.[37]

The left-wing press boasted 'that the flowering commonwealth of the Greater Berlin area, which is infused with a liberal spirit, is a counterweight that casts shame on bureaucratic and feudal backwoods behaviour'.[38] Even with the block on incorporating neighbouring districts Berlin had an annual budget equal to one of the medium sized German states. In 1910 city expenditure reached 309.8 million marks compared to 17.8 million in 1871.[39] And if the Conservatives held entrenched positions in the upper ranks of the Prussian civil service, the left-liberal leaders in the Berlin council chamber were equally well-established. When doctor Paul Langerhans stepped down as the head of Berlin city council in January 1908 it was after fifteen years in office. He continued in his thirty second year as a councillor and also represented a Berlin constituency in the Prussian House of Deputies. Michelet, Langerhans' successor, had already been in public life for forty years.[40] The new deputy chairman Ernst Cassel was another left liberal with long years of public service.

The continued rivalry between the Prussian state and Berlin was reflected in the obituaries for Martin Kirschner in September 1912. The press noted the Prussian state's continued opposition to Kirschner's call for a single Greater Berlin authority, and his dissatisfaction with the limited co-ordinating body

(Zweckverband) established in 1911. The ministry of public works had thwarted Kirschner's aim of bring a large part of Berlin local transport under municipal control by extending the Grosser Berliner Strassenbahn's concession for fifty years over the heads of the city council. Kirschner objected to the Prussian police's role in Berlin jails, insisting that imprisonment was a function reserved to the Reich according to the 1871 constitution. Kirschner's presence at the funeral of Berlin socialist leader Paul Singer was a pointed contrast to the Prussian state's refusal to have anything to do with the Social Democrats.[41]

As Kirschner's obituaries implied, Conservatives continued to grasp the levers of power in the Prussian bureaucracy and legislature. But by the eve of the First World War it was ultra Conservatives rather than the ideas of progress symbolised by Berlin that were on the defensive, battered by the tides of economic and social change and public opinion. In January 1914 Count York von Wartenburg brought a motion before the Prussian House of Lords calling for a return to past Prussian dominance, while the Prussian League (Preussenbund) gathered to support the core Prussian values that were being threatened by Berlin. Critical responses were evident far beyond the left-wing Berlin press. Turning on recent allies, the *Kölnische Volkszeitung* declared: 'the Conservatives are deceiving themselves if they think that today Conservative politics can be made and Conservative successes attained by the Landrat and police measures alone'.[42] The Catholic daily condemned Oldenburg-Januschau's 1910 speech that the monarch had the right to order an army lieutenant and ten men to close the Reichstag, or Conservative support for the army's mistreatment of civilians in the Alsatian garrison town of Zabern in November 1913 as examples of false Prussianism. As the National Liberal *Kölnische Zeitung* concluded, 'public opinion had to be reckoned with as a force in the state, whether you like it or not'.[43]

Whilst von Jagow's period in office brought out division, the long career of the Hessen architect Ludwig Hoffmann as city building director offered a more consensual view of Berlin. His municipal appointment in 1896 may have come in competition to the state.[44] Hoffmann chose Berlin in preference to a position in the Reich Office of the Interior. It was also accompanied by Agrarian mutterings that he owed his new position to his marriage to a Berlin Jew. Yet after an initial pause Hoffmann developed a major public building programme. By the time he celebrated his sixtieth birthday in July 1912 Hoffmann had carried out 85 public building projects to a value of 160 million marks. The span of proposals for which he acted as consultant, judge or advisor was even broader. Hoffmann corresponded with the emperor over the new opera house and the Berlin Social

Democrats about the design of Paul Singer's gravestone; Tietz over department stores and the Agrarian League over new offices; chancellor Bethmann Hollweg over a new government building in the Wilhelmstrasse and the committee for the erection of a monument to the left liberal party leader Eugen Richer in Berlin. Hoffmann's contacts were even more eclectic than his architecture.

What Hoffmann built was also significant in raising Berlin's reputation. Improved educational and public health facilities were at the core of his architecture financed by the city council. The building of municipal baths was continued with a majority of councillors rejecting calls to reduce facilities or raise prices to avoid damaging private operators. A series of new schools and hospitals were constructed to respond to growing demand. The health facilities opened at Buch on the northern edges of Greater Berlin were the subject of particular interest and praise. Celebrated in a 1911 article reprinted in the provincial press, Paul Westheim acclaimed Buch as 'a social creation of the modern bourgeoisie'.[45] The peaceful setting, Heimat-inspired architecture was combined with modern medicine and more humane treatment of the elderly infirm.

This expansion of municipal spending and services meant Berlin could no longer be considered the epitome of Manchesterite opposition to Bismarckian state socialism. In 1914 the council rejected a Prussian interior ministry edict on cutting hospital building costs, voting 6,500,000 marks to expand Moabit hospital.[46] Indeed, one of Hoffmann's buildings, the *Stadthaus*, was a monument to larger city government, housing over a thousand municipal employees. Predictably the building was celebrated by the liberal metropolitan press as a symbol of Berlin's achievements. Its imposing tower was labelled the tower of municipal self-government and its architect lauded as 'the glorifier (Verherrlicher) of bourgeois power'. Marvelling at the building's baroque hall that could hold 1,500, the *BZ am Mittag* proclaimed that 'the self-confident power and might of a massive municipality could not be more proudly expressed than in this splendid room'. The building was a worthy representation of 'the Berlin of today with its earnest industry and upward-striving greatness, its arts and its adept artisans'.[47]

However, the right's response was more positive than negative. The Agrarian *Deutsche Tageszeitung* was keen to infer Berlin's reliance on the province from the use of Brandenburg stone: the building material for the metropolis 'lies far away, on the horizon of the woodlands and ploughed acres'. The *Tägliche Rundschau's* commentator, with some justice, found the building 'more Paganini than Beethoven'. But reports on the *Stadthaus* in the *Schlesische Zeitung*, the *Norddeutsche Allgemeine Zeitung* and *Die Post* were all favourable.[48]

Even the most notorious of Berlin critics, Kaiser Wilhelm II, appeared to become less hostile. He was amongst the admirers of Buch, visiting the new buildings in October 1910. The emperor's interest in Cadiner ceramics led him to inspect the Berlin zoo restaurant and the imperial room in the Kempinski wine house.[49] Left-wing papers cited with approval Wilhelm's expressed support for the preservation of the Grünewald and for a tunnel beneath Unter den Linden to relieve Berlin's traffic problems. The Kaiser attended the red town hall in 1908 to mark the centenary of Freiherr vom Stein's municipal code. The following year King Edward visited the building, a response to Wilhelm's reception in the Guild Hall on a state visit to London. To be sure, such instances did not erase all differences. The 'travelling emperor' still spent a large part of the year away from the capital, whether residing in Potsdam, hunting on East Elbian estates, visiting his Corfu villa in spring, attending sailing weeks or military manoeuvres, steaming on the Norwegian fjords in July, or on state visits. At the 1908 centenary celebrations the press could not resist commenting that it had been a long time since the emperor had last been seen in the red town hall. On Edward VII's visit the king raised the profile of the occasion by giving an impromptu speech. He was also noted lingering in front of the portrait of Friedrich III, whose Prussian liberal sympathies were far more in tune with Berlin than the views of his son Wilhelm.[50]

For all that Prussian officialdom found Berlin uncongenial, it was even more reluctant to allow new government institutions to be founded away from the capital. State and military officials, for example, were aghast at parliamentary suggestions that a Reich mechanical-technical institute be set up under Count Zeppelin's leadership in Friedrichshafen on Lake Constance. The institute ended up in Adlerhof, close to Berlin.[51] The economic dividing line between Berlin and Brandenburg was also less clear-cut than critics like the *Deutsche Tageszeitung* or indeed supporters of Berlin admitted. Although Silesians in the 1870s or Poles and Gallicians in the early twentieth century were the most commented on immigrants to Berlin, far more Brandenburgers moved to the Reich capital in the 1870s and 1880s. In 1907 over 360,000 Berlin inhabitants, 18% of the total, had been born in Brandenburg.[52] Even among those who remained, the more substantial and enterprising Brandenburg peasants recognised the value of Berlin as a market for meat, milk, fruit and vegetables. And just as Brandenburgers were drawn to Berlin, so the big city was increasingly tied to its surrounding area. The modern sewerage system developed in late nineteenth century Berlin required agricultural areas where the effluent could be treated and spread on the land. Similarly, the city depended on the surrounding areas for its water supply and for peaceful recreation in the woods and lakes of the region.

While relaxation could still be found in the Grünewald, or on the Lanke estate bought by Berlin city council in 1914, parts of Brandenburg were transformed by urbanisation and industrialisation. This was the major cause of immigration into Brandenburg in the years after 1890 following decades of emigration or stagnation. The province had a net population inflow of 609,000 between 1901 and 1911. The process was strongest in what was to become Greater Berlin in 1920.[53] But even in Potsdam, 'my eldorado' according to Wilhelm II, social and economic change outweighed royal and army tradition. The city elected the radical Social Democrat Karl Liebknecht to the Reichstag in 1912, and, ironically, it was the Berlin royal palace that remained out of the Socialists' grasp.

Less important, however, to many middle-class Berliners than ambiguity, or grudging acceptance by the state, was a strong sense of their own worth and achievements. This was reflected in the confident words of the journalist and architectural commentator Max Osborn in 1909:

> *Almost everywhere it is the middle-classes that have made the steps towards progress in the last decade. The city government, the spirit of private enterprise, the artistic tastes of the inhabitants have taken the lead. The court and the state, to which Berlin once owed everything, have, with all good will and despite all the riches at their disposal, been left far behind. Only after a hard fight could the healthy and forward-looking tendencies assert themselves. Nevertheless, their final victory is certain.[54]*

Notes

1. I wish to thank the Leverhulme Trust for its financial support of this research.
2. Else Grüttel, *Im Luftfahrt über Berlin and Umgebung* (Stuttgart, 1914).
3. Brian Ladd, *The ghosts of Berlin: confronting German History in the Urban Landscape* (Chicago and London, 1997), pp. 55, 83–88.
4. On this 'Berlin of surrogates' see Benjamin Carter Hett, *Death in the Tiergarten: Murder and Criminal Justice in the Kaiser's Berlin* (Cambridge Mass., 2004), pp. 56ff.
5. Kai Michel, "'Und nun kommen Sie auch gleich noch mit'ner Urne. Oder is es bloss'ne Terrine?" Das Märkische Provinzial–Museum in Berlin (1874–1908)' in Thomas W. Gaehtgens and Martin Schieder (eds), *Mäzenatisches Handeln: Studien zur Kultur des Bürgersinns in der Gesellschaft* (Zwickau, 1998), pp. 60–81.
6. *Frankfurter Zeitung* 31.5.1908 and *Vossische Zeitung*, 1.6.1908.
7. Cited in Dorothy Rowe, *Representing Berlin: Sexuality and the City* (Aldershot, 2003), p.25.
8. Detlef Briesen, *Berlin die überschätzte Metropole* (Berlin, 1992).
9. *Deutsche Tageszeitung* no. 363, 21.7.1914.
10. 'Fremde in Berlin', *Berliner Volkszeitung*, no. 249, 18.5.1908.
11. Gerhard Masur, *Imperial Berlin* (London, 1971), pp. 125–26.
12. Emil Dovifat, 'Das publizistische Leben', in Hans Herzfeld (ed.), *Berlin and die Provinz Brandenburg im 19. and 20. Jahrhundert* (Berlin, 1968), p. 765; Michael Erbe, 'Aufstieg zur

Weltstadt', in Werner Süss and Ralf Rytlewski (eds), *Berlin. Die Hauptstadt. Vergangenheit and Zukunft einer europäischen Metropole* (Bonn, 1999), p. 69.

13. Adeptly evoked in Peter Fritzsche, *Reading Berlin 1900* (Cambridge Mass. and London, 1996), esp. pp. 19–86. Thomas Lindenburger, *Strassenpolitik. Zur Sozialgeschichte der öffentlichen Ordnung in Berlin 1900 his 1914* (Bonn, 1995) is an incisive study that underscores the value of Berlin newspapers as a record of everyday attitudes and events.

14. Berliner Lokal-Anzeiger, no. 106, 27.2.1908. Cf. Uwe Fraunholz, *Motorphobia: Anti-Automobiler Protest in Kaiserreich und Weimarer Republik* (Göttingen, 2000).

15. *Berliner Tageblatt*, no. 97, 22.2.1908.

16. *Kreuzzeitung*, no. 118, 10.3.1908.

17. *Deutsche Tageszeitung* no. 609, 31.12.1907; *Pommersche Tagespost* no. 442, 20.9.1913.

18. Kurt Tucholsky, `Berlin and the Provinces' (1928) in Anton Kaes et al. (eds.) *The Weimar Republic Sourcebook* (Berkeley, 1994), pp. 418–20.

19. Max Osborn, *Berlin* (Leipzig, 1909), pp. 248ff. and Osborn's article on new Berlin buildings in *Berliner Morgenpost*, 4.12.1910.

20. Andrew Lees, *Cities, Sin, and Social Reform in Imperial Germany* (Ann Arbor, 2002), ch. 2; Ralf Thies and Dittmar Jazbinsek, 'Berlin - das europäische Chicago: über ein Leitmotiv der Amerikanisierungsdebatte zu Beginn des 20. Jahrhunderts', in Clemens Zimmermann and Jürgen Reulecke (eds.), *Die Stadt als Moloch? Das Land als Kraftquell? Wahrnehmungen and Wirkungen der Großstädte um 1900* (Basel, 1999), pp. 74–87.

21. *Simplicissimus*, 22.2.1909.

22. *Berliner Volkszeitung*, no. 75, 14.2.1908.

23. *Berliner Tageblatt*, no. 97, 22.2.1908. On the low rate of violent crime in German cities sec Eric A Johnson, *Urbanization and crime: Germany 1871–1914* (Cambridge, 1995).

24. See, for example, *Vossische Zeitung*, 1.6.1908 and 30.10.1911; *Berliner Tageblatt*, 29.3.1911.

25. *Freisinnige Zeitung*, 13.1.1914; *Berliner Tageblatt*, 29.3.1911.

26. *Berliner Volkszeitung*, no. 98, 27.2.1914.

27. *Berliner Volkszeitung*, no. 373, 11.8.1908.

28. *Berliner Tageblatt*, no. 416, 13.8.1908.

29. *Neues Wiener Tageblatt*, 30.10.1911.

30. *Vossische Zeitung*, no. 575, 11.11.1913.

31. In Prussian state elections the degree of plutocracy in voter classification was somewhat less extreme. But as the three classes each elected a third of electoral delegates in each constituency the around 80% of electors in the third class were usually outvoted and therefore even more crassly under-represented than in the city councils. Thomas Kühne, *Dreiklassenwahlrecht and Wahlkultur in Preussen 1867–1914. Landtagswahlen zwischen korporativer Tradition and politischem Massenmarkt* (Düsseldorf, 1994) and Berthold Grzywatz, *Stadt, Bürgertum and Staat im 19. Jahrhundert. Selbstverwaltung, Partizipation and Representation in Berlin und Preussen 1806 his 1918* (Berlin, 2003) are informative, but tend to underplay opposition to the Prussian franchise.

32. *Vorwärts*, 8.5.1906 and 21.2.1914.

33. *Simplicissimus* 22.3.1909.

34. *Berliner Tageblatt*, no. 416, 13.8.1908.

35. For the following see Landesarchiv Berlin, Rep. 000-02-01, Stadtverordnetenversammlung Berlin, 2071.

36. Lindenburger, *Strassenpolitik*, esp. pp. 285–90, 341ff.

37. Landesarchiv Berlin, Pr. Br. Rep. 30 Polizei-Presidium 95, Sect 7, 15997, fos. 144-45; and Rep.

000-02-01, 2250, council minutes 27.3.1913 and 12.3.1914.

38. *BZ am Mittag,* 23.2.1914.

39. *Berliner Tageblatt,* 30.10.1911.

40. *Vossische Zeitung,* no. 3, 3.1.1908.

41. *Vorwärts,* 15.9.1912; *Frankfurter Zeitung,* no. 256, 159.1912; *Berliner Tageblatt,* no. 416, 14.9.1912.

42. *Kölnische Volkszeitung,* no. 29, 10.1.1914.

43. *Kölnische Zeitung,* no. 41, 12.1.1914.

44. The following is drawn from Hoffmann's papers in Landesarchiv Berlin, E Rep. 200-50.

45. Landesarchiv Berlin, E Rep. 200-50, no. I I, fo. 96.

46. *Berliner Morgenpost,* 27.3.1914.

47. *Berliner Tageblatt,* 25.10.191 1 and 30.10.1911; *Vossische Zeitung,* 26.10.191 1; *BZ am Mittag,* 27.10.1911.

48. *Deutsche Tageszeitung,* 30.10.191 1; *Tägliche Rundschau,* 31.10.1911; *Schlesische Zeitung,* 29.10.1911; *Norddeutsche Allgemeine Zeitung,* 29.10.1911; and *Die Post,* 28.10.1911.

49. *Berliner Lokal-Anzeiger,* 25.10.1911 and 21.12.1913; *Vossische Zeitung* 130, 12.3.1914.

50. *Berliner Tageblatt,* no. 302, 16.6.1908; *Berliner Volkszeitung,* no. 373, 11.8.1908; *Vossische Zeitung* 548, 21.1 1.1908.

51. Geheimes Staatsarchiv Berlin, Ministry of Public Works Rep. 120 Tn, no. 11, vol. 1.

52. Gerd Hohorst *et al.* (eds), *Sozialgeschichtliches Arbeitsbuch II. Materalien zur Statistik des Kaiserreichs 1870-1914* (Munich, 1975) p. 40.

53. H. Silbergleit (ed.), *Statistisches Jahrbuch der Stadt Berlin* 32nd vol. (Berlin, 1913), pp. 55-59; *Sozialgeschichtliches Arbeitsbuch II,* p. 41.

54. Osborn, *Berlin,* p. 274.

Part Five

Region and Culture

Chapter Fifteen

The old cultural regionalism – and the new

Peter Aronsson

Contemporary globalisation is often presented as a modern master-story, undermining the hegemony of nationalism and emancipating local, regional narratives on the one hand and cosmopolitan and multicultural ones on the other.

Several overlapping arguments both illustrate and complicate this view by means of Swedish examples of uses of history in regional settings. A regional-national dynamic is an intertwined process, which should not be analyzed as a phenomenon qualitatively different from other identity processes with a territorial dimension involved. Recent multi-cultural approaches attempt to up-date the territorial representation of diversity to a diversity of ethnicity in the twenty-first century have a similar integrative feature. Regional movements used to be and are still dialectic and ambiguous in relation to their cultural–political effects. Earlier regional divisions and now multi-culturalism might reinforce a national understanding – or undermine it. A one-sided focus on the political aspects of regional processes and narratives fails to fully understand the attraction and power of certain projects in comparison with other projects. This becomes perhaps even more evident when we move from historical to contemporary regional dynamics.

Place is often used as an analytical category other than region and, above all, nation. Face-to-face relations, praxis and everyday experience are contrasted with the cultural construction and institutionalized framework of larger communities. There is, however, a constructed narrative structure also in individual biographies and local communities. These, too, need representation, even if their meaning could be more embedded and in need of non-textual contextualisation. The analytical dichotomy needs to be questioned in order to theoretically approach the varying resonance that different projects have in historical culture at large. Concepts like meaning (identity, history), territory and power are a more productive analytical set to start out from than the territorial hierarchy of nation, region and place.

All the arguments lead towards the need for a comprehensive theory of the use of history in the construction of identity, which identifies the possible and perhaps necessary dynamics between different parts of historical culture.

A long-term regional-national dynamic pattern

Norway, Denmark, Sweden and Iceland often used to boast about belonging to the exclusive group of nation states that actually lived up to the idea of one people, one country and one state, statements that were continuously repeated during the nineteenth century. Although there seems to have existed a layer of description which recognized the Nordic peoples (Scythic, Indo-Germanic by descent) and Scandinavia as a natural or desirable territory for co-operation and cultural similarities, the very *late* nation states of Denmark (1864/1920) Norway (1814/1905), Finland (1809/1917) and Sweden (1809/1905) have managed to be established as the natural and desirable eternal shape of states in the region.[1] Iceland and Sweden are often presented as among the few regions in the world that match the ideal of one nation, one state. This view has in theory been problematised by the impact and now firmly installed perspective of cultural constructivism. Not even by scholars who move the establishment of national sentiment a few centuries back in history is the perspective of constructivism challenged, only the idea of the close relationship between modernization and nationalism.

There are, however, fewer differences than one might think between Scandinavia and other European countries in regard to regional questions. A millennial and Nordic perspective would help us, instead of ideal nation states, to paint the picture of a dramatic failure to measure up to the medieval unionist project, centuries of federal complexity, ethnic diversity, endless wars between the aspiring Baltic empires of Sweden and Denmark, national movements within the emerging states of Norway, Finland, Iceland and border areas with uncertain loyalties and ethnic minorities lingering on, creating and dissolving empires well up to the twentieth century (Schleswig and Holstein, Jämtland, Skåne, Carelia, the Sami regions, Iceland, etc).[2]

To make a long history short: a fairly ordinary European experience could be sketched as regards the potential region-national complications in Scandinavia. What might need an explanation is why this heritage of potential injustices for most of the provinces was not utilized for aggressive nationalist purposes in the age of nationalism, or later in the age of regionalism. It is my argument that a triple integrative strategy construction has been at work: The establishment of a *Nordic* cultural nation and historical culture is the first important factor in the process of building the Nordic *nation states*. The second is, of course, the successful investment in a national (historical) culture in many spheres of life: sports, language, politics, literature and welfare politics. However, the third integrative strategy has been less appreciated: the ability to deal with regional differences as a national cultural orchestration, and later as a purely administrative aspect of allocating equal opportunities, moved the question of diversity from a potential political arena of identity and power to that of cultural heritage and personal sentiment.[3]

There is no doubt that academia has taken a massive part in this integrative dynamic. To put it very short, the traditional division of labour between the disciplines has enhanced the integrative function: history forgets regions and naturalizes nation states, ethnology culturalises regional differences and social science instrumentalises regions. The net sum is a massive naturalization of the present order. The dominance of a constructivist approach is furthermore in phase with flexible capitalism – teaching citizens reflexivity and the ability to change and adjust, which today is more valuable than the capacity to sacrifice the lives of soldiers at war.[4]

Changing regional dynamics?

Provincial strategies might, however, vary in a way that is not to easy to reduce to ready-made explanations. It is possible to see five different ideal types, here exemplified in the Swedish regional landscape:

1. Self-government – federation – periphery/centre. This is the long-term classic integrational struggle between regions with different aspirations in the nation-building project. The typical trajectory through history is from the perspective of the region a combination of a federative status and self-government, where the federative aspect has been gradually diminished and the self-government aspect more and more a rhetorical residual, while it has de facto developed into more of a local state.

2. Resistance. If the first strategy is a negotiating position, this implies a harsher attitude of resistance. Its military aspect was real until the Dacke feud in 1541 and Skåne in the 1670s, but it has had outbursts which even more implanted fear into the central government, a fear that was alive well into the 19th century. Today, it rather takes the forms of ridicule and even civil disobedience with reference to the lack of legitimacy of the Swedish occupational government – this is the attitude most commonly fostered in the regions conquered in 1645/58, Jämtland, Skåneland, and in the rest of the country in a milder form against people from the capital.

3. Cultural mapping, cultural credit in a national framework. This is the major strategy of regional cultural elites, going back as far as the 17th century, but becoming a main part of historical culture from the mid-19th century. (Dalarna, Småland).

4. Winning regions. If the idea of resistance regions had a renaissance in the 1970s, it was soon to be followed by the even stronger demands from the strong regions to revolt against supporting the less fortunate ones over the tax-bill. (Mälardalen, Öresund).

5. Attraction landscapes. As part of a leisure and experience economy a new regional landscape is constructed which aims both to give an impetus to civil society, networking, and life-value within the local community and to produce assets worth selling to visitors coming for tourist purposes or even moving into the landscape as resident tax-payers to help counteract the continuing massive trail from the countryside, and from smaller towns into the three or four main urban regions in Sweden (Gotland, Österlen, Arnland).

6. Indistinct regions: All regions do not choose a strategy, or at least they do not succeed equally well in being recognized in any of the strategic landscapes. Blekinge and Halland might be seen as examples of this.

I will now continue to say something of three forms of regional cultural dynamics that are the most prominent in contemporary Sweden: resistance, winners and attraction landscapes – not seldom in conglomerate combinations: peripheries form a resistance identity as part of an attraction landscape to challenge the winning regions. The starting-point is the well-established imagery that Sweden is built up of natural provinces, *landskap*, literarily "landscapes". Ever since the nineteenth century they have organized geography, text books, literary images, tourist imagery – but, and this is a crucial point in their earlier function as cultural regions, without administrative or political functions.[5]

Changing landscapes: Jämtland

One of the most researched cases of regional movement and identity in Sweden is Jämtland. The argument here is that the construction of a regional identity is no less complex than that of a national identity. It is moulded out of conflicts within the region, with neighbouring regions and in relation to the nation state. However, there are also changing elements in the construction depending on what coalitions and strategies for the future are preferred.[6]

The construction of a deep medieval history is not seldom triggered by rapid change and a search for legitimate unity when threatened by class struggle or regional disintegration.[7] It might be suggested that the very rapid economic cycle for the timber industry in western Jämtland 1880–1900 can be seen as an example of how an exploiting industry which does not meet a developed local counterpart will have an almost colonial dynamic: a short swing upwards for a mono-cultural economy followed by a long period of more or less chronic crises.[8] The social forces in this turmoil were to a large extent migrants from outside the region. This goes both for capital and workforce, also challenging the inhabitant normatively by an excessive use of alcohol, triggering both the temperance and the local history movement. It can be looked upon as a cultural front, excluding the immigrants from the regional narrative, but of course it also gives an opportunity to "learn" both a tempered disciplined way of living and to internalize a historical narrative to become part of a regionally defined identity. Perhaps this is a social explanation of the impact of the regional dimension: the opportunity to integrate in a local community is more difficult since that is more tightly connected with birth and a way of life than a learned narrative. Nevertheless, it is obvious that the regional elite, who are the main bearers of the regional narrative, do not overlap with either the contemporary construction of a local narrative and cultural heritage of the only city, Östersund, or the many local historical societies.[9]

The narrative consists of the strong and early institutionalised establishment of the region as a historical subject, as an early medieval "Republic of Jämtland" only loosely collaborating with other nations such as Norway. *The Frösö Thing* (Jamtamotet) used to be the central institution for the independent political unit, uniquely in use until 1862. The existence of a regular Jamt language, not only a dialect, is part of the national argument. Consequently, the decline of the Republic corresponds with the rise of the strong nation states. The development is suppressed, first by Denmark-Norway (direct rule from 1536) and later by Sweden (occupation since 1645). The second heyday of the culture is connected with a special blend of trading farmers (forbönder) in 1750–1850, exploiting the regional position between the two states. The growing importance is verified by the establishment of the regional centre of Östersund in 1786. The short industrial exploitation of the forest resources at the beginning of the twentieth century is followed by a long era of emigration, caused by the oppression and neglect of outside forces.

In the regional history of Jämtland we can clearly see the relationship to the centre and the power of the state becoming one of conflict. Competition with neighbouring regions was a prominent feature as early as the start of the twentieth century.

The local culture and history movement reinforced the patriotic currents at the turn of the century even more explicitly. Even if the narrative might look anti-national, it is striking that the territorial border of the historical subject for no good cultural historical reason follows the county territory – including the two provinces of Härjedalen and Jämtland proper, and within these quite different ecotypes and ways of life, from Sami minorities and forested peripheries to the central farming district around Lake Storsjön. It was the latter that formed the model for the identity of the region. The regional elite was, however, never uncontested. In Härjedalen tradesman Erik Fundin established his own alternative institutions in Funäsdalen, but he was not supported by the important power elite and formal institutions of Östersund (in the province of Jämtland) and could not challenge the hegemony built up around Jämtland's antiquarian association in 1886, the Arts and Craft of Jämtland, *Jämtslöjd*, 1908 (founded by the wife of the governor), the building of an outdoor museum in the 1910s, instituted as Old Jamtli, *Fornbyn Jamtli*, in 1912 under the leadership of Eric Festin. Other acts of creation, such as the revitalization of the Jamtamot, the Song of Jämtland, and Arnljotspelen, an epic play about the origin of the country by the famous composer Wilhelm Peterson-Berger performed from the early twentieth century onwards, mediate to the public the idea of a community based on a grand regional past. These societies, phenomena and books are sanctioned by the state when their national romantic buildings of a county archive together with the county museum create a cultural agora at the gates of Jamtli, in intense competition with the coastal town of Härnösand. In 1930 the imposing milieu is inaugurated as a monumental proof of the existence of a real historical background to the regional narrative.[10]

When the tide turns once again in the late 1950s and early 1960s the rapid transformation and outward mobility trigger a new flavour of regionalism, as in many parts of Western Europe. A Freedom movement is created in connection with a festival, *Storsjöyran* and the first president is elected, the entertainer Yngve Gamlin, again an exile Jamt. Government policy was seen as the main enemy, crowned by the suggestion by a committee in 1967 to merge the county of Jämtland with the county of Västernorrland and make Östersund's rival city, Härnösand, the capital. A humorous touch balances the alleged parallelism with liberation armies in the third world. The movement abates somewhat in the 1970s when low temperature in the economy elsewhere to some extent reduces the demographic movements. In the 1980s it regains momentum and the aggressiveness is communicated with the establishment of JRA, *Jamtlandska*

Republikanska Armén (1983) and a new exile entertainer, Moltas Eriksson, as President declares that "the Republic is 51% fun and 49% serious". The army works as a guard of honour for the president and appears as a mock border-controlling guard during the festivals, nevertheless in a carnivalistic manner communicating a territorial message. References are made both to contemporary European liberation movements, nurtured by not only the medieval story but also by the fact that the region was part of the provinces conquered from Denmark-Norway by Sweden in the mid-seventeenth century. Rituals produced in this setting are packed in symbols like the flag and everyday references to the republic as an identity-marker and are again institutionalized in narratives of institutions like Jamtli under the distinct regionalistic and publicly successful leadership of Sten Rentzhog.[11]

Within the movement the need for balance between excluding and including strategies has been recognized. The historically based narrative tends to contain an ethnic or even racist bias which makes it difficult to include newcomers and also to be accepted outside a fanatic core. The other way of constructing a community is to make belonging a question of option and voluntary identity choice. In the 1995 presidential speech it is once more stated that being a Jamt is a question of attitude, a "longing for freedom and uncompromising struggle against chauvinist Swedishness".[12]

The topographically rooted novel, especially the historical novel with its modern mediated counterparts, has had an important impact on the creation of the above-mentioned resistance landscapes. To become successful as such does not only require that the social and political preconditions have to be fulfilled. There must also be a rather precise presupposition of the unity at play, of its facticity, symbolic representations and narrative messages to later generations. It is not a coincidence that so many cultural workers and media professionals are active also in Jämtland. One of the more active in the twenty-first century is Carl-Göran Ekerwald, famous for his literary-cultural books and many biographies on prominent figures in European intellectual history. But he has also engaged in writings on Jämtland and Jamt identity, the latest book arguing for the real existence of the Old Jämte against the relativising activities from the museum officials and other academics.[13] He explains the animosity between the defenders and attackers of the idea of the republic and the Old Jämte as "tribal thinking". By this he means that the attacks on the idea of the existence and prevalence of a distinct Jamt culture, denying the differences in skull formation, the evidence of the runic stones and patterns of inter-marriage emanate from sub-conscious chauvinist Swedish tribal sentiments fostered at Uppsala University. The truth is there, but it is easier to discern from the marginal. That is why the classic professional breakthrough in Swedish historiography was made from Lund and Skåne, by Lauritz Weibull of Danish descent, writing the history of the province. The lesson to be learned is however, according to Ekerwald, not political, but personal. But on that level it is a lesson with implications – for those who care to listen.[14]

Here the argument is still firmly rooted in the legitimate existence of past actions and realities. The importance of the lesson is not entertainment, tourism or local development. The opposite might be the case. These phenomena threaten to diminish the sense of reality and make a vulgar *commedia dell arte* of the regional. That the road to recognition is at least using "edutainment" as a tool, and sometimes more than that, is however the main strategy used by many pretenders to success. Even Jamtli Historyland might be seen as choosing this path as a tool. Gotland with Visby is the best explored example in Sweden, but many ecoparks and edutainment landscapes have been developed all over the world, exploring the dynamics of the experience economy, making more or less use of historic reality as a source of imagination.

The complicated relation to the construction of a homogenizing identity based on a very selective culture has its parallels in academic and political debates all over the world. The interesting thing here is that it is mirrored also on the regional level. One of the major institutions for securing the reality of Jämtland's separate and unique culture is the County Museum and its extraordinarily popular outdoor museum, Jamtli. It has for some decades also served as a bridge between scientific legitimacy and the popular construction of regional identity. The basic exhibition in the new museum building from 1995 must still in 2004 be said to communicate the grand narrative of the region as a country, added with Sami culture in a well defined corner: a mythical Viking founding era is complemented with the celebrated heydays of the trading farmers of eighteenth- and nineteenth-century pre-industrial society and in between the troubles of the conquest and occupation by Swedish troops.[15] This is a function that has recently been questioned in both thematic exhibitions and by adding more troublesome dimensions to the outdoor museums since the successful main theme of the 1970s: History is fun!

The change in policy resulted in an intense public debate around the question-mark after the exhibition in summer 2003: *Urjämten – finns han?*, "The Ur-Jamt, does he exist?" The new regime of the county museum set up by the recently appointed Danish director Henrik Zip Sane in 2002, reinforced by a national assignment to develop the outdoor museum, confronted the set of ideas accumulated in the twentieth century. The question mark after regional identity was registered as an insult and the common academic constructivist approach as an accusation of building identity on a conscious lie. The traditional argument in favour of the existence of an autonomous Jamt tribal culture was by association connected with biologist and even racist arguments typical of the 1930s and earlier. The newspaper debate came to circulate around an accusation, even brought to court, that the museum associated narratives with a tribal, biologist and racist discourse, and by association with Nazism. The museum director, on the other hand, investigated the possibility of taking legal action as a reply to what he thought of as defamation. The struggle raged in the regional media in 2003, among not too many people, but with a grave intensity. The defender of the traditional viewpoints had proponents in one of the newspapers, *Länstidningen*, and a group of well-known cultural workers and journalists assigned the titles like "Foreign Minister" and "National Source of Knowledge", respectively, by the "Government of the Republic"[16] , in association with local historians. The proponents are both the newspaper *Östersundsposten* but above all a group of professional academics arguing for a more modern and updated, one might say, politically and scientifically correct perspective: universal human rights, pluralism, differing interpretations and the like. The program of the museum reflects this change in its overall activities, dealing with less happy and cheerful topics than before and treating subjects like war, migration and refugees. As mentioned, this is in tune not only with developments within cultural sciences, but also in national cultural politics, like the national reform program for cultural heritage brought to a conclusion in 2004, *Agenda Kulturarv*.[17]

Somewhat surprisingly, one might describe the position once again as the culture and worldview of the national institution imposing over strong regional narratives. The message once formed and legitimized by government and scientific institutions to enhance the position in the national system has been expelled to popular culture. The academic leadership in coalition with modernizers argue for the need to expel the idea of Jamt identity as a basis for community-building and exchange it for universal human rights and a functional need to cooperate in the region where one happens to live. However, in a territorial power perspective this position under-communicates its national agenda. It might be looked upon as a strategy to once again reinforce and legitimate the power structure of the Swedish nation state, but with a rhetorical anti-nationalist nationalism. The proponents for a traditional Jamt narrative are on the other hand not 'ordinary people' but rather organic intellectuals in Gramsci's sense, at least in their articulation of a sceptical outlook on constructivism, relativism, the higher academic esteem of long roots and traditional ways of life. Most of the activists are, however, people who are either immigrants to the republic or professional emigrants. These life experiences make it more necessary to establish a conscious and a reflected narrative around what for most people remains unarticulated everyday life experience.

The contemporary and conflictual alternative to a Jamt identity can be compared with the construct of a Sami identity. The ethnic definition has been very strong here since both the Swedish majority culture and the minority group itself had a common interest in the establishment of a strict dichotomy between the cultures and ethnicities in the late nineteenth century – steadfast farmers on the one hand and nomadic reindeer economy on the other, disregarding parallel diversities in the real culture of both groups. The establishment of Sami reserves, Sami villages for an exclusive reindeer economy, was the result of this.[18] When in the 1980s another strategy, namely that of claiming property rights, was tried out, it did not succeed. The power of written evidence should have discouraged any oral culture from attempting such a strategy.[19] Today the cultural construction of an ethnic past going back to the Stone Age is also pursued by official institutions that would not even consider the same argument (openly) for the majority culture. In the official cultural policy, cultural diversity in ethnic and territorial terms is proposed as the alternative to obsolete nationalism.

Struggling to become a winning region: Skåne

Parallel cases of protest identity and other strategies for regional formation are also to be found in Skåne. The rhetoric to integrate a province conquered in the second half of the seventeenth century, and to articulate resistance, has shifted over the years. An open-air museum was opened in Lund, the cultural capital of Skåne, in 1892, only a year after the Skansen museum in Stockholm.[20] But here one can discern three parallel narratives without the intensity of the struggle for hegemony that has been possible in Jämtland. In Skåne there is a parallel protest identity, struggling for liberation, but without the characteristic Jamt smile. That the occupation power should return the stolen cultural heritage to where it belongs is the message from the *Resistance region.*

At the other extreme, there is regional presentation as a clear example of a *Winning region* ambition. This concept was refined in the first enthusiasm for the Öresund

Bridge and emphasises the trans-national Öresund region as a high-tech metropolitan region defined by fast communications, world-leading biotechnology and a dense university structure.[21] A more neutral presentation in continuation of the one proposed by county officials and tourist boards is what might be called the *Official or EU province*, with its distinct blend of local uniqeness and the idea of being encompassed within a European family, in sharp contrast to the more solitary (and anti-EU) otherness fostered in Jämtland.

The three different regions are taken for granted and developed in their respective cultural genre and historical culture.[22] They are also presented very demonstratively on their respective homepages: *Skånes Framtid* (resistance), *Region Skåne* (official) *Öresundskommittén* (winning). The fate of the regions differs according to varying desires and threats projected into the future. The varying logic among these three shows clearly how the representation of the past relates to the future, which determines their structure and narrative. The official homepage is a negotiated story where the politicians' wish to underpin regional identity has met the professionals' unwillingness to do so (they would prefer either to be more local or more universal).[23] Should history create a dark obsolete background (old industry) to a bright high-tech (bio-medicine) future? Should it give critical examples of abuse from occupation forces or create local space to identify with and feel at home in?[24]

In the region of Skåne there are more interpretations on the public arena, especially the stronger stance for the modernistic master-narrative, which prefers to look into the future to looking back for legitimacy. The separatist voice lacks the ambivalent overtone of laughter and good humour, and is hence more marginal than in Jämtland. Both landscapes do make excessive and multi-dimensional use of their history in order to suggest to the present a way or several ways into a threatening future.

A theory of the uses of history

Developments within science and contemporary history have led to an increased interest in how history is (re)created in other arenas than the scientific. This article suggests that such concepts as the culture of history, the uses of history and historical consciousness are just as potentially important concepts in historiography as are social aspects, culture, mentality and gender in terms of their potential for changing the perspective of research.

The culture of history consists of the artefacts, rituals, customs and assertions with references to the past, which allow us to link the relationship between the past, present and future. Occasionally they are direct and explicit interpretations of this link. *Uses of History* is a concept including the processes where parts of the culture of history are activated to form definite opinions and action-oriented totalities. *Historical consciousness* comprises those views of the link between the past, present and future which steer the use of history and which are established and reproduced in its use. A certain selection of the culture of history is activated as communities of memory and forms a historical consciousness. The concept of the historical categories *space of experiences* and *horizon of expectations* fits well into this framework. Knowledge and descriptions of the past create opportunities for certain assumptions about the future. The hopes and fears created by images of the future in the present influence the way the relationship between memory and that which is forgotten is organized in the spaces of experience. The uses of history take place in the dynamic process that links the spaces of experience and horizon of expectations in a specific situation.

The field of cultures of history might be separated into communicating spheres, where some are more explicit and some more implicit in their use of history: Two hypotheses related to this graph are:

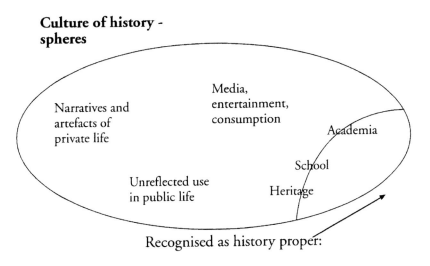

**Culture of history -
spheres**

Figure 1.

1. The impact of a specific combination is dependent on the intertwined combination of uses in several spheres. When an epoch like the medieval reaches an epochal interest above others, or when a regional level is articulated more then national or local levels, this is possible because it speaks through all these channels. The production of meaning is often enhanced, rather then undermined, by contradictory combinations.

2. The source of legitimacy heavily invested in the right side of the graph has spread more evenly during the last few decades. Legitimate uses of the past are legitimately and publicly recognized both as private experiences, political community-building and commercial goals, the striving for knowledge being only one special interest. The interaction between them seems to be a matter of legitimacy by cross-reference rather than contradiction, which used to be the foundation of the traditional evaluation of critical science.

The storyline, the inner meaning, can change over time, but the forms are restricted to four logically possible narratives of historical consciousness. These four can be logically constructed by their way of relating past-contemporaneousness-future:

1. The past as the *Good old days*, where the grass was greener, people finer and more real (Classic Jamt, Skånes framtid).

2. The story about continuing *Progress*, where little by little or by revolutionary acts the bad old days develop into our own time with ourselves as the crown of historical development. From poverty to welfare capitalism (the main story of the Western world) (High-tech, transnational Öresund).

3. History as a *Never-never-land* indisputably and qualitatively separated from our own presentness (tourist landscapes).

4. And the opposite idea: *There is nothing new under the sun*. Humans are basically the same and we live in one time-space of experiences to learn from, be seduced and horrified by (providing the subjective opportunity of empathy).

Many good stories contain a combination of these four narrative genres, thereby allowing the tale to respond to different needs. These four types designate the formal connection between the past and the present in the narratives. However, their meaning is not restricted to the storyline but is also attached to their capacity to work as symbols and metaphors.

This might seem like a contrary way of organizing experience through symbol, icon, metonymy and metaphor. A symbol might seem as a frozen statement without the chronology of the narrative. When it works as metonymy, however, there is an effective interplay between the storyline and the symbolic use, a kind of shorthand, where it is possible to connect metaphors both as the effective outcome of a narrative and as a necessary framework for a narrative to work. Epochal designations like 'medieval' might be used both ways. The use of symbols to communicate meaning is then not contrary to the narrative approach but the two have rather to be combined to make understandable the strength and effect they might produce in combination. By connecting both identity and difference in an open manner, metonymy has a capability to create authentic experiences in a way that more precise concepts are unable to.[25] Using this perspective in historical experience seems most appropriate, since it can give a mimetic reflection of the impossibility of a 'historical experience' proper. It has to be produced in a metaphoric process combining the past with the present. The logic of this process is given only when we bring the future into the horizon. Understanding is an action which relates to a "full" perspective of connecting an experience of the past with fears and longings regarding future realities, horizons of expectations, and brings them into the realm of present understanding and action.

space of experiences　　　　　　　　　　　　　　　　　*horizon*

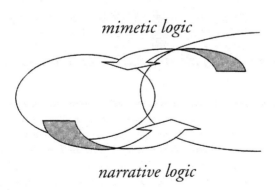

Figure 2.

New regional dynamics – playing with identity, mass media and regional development

The examples have illustrated both continuities and changes in the way regional histories are put to play over the centuries. As positive *projects* they are still relevant with their pseudo-national ambitions but perhaps more often so by establishing new economic clusters in an experience economy. As proponents for a strategy of *resistance* claims can be raised for a more aggressive strategy, exemplified by Jämtland, or a more begging one, asking for support nicely. The national rationale for supporting this, as well as the regional rationale in an inwards dynamic is *integration*, often through balancing a homogenizing narrative with the idea of unity in diversity. This strategy is close to the integrative function also reproduced by all academic and educational activity: unity by knowledge, producing meaning, around and by historical subjects, territories and events and thereby giving them a reflected existence.[26] This may all be seen as part and parcel of the old regional dynamics. Added to these, I would state that what is more typical of a contemporary set of conditions is when historical regions are set up, as is the case for example in a grand scheme in the county of Västernorrland to reactivate the industrial past with European Union money (180 million SEK in six years). Here the context is development, rather than national politics. Of course the nation is still important for allocating resources, also from the EU, but the faith in political decisions *per se* is not there any more. Connected with the hopes of making culture revitalize a visiting economy are often hopes and strategies to contribute to new business, often via enhancing social networking, in other words, trust, coherence and flexibility through cultural investments. Branding a community, making it a trademark, is often seen as a general tool for attracting both citizens, visitors and entrepreneurs to the region. As an extra bonus, if these rather direct hopes do not measure up, there are irreducible life values to add: health, well-being, knowledge.[27]

The construction of regional challenges to other levels of identities, local, national and universal, is not new. It has been suggested that we can view ancient monuments as communicators of ambitions of this sort.[28] In Sweden it is well known that regionalistic ambitions on the political scale, so frequent until the 16th century, change to more cultural forms in the seventeenth century. Even at this early stage the standard formula is to develop the argument that the region is in fact not a periphery but the legitimate centre of the early birth and growth of the nation. For regions where this seems like a hopeless strategy there still remains the classic historical capital in showing old settlements, the unique culture within the preferred territory, creating a historical subject to take part in the orchestrated national ensemble.

All the uses are in Friedrich Nietzsche's sense monumental and not critical, at least in their message to outsiders. There might also for several of the readers and participants be uses which more resemble the antiquarian mode, relating the individual to a more existential, less directly political and more emotive landscape of inheritance and layers of meaning producing a sense of home with more dimensions then what is otherwise possible.[29]

The monumental mode is connected with the narrative trope of the Golden Age, often combined with a clear, nostalgic and fantasy-opening distance between Now and Then, producing a Never-never land to play in. The latter is especially clear when it comes to medieval landscapes. When regional history is utilized as a political force, some of the traits might seem unchanging: the Swedish occupation of the seventeenth century really never ended for Skånes Framtid or JRA, it just took on new forms of capitalist extortion or state policy of bringing both cultural goods and natural resources out of the province without any real reimbursement. But even more so, this trope is at play when people have an empathic viewpoint of the age, people and places they interact with.

On a more general level, the answer to the introductory questions is that regional projects and their uses of the past must be understood as negotiating meaning in the face of fears or longings projected on the future. The need for a theoretical development of the uses of history is urgent to regional history. When the legitimacy of traditional institutions is eroding, the constructionist perspective and the political function of academia become more open and contested – as one of many aspirants to legitimate knowledge. The academic production of knowledge should not only be regarded as the external organization of cognition. It is at least functionally part of a division of labour with fundamental consequences to the production, representation and legitimization of territories. This does not change because the focus changes from nation to region. On the contrary, as politics and economics increasingly become politics of identity and the market looks to culture as a major resource, it integrates cultural sciences in a new societal division of labour. But the perspective also helps towards a radical historization of both the relationship between region and state, region and other divisions and, above all, the active role interpreters and knowledge producers have as not only mapping but also making the regional landscapes.

References

Amft, A. (2000) *Sápmi i förändringens tid: en studie av svenska samers levnadsvillkor under 1900-talet ur ett genus- och etnicitetsperpektiv.* Kulturgräns norr: Umeå.

Aronsson, P. (1995) *Regionernas roll i Sveriges historia.* Östersund: Expertgruppen för forskning om regional utveckling: Stockholm: Fritze.

Aronsson, P. (2000a) Regionbegreppets funktion för skilda akademiska discipliner och samhällsutvecklingen, *Kontinuitet och förändring i regionala rum.* Lars-Erik Edlund & Anna Karolina Greggas, (red.), Umeå.

Aronsson, P. (red.) (2000b) *Makten över minnet. Historiekultur i förändring.* Studentlitteratur: Lund.

Aronsson, P. (2001) *Historia som färskvara?, Historien som ferskvare. Rapport fra konference for arkiver og museer omkring Öresund på Malmö museer 11 oktober 2000.* Henrik Zip Sane & Bjarne Birkbak, (red.), Farums arkiver & museer: Farum.

Aronsson, P. (2003) Historiens brunn – kulturarvet som ok, spann eller vatten för samhällsbygget?, *Hur djup är kulturens brunn? En antologi.* Gösta Blücher & Göran Graninger, (red.), Linköpings universitet: Linköping.

Berg, Per Olof, Anders Linde-Laursen & Orvar Löfgren, (red.) (2002) *Öresundsbron på uppmärksamhetens marknad: regionbyggare i evenemangsbranschen.* Studentlitteratur: Lund.

Bergman, Karl (2002) *Makt, möten, gränser: Skånska kommissionen i Blekinge 1669–70.* Nordic Academic Press: Lund.

Blom, K. Arne, Staffan Johansson & Jan Moen (1986) *Slagfält i Skåneland.* LiberFörlag: Malmö.

Bradley, Richard (2002) *The past in prehistoric societies.* Routledge: London.

Carlqvist, Anna & Peter Aronsson (2003) *Regional museipolitik – Tre år av erfarenheter med Museiprogram för Skåne.* Linköpings universitet: Norrköping.

Castells, Manuel (2003) *The power of identity.* Blackwell: Malden, Mass.

Ekerwald, Carl-Göran (2004) *Jämtarnas historia intill 1319.* Jengvel – Förlaget för Jemtlandica: Östersund.

Fewster, Derek (2002) Vision of National Greatness: Medieval Images, Ethnicity, and Nationalism in Finland, 1905–1945; *On Barbarian Identity. Critical Approaches to Ethnicity in the Early Middle Ages.* Andrew Gilett, (ed.), Brepols: Turnhout.

Funke, Mikael (2004) *Historien i formering av regional idenitet. En analys av historiesyn, historiebruk och regional identitet utifrån debatten om utställningen 'Urjämten – finns han?' (opubl C-uppsats, Historia, Stockholms universitet).* Stockholm.

Hansen, Kjell (1998) *Välfärdens motsträviga utkant: lokal praktik och statlig styrning i efterkrigstidens nordsvenska inland.* Historiska media: Lund.

Hansen, Kjell (2001) Retoriska alternativ: en analys av bruket av historieskrivning och kulturhistoria i formerandet av alternativa politiska offentligheter, *Historisk Tidskrift för Finland,* 86, 493–515.

Häggström, Anders (2000) *Levda rum och beskrivna platser: former för landskapsidentitet.* Carlsson: Stockholm.

Idvall, Markus (2000) *Kartors kraft: regionen som samhällsvision i Öresundsbrons tid.* Nordic Academic Press: Lund.

Lerbom, Jens (2003) *Mellan två riken: integration, politisk kultur och förnationella identiteter på Gotland 1500-1700.* Nordic Academic Press distributör: Lund.

Lindén, Jan-Ivar (1987) Metaforen. En ricoeurisation, *Res Publica,* pp. 141-165.

Lundmark, Lennart, Kulturgräns norr & Norrbottensakademien (2002) *"Lappen är ombytlig, ostadig och obekväm-" : svenska statens samepolitik i rasismens tidevarv.* Norrlands universitetsförl: Bjurholm.

Nietzsche, Friedrich (1980) *On the advantage and disadvantage of history for life.* Indianapolis, Ind.

Paasi, Anssi (1986) The institutionalization of regions: a theoretical framework for understanding of the emergence of regions and the constitution of regional identity, *Fennia*, 164.

Paasi, Anssi (1996) *Territories, boundaries and consciousness: the changing geographies of the Finnish-Russian border.* Wiley: Chichester.

Rentzhog, Sten (1984) *Jämtland.* AWE/Geber: Stockholm.

Ricoeur, Paul (1978) *The rule of metaphor: multi-disciplinary studies of the creation of meaning in language.* Routledge & Kegan Paul: London.

Röndahl, Uno (1993) *Skåneland utan förskoning: om kungahusens och den svenska överklassens folkdråp och kulturskövling i Skåneland:en studie av omnationaliseringens tragik.* Lagerblad: Karlshamn.

Röndahl, Uno (1996) *Skåneland ur det fördolda: en upprättelse av de skåneländska frihetskämparnas minnen och historia : en studie av omnationaliseringens tragik.* Lagerblad: Karlshamn.

Sane, Henrik Zip (2005) Makten över historien i Jämtlands län, *Fornvårdaren.* Jämtlands läns museum: Östersund.

Sennett, Richard (1998) *The corrosion of character: the personal consequences of work in the new capitalism.* W.W. Norton: New York.

Skansjö, Sten (1997) *Skånes historia.* Historiska media: Lund.

Stråth, Bo & Øystein Sørensen, (ed.) (1997) *The cultural construction of Norden.* Scandinavian Univ. Press: Oslo.

Tengström, Lena (2003) *"Landet Annorlunda". En etnologisk studie av konstruktionen Jämtland och "urjämten" (opubl D-uppsats i Etnologi, Umeå universitet).* Umeå.

UNESCO (1996) *Vår skapande mångfald: rapport från Världskommissionen för kultur och utveckling.* Svenska unescorådet: Stockholm.

Weissglas, Gösta, *et al.* (2002) *Kulturarvet som resurs för regional utveckling. En kunskapsöversikt.* RAÄ: Stockholm.

Notes

1. *The Cultural Construction of Norden*, ed. Øystein Sørensen and Bo Stråth (Oslo: Scandinavian University Press, 1997); Uffe Østergård, *Europas Ansigter. Nationale stater og politiske kulturer i en ny, gammel verden* (Copenhagen, 1992).

2. Paasi, 1986; Paasi, 1996; Aronsson, 1995.

3. Some historians have dwelled especially on the Nordic dimension. Harald Gustafsson, "Statsbildning och territoriell integration. Linjer i nyare forskning, en nordisk ansats samt ett bidrag till 1500-talets svenska politiska geografi", *Scandia* 1991:2, Gidlund, Janerik & Sörlin, Sverker, *Det europeiska kalejdoskopet* (SNS, 1993). Stråth & Sørensen, 1997.

4. Sennett, 1998; Aronsson, 2000a.

5. Aronsson, 1995.

6. Cf. Häggström, 2000; Hansen, 1998; Hansen, 2001.

7. Fewster, 2002.

8. Edquist, 1989.

9. Aronsson, 1995. Sane, 2005.

10. Sane, 2005; Tengström, 2003.

11. Rentzhog, 1984; Hansen, 1998; Hansen, 2001; Häggström, 2000; Tengström, 2003.

12. Hansen, 2001, *cit.* p. 509, the author's translation.

13. (Ekerwald, 2004).

14. Ekerwald, 2004.

15. Articles in Östersundsposten and Länstidningen 2003, 0718, 0809, 0811, 0812, 0813, 0814, 0815, 0816, 0819, 0826, 0902, 0911, 0913, 0931. Described and analyzed in Tengström, 2003.

16. http://www.storsjoyran.se/ftp/republiken/rep_reg.asp, 2004-06-17.

17. Funke, 2004.

18. Lundmark, Kulturgräns norr & Norrbottensakademien, 2002; Tengström, 2003; Amft, 2000.

19. It is tempting to compare with the Maori struggle in New Zealand where the very existence of a written 'constitutional agreement' between the British and Maori makes a foundation for the legal and cultural settlement of disputes. Where this is lacking, as for the Aborigines in Australia, minority rights seems to be the only way to enhance the legal position of a minority in a liberal democracy.

20. The "Swedifying" processes are again under debate in the historical literature. See e.g. Lerbom, 2003; Bergman, 2002, articles in *Kulturen* 1995 and 2000.

21. Idvall, 2000; Berg, Linde-Laursen & Löfgren, 2002, xxx homepages.

22. Cf. e.g. Röndahl, 1993; Röndahl, 1996; Blom, Johansson & Moen, 1986 with Skansjö, 1997 and Berg, Linde-Laursen & Löfgren, 2002.

23. Carlqvist & Aronsson, 2003.

24. Aronsson, 2000b; Aronsson, 2001. http://www.ts.skane.se/; http://www.scania.org/main.html; http://www.oresundskomiteen.dk/index.php.

25. Ernst Cassirer on symbols. Ricoeur, 1978, s. 154f, cited from Lindén, 1987.

26. Cf. UNESCO, 1996; Castells, 2003.

27. Aronsson, 2003; Weissglas, 2002

28. Bradley, 2002.

29. Nietzsche, 1980.

Chapter Sixteen

Culture and the formation of northern English identities from c.1850

Dave Russell

This chapter is concerned with the role of culture, defined widely as both text and practice or activity, in the construction and expression of northern English identities across a broad section of the region's population since the mid-nineteenth century. After a discussion of the nature of northern identities, it examines the part played by culture and cultural organisations in the establishment of loyalty to place either by the provision of personal physical experience of, and/or the opportunity for active commitment to, a particular region or sub-region. The third section focuses on the role of cultural representation in the construction and articulation of regional and sub-regional identities, while a brief final comment considers the problematic nature of northern identities in recent decades. As is so often the case, the discussion draws rather more heavily on material from Yorkshire and Lancashire than is perhaps healthy and its breadth of coverage and width of chronology will inevitably lead to some ironing out of subtle variation.

The main interest here is with specific territorial loyalties and affiliations. These are not seen here as being of more importance than the rival claims of nation, class, gender, ethnicity, race, religion and the innumerable other forms of personal and collective identity that shape northern worldviews. One of the great attractions of the North for historians of identity is the sheer richness of the mix of identities available and one of the most stimulating tasks ahead is a far greater consideration of the ways in which they inter-relate. That is not, however, the objective here. There is also no attempt to claim culture as the sole producer of northern identities. Landscape, family and kinship ties, economic structures and occupational patterns all have enormously important parts to play in building and negotiating territorial allegiances. Nevertheless, the central premise here is that, particularly through the representations it offers and the critical discourses that surround it, culture has consistently provided one of the most potent methods through which individuals and groups come to "know" and feel affinities with territories of which, for all the objective experiences that will be discussed, they have little or no actual personal knowledge.

The North and Northern identities

Exactly what constitutes the North of England will always depend on context, chronology and a myriad of individual perspectives: neat lines on maps will never capture what is essentially a habit of thinking. For the sake of convenience, this study defines the region as that territory comprising the seven historic counties of Northumberland, Durham, Cumberland, Westmorland, Yorkshire, Lancashire and Cheshire. Some would want to exclude much of Cheshire, others to include all or parts of Lincolnshire, Nottinghamshire, Derbyshire and Staffordshire and strong arguments could be made for such cases. Interestingly, when in 1932 Newcastle United became ambassadors for "many in the North" after their Cup Final defeat of Arsenal, it was "from Grantham onwards [that] there were crowds at every wayside station, big and little" to salute the conquerors of London's wealthy and high profile representatives.[1] For all its false tidiness, however, and for its exclusion of so many football fans of exemplary taste the version of the North used here at least has the advantage of being recognisable both to most of it inhabitants and to informed observers beyond.[2]

As most historians have long acknowledged, the North, however defined, is extremely diverse in terms of physical geography, economic structure and history and is riddled with internal conflicts which have reached their apotheosis in the battles between the "city-states", especially Manchester and Liverpool, that grew to prominence from the late eighteenth century. The emphasis, then, must always be on identities, on a family of northern mentalities operating sometimes in concert, sometimes in conflict at different spatial levels. In order to impose some necessary order on what is often in reality enjoyably chaotic, three main levels are identified here termed the "local" (a particular town or city) the "sub-regional" (the intermediate units that lie between these and the seven-county North as a whole, with the county is the most obvious) and the "regional" (the seven-county North in totality). Attachment to these various territories, either in isolation or, more normally, in quite complex inter-relation, is most usually demonstrated by attachment to particular bodies or organisations and by some degree of acceptance of and adherence to, a set of myths that both define the special characteristics that mark a community and distinguish it from others. There is still much to be learnt about the origin and development of these myths but a self-defined "northern character" does appear to have been a fairly settled issue by the middle of the nineteenth century. The people of the "North" (usually coded as masculine) saw themselves as, *inter alia*, hard-working and hard-playing, physically tough, blunt, shrewd, homely, unpretentious, independent of outlook, assertive and possessed of a strong spirit of justness and fairness. An ill-defined "South" that usually equated with London and what became known as the Home Counties, provided the significant "other", a place of over-weaning ambition that absorbed the wealth that the North created. The familiarity of this litany should disguise neither the longevity nor the power of such notions within the emotional structures of modern English history.

There have certainly always been distinctive self-images *within* the North that distinguish certain parts from others. In some cases a particular characteristic is emphasised as with the supposed "forthrightness" of Yorkshire folk or the friendliness of Lancastrians. In others, a common northern trait is heralded as being particularly well developed within one of its constituent parts. (After suggesting in my *Football and the English* (1997) that there was possibly hard evidence in support of the north-east's claim for an especially intense sporting passion, I received a well-argued six-page letter accusing of me of "typical Geordie bias" – an interesting experience for a southerner – and arguing the case for east and central Lancashire.) Quite rightly, then, any simplistic sense of northern homogeneity is rapidly lost. The rather dour West Riding "Tyke" seen by one local observer as "rather ponderous and slow to quicken" "brusque" and rather lacking in humour – "what passes for humour is a form of ingenuousness, a naïveté of utterance" – sits a little uneasily with both the easy-going bonhomie of the "Bob Cranky" figure that emerged within Tyneside popular culture from the late eighteenth century or the "Scouser" from the early twentieth, all non-conformity, verbal wit and invention.[3] For all these variations, however, there are clearly enough unifying threads, enough of a common master narrative, to allow for a recognisable "northern" standpoint to emerge.

The relationship between local, sub-regional and regional identities is an intricate one. It is not uncommon for the smaller units to be described as building blocks for, or stepping-stones toward, the larger ones; I have indeed adopted such terminology in the past.[4] However, while there are occasions when this progressive model works, it is probably more accurate to think of these identities as constantly cross-cutting and cross-fertilising with individuals balancing them in a variety of combinations as the situation demands. In terms of the relative balance of power between the different levels, it is hard to disagree with John Marshall's claim that the "most keenly felt sense of place is in the main the local, not regional". (This argument surely remains largely convincing even in the post-modern, globalised environment of the early twenty-first century.[5]) Loyalty to sub-region and perhaps especially to region, is generally far thinner than that to both the locality and the nation that compete so effectively with these identities of the middle ground.

However, while John Walton is probably correct to see identification with "a wider and more nebulous entity called 'the north'" as most likely to occur when individuals were "away from [the region] and presenting themselves to others", a sense of pride in belonging to something individuals call the "North", the "North Country" or the "Northlands" is an insistent part of the historical record. This is perhaps especially the case from about the 1920s. We have as yet no detailed history of these terms and their usage but there is an impression that most northern commentators in the Victorian period at least, professed loyalty to rather narrower units, very often based on the county or some division of it. Although locality and sub-region often continued to take preference or to form the particular through which the more general North was imagined, increasing discussion of the "North-South" economic-divide during the inter-war years may well have inaugurated a more frequent use of the wider term. Irrespective of the chronology, for all the undoubted limits to its power as a focus for identity, especially collective identity, the North remains the only major English region strong enough to give its name to a form of attachment and loyalty to it provides an important emotional resource for many within its boundaries.

Experiencing the North

As argued at the outset, the main role of culture in the construction of territorial identities has been either to provide actual physical experience of a particular place and/or its institutions and representatives or to generate the representations that carry and embellish the myths upon which identities are built. The process is not as neat as this suggests; personal experience is always coloured by and indeed, ultimately dependent upon, exposure to a variety of cultural forms. Nevertheless, this formulation provides a useful organisational structure for what follows. In an academic climate where symbolic forms of knowledge and communication are so much the centre of interest, it is crucial to remember the importance of "being there". Two obvious but important points emerge in this regard. First, many cultural pursuits have encouraged a geographical mobility that, while in no sense undermining attachment to the locality, can only have helped to increase knowledge of the North or at least its intermediate regions. Tourists enjoying "the sites", sportsmen (and it was usually men) and their supporters travelling to matches, bandsmen and choral singes *en route* to concerts and contests, all had varying degrees of opportunity to visit new places and learn new personal or collective geographies. Tourism in particular, perhaps came closer than any other practice in defining the iconic sites – York Minster, Blackpool Tower, the Lakeland fells – that helped give substance to the idea of a region or sub-region.

Partly stimulated by, partly stimulating this new mobility, a range of institutions and activities emerged over the period that helped articulate allegiance to existing but often indistinctly imagined socio-spatial formations or, in some cases, give rise to new ones. Most examples here are drawn from sport, arguably the most fertile arena in this context, but further illustrations could be provided by the societies dedicated to antiquarianism, art, dialect, folklore, literature, music and much else that blossomed from the later nineteenth century. Formal mechanisms for the expression of extra-local allegiances, especially those that mobilised wide sections of society, were relatively infrequent in the North and in England as a whole before about the mid-nineteenth century. There was certainly a strong sense of a "county community" within English society from the seventeenth century, while a growing, cross-county sub-regional consciousness generated by industrialisation increasingly marked the period from the mid-eighteenth century in the West Midlands, the Black Country, the West Yorkshire Textile District, Tyneside and elsewhere. While the associated institutions, symbols and rituals were most typically shaped and experienced by the gentry and the middling sort, subordinate social groups could never be completely untouched whether as the result of casual observation of the county town social round or a more substantial involvement with the patterns of local trade.[6] However, it was the changed context created by rising living standards and the communications revolution from the mid-nineteenth century that made anything resembling mass engagement with regional and sub-regional institutions a possibility.

These organisations were probably at their most potent between about 1860 and 1914 although, even from that point and despite the emergence of and/or increased importance of county regiments, county councils and the county as postal district, people were only relatively infrequently asked to "think regionally". Cultural life thus helped fill a large gap. As already strongly implied, the county was unsurprisingly the greatest beneficiary. The second half of the nineteenth century saw a significant expansion of countywide bodies within the cultural arena rooted in at least some degree in a reasonably broad social constituency. The county cricket clubs of Lancashire and Yorkshire were arguably the two most powerful institutions in this regard. Although enjoying relatively small and often quite socially exclusive memberships – figures stood at between 5,000 and 6,000 for both counties during the 1930s – and playing for the most part at times of the week and day that rendered attendance by the majority of the working population impossible, they had the power to mobilize high levels of popular interest on days when working- and lower-middle class attendance was possible. On August Bank

Holiday 1923, for example, 23,000 packed into Bradford's Park Avenue ground to the see the two rivals in the "Roses" match with an estimated 50,000 locked outside.[7] Not the least significant of county cricket's contribution was the fact that for five months of the year, the teams moved around the county playing in anything up to seven or eight different locations, thus drawing disparate communities together in a shared sporting embrace. In Yorkshire, the West Riding certainly dominated in terms of venues and in other ways (Sheffield and then, from 1902, Leeds acted as headquarters), but annual visits to Middlesbrough, Hull and Scarborough helped make Yorkshire a little more a sum of its parts. Through its sporting representatives, the county was made real. The Great Yorkshire Show, admittedly only partially a cultural event, fulfilled a similar function during its peripatetic phase from 1838 to 1951 as did the many smaller organisations whose members travelled to events, opened newsletters, read yearbooks and engaged in a variety of scholarly and other activity that brought the abstract territorial unit alive.[8]

There are clear limits here. The numbers involved were often small and "activists" were largely drawn from the middle class. The modern county has perhaps always been of greatest significance for the middle-class, a middling space for the middling sort. Again, not all northern counties showed the same level of intensity in activity of this type. In the cricketing context, for example, Lancashire and Yorkshire were, until Durham's elevation to the County Championship in 1992, the only northern counties to play the First Class game and thus cannot be seen as typifying the North as a whole. Cheshire seems to have had a particularly weak cultural project. Its three leading historical and antiquarian societies were paired with Lancashire and, albeit using an example here from beyond the purely institutional arena, it produced a remarkably low number of regional novels in comparison with other northern counties; our most detailed survey records a mere fourteen novelists producing just twenty titles between 1800 and 2000 in comparison with figures, for example, of 235 and 387 in Northumberland and 368 and 939 in Yorkshire.[9] It is also unsurprisingly the case that the "cultural" county rarely mapped onto its administrative or historic equivalent. David Neave has used the undeniable weakness of East Riding representation within the new "Yorkshire" organisations of the late nineteenth century to challenge the notion of Yorkshire, with its "new heart" in the industrial West Riding, as a unified cultural entity.[10] There is some evidence for this and Neave is undeniably correct to argue for an East Riding distinctiveness. Nevertheless, although 87% of Yorkshire County Cricket Club membership in 1911 came from the West Riding, that is not exceptionally out of line with its share of the county's population (77%) and by no means all of them were based in its industrial core. The much smaller but influential Yorkshire Dialect Society drew a suitably proportionate 79% of its members from the West Riding and managed at least a scattered presence across the whole county. Some important county bodies did speak for a wide constituency, even if other territories made equally insistent calls.

As well as giving greater texture to the idea of the county, cultural life, with sport again highly prominent, could also help build new forms of sub-regional allegiance. In an important examination of the ways in which the sporting culture of east Northumberland pit villages came to embrace not only an intense localism but also a wider regional outlook, Alan Metcalfe has shown how support for Newcastle United Football Club in the late 1890s and early 1900s helped miners:

> ...to perceive themselves as Northeasterners rather than as members of isolated mining villages...for the first time the miners did not look on Newcastle as the arch enemy but rather as carrying the pride and hopes of the northeast.[11]

Late Victorian and Edwardian Newcastle, already one of England's few, undisputed regional capitals and, unlike, for example, Manchester, not faced with several powerful footballing rivals in neighbouring towns, may have been something of an exception here. It would nevertheless be interesting to see how support for other big city clubs in the North impacted on the identities of fans in the hinterlands. Studies focused on other smaller communities would also be interesting. From relatively early in its history, Burnley Football Club (1881), based in an industrial outlier on the east Lancashire border, drew a significant number of fans from rural and small town communities within the West Riding of Yorkshire.[12] Were such fans drawn into a type of south Pennine identity that transcended sport in the way that Metcalfe suggests for the miners of east Northumberland or were they merely (if that is not too demeaning) part of a "football community" that existed only for one purpose?

Indeed, we need far more historical geography of cultural activity, a mapping of networks that allows us to view more clearly the highly distinctive cultural regions that have emerged over the last two centuries. Some work of this type has been undertaken, most notably within sports history and usually focused on the growth and diffusion of specific games. There is scope for much more work, but with a different emphasis. We should capture the exact geographies experienced by a brass band, a football team, a hiking club or of the constituencies built by sports teams and then attempt to see if these cultural regions were only that, spaces in which particular activities were carried out by particular people, or whether that space became "time-thickened" to produce a real sense of place and loyalty to it.[13] In such cases as brass banding, crown green bowling, league cricket and rugby league, where the cultural activity is strongly associated in the popular imagination with "northernness", it may well be that adherents gain an enhanced sense of northern identity, made more explicit by meeting others of like mind in new places.

Rugby league is interesting here. Although it has never established itself throughout the North, it is probably closer than any other significant cultural form to being distinctively and fully a "northern" phenomenon. It was initially rooted in a breakaway by twenty-two clubs from Lancashire, Yorkshire and Cheshire in 1895 from what one newspaper called "the thraldom of the southern gentry", following, amongst other things, the refusal of the London-based Rugby Football Union to sanction payments for working-class players forced to miss work.[14] The game has developed a very distinctive geography becoming rooted most notably in south-west Lancashire, west Cumbria, the textile regions of west Yorkshire and Humberside.[15] The game has pulled into knowable community disparate elements of the North not normally united in any other way. This is especially important for Rugby League strongholds in more isolated areas that are rarely "imagined" as part of the North, such as the West Cumbrian towns of Barrow, Workington and Whitehaven, and even the city of Hull in east Yorkshire. Their presence on the Rugby League map has rendered them both visible and visibly northern.

Representing northern identities

For all the importance of objective experience, it is nevertheless the case that, ultimately, cultural representations play the most important part in the construction of most territorial identities beyond the local; even there, they remain potent. The limits on personal knowledge simply demand this. Although journalist Graham Turner began his fine work *The North Country* (1967) with the words "I have always instinctively thought of myself as a Northerner", he willingly acknowledged that he "had never seen most of it".[16] Even at a very local level, the structures of physical and economic geography often ensure that a community can be largely ignorant of another only a few miles away. Similarly, as has already been noted, actual physical experiences invariably require mediation from cultural commentators or from the stock of popular knowledge in order to gain or develop meaning. Yorkshire cricket supporters did not feel more "Yorkshire" just by sitting at a game but because that act was given meaning by journalistic and conversational discourses that wedded older notions of Yorkshire specificity and superiority – competitiveness, physical hardness, extreme loyalty to county – to the sporting context that helped inform their interpretation of events. Moreover, far more of them will have experienced the team through the media than by watching them on the field of play.

The representations that allow communities to be imagined and loyalties forged can come from literally any cultural form.[17] Dialect writing was an important internal source from about the 1840s, although it was not universally popular across the North and had lost much of its purchase by the 1930s. Other important contributions from the late nineteenth century and onwards have come from the stage, cinema and television. Probably the most consistently influential across the whole period, however, have been the novel, travel literature, the press, especially at local and regional press and that loose body of writing embracing local and regional history, folklore and topography. While the local press and local histories have been thoroughly mined by historians, their particular contributions to identity formation have not generally been looked at in a systematic way. Detailed projects on the provincial press (mapping of circulation areas might illuminate the process through which communities have defined themselves and been defined) and the thousands of books, pamphlets and magazines that have been such a feature of popular literary culture in northern England would be invaluable.

Those producing the representations might most easily be divided into the "internals" who had enjoyed some longstanding connection with the North and the "externals" who were either short-term visitors to it or, indeed, who had little or no experience of it at all. While the concentration to date has been upon northern self-depiction, as Helen Jewell in particular has shown so well, external myths and versions of the North also have a long history and a powerful influence.[18] While there is generally broad congruence between the internal and external view of the region and its inhabitants, there is often a crucially different reading of perceived characteristics; what a northerner might see as competitiveness, for example, an outsider (especially a southerner) might see as an unhealthy desire to win at all costs. It is this fertile repertoire of contested imagery that has been the engine for so much of the cultural politics of the English regions.

Although the analysis that follows tends to a narrative pitting locally-born Northern patriots against external detractors, the reality was always far more complex. There have always northerners with little that was good to say about their native heath and outsiders with little that was bad. Again, not all regional and sub-regional champions have necessarily been born or even spent their formative years in the places they are most closely associated with. An Edwardian writer noted that it "has been a source of amusement to many" that the Yorkshire Dialect Society chairman was from East Anglia, the secretary from Wiltshire and three committee members from Cornwall. (He was pleased to record that, in accordance with the county stereotype, "The treasurer, however, is a Yorkshireman".) Archie Harding, a southerner educated at public school and Oxford University and who, as the BBC Northern Region's Director of Programmes from 1933–36, did much to pioneer the broadcasting of northern voices, was described by one contemporary source as a man "bitten by that awful bug which gives a man delusions about the north" and makes him see it as "more full of integrity" than the South.[19] Although the most commented upon and probably the culturally more significant personal journey in English society has been that from North to South (usually London and the Home Counties), there were many journeys in the other direction and many making them were to "go native" to varying degrees. The "Otherness" of the North with its rich cultural resources and association with struggle, hardship and "authenticity" has proved attractive to many seeking, if not new identities, then at least a reshaping of existing ones. Historians of regional identity might be well advised to consider the history of incomers as much as the leave-takers who have tended to preoccupy us to date.

Although northern identities have ultimately been constructed from within, external visions have also played a highly important and sometimes critical role. It may indeed be the case that external commentators were, at least initially, the most vocal in "speaking" the North, in the sense of gathering together and providing a collective noun for a set of cities and sub-regions. As already suggested, northerners seem often to have shown a preference for identifying and identifying with, smaller units. At the same time, powerful and insistent external commentary constructing the North as "other", as an undifferentiated, industrial "Black England" has stimulated a process of vigorous contestation within. Often insecure about both the region's and their own status within the national culture, the North's cultural spokesmen and women have taken offence to great effect.

This is most noticeable in the powerful strand of anti-metropolitanism that so marks northern discourse. This mentality indeed comes the closest to forming a unifying northern ideology, something that, even if often expressed with a local or sub-regional grievance in mind, is at least recognisable to a large constituency across the region as a whole.[20]   Obviously, external representations have not necessarily emanated exclusively from the capital and indeed, at least in recent years, some of the most negative images of particular parts of the North have been perpetuated within the region as a whole. The 1980s construction of Liverpool as a city typified by dole claimants and self-pity was enthusiastically endorsed in the popular culture of many other northern towns and cities. However, London's place at the core of the media industry and its overall power within the national culture made the capital the inevitable focus for retaliation. London as a city has, of course, been enormously attractive to many northerners who have variously recognised it as a place of excitement and opportunity, the capital of Empire, one of the world's great cities and a cultural cornucopia. In Willy Russell's play *Educating Rita* (1980), Rita's excited comment to her Open University tutor that her visit there was, "fantastic. Honest it was – ugh", inelegantly but neatly captures some of its imaginative and actual power.[21] Numerous northerners have moved to the capital in search of work and escape from the restrictions of provinces and their experiences have formed the substance of innumerable novels, plays and films. There has also often been a need to experience the approbation of the capital's specialist elites. When in 1932 the Huddersfield Choral Society appointed as conductor, Malcolm Sargent, then a rising star of the musical firmament, the local newspaper noted that:

> *It is also something a of a compliment to the reputation of the Huddersfield Choral Society that a young conductor with so many avenues of employment open to him, with an established place in London, should have consented to come to another provincial society.*[22]

Northern hostility to the capital has come then, not from an intrinsic dislike of the place or of its people, but from opposition to its dominance of the nation's economy, politics, administration and culture. "London" becomes useful shorthand through which to express opposition to this accretion of power and, above all, to any metropolitan representation that even hinted at a superior or patronising tone. By the later twentieth century, cultural expression of this opposition had long since solidified into a commonplace categorisation of the South as effete and parasitic upon the hard work of the North and the provinces more generally, a trope well captured by Malcolm Bradbury in his novel *Stepping Westward* (1965) at the moment where a character takes the well-trodden path from the North. "Behind now, lay decency, plain speaking, good feeling; ahead lay the southern counties, all suede shoes and Babycham".[23]   Behind this slightly ironic take on North-South relationships, however, lies a long history of northern resentment.

Nevertheless, while anti-metropolitanism was often a response to supposed external slight, like other forms of northern sensibility, it was always far more than just a response to outside commentary, a reworking of external viewpoints. The North was ultimately scripted far more from within than without. Although regional and sub-regional cultural representatives frequently addressed the supposed "otherness" of their constituencies, they had many other agendas and worked from many motives including local and regional pride, a thirst for knowledge of self, the desire to obtain status (and income) through the production or management of cultural capital and much else. Much northern culture was produced, at least initially, for internal audiences and tried in a variety of modes to make sense of the social and economic changes the region had passed through. This was a process that would have been necessary irrespective of any external considerations.

It was also essential to the working out of internal rivalries that so marked the North and it is once again significant that much self-representation was largely produced at the level of the locality or sub-region rather than the North as totality. The sub-region in its turn was usually only quite modest in scope and certainly not constrained within any administrative boundaries. Although we tend to categorise regional novelists, for example, in terms of county affiliation, most took for their creative space either a town and its hinterlands or an area defined by natural features or economic processes. While sailing under county flags of convenience folklorists and antiquarians also sometimes articulated regions that had no place on a standard map. In his *Lancashire Humour* (1900), for example, Thomas Newbigging talked of an area of the county east of a line running from Manchester to Bolton, Blackburn and ending at Clitheroe "in which the purest breed of Lancashire men and women will be found". (Within this, he defined an even tighter inner core that included his native Rossendale Valley.) According to Newbigging, the county's inhabitants became "more mixed" as one approached the coast and "it is only by an incursion into the interior that the unadulterated aboriginals are to be found in their native purity".[24] As Newbigging shows in unusually stark form, at least until the 1950s, at the heart of much cultural representation lay a desire to unveil the "character" that defined the people of their chosen locality or region, something usually explained in terms of either or both racial (most frequently asserted in the nineteenth century) or environmental factors. Much popular cultural production was structured around the creation of sets of *dramatis personae* that displayed in balanced concert the necessary requirements of locality and region, a family that allowed the inhabitants of a particular territory to see themselves as they would have wished to be seen. Thus emotionally armed, northern communities were ready both to pursue local matters and to recognise, albeit often reluctantly, their wider allegiances with others who bore a distinct family resemblance.

Culture and identity in the modern North

Much of the culture discussed here was at its zenith during the period from about 1880 to 1950. From that point, northern culture and cultural institutions have come under pressure in ways that have been problematic for the nature and expression of northern identity. The de-industrialisation of the region made it an inevitable (and often justifiable) focus for the "decline of England/Britain" narratives that were so prevalent from the late 1970s to the early 1990s. The regeneration from the 1990s has led to far more positive imagery, but the North, and especially its smaller and middle-sized towns still seem to attract a large amount of sepulchral coverage. Partly, although far from exclusively because of the shifts in the regional economy, many of the region's cultural icons have declined and its cultural capital devalued. The decline in the status of county cricket has eroded the power of Lancashire and Yorkshire Cricket Clubs to speak for large communities. Even football, powerful within the national culture as never before, offers fewer really valuable northern signifiers than before. It was difficult enough in the 1930s for Newcastle manager Andy Cunningham with six Scotsmen in his side, to reflect back the glory of his team on their fans by claiming that "he knew North Country grit and determination would triumph".[25] How much harder seventy years later when players come from all over the globe and can earn in a season far, far more than most fans will earn in a lifetime.

There have also been changes, or new emphases, in the nature of cultural representation. In the increasingly iconoclastic public culture that has emerged from the late 1950s, the "North" became an easy target for parodic humour. That staple of the comedian's art, the "Grim North", was born and continues to flourish. In essence, the representation of the "northerner" whether as composite supra-character or more local figure, had long hardened into cliché by the mid-twentieth century. Character had become caricature and a new generation were quick to seize on the comic possibilities. Some of the humour stemmed from outsiders but, crucially, a substantial amount came from within. At the very moment when the North was briefly made fashionable by a small coterie of novelists, film directors and playwrights, a parallel and far longer lasting version of the North was set in motion. Indeed, one of those very novelists, Keith Waterhouse, played a major contribution to the new strand through the comic treatment of traditional northern life by leading character Billy Fisher and his friend Arthur in *Billy Liar* (1959). From Reg Smyth's *Andy Capp* cartoon in the northern edition of the *Daily Mirror* from 1957, through to Michael Parkinson's comic memories of Barnsley football in the *Sunday Times*, cartoonist Bill Tidy's depictions of "northern Lancashire seen through the eyes of a Liverpudlian" ("I am a Scouser...The idea of Preston or Blackburn or Oldham used to bring tears of laughter to our eyes"), the novels and TV scripts of Peter Tinniswood and beyond, the comic North took shape.[26] Internal parody of the region was nothing new with individuals as diverse as comedian George Formby senior and *Manchester Guardian* music critic and cricket writer Neville Cardus proving masters of the trope earlier in the twentieth century and knowingly running the risk of making outsiders laugh *at* a culture that insiders laughed *with*. However, while they wrote at a time when the North was reasonably secure about its economic position and its working-class culture remained essentially intact, the newer modes were created in a much altered and much less secure context and the jokes thus far more troublesome.

There have also been other shifts in the cultural register that have flowed from the social and cultural changes already sketched in. Although the North obviously had no unique claim to be considered the land of the working-class, its objectively strong association with "traditional" working class culture has led to such an image at the heart of its imaginative construction. As working-class culture began to change irrevocably from the 1950s under the impact of innumerable forces including the rise of consumption, the decline of heavy industry and consequent unemployment and/or new non-place specific employment patterns, South Asian and Afro-Caribbean immigration and much else, nostalgia for lost community perhaps inevitably often took the form of an affectionate turn to an idealised version of the northern industrial community. David Gervais has talked of the "axis of Englishness" moving northward over the twentieth century and it is certainly possible to see, if not a displacement in the national imagination of the rural "South Country" by the northern terrace street, then at least a significant jostling for position.[27] Particularly through Granada Television's *Coronation Street* (1960) (at least in latter decades), the many autobiographies of northern childhood – William Woodruff's *The Road to Nab End* (2000) is perhaps the most popular – and the ever growing body of saga fiction that has been such a feature of the popular literary ecology from the second half of the twentieth century, the cultural depiction of the North has helped reacquaint many with a world of tight community they believe they have lost.[28] Problematically for the North, the version of the region that emerges is often a bleak one, with the hardships of the nineteenth century and the 1930s notably popular themes, and one that looks back and thus fixes a distinctive and often outdated picture upon the region as a whole.

The rise of the comic North and the lost North, has potentially damaging implications for the expression of northern identities. Always to some extent rooted in a defensive posture against detractors in the capital, these new forces are highly likely to reinforce that defensive mode of expression. Those who feel patronised will sound the more strident and those seeking to sell a new image as cities and towns begin to reinvent themselves for a post-industrial future, ever more anxiously insistent. This is not to deny the existence of highly positive forms of northern consciousness or of able and vocal representatives within the cultural field. Nevertheless, they have much to contend with. Keith Wrightson was surely correct when he called in 1995 for a northern consciousness that offers:

> ...inoculation against the two least constructive forms of response to the uncertainties and insecurities of the northern present – a cringing deference to the currently dominant values and perceptions of the English establishment on the one hand, and, on the other a strutting in-your-face, manifestation of the imputed characteristics of northernness.

However, his call to heed the reminder of Australian Robert Hughes that "the Right attitude is neither cringe nor strut, but a natural and relaxed uprightness of carriage" will not always be easy; there will, after all, still be an awful lot of cultural assumptions to step around.[29]

Notes

1. *Yorkshire Observer* 23 and 26 April 1932.
2. On definitions, S. Rawnsley, 'Constructing "The North": space and a sense of place', in N. Kirk (ed.), *Northern Identities* (Aldershot: Ashgate, 2000), pp. 3–22; D. Russell, *Looking North. Northern England and the National Imagination* (Manchester: Manchester University Press, 2004), pp. 14–18.
3. J. Hambley Rowe, *An Investigation into the Character of the West Riding Personality* (Bradford: author published, N.d c.1910), pp. 4–8; R. Colls, *The Collier's Rant. Song and Culture in the Industrial Revolution* (London: Croom Helm, 1997); Belchem, '"An accent exceedingly rare": Scouse and the inflexion of class', in his *Merseypride. Essays in Liverpool Exceptionalism* (Liverpool: Liverpool University Press, 2000), pp.31–64 and G. Turner, *North Country* (London: Eyre and Spottiswoode, 1967), pp. 140–58.
4. D. Russell, 'Sport and Identity: The case of Yorkshire County Cricket Club, 1890–1939', *20th Century British History*, 7, 2, 1996, p. 216.

5. J.D. Marshall, *The Tyranny of the Discrete* (Aldershot: Scolar Press, 1997), p. 105. On local and global in the North see I. Taylor *et al.*, *A Tale of Two Cities. A Study in Manchester and Sheffield* (London: Routledge, 1996).

6. J. Langton, 'The industrial revolution and the regional geography of England', *Transactions of the Institute of British Geographers*, new series volume 9, 1984, pp. 146–167.

7. D. Hodgson, *The Official History of Yorkshire County Cricket Club* (Ramsbury, Wilts: Crowood Press, 1989), p. 112.

8. V. Hall, *A History of the Yorkshire Agricultural Society, 1837–1987* (London: Batsford, 1987), pp. 206–09.

9. J.K. Walton, 'Doing comparative social history: north-west England and the Basque Country from the 1830s to the 1930s' (Lancaster: Lancaster University, 1996) p. 8; figures extracted from K. Snell, *The Bibliography of Regional Fiction in Britain and Ireland, 1800–2000* (Aldershot: Ashgate, 2002).

10. D. Neave, 'The identity of the East Riding of Yorkshire', in E. Royle (ed.) *Issues of Regional Identity* (Manchester: Manchester University Press, 1998), p. 189.

11. A. Metcalfe, 'Sport and community: a case study of the mining villages of East Northumberland, 1800–1914', in J. Hill and J. Williams, *Sport and Identity in the North of England* (Keele: Keele University Press, 1996), p. 30.

12. G. Mellor, 'Football and its Supporters in the North West of England, 1945–1985', (Unpublished PhD thesis, University of Central Lancashire, 2003).

13. M. Craig, *Cultural Geography* (London: Routledge, 1998), p. 103.

14. Quoted in T. Collins, *Rugby's Great Split. Class, Culture and the Origins of Rugby League Football* (London: Frank Cass, 1998), p. 157.

15. T. Collins, *Rugby League in Twentieth Century Britain. A Social and Cultural History* (London: Routledge, 2006, p. frontispiece map.

16. Turner, *North Country*, pp. 11–12.

17. The range of material is far too great to allow for even the most cursory analysis here. See Russell, *Looking North*, passim, for detail.

18. H. Jewell, *The North-South Divide. The Origins of Northern Consciousness in England* (Manchester: Manchester University Press, 1994),

19. Rowe, Investigation p. 8; quoted in P. Scannell and D. Cardiff, *A Social History of British Broadcasting*, vol.1, 1922–1939 (Oxford: Basil Blackwell, 1991) pp. 339–40.

20. D. Russell, *The Heaton Review*, 1927–1934: culture, class and a sense of place in inter-war Yorkshire', *Twentieth Century British History*, 17, 3, 2006, pp. 323–49.

21. (London: Longman, 1991 ed.), pp. 29–30.

22. *Huddersfield Examiner*, 22 Feb 1932.

23. Quoted in D. Elliston Allen, *British Taste. An Enquiry into the Likes and Dislikes of the Regional Consumer* (London: Hutchison, 1968). The ultimate destination was America.

24. Thomas Newbigging, *Lancashire Humour* (London: Dent, 1900), pp 1–3.

25. *Yorkshire Post*, 26 April 1932.

26. *Bill Tidy. Drawings 1957–1986* (Liverpool: Walker Gallery, 1986), p. 7.

27. D. Gervais, *Literary Englands. Versions of Englishness in Modern Writing* (Cambridge: Cambridge University Press, 1993), pp. 271–2.

28. David Law, 'Northern identities: five autobiographies of inter-war childhood' *Manchester Region History Review*, 17, 1, 2004, pp. 18–27.

29. K. Wrightson, 'Northern identities: the long durée', *Northern Review*, 2, 1995, p. 34.

Chapter Seventeen

Imagining regions in comparative perspective: the strange birth of North-West England

John K. Walton

Regions are, by their nature, complex entities, whether the preferred mode of definition involves shapes on the ground (geographical or administrative boundaries) or more overtly discursive constructions (representations of "regional" characteristics and cultures). As envisaged in this chapter, they cover broader territories (physical and imaginary) than a single administrative county, province, department or equivalent, and constitute the largest and most extensive intermediate collectivity between the individual and the nation state. Within them nest the lesser categories of provinces or counties, lesser territorial entities of government, cities, towns and smaller, more local communities, to each of which individuals and families owe allegiances which may be mutually reinforcing, contradictory or conflictual according to the circumstances in which the various layers of loyalty and instrumentality come into contact. Taking a European perspective, and setting aside Pollard's international economic regions for present purposes[1], we can regard the region as one of a small number of substantial geographical divisions within a nation that both generates subjective identification with its imputed collective characteristics, and constitutes an heuristic device (for bureaucrats as well as historians) that helps us to make sense of variety without losing ourselves in diversity.

On such a definition, the concept of a region is particularly problematic in the modern English setting. Here, the lack of deep-rooted and mutually congruent governmental and administrative divisions, and of well-defined linguistic and cultural characteristics that can be seen to be shared across extensive sub-national territories, imposes an arbitrary and debatable quality on all attempted definitions, including those based on post-Heptarchy administrative divisions and on more than an individual literary text or visual representation (and if one is chosen, how can one justify the choice?). Even the North-South divide, which itself features fluctuating and conflicting definitions both of the North and of the metropolitan "other" (as seen from "here", wherever exactly that may be) that tends to do duty for the South (except when it is represented in rustic, bucolic, romantically archaic countryside mode), generates debate over the extent and significance even of the most quantitative of adduced economic contrasts, even if we could agree on what should be compared. This apart, and even taking account of the relatively strong identity of the West Country (which is itself ultimately nebulous and subject to ebb, flow and changes of perspective according to vantage point, and overlaps with the imagined territory of "Wessex", with its literary and historical connotations, without being in any sense coterminous with it), the characteristics of English regions are particularly difficult to identify in a consensual way, despite the determined efforts of romantic topographers and tourism propagandists to construct them for their own purposes. The absence of contributions to this volume dealing with (for example) the English midlands, or the "south" (as opposed to the metropolis), or even the south-west (as opposed to Cornwall), is telling in this context. The English seem to be more at home with localities, cities and even counties than with more generously-proportioned intermediaries between the individual and the nation, with or without a state.

Any attempt to discuss "regional culture" in an imagined sub-division of the shape-shifting "North"[2] is therefore a challenging enterprise, especially as there are several different current versions of the "North West", involving various combinations of the counties of Cheshire, Lancashire (sometimes divided at the River Ribble, and carved up in a particularly complicated manner in the redrawing of local government boundaries in 1974), and what has for thirty years been known as "Cumbria", which might equally be incorporated into Fawcett's version of a northern region extending across from Northumberland and Durham, or into Charles Phythian-Adams's "archipelago England".[3] The area covered by the proposed North West Regional Assembly, part of the project of limited internal devolution in some English regions, covers Cheshire, Lancashire, Greater Manchester, Merseyside and Cumbria,[4] while the remit for North West Arts extends into the Peak District of north-west Derbyshire, an anomalous hybrid upland area "in the North but not of it",[5] and the British Library categorises William Tunnicliff's topographical survey of Staffordshire, Cheshire and Lancashire under the heading, "North West England: geographical features".[6] This is the most "southerly" definition of North West England I have found, although it lacks the ready visibility of the other examples given here. I myself have taught a regional history course on a "North West" covering Lancashire and Cumbria, while writing for the *Cambridge Social History of Britain* on a "North West" interpreted as constituted by the counties of Lancashire and Cheshire, a very different entity despite the importance of its shared Lancashire core; and other academic versions of North West England are also available, such as Jon Stobart's analysis of eighteenth-century urban networks in a "North West" composed of Cheshire and Lancashire south of the River Ribble.[7] Parts of a notional "North West" have also been subsumed into an alternative transpennine formulation of the "near North" or "M62 corridor" (with antecedents going back far beyond the eponymous motorway and the efforts of Will Alsop to promote a linear city along it), while Cheshire finds an alternative home in the Midlands or Welsh Borders and Cumbria is often assimilated into a Fawcettian "far or true

North" that links it with Northumberland and Durham.[8] These latter counties are in turn sometimes treated as if they alone constitute the "North", or represent an imagined core of genuine Northern values.[9] When what eventually became the Beamish open-air museum for the North of England was originally proposed in the mid-1960s, its promoter Frank Atkinson envisaged participation from Carlisle, Cumberland and Westmorland, but failed to obtain the necessary local government backing from that side of the Pennines, and fell back on a north-eastern vision of the North, which perforce ignored the industrial North West.[10] The core of that North West, for many purposes, is the old Lancashire industrial belt that occupies the triangle between Manchester, Liverpool and Preston and stretches fingers of desire outwards to the commuter and retirement estates and entertainment centres of the Irish Sea coast, and towards the Lake District as regional playground; and historians have often been tempted to write about the old "cotton towns" as if they were somehow the essence of the pre-1974 county of Lancashire, which covered a much wider area and diversity of topographies and economic characteristics, and as if discussing their distinctive features did duty for the county as an imagined whole, and in turn for the whole of a broader North-West "region".[11] References to a "Manchester region", however, tend to allude overtly to a smaller area within the North West more broadly conceived,[12] as do those to Merseyside, although John Belchem's representation of the latter might pay more heed to Liverpool's long-standing status as "capital of North Wales", with (for example) its notorious Welsh builders and (for many years) flourishing Welsh Methodist chapels.[13] This extends the ascribed aura of part of the imagined North West across an additional boundary.

Part of the problem is that notions of "the North West" as a regional descriptive or analytical category in England have a very limited pedigree. There is no deep regional mythology on which to build, spanning any version of the imagined region: neither Strathclyde nor Rheged map on to it, and there is nothing to match the impetus to territorial myth-making that is afforded on the other side of Northern England by Northumbria.[14] It seems clear that the use of North West England as a regional descriptor came into widespread use mainly through the planning discourse of the 1960s (not even the earlier versions of the 1930s or the immediate post-war years), and that the eight planning regions advocated by the short-lived Department of Economic Affairs under the Wilson government in 1965, or the rejected vision of eight regional planning councils proffered by the Redcliffe-Maud report on the future of local government in 1969, lie close to the roots of this territorial vision.[15] The Department of the Environment's Strategic

Plan for the North West, prepared in 1973 and published in the following year, was obviously a highly significant influence on attitudes and spatial imaginings.[16] A book title search through the British Library catalogue revealed that the term "North West" only came into frequent use in this context from the late 1960s and especially the early 1970s, as notions of regional planning beyond the individual city and its hinterland began to make headway among policy makers and their advisors. It was at this point that geographers began to write text-books and surveys of the regional geography of such an entity: where in 1966 Freeman, Rodgers and Kinvig had called their regional historical geography survey "Lancashire, Cheshire and the Isle of Man",[17] Marsden (1975) and Dobson (1977) adopted the new regional label, as did David Stenhouse in his "Past-into-Present" history for Batsford.[18] The foundation of Lancaster University's Centre for North West Regional Studies in 1973 also fits this pattern, with a geographical emphasis on north Lancashire and Cumbria, although John Marshall, the Centre's founder, had been teaching undergraduate and postgraduate courses on "The Regional History of North-West England" in the University since the late 1960s.[19]

Before this watershed, British Library title references to "the North West" as a region were few and far between. Significantly, the systematic use of the term was pioneered by an organization devoted to supporting business development, originally in Lancashire in the 1930s; and the early reports of the relabelled North West Industrial Development Association, from 1948 onwards, dealt with the industries of that county even as the new title suggested involvement on a wider stage.[20] Histories of religious bodies were even earlier in using the label: Whitley's *Baptists of North West England* pioneered the usage in 1913, and 34 years later Taylor's *The Valiant Sixty*, a history of the early Quakers published in 1947, had the region in the subtitle.[21] But the NWIDA was the first to incorporate it into the titles of a series of economically significant publications. During the 1950s we find references to the Incorporated Association of Headmasters conducting a survey of grammar schools in the "North West", and to the North-West Region of the National Federation of Painters and Decorators, no doubt the tip of an iceberg, while tourism, which was to become so prominent in the promotion of regional identities based on imagined cultures and characteristics (such as the imaginative "Heart of England" designation for the West Midlands), also began to use the term in bed and breakfast guides and the British Railways "Holiday Haunts" series, although in both cases the "North West" was combined with Wales.[22] In all these cases, even the tourist publications, the region appears to be merely a convenient administrative or descriptive sub-division, and the wider range of themes involving North-Western titles in the following decade fell into the same category, whether they dealt with the region's secret rooms, chapbook mummers' plays, natural history, shopping centres or railway history in pictures.[23] Up to this point economic and cultural organizations covering areas beyond the locality within future versions of the North West had organized themselves on the bases of counties or city regions, sometimes combined (Lancashire and Cheshire, Cumberland and Westmorland), from the Lancashire and Cheshire Historic and Antiquarian Societies and their Cumberland and Westmorland Archaeological and Antiquarian Society counterpart, along with the Chetham Society and the Record Society that emerged and survived from the boom in regional antiquarianism and the search for the validation of provincial identities through the elaboration of historical roots that began in earnest in the second quarter of the nineteenth century, to the Lancashire Industrial Development Association of 1931, mentioned above, which lived on after the Second World War as the NWIDA or Norwida.[24]

Viewed through the (possibly distorting) lens of the publications that reached the British Library catalogue, the late 1960s and early 1970s saw an explosion of voluntary organizations and government bodies with a North West prefix, or branches of national bodies that took the regional label rather than the available geographical alternatives. Thus, as well as the North West Arts Association, we have the Civic Trust for the North West, the North West Council for Sport and Recreation, the North West Roads Group (a branch of the British Roads Federation), the North Western Society for Industrial Archaeology and History, the North West Museum and Archaeology Service, and the North West Player Piano Association, not to mention the north-western incarnations of the nationalized utilities and arms of the Welfare State: North West Water Authority, North West Gas, the North West Regional Health Authority, the North Western Electricity Board and the North West region of the Department of Health and Social Security. The Civic Trust for the North West was in existence by 1969. As this official or quasi-official usage rapidly became current, so authors and compilers adopted it in their book titles. The first commercial directory to use "North West" in its title and achieve British Library catalogue listing was Kelly's in 1980, although this finding is particularly vulnerable to more detailed local research. Writings on transport history were early in the field, and Hadfield and Biddle covered the canals of North West England in 1970.[25] A book on North West railway history in pictures had already appeared in 1968,[26] perhaps influenced by the region's status as last bastion of the steam locomotive in that year, while G.O. Holt wrote about the railways of North West England in 1978,[27] and books on railways in the North West proliferated thereafter, despite the lack of a British Railways North Western region (though there had been a London and North Western Railway, which had a very high profile before being absorbed into the London, Midland and Scottish in 1923, but there was no regional equivalent of the North Eastern Railway, as a regional unifier east of the Pennines). Alan Lockett extended the theme to North West ships and seamen in 1982.[28] Owen Ashmore, author of an earlier book on the industrial archaeology of Lancashire, extended his remit to the North West in 1982.[29] The implications of all this for a distinctive kind of regional tourism were becoming apparent, as old industries declined and various incarnations of the "heritage industry" arose in their stead.[30] In 1988 Steve Beioley and Richard Denman published *Tourism and the Industrial Heritage of North West England* for yet another regional entity, the North West Tourist Board.[31] The idea of a distinctive North West industrial heritage was also used as part of a campaign to attract contemporary industry, as the North West Industrial Development Association personified and promoted it as "the most experienced industrial region in the world".[32] Economists began to focus on the North West as an area for study, helped by new conventions of statistical compilation, and stimulated by the problems posed by recession, unemployment and industrial re-location.[33] Topographers and travel writers began to use the term: the prolific Jessica Lofthouse adopted it in 1980, when the playwright David Pownall used it as a context for his musings on the area "between Ribble and Lune".[34] In the following year the RAC produced a guide to a North West England that extended from Cheshire to Cumbria.[35] The pioneering religious theme developed further, as the journal *North West Catholic History* was founded in 1971 (swiftly followed in secular vein by *North West Labour History*), and Roger Richardson published on *Puritanism in North West England* (actually Lancashire and Cheshire) in the following year.[36] In more eclectic vein, Peter Underwood published on the ghosts of North West England in 1978, while ten years later the Murder Club issued its guide to the region.[37] Use of the region as a geographical and perhaps a cultural marker had spread swiftly from bureaucratic convention into popular culture, no doubt assisted by the use of the terminology of the North West by regional broadcasters (although even Granadaland, based in Manchester, gave way to the Border Television franchise at fluctuating points within Cumbria); but there was never a newspaper or magazine with a North West remit, as opposed to providing coverage of smaller areas within the region, as in the case of *Lancashire Life* or the *Dalesman*. The use of the label North West to cover Lancashire and Cheshire, in (for example) the Manchester press, may have deeper antecedents and would be worthy of investigation; but that would require a substantial research project. But it is clear that from the 1980s onwards the use of "North West" became widespread and commonplace, with a particular proliferation of poetry publication (especially Christian poetry), based mainly in Peterborough and running on strongly through the 1990s without ever approaching the prestige of the North East's Bloodaxe imprint,[38] to set alongside the continuing use of the term by official bodies in spite of the demise of the regional utilities after privatisation.

This evidence on the recent nature of the emergence of what might be called "North West consciousness" has important implications for any attempt to discuss the cultural characteristics of this region. It would be interesting to compare these findings with other regions that might lay claim to older-established and more cohesive identities, founded on shared myths, stories and perceptions of shared characteristics, such as the North East (or Northumbria), the West Country (or Wessex), East Anglia or the Home Counties (or Hilaire Belloc's South Country). It would certainly be hard to sustain an environmentally deterministic approach to North Western identity, however robust the geographical boundaries of Irish Sea, Solway Firth, Pennines and Mersey (but only if we exclude Cheshire and Staffordshire) might look, and especially if we bear in mind that mountain ranges (if the Pennines deserve that label) and rivers can promote cultural unity across imposed administrative boundaries, based on shared ways of life and use of resources, as well as acting as agents of division: perceived frontiers of this kind are always permeable and often, for many purposes, illusory. Angus Winchester is right to suggest that the North West is an "almost meaningless expression at grass roots level" in the medieval and early modern period, providing little more than an aggregation of local experiences which facilitates "compare and contrast" exercises; but what this trawl through the publications record suggests is that the same would apply to the Industrial Revolution years and after, and that the North West lacks meaning as an overarching regional concept until around 1970, when the terminology comes into use alongside, rather than instead of, the older attachments to smaller regions, counties, cities, towns and localities.

Perhaps the nature of the publishing patterns that do emerge from this exercise may give us some clues as to perceptions of the common threads that might be thought to bind together a greater North West. Transport and industrial history are clearly important, with perceptions of the region as a cradle of early industrialization and related transport innovation very much to the fore. As perceived attributes of "the North West" rather than localities or particular lines of route within it, these are most strongly focused in south Lancashire, which did, however, act as a focus for migration from the rest of the region as well as beyond it, and in turn generated (for example) demand for tourism and leisure that affected much of the region, whether as providers, consumers, or both. Religious distinctiveness, in the form of Roman Catholic survival and importation alongside the Dissenting traditions of (especially) Quakerism and the Baptists and Congregationalists, is also to the fore in the literature. Ideas about a dominant North Western landscape, or art, or literature, or indeed poetry, might also be worth pursuing, although they would be likely to run into the sands of intra-regional diversity. The most important research project arising from these initial investigations would, indeed, be focused on the rise of the idea of the North West in the late twentieth century, where it came from, exactly what its content was, how and to what extent it took root, and what its cultural meanings have been. This would be well worth pursuing. A crucial question, however, is: who, and under what circumstances, without very specific prompting as in "Which region do you belong to?", would define themselves primarily, as their core identity, as inhabitants of North West England ahead of whatever other options were available to them?

When I compare North West England with my other main area of research, the Basque Country, I am struck by the much deeper roots of what might be called "regional identity" in what is actually not only a nation without a state, but one that straddles national boundaries, although the four provinces on the Spanish side of the border (Vizcaya, Guipúzcoa, Alava and, on the eastern fringes and more controversially, Navarra) have been much more assertive in promoting a sense of shared identity than the three on the French side.[39] The situation here is far from straightforward, as anyone who has followed the conflicts over the terrorist organization ETA and its associated political incarnations will be aware; but the conflicts themselves, violent and severe as they have been over the last thirty years, revolve around aspects of imagined collective identity, of a kind that would be unthinkable in North West England (Wales, of course, would be a different matter). Here there is a shared language, although one that divides its own speakers from those whose lives are lived through Spanish and French, and between the speakers of the seven (or eight) varieties of Basque, while the extent of Basque speaking and the visibility of Basque culture varies widely between and within the provinces. The Basque Country also has a set of shared myths of origins and stories about shared characteristics and virtues, although these also vary in some respects: the hospitable and open set of virtues attributed to the Basques by the rhetoric of tourism promoters sits uneasily alongside the toughness and asceticism attributed to the upland farmers, on an idealised version of whom the foundation myths of Sabino Arana's PNV (Basque Nationalist Party) are based.[40] Significantly, however, that party was founded at the end of the nineteenth century in the industrial city, provincial capital and international trading centre of Bilbao, and it was able to build on enduring indignation at the loss of the remaining *fueros* of the Spanish Basque provinces in 1876, which had removed historic exemptions from national taxation and conscription. It was also able to advance a vision of Basque democracy, based on shared nobility, which undermined the salience of economic divisions and rendered notions of class conflict alien to this version of Basque society. Arana's vision of Basque nationhood was founded in stories of racial identity as well as linguistic distinctiveness and autochthonous antiquity, involving (for example) shape of cranium and blood type, and a perception that Basques, as exceptionally good Catholics, were naturally virtuous, almost all of the crime being committed by immigrant *maketos* who could not share the Basques' innate aversion to vice. A supporting story explains that the Basques are so virtuous because, during a seven-year residence among them, the devil was unable to learn their formidably difficult language and therefore could not tempt them.[41]

Mainstream Basque nationalism has steadily retreated from these strong positions throughout the succeeding century. The Basques are both a farming and a maritime people, with corresponding contrasts in ways of life which are reflected in everything from social organisation (the fishermen's guilds or *gremios* in ports like Bermeo) to culinary traditions, and a contrast between outward-looking maritime societies (Bilbao for commerce and industry, San Sebastián for national and international tourism) and inward-looking farming or old industrial ones, although Basque speaking and PNV support have balancing strengths and weaknesses in both areas.[42] In the first third of the twentieth century the nationalists took care, alongside aristocratic traditionalists drawn mainly from the monarchist parties, together with sporting entrepreneurs and (uneasily) tourism promoters, to sustain or revive a set of shared traditional sports, dances and cultural and artistic traditions. The characteristic Basque sport of *pelota* or *jai-alai* was already becoming commercialised at the highest levels, with professional players and paying spectators in dedicated arenas, by the 1870s, and high levels of gambling accompanied all Basque sports, not excluding the rural ones involving the competitive cutting of tree-trunks or lifting of stones. Some commentators also remarked on a Basque propensity for alcoholic excess, which undermined

Arana's rhetoric of rustic virtue.[43] But perceptions of Basque characteristics of strength, power and virility were capable of being transferred to an imported sport like football, which Basque nationalism was eventually prepared to adopt and which provided a focus for inter- and intra-provincial rivalries within the Basque Country, especially between Bilbao/Vizcaya and San Sebastián/Guipúzcoa.[44] The enduring popularity of bullfighting, seen as essentially a Spanish spectacle and a dangerously corrupting import into Basque society, was a considerable embarrassment to proponents of a virtuous and rational Basque identity. Alongside all this, the Basque Country within Spain has, since the transition to democracy of the late 1970s after the death of Franco, and especially since the emergence of autonomous regions after the statute of 1983,[45] developed a strong regional government with powers of patronage and cultural support that are reinforced by provincial assemblies and institutions like savings banks; a regional police force operating alongside the national one; a regional narrow-gauge railway system operating alongside RENFE; two television channels, one in the Basque language; and an accelerating drive to make the Basque language the dominant vehicle of administrative and cultural expression. This marks a return to an agenda that was already strongly signalled under the Second Republic in the years immediately preceding the Civil War. What all this adds up to is a strong sense of shared identity that overcomes provincial differences and rivalries, and the anomalous status of Navarra, which is in many ways a semi-detached and divided province at the eastern edge of the Basque Country, with its own identity and politics alongside a strong and vociferous Basque presence. It even copes with the divisions in Basque politics that are associated with the tensions between ETA and its political wings, the Basque Nationalist party and the Basque branches of the Spanish political parties.[46]

What is striking about this is the complete absence of all of these themes from North West England. Here there is no historic sense of regional identity, no language issue, no campaign for the lost liberties of the Duchy of Lancaster or the reconstitution of the nation of Rheged, no sporting or cultural ties that can be represented as binding this collection of counties and (almost) city-states into an identifiable region, no regional cooking styles or sporting attributes, no myths about the racial or cultural distinctiveness of a North Western people. We can find pallid echoes of some of these themes at county level, especially in Lancashire, but there is nothing remotely resembling the Basque sense of shared identity, its historical depth or the sometimes obsessive and damaging ways in which it is pursued. The comparison is an extreme one, of course: North West England is situated towards the opposite end of a notional spectrum of regional identity from the Basque nation without a state, for better and worse; but over much of Europe regional identities are closer to the Basque pole than the North Western one, and English regions generally, with the possible exception of the North East/Northumbria, are clustered towards the weak end of the European regional spectrum. Even the assertive public display of the black and white Northumbrian flag is a very recent phenomenon. What needs explaining, however, is the rise of some sort of regional consciousness, however attenuated, even on the unpromising territory of the imagined North West since the late 1960s. Here can be found ample scope for comparative contemporary history.

Notes

1. S. Pollard, *Peaceful Conquest: the Industrialization of Europe 1760–1970* (Oxford University Press, 1981).

2. Dave Russell, *Looking North. The North in the National Imagination* (Manchester University Press, 2004) draws attention to such issues and refers back to earlier debates.

3. C.B. Fawcett, *Provinces of England* (London: Williams and Norgate, 1919), and commentary by Bill Lancaster; Charles Phythian-Adams, 'Differentiating Provincial Societies in English History: Contexts and Processes', this volume.

4. http://www.nwra.gov.uk/ accessed 6 Sept. 2004.

5. http://www.craftscouncil.org.uk/craftmap/nwa.html accessed 6 Sept. 2004; Melanie Tebbutt, '"In the Midlands but not of them": Derbyshire's Dark Peak', in N. Kirk (ed.), *Northern Identities* (Aldershot: Scolar Press, 2000).

6. William Tunnicliff, *Topographical Survey of Staffordshire, Cheshire and Lancashire*, catalogued under 'North West England: Geographical Features', British Library On-line Catalogue, accessed 6 Sept. 2004.

7. J.K. Walton, 'Lancashire and Cheshire, 1750–1950', in F.M.L. Thompson (ed.), *The Cambridge Social History of Britain* (Cambridge University Press, 1990), vol. 1, 355–414; Jon Stobart, *The First Industrial Region* (Manchester University Press, 2004).

8. S.A. Caunce, 'Northern English Industrial Towns: Rivals or Partners?', *Urban History* 30 (2003), 338–58.

9. R. Colls and B. Lancaster (eds), *Geordies* (Edinburgh University Press, 1992).

10. Frank Atkinson, *The Man who Made Beamish* (Gateshead: Northern Books, 1999), 94–5.

11. Patrick Joyce, *Visions of the people* (Cambridge, 1991) is a good example. An even better one is Barbara J. Blaszak, 'The Gendered Geography of the English Co-Operative Movement at the Turn of the Nineteenth Century', *Women's History Review* 9 (2000), 559–83; and see also critique by John K. Walton, *idem.* 12 (2003), 477–88.

12. The *Manchester Region History Review*, for example, was founded in 1987.

13. John Belchem, *Merseypride* (Liverpool University Press, 2000); J. R. Jones, *The Welsh Builder on Merseyside* (Liverpool: J.R. Jones, 1946); R. Merfyn Jones and D. Ben Rees, *The Liverpool Welsh and their religion* (Liverpool: Modern Welsh Publications, 1984).

14. Rheged's most prominent current incarnation is a tourist development near Penrith, which emphasizes the Dark Age kingdom's connection with Cumbria and the Northern Pennines,

although at the height of its influence in the sixth or seventh century it may have extended as far south as what is now Oldham, as far north as Galloway or Morayshire and as far east as Northumberland. But it has never attained the popular visibility or historical respectability of Northumbria and its antecedents: http://www.rheged.com accessed 12 Sept. 2004.

15. Peter Calvocoressi, *The British Experience 1945–75* (Harmondsworth: Pelican, 1979), 171–2.

16. Department of the Environment, North West Joint Planning Team, Strategic Plan for the North West, *Report*, 1973 (London, 1974).

17. T.W. Freeman, H.B. Rodgers and R.H. Kinvig, *Lancashire, Cheshire and the Isle of Man* (London: Nelson, 1966).

18. W.E. Marsden, *North West England* (Cambridge University Press, 1975); F.R. Dobson, *The North West: a Regional Study* (London: Hodder and Stoughton, 1977); David Stenhouse, *The North West* (London: Batsford, 1977).

19. http://www.lancs.ac.uk/users/cnwrs/ accessed 12 Sept. 2004.

20. North West Industrial Development Association, *Report Nos.1 and 2*, covering the Furness area and the Lancashire weaving district, 1948.

21. W.T. Whitley, *Baptists of North West England* (Preston, 1913); E.E. Taylor, *The Valiant Sixty* (Bannisdale Press, 1947).

22. Incorporated Association of Headmasters, *The Staffing of Grammar Schools… in the North West* (Liverpool University Press, 1954); National Federation of Master Painters and Decorators, *Regional Review*, 1957 onwards; P.S. Williams (comp.), *Bed and Breakfast in Wales and North West England: the Tourist's Handbook* (Croydon, 1959); British Railways, *Holiday Haunts: North West England and North Wales, including the Isle of Man*, 1950 onwards.

23. Winifred I. Howard, *Secret Rooms of North West England* (Clapham via Ingleton: Dalesman, 1964); *The Changing Scene: A Review of Natural History in the North West of England* (Kirby Lonsdale, 1960 onwards); Victoria University (Manchester), Department of Town and Country Planning, *Regional Shopping Centres in North West England* (Manchester, 1964); J.A. Patmore, *Railway History in Pictures: North West England* (Newton Abbot: David and Charles, 1968).

24. Alan Crosby, *A Society with no Equal: the Chetham Society, 1843–1993* (Manchester: The Chetham Society, 1993); Philippa Levine, *The Amateur and the Professional* (Cambridge University Press, 1986); *Norwida: Fifty Years of Service 1931/1981* (Manchester: The Association, 1981).

25. Charles Hadfield and Gordon Biddle, *The Canals of North West England* (Newton Abbot: David and Charles, 2 vols., 1970).

26. Patmore, *Railway History in Pictures*.

27. G.O. Holt, *The North West* (Newton Abbot: David and Charles, Regional History of the Railways of Great Britain series, 1978).

28. Alan Lockett, *North West Ships and Seamen* (Preston: Editorial Workshop, 1982).

29. Owen Ashmore, *The Industrial Archaeology of North West England* (Manchester University Press, 1982).

30. Robert Hewison, *The Heritage Industry* (London: Methuen, 1987).

31. Steve Beioley and Richard Denman, *Tourism and the Industrial Heritage of North West England* (Leisureworks for the North West Tourist Board, 1988).

32. NWIDA, *North West England: the Most Experienced Industrial Region in the World* (Manchester, n.d.).

33. P.E. Lloyd, *North West England 1975–1980: industrial change and job generation under conditions of recession* (University of Manchester, 1983); P. L. McLoughlin, *Semi and non economic factors in the formation of manufacturing plant in the North West region of England 1972–1975* (University of Reading, 1982).

34. Jessica Lofthouse, *Borders of the North West* (London: Hale, 1980); David Pownall, *Between Ribble and Lune: Scenes from the North West* (London: Gollancz, 1980).

35. Ken Ward, *Northwest England: Cumbria, Cheshire, Greater Manchester, Lancashire, Merseyside* (London: Travellers Realm, 1981).

36. R.C. Richardson, *Puritanism in North West England* (Manchester University Press, 1972). Richardson's book, which originated as a doctoral thesis, emerged a year after the completion of another doctorate with a similar geographical remit: John Baxendale, 'The Liberal Party in North-West England, 1885–1900', D.Phil. thesis, University of Oxford, 1971. Here again, the North West in question was Lancashire and Cheshire: my thanks to Dr Baxendale for his helpful comments on this issue.

37. Peter Underwood, *Ghosts of North West England* (London: Fontana, 1978); *The Murder Club Guide to North West England* (London: Harrap, 1988).

38. For example Rachael Walton (ed.), *North West Poets* (Bretton: Arrival, 1992); Andrew Head (ed.), *Anchor Poets for the North West* (Peterborough: Anchor, 1995).

39. For an accessible comparative study in English, L. Castells and J.K. Walton, 'Contrasting Identities: North West England and the Basque Country, 1840–1936', in Edward Royle (ed.), *Issues of Regional Identity* (Manchester University Press, 1998), 44–81.

40. See most recently Ludger Mees, *Nationalism, Violence and Democracy: the Basque Clash of Identities* (Basingstoke: Palgrave Macmillan, 2003).

41. Mark Kurlansky, *The Basque History of the World* (London: Jonathan Cape, 1999), pulls together a lot of this material in accessible form.

42. Ander Delgado and John K. Walton, 'La Pesca y los Pescadores en Inglaterra y el País Vasco, siglo XIX – 1930', *Itsas Memoria* 4 (2003), 563–82.

43. J.K. Walton, 'Tradition and Tourism: Representing Basque Identities in Guipúzcoa and San Sebastián, 1848–1936' in Kirk (ed.), *Northern Identities*, 87–108.

44. J.K. Walton, 'Basque football rivalries in the twentieth century: Real Sociedad and Athletic Bilbao', in G. Armstrong (ed.), *Fear and Loathing: Local Rivalries in World Football* (Oxford: Berg, 2001), 119–33; F.J. Caspistegui and J.K. Walton (eds.), *Guerras Danzadas* (Baranain, Navarra: EUNSA, 2001), a bilingual collection in English and Spanish on football and local identities.

45. Jeremy MacClancy, *The Decline of Carlism* (Reno, Nevada: University of Nevada Press, 2000), is the most recent treatment of Navarra's distinctive political history and its legacy to Basque nationalism.

46. Mees, *Nationalism, Violence and Democracy*, and references cited there.

Chapter Eighteen

The North and the dynamics
of regional identity in later
medieval England

Matt Holford

The North is a difficult subject. It is indisputably an area with vague and shifting boundaries, encompassing great diversity; equally clearly, it is a concept which has formed the basis of powerful loyalties and identities.[1] But medieval historians, perhaps understandably, have been happiest emphasizing the region's diversity. They have argued that in social, economic, and political terms the region is too "large, diverse and ill-defined" to warrant study in itself;[2] and that "identities, like social and economic patterns, varied greatly in different parts of the region".[3] It has also been argued that identification with the broader North was submerged either by national loyalties, or by allegiances to smaller communities.[4] As a result Northern identities – identities based around ideas of the North – have been overlooked. Undoubtedly such identities can be elusive and insubstantial. They lack, in the words of Rees Davies, "hard institutional substance and ample archival sediment".[5] But although the North was an "idea" rather than a geographical or social "reality", that idea could still have an important influence on social and political identities in the region.

The power of "the North" as an idea also sheds broader light on the formation of regional identities in medieval England. This power resulted from the consistent characterization of the region and its inhabitants in national political culture, particularly after the outbreak of war with Scotland from 1296. The idea of the North was largely the creation of people from outside the region: but it was nevertheless a powerful vehicle for identification within the region itself. It was so all the more because the North was often defined by contrast or conflict with the south, and because the region came – again as a result of war – to have a relatively clear geographical delimitation.

The consistent characterization which the North received in medieval English culture is relatively well-understood: broadly, from the twelfth century onwards, the region was portrayed as wild, uncivilised, and poor.[6] These stereotypes remained much the same throughout the Middle Ages. The caricature of the "fierce northern people", for example, changed little from William of Malmesbury in the twelfth century to Polydore Vergil in the sixteenth.[7] "Northerners, stronger in arms, readier to war", in the words of a fifteenth-century writer.[8]

The outbreak of long-term hostilities with Scotland in 1296, however, did lead to significant developments in how the North was imagined. Uniquely among English regions, the North came to have a clearly defined function within the national polity: the defence of the realm against the Scottish enemy. This role was sometimes allotted to a vaguely defined "north parts": for the Westminster chronicler, writing at the end of the fourteenth century, "the northern lords" were "most expert in Scottish wars".[9] But war also led to the North acquiring greater geographical definition. The area north of the river Trent became increasingly associated with defence against the Scots, and the North in turn became associated with the area beyond the Trent.

The river had acted as a division in royal administration from the early thirteenth century; but it really began to shape wider political consciousness with the outbreak of long-term hostilities between England and Scotland.[10] The Trent became a frequent means of defining the northern area which should bear particular responsibility for that war: royal lieutenants were established from the Trent northwards; the faithful men of the counties beyond the Trent treated amongst themselves for the welfare of that region; men were levied from the Trent northwards, and so on.[11] War did not, of course, affect all parts of this region equally, and it was Northumberland and Cumberland which became most thoroughly militarized, and which acquired distinct legal and jurisdictional status as the East and West marches respectively.[12] Nor was the Trent the only border used to delimit "the north", and it was not a fixed and definitive boundary with a significant influence on social and political life.[13] To some extent, indeed, it was only "a convenient geographical phrase", simply a short-hand for referring to the counties north of the river.[14] But the Trent did, nevertheless, become the most widespread and prominent of the region's southern boundaries. It offered a relatively fixed and widely shared way of delimiting the North which became central to how the region was understood. As early as the 1340s, the commons in parliament successfully petitioned that taxes granted from "north of the Trent" should be used "in defence of the North" or to attack the Scots.[15]

In one sense, therefore, war with Scotland led to "the north parts" becoming increasingly integrated with the realm as a whole, as the region's distinctive contribution to national security was recognized and defended by wider political society. On the other hand, however, the region's distinctive responsibilities came to set it apart from the rest of England. Firstly, war seems to have given renewed currency to perceptions of the region's wildness and the hot temper of its inhabitants. Observation of these characteristics becomes increasingly common from the fourteenth century.[16] Secondly, the region could be seen as contaminated by its proximity to Scotland. "Northerners", when they failed to protect the kingdom against attacks, were easily imagined as complicit with the enemy. The Westminster chronicler considered that "our northerners", once active and vigorous, had recently and regrettably become lazy and spiritless and were failing to defend the border.[17] Such distrust of "northerners", in fact, was typical of the 1380s, when Scottish attacks reached deep into England.[18]

War thus contributed to the development of an "oppositional" way of seeing the North,[19] which emphasized its difference from, and usually its inferiority to, the south. Thomas Walsingham, another chronicler writing towards the end of the fourteenth century, described Northerners as a *gens* or people, rash and impulsive by nature, who barked rather than spoke, and his comments were echoed in the fifteenth century.[20] As we have seen above, most of the stereotypes which characterized this *gens* changed little throughout the Middle Ages; but in some ways, they did develop in line with changing political circumstances. The idea of the rude or backward north thus shifted in the 1530s, as the region became associated with doctrinal conservatism or heresy in the minds of some of the government's ministers. One, writing to Thomas Cromwell in 1535, described "the rude people of the north... more superstitious than virtuous, long accustomed to frantic fantasies and ceremonies".[21] It could easily be argued that such stereotypes and literary conventions had little relationship to reality: how could it be otherwise, when the area north of the Trent was characterized above all by social and economic diversity? All the same, these conventions deserve our attention: they represent "the world as contemporaries saw it" – or at least, as they chose to see it, some of the time.[22]

For the cultural frameworks which defined North and south in opposition to one another could on occasion become highly significant. As Tony Pollard has pointed out, it seems ridiculous to imagine "a deeply divided society in which North and south looked upon each other in mutual hostility".[23] But several later-medieval writers do refer to ill-feeling as if it were commonplace – "Northerners and Southerners, in general, do not love one another".[24] At moments of crisis, hostility could easily come to the fore, and opposition between North and south was one of the frameworks through which contemporaries understood political conflict. In the turbulent days of late 1460 and early 1461, for example, Lancastrian forces were widely perceived as "northern" rebels.[25] There were reports that "northerners and their supporters" wanted to kill all the Franciscan friars "on this [the south] side of the river Trent", and an English poem described how these northerners had been resisted by "all the south of England unto the water of Trent."[26] The Trent even became a concrete boundary between the loyal south and the rebellious North. In a proclamation of 6 March 1461, Edward IV forbade anyone to cross the Trent without special licence, and the abbot of Fountains was later forbidden to travel north of the river.[27] Distrust of "the North" continued in the later fifteenth century, especially during Richard III's reign;[28] and opposition between "North" and "south" was again noticeably prominent during the rebellion of 1536 known as the Pilgrimage of Grace. From early on, the rebels were widely perceived as "northern men", the "commons of the north" or "northern rebels".[29] They also had the characteristics appropriate to their region. A royal herald described the "northern men" as "very cruel fellows"; in Boston it was thought that one man from the northern army "would be good enough for two of the best from this country".[30] The North-south divide was, it appeared, increasingly real.

Much of the evidence about "the North" relates only to outsiders' perceptions of the region. The "construct of the North", indeed, has been described as merely a fantasy "of those who lived elsewhere", something of no significance to natives of the region.[31] But such a judgment is over-hasty. The ideas we have surveyed above did matter to inhabitants of the region.

First, the region's place in the national polity, defending the realm against the Scottish enemy, was recognized and exploited by Northerners themselves. It was natural for a Durham writer to describe the Scottish war as the concern of "northern lords", and for another in 1346 to see the Scots as "resolved to destroy the whole of the North", and to describe the relief of "the North parts" at their defeat.[32] Institutions petitioning the crown for assistance portrayed themselves as central to the region and its role in the defence of the realm. It was in this context that, around 1380, Tynemouth Priory was described as "a notable fortress of the North", and Hull as "the key of the North parts";[33] while in the late fifteenth century the city of York argued that it was in danger of becoming so poor that "the north parts of this your realm – by whom your old enemies the Scots are commonly resisted in their malice ... – should be greatly dishonoured and hurt".[34]

Especially when interacting with central government, then, northerners identified with a region that was very much a member of the wider body politic. This reflected one way in which the region was constructed in political discourse. But definitions of the North as "other", as uncivilized and inferior, also had their influence on northern identities, which also took shape in clear contrast to a "south". Such oppositional identities, in fact, could be particularly important to what it was to be northern.

This was perhaps especially the case in periods of political crisis and dislocation, when the interests of centre and provinces seemed particularly at odds. One such period was the 1310s and 1320s, when Scottish attacks on northern England were notably severe, and when it was felt that that the region had been abandoned by a royal government with interests elsewhere. The Northumbrian knight Thomas Gray criticized Edward II for leaving the northern marches "in great tribulation" and retiring "to the south" in 1319,[35] while the Scottish historian John Barbour recorded that in the same year the English were divided, with "southern men" urging the king to continue the siege of Berwick and "northern men" urging him to abandon the siege and protect their estates.[36]   Other signs of regional dislocation from the crown included the widespread forging of local truces with the Scots, and the open rebellion of Gilbert of Middleton in 1317. Middleton, who claimed the title of duke of Northumberland or Northumbria (*dux Northumbrie*), may even have appealed to regional loyalties of some kind.[37]

Such dislocation helps to explain a tangible opposition between North and south that can be detected around this time. The "Lanercost" chronicle from Carlisle described the election of a bishop of Carlisle in 1325, when the canons' choice was set aside in favour of a papal nominee. The replacement was identified rather scornfully as "a southern man". The same chronicle, describing Edward II's progress against Thomas of Lancaster in 1322, saw the king as accompanied by "all the forces from south of Trent". This is a highly distorted view of events: but one which reveals a potent sense of regional opposition in the writer's mind.[38] In 1327 a petition from "the men north of Trent" was added at a late stage to parliamentary proceedings, presumably as a result of regional pressure, and perhaps for the same reason knights from both north and south of Trent were present in the deputation from parliament which visited Edward II before his deposition.[39] It is perhaps no coincidence that conflicts between northern and southern students in London were recorded in 1326.[40]

After this period there is little direct evidence of oppositional northern identities until the mid fifteenth century, another period when political dislocation acquired a regional element.[41] In 1460–61, when Yorkist and Lancastrian forces fought for the throne of England, Lancastrians were widely perceived as "northerners". They were described as "appointed to ... give away men's goods and livelihoods in all the south country", and as having license to plunder as soon as they arrived south of the river Trent; and they were said to think that one of their number was a match for a thousand southerners.[42] Whether the words of these hostile commentators bear any relation to northern self-perceptions is, unfortunately, unclear, but later evidence does suggest the development, towards the end of the fifteenth century, of northern identities increasingly distanced from the south. Richard III claimed in 1483 that southern forces were aiming to destroy "the North parts".[43] In 1485, after the battle of Bosworth, Richard's death, and the deaths of "many other lords and nobles of these North parts", was noted at York, and the city planned at one stage to memorialize these men in a list.[44] In 1489 an anonymous proclamation attempted to raise "all the north parts of England" in rebellion against the crown.[45]

It is with the rebellion of 1536, however, commonly known as the Pilgrimage of Grace, that the importance of political identities focused on the North can most clearly be seen. At heart, the Pilgrimage was a reaction against the religious and political changes of the 1530s.[46] But it gained a considerable amount of support and momentum through appeals to long-established ideas of the North. The region was not simply opposed to a "south". It had the characteristics of bellicosity and rudeness that were widely attributed to it by outsiders, but these characteristics were presented by the rebels in a positive, not a negative light.
This is most clearly seen in the verse "exhortation to the nobles and commons of the North" written by John Pickering, a Dominican friar, which circulated widely among the Pilgrims. The opening lines called on the "faithful people of the boreal region / Chief bellicose champions by divine providence", and the poem went on to claim that, although "the northern people in time long past / Hath little been regarded of the austral nation", the pilgrims would soon win renown from "these southern heretics", and overthrow them: "their faith is untrue".[47] Such appeals deserve more attention than they have hitherto received. The crown's officers, at least, realized their power. Interrogating Pickering after the rebellion, they asked what could encourage the rebels more than the claim that they had long been despised by "the southern men". Pickering answered that he had "put in as much matter as he could" to encourage the rebels.[48]

Much other evidence confirms the importance of "the North" to the rebels. The rebel army as a whole characterized itself as "the barons and commonalty of the North",[49] and resolved to keep to its purpose "in all this North land".[50] For many rebels the ideological concerns behind the pilgrimage were bound up with the claims of regional solidarity; for some, indeed, regional antipathies seem to have been more significant than any of the "official" aims of the pilgrimage. At an early stage there was talk in the marketplace at Beverley of bringing home the goods of Cheapside and the south; when Sir Francis Bigod attempted to lead a new rising early in 1537 he claimed that its costs would be met by "the fat priests' benefices of the south". In the aftermath of the rebellion a sympathetic writer mocked the "southern boys" who were threatening enough at home, but cried like "maid men" at the prospect of actual battle with the northerners.[51]

It would still be misleading to describe the pilgrimage as a northern rebellion which illustrates a "North-South dichotomy".[52] Few of the Pilgrims' demands were regional or local in character; nor was the image of a rebel North wholly accurate. Significant areas of the region remained loyal to the crown, and conversely, the Pilgrims had their supporters and sympathizers in the south. One man was sold his shoes cheaply in London because he was a "northerner" and his fellows had "done well there".[53] It is for such reasons that interpretation of the pilgrimage as in any way a "northern" rebellion finds little favour in modern accounts.[54]

Nevertheless, the idea of the North clearly enabled the construction of an "imagined community" in which individual differences were subsumed by a larger common purpose. It was an idea largely derived from the conventions of national political culture explored above. The North was an area whose poverty contrasted with southern wealth, whose manliness contrasted with southern effeminacy, and whose rudeness' became, in the avoidance of doctrinal innovation and "heresy", a positive virtue. These were stereotypes with only a crude relation to life on the ground: but they were nevertheless part of what sustained the rebellion.

Part of what gave northern identities their power was, therefore, the coherent characterization of the region as a discrete area potentially under threat from or in conflict with a "south". In some contexts, divisions between North and south were enshrined in institutional arrangements, as at the universities of Oxford and Cambridge, where conflicts between "northern" and "southern" students were common.[55] At Oxford, antagonism between northerners and southerners has been described as "deep-seated and continuous" and "a touchstone which needs to be applied in any attempts to explain the causes which underlay every sort of quarrel and controversy."[56] Outside such contexts, identification with "the North" was more occasional, often stimulated by particular local or national crises. But it was probably only because of a more general readiness to identify with "the north" that northern identities did powerfully come to the fore at particular moments.

The other factor which gave particular force to northern identities was the region's geographical definition. Often, of course, the exact area to which "the North" refers is unclear: and it could be argued that it was precisely this vagueness which made the idea of the North widely available and attractive. But on the other hand, as we have seen above, the North was in many contexts defined as the area north of the river Trent. Within the region, too, the Trent gave solidity to the definition of northern identities. As early as 1327, as we have seen above, a petition from "the men north of Trent" was presented in parliament; and at the end of our period, during the Pilgrimage of Grace, the river again defined the North.[57] As well as asking for parliament to be held "in a convenient place" at Nottingham or York, the pilgrims demanded that men "from north of Trent" should be allowed to answer most subpoenas at York.[58] But the significance of the river is perhaps best seen in other contexts, and we can again take examples from either end of our period. First, in 1309, it was alleged that monks in Durham Priory had conspired "that no-one should be received as a monk, who was born on the other side of the Trent, or other fixed limits".[59] The charge reflected conflicts within the priory resulting from a serious dispute with bishop Antony Bek that had begun in 1300. Several of the monks who had supported Bek's cause were from the bishop's home county of Lincolnshire, and it was apparently felt that men from further north would have been less divided in their loyalties to the priory. The region's boundary potentially enabled northern solidarities to be clearly defined and enforced.

This was also the case at the other end of our period, when Thomas Thomson (d. 1540) established a fellowship at St. John's College, Cambridge, with a marked regional bias. Fellows were to be men from Yorkshire (particularly the area of Cleveland); if such could not be found, men were to be chosen from Richmondshire or the bishopric (that is, modern county) of Durham; and finally from any county north of the river Trent.[60] Loyalty to the wider north was not, therefore, the most important of Thomson's local and regional solidarities: but such loyalty was nevertheless present, and the region's recognized boundary enabled this loyalty to be expressed in real and concrete form.

Conclusion

Thomas Thomson's foundation is a good place to end this survey. It is a reminder of the complexity and elusiveness of regional identities. Thomson is unlikely to have been alone in imagining himself in relation to several neighbouring or overlapping localities, of which "the North" was by no means necessarily the most important.

Inevitably the kind of broad survey attempted here can capture relatively little of this complexity and elusiveness. But such a survey can still contribute something to an agenda for regional history. First, "the North" reveals the importance of examining contemporary ideas about regions. As we have seen, few if any modern historians would recognize the North as a region with geographical, cultural, or social coherence. The North was not a "cultural province" of the kind identified by Charles Phythian-Adams: as a genuine cultural boundary, the Tees seems to have been more important than the Trent.[61] Nevertheless, contemporaries recognized and identified with an increasingly well-defined idea of the North. Even if such identities were only fleeting and occasional, they could nevertheless be very real. They should be as important to regional history as the social, economic, or geographical "realities" of the regions around which they were based.

Second, the North reveals something about the dynamics of regional identity in medieval England. This was very different to the creation of regional identities in an area like Brittany in France.[62] Like many other regional units in Western Europe, Brittany could be described as a state within a state. Its relationship to the kings of France only became clearly defined in the thirteenth century; and in the later middle ages Brittany was ruled by dukes with extensive judicial and financial powers over their subjects, and with the will and resources to mould local attachment to the region. There were few such areas in the precociously-centralized kingdom of England – although some parallels are offered by highly-privileged liberties like the "counties palatine" of Durham and Chester, both areas with a strong sense of local identity and particularism.[63]

In contrast, the only real "institutional expression of northern identity" has rightly been identified as the ecclesiastical province of York.[64] The convocations in which this body assembled functioned primarily to grant taxes from the northern clergy to the crown.[65] No nobleman in late-medieval England had anything approaching the authority of earlier rulers of Northumbria: the wish of Henry, fifth earl of Northumberland (d. 1527), to "rule all from Trent north" was, simply, a wish.[66] Such institutional or political coherence as the North possessed was thus largely the result of central royal administration: the only men with formal authority over the whole area beyond Trent were the lieutenants sometimes appointed by the crown.[67] Culture or institutions within the region itself made little contribution. The Pilgrims of Grace may have marched with the banner of St Cuthbert before them, but the saint had no settled or enduring association with "the North" as a whole.[68]

Identification with the North became increasingly shaped by the structures of royal government. More widely, in fact, there is strong evidence that the state was fundamental in shaping local identities in medieval England: the county, a primary focus of local identification, was after all essentially a unit of royal government.[69] Northern identities were also, however, shaped by the stereotypes of wider political discourse – the ideas of northern bellicosity, barbarity, and inferiority explored above. All this gave the North unique importance as a region. It is difficult to think of an area or "country" in medieval England, above the level of the county, with comparable power.[70] Other "countries" also had geographical definition: notably those comprised of groups of counties, such as Norfolk and Suffolk (comparable to the modern region of East Anglia), or Northumberland and Durham (essentially the modern "north-east").[71] But such regions lacked the strong characteristics which "the North" acquired. They did not have a comparably well-defined place in the national polity, they were not consistently associated with a limited set of characteristics; most of all, perhaps, they had no "other" against which they could be set. The North was a region created by outsiders. Paradoxically, it was precisely for that reason that the region could matter so much to its inhabitants.

Notes

1. J. le Patourel, 'Is Northern History a Subject?', *Northern History*, 12 (1976), pp. 1–15. The best survey remains Helen M. Jewell, 'North and South: The Antiquity of the Great Divide', *Northern History*, 27 (1991), pp. 1–25, and more broadly, her *The North-South Divide: The Origins of Northern Consciousness in England* (Manchester, 1994).

2. R. B. Dobson, 'Politics and the Church in the Fifteenth-Century North', in *The North of England in the Age of Richard III*, ed. A. J. Pollard (Stroud, 1996), pp. 1–18 (p. 3); A. J. Pollard, 'The Characteristics of the Fifteenth-Century North', in *Government, Religion and Society in Northern England 1000–1700*, ed. John C. Appleby and Paul Dalton (Stroud, 1997), pp. 131–43 (pp. 131–2).

3. Alastair J. Macdonald, 'John Hardyng, Northumbrian Identity, and the Scots', in *North-East England in the Later Middle Ages*, ed. C. D. Liddy and R. H. Britnell (Woodbridge, 2005), pp. 29–42 (p. 39).

4. Pollard, 'Characteristics of the Fifteenth-Century North', pp. 141–2; Bruce M. S. Campbell, 'North-South Dichotomies 1066–1500', in *Geographies of England: The North-South Divide, Material and Imagined*, ed. Alan R. H. Baker and Mark Billinge (Cambridge, 2004), pp. 145–74, esp. p. 167.

5. R. R. Davies, 'The Peoples of Britain and Ireland, 1100–1400', *Transactions of the Royal Historical Society*, 6th series 4 (1994), 1–20 (pp. 2–3). For comparable approaches to regional history see Edward Royle, 'Introduction: Regions and Identities', in *Issues of Regional Identity: In Honour of John Marshall*, ed. Edward Royle (Manchester, 1998), pp. 1–13; *Geographies of England*, ed. Baker and Billinge; *Identité régionale et conscience nationale en France et en Allemagne du moyen âge à l'époque moderne*, ed. Rainer Babel and Jean-Marie Moeglin (Sigmaringen, 1997).

6. For a recent survey, see A. J. Pollard, *Imagining Robin Hood: The Late-Medieval Stories in Historical Context* (London, 2004), pp. 63–71; for background, see Jewell, *North-South Divide*, pp. 33, 37–38; Pollard, 'Characteristics of the Fifteenth-Century North', pp. 140–41.

7. *The Anglica Historia of Polydore Vergil, 1485–1537*, ed. D. Hay, Camden Society, 3rd series 74 (1950), pp. 9–10.

8. *Registrum quorundam abbatum monasterii S. Albani*, ed. H. T. Riley, 2 vols., Rolls Series 28/6 (London, 1863–69), I, 171.

9. *The Westminster Chronicle 1381–94*, ed. and tr. L. C. Hector and B. F. Harvey (Oxford, 1982), pp. 394–95.

10. Jewell, *The North-South Divide*, p. 23. Jewell shows that the modern historian can identify some kind of north-south frontier in the region of the Trent from a much earlier period. But it is unusual for contemporaries to identify the boundary in terms of the river before the fourteenth century.

11. *Rotuli Scotiae*, ed. D. Macpherson, J. Caley, W. Illingworth, 2 vols. (London, 1814–19), Vol I, 130, 136, 139–40, 147, 148, 167, 190, etc.

12. See, for example, Henry Summerson, 'Responses to War: Carlisle and the West March in the Later Fourteenth Century', in *War and Border Societies in the Middle Ages*, ed. Anthony Goodman and Anthony Tuck (London, 1992), pp. 155–77; Cynthia J. Neville, *Violence, Custom, and Law: The Anglo-Scottish Border Lands in the Later Middle Ages* (Edinburgh, 1998).

13. For alternative boundaries, see Pollard, *Robin Hood*, p. 67.

14. E. R. Stevenson, 'The Escheator', in *The English Government at Work II: Fiscal Administration*, ed. W. A. Morris and J. R. Strayer (Cambridge, MA, 1947), pp. 109–67 (p. 116); cf. Jewell, *North-South Divide*, pp. 23–24; J. C. Holt, *The Northerners: A Study in the Reign of King John*, rev. edn (Oxford, 1992), pp. 14–16. For some of the potential complexities which resulted when the river was used as a real boundary, see S. T. Gibson, 'The Escheatries', *English Historical Review 36* (1921), pp. 218–25 (pp. 220–22); *Rotuli Scotiae*, I, 655; *Calendar of the Close Rolls 1343–6* (London, 1904), p. 471.

15. *Rotuli Parliamentorum, ut petitiones et placita in parliamento*, ed. J. Strachey, 6 vols. (London, 1767–77), Vol II, 148, 150, 201, 202; M. Jurkowski, C. L. Smith, and D. Crook, *Lay Taxes in England and Wales, 1188–1688* (Kew, 1998), pp. 46–7, 50–1.

16. In addition to the references below, see, from 1327, *Literae Cantuariensis: The Letter Books of the Monastery of Christ Church, Canterbury*, ed. J. Brigstocke Sheppard, 3 vols., Rolls Series 85 (London, 1887–89), Vol I, 224.

17. *Westminster Chronicle*, ed. Hector and Harvey, pp. 138–9.

18. Alastair J. Macdonald, *Border Bloodshed: Scotland and England at War 1369–1403* (East Linton, 2000), pp. 212–3.

19. *The St Albans Chronicle*, ed. Taylor, Childs and Watkiss, pp. 366–7 (*latrantes; prout moris est illius gentis*), pp.568–69.

20. *Registrum quorundam abbatum*, ed. Riley, Vol I, 388–90, 399–400.

21. *Letters and Papers, Foreign and Domestic, of the Reign of Henry VIII*, ed. J. S. Brewer, J. Gairdner and R. Brodie, 21 vols. (London, 1862–1920 – henceforward *L&P*), VII, 955.

22. Davies, 'Peoples of Britain and Ireland', p. 16.

23. A. J. Pollard, *North-Eastern England During the Wars of the Roses: Lay Society, War, and Politics 1450–1500* (Oxford, 1990), p. 27.

24. *Gesta abbatum monasterii Sancti Albani*, ed. H.T. Riley, Rolls Series 28/4, 3 vols (London, 1867–69), Vol I, 271; cf. G. R. Owst, *Literature and Pulpit in Medieval England*, 2nd edn (Oxford, 1961), p. 563; *Humanist Scholarship and Public Order: Two Tracts against the Pilgrimage of Grace by Sir Richard Morison*, ed. D. S. Berkowitz (Washington, 1984), p. 132.

25. Pollard, *North-Eastern England*, pp. 25–26.

26. *Paston Letters*, ed. Davis, II, 213; *Early English Carols*, ed. R. L. Greene, 2nd edn (London, 1977), no. 431; and compare Richard Beadle,' Fifteenth-Century Political Verses from the Holkham Archives', *Medium Aevum*, 71 (2002), pp.101–21. The Trent did not mark an

administrative division for the English Franciscans: J. Burton, *Monastic and Religious Orders in Britain 1000–1300* (Cambridge, 1994), p. 122 and n. 44.

27. *Calendar of the Close Rolls 1461–8* (London, 1949), pp. 54–5, 72; cf. Cora L. Scofield, *The Life and Reign of Edward IV*, 2 vols. (London, 1923), Vol I, 155–6, 167–8.

28. See, for example, Historical Manuscripts Commission, *The Manuscripts of the Duke of Rutland*, 4 vols. (London, 1888–1905), pp.I, 3–4; *Paston Letters and Papers of the Fifteenth Century*, ed. N. Davis, 2 vols (Oxford, 1971), pp. I, 431, 440; Pollard, *North-Eastern England*, pp. 367–70; Jewell, *North-South Divide*, pp. 48–52.

29. *State Papers: King Henry the Eighth*, 11 vols. (London, 1830–52), I, 496; *L&P* XI, 1319; XII/1, 193, 990.

30. *State Papers: King Henry the Eighth*, I, 485, 488; *L&P* XI, 920.

31. Pollard, 'Characteristics', pp. 141–42.

32. Durham University Library, Archives and Special Collections, Durham Cathedral Muniments, Miscellaneous Charter 6046; *Historical Papers and Letters from the Northern Registers*, ed. James Raine, Rolls Series 61 (London, 1873), pp. 388, 390.

33. Northumberland County History Committee, *A History of Northumberland*, 15 vols. (Newcastle, 1893–1940), VIII, 97 n.2; Kew: The National Archives, Public Record Office, SC 8/119/5924.

34. *York House Books 1461–1490*, ed. L. C. Attreed, 2 vols. (Stroud, 1990), I, 390–1 (my punctuation). See L. C. Attreed, 'The King's Interest: York's Fee Farms and the Central Government 1482–92', *Northern History*, 17 (1981), pp. 24–43.

35. *Sir Thomas Gray: Scalacronica 1272–1363*, ed. Andy King, Surtees Society 209 (2005), p. 87, and cf. 79.

36. John Barbour, *The Bruce*, ed. A. A. M. Duncan (Edinburgh, 1997), pp. 658–59.

37. Colm McNamee, *The Wars of the Bruces: Scotland, England and Ireland, 1306–28* (East Linton, 1997), pp. 129–40; Andy King, 'Bandits, Robbers and *Schavaldours*: War and Disorder in Northumberland in the Reign of Edward II', *Thirteenth Century England*, 9 (2003), 115–30 (p. 127). *Johannis de Trokelowe Annales*, ed. H.T. Riley, Rolls Series 28/3 (London, 1866), p. 101, refers to the rights claimed by Middleton and his brothers in *comitatu Northumbriae*.

38. *Chronicon de Lanercost*, ed. J. Stevenson (Edinburgh, 1839), p. 253 (the man involved was John Ross, of Ross in Herefordshire), 242. The chronicle's origins are discussed by Antonia Gransden, *Historical Writing in England II: c. 1307 to the early sixteenth century* (London, 1982), pp. 12–17. Compare Roy Martin Haines, *King Edward II* (Montreal, 2003), pp. 137–41.

39. *Rotuli Parliamentorum*, II, 10; *Rotuli Parliamentorum Anglie hactenus inediti MCCLXXIX–MCCCLXXIII*, ed. H. G. Richardson and George Sayles, Camden Society 3rd ser. 51 (London, 1935), pp. 101–102.

40. *Chronicles of Edward I and Edward II*, ed. W. Stubbs, 2 vols., Rolls Series 76 (London, 1882–3), Vol I, 313.

41. For possible indirect evidence from the later fourteenth century, see Macdonald, *Border Bloodshed*, ch. 6 *passim*. An exception must be made for particular contexts such as Oxford University, for which see below, at nn. 55–6.

42. *Registrum quorundam abbatum*, ed. Riley, I, 388, 394; *Paston Letters*, ed. Davis, I, 198.

43. *York House Books*, ed. Attreed, II, 713–4.

44. *York House Books*, ed. Attreed, I, 369.

45. *Paston Letters*, ed. Davis, I, 659.

46. For a recent review of the historiography, see M. L. Bush, 'A Progress Report on the Pilgrimage of Grace', *History*, 90 (2005), 566–78.

47. Godfrey Anstruther, 'The Rime of John Pickering, OP', *Dominican Studies*, 2 (1949), pp. 16–29. For discussion, see M. Bush, *The Pilgrimage of Grace: A Study of the Rebel Armies of 1536* (Manchester, 1996), p. 49 n. 132, p. 62 n. 205.

48. Anstruther, 'Rime of John Pickering', pp. 22, 24.

49. Examples include *L&P*, XI, 1079, 1115, 1155; 'Letters of the Cliffords, Lords Clifford and Earls of Cumberland, c. 1500 – c. 1535', ed. R. W. Hoyle, in *Camden Miscellany* 31, Camden Society, 4th ser. 44 (1992), pp. 1–191 (p. 79).

50. *L&P* XI, 892; XII/1, 163/2.

51. *L&P* XI, 841; E. Milner, *Records of the Lumleys of Lumley Castle*, ed. E. Benham (London, 1904), p. 40; L&P XII/1, 798.

52. *Pace* Campbell, 'North-South Dichotomies', pp. 145–47 (at p. 145).

53. *L&P* XII/1, 201/vi.

54. Michael Bush reviewed and discounted the evidence for such an interpretation in an unpublished paper delivered to a conference on 'Regional Identities: Shifting Boundaries and Contested Meanings' at Manchester Metropolitan University, September 2000.

55. A. B. Emden, 'Northerners and Southerners in the Organization of the University to 1509', *Oxford Studies presented to Daniel Callas*, Oxford Historical Society, n.s. 16 (Oxford, 1964 for 1959–60), pp. 1–30; P. Kibre, *The Nations in the Medieval Universities* (Cambridge, MA, 1948), p. 167.

56. Emden, 'Northerners and Southerners', p. 16

57. See also *L&P* XI, 909; XII/1, 466, 1186; *State Papers: King Henry the Eighth*, I, 492.

58. R. W. Hoyle, *The Pilgrimage of Grace and the Politics of the 1530s* (Oxford, 2001), p. 462. The evolution of these demands is discussed ibid., pp. 347–53.

59. *Records of Antony Bek, Bishop and Patriarch 1283–1311*, ed. C. M. Fraser, Surtees Society 162 (London, 1953), p. 151; C. M. Fraser, *A History of Antony Bek, Bishop of Durham 1283–1311* (Oxford, 1957), p. 171.

60. *North Country Wills 1383–1558*, ed. J. W. Clay, Surtees Society 116 (Durham, 1908), pp. 286–87.

61. Charles Phythian-Adams, 'Frontier Valleys', in *Rural England: An Illustrated History of the Landscape*, ed. Joan Thirsk (Oxford, 2000), pp. 236–62.

62. For what follows see M. Jones, '"Mons Pais et Ma Nation": Breton Identity in the Fourteenth Century', in id., *The Creation of Brittany: A Late Medieval State* (London, 1987), pp. 283–307.

63. Tim Thornton, *Cheshire and the Tudor State, 1480–1560* (Woodbridge, 2000); M. L. Holford and K. J. Stringer, *Liberties and Loyalties: North-East England, 1200–1400* (Edinburgh University Press, forthcoming).

64. There was a king's 'Council of the North' which existed briefly in the reign of Richard III, but it was not permanently established until after the Pilgrimage of Grace: R. Reid, *The King's Council in the North* (London, 1921).

65. R. B. Dobson, 'The Northern Province in the Later Middle Ages', *Northern History*, 42 (2005), pp.49–60 (p. 52).

66. *Letters of Richard Fox*, ed. P. S. and H. M. Allen (Oxford, 1929), pp. 43–44.

67. These lieutenants have been little studied; for some references, see above n. 11.

68. Bush, *Pilgrimage*, pp. 376, 380.

69. Peter Coss, *The Origins of the English Gentry* (Cambridge, 2003), pp. 202–15.

70. For the notion of 'country' see M. L. Holford, '*Pro patriotis*: "Country", "Countrymen", and Local Solidarities in Late Medieval England', *Parergon*, 23 (2006), pp.47–70.

71. For the north-east, see *Regional Identities in North-East England, 1300–2000*, ed. Adrian Green and A. J. Pollard (Boydell, forthcoming).

Chapter Nineteen

"A Duchy in every respect un-English": discourses of identity in late modern Cornwall

Philip Payton

Bill Lancaster, distinguished historian of North-East England, has confidently asserted that the North East is "the most distinctive region in England".[1] It is an opinion that would be hotly contested in Cornwall, and a recent poll has indicated that of all local identities in England, "Cornish" is by far the strongest.[2] And yet, an equally vociferous body of Cornish opinion would insist that Cornwall was not actually part of England at all, and that – historically, constitutionally, even ethnically – Cornwall was (and is) nothing less than a "Celtic" nation in its own right. In such a view, Cornwall is neither region nor county, and should be compared – not with English regions such as the North East nor English counties such as Yorkshire – but with other European small nations: notably "Celtic" Wales and Brittany.[3]

To even informed observers of British territorial diversity, the existence and strength of such feeling often comes as a surprise. For example, even as the North East rejected emphatically the proposal for devolutionary regional government, a Cornish Constitutional Convention was able to marshal a petition of some 50,000 verifiable signatures (10 % of the Cornish population) calling for just such an assembly for Cornwall. Moreover, while national political attention was focussed with great intensity upon the referendum in the North East in 2004 – with the Labour government putting all the means at its disposal behind the "Yes" campaign – so the popular movement for a Cornish devolutionary assembly was all but ignored by both media and government. For the latter, Cornwall was merely one county component of a much larger construct – the "South West" – which in any case was not scheduled to appear on the devolutionary agenda until apparently more pressing work in the North had been attended to.[4]

But more than this, as Mark Sandford has made plain, the government's inability to take Cornish claims seriously was also a function of its widely different attitudes to Cornwall and the North East.[5] The former – an "inconvenient periphery"[6] as one observer has dubbed it – was never likely to appear on the government's agenda, the basic tenets of its claims for separate or privileged treatment – Celtic origins and historical identity – not understood (or anathema) in Labour circles. This was in marked contrast, Sandford explained, to the North East where there was a recent and powerful history of alignment between regional aspirations and Labour Party policy. As Sandford noted wryly, contrasting governmental attitudes to Cornwall and the North East were exemplified neatly in the differing perceptions of the two territories presented in the recent popular television series *Wild West* (set in Cornwall) and *Our Friends in the North*.

Governmental inability to understand or consider Cornish claims was mirrored – until very recently at least – in the relative invisibility of Cornwall and the Cornish as a territory and a people in British national historiography. This shortcoming is only now being addressed in the so-called "new British historiography", with its eschewing of hitherto Anglocentric presentations of British history and its emphasis instead on the component but interlinked experiences of each part of the "Atlantic Archipelago" (the British Isles). However, even here the accommodation of Cornwall is not without difficulties, threatening as it does to subvert the recently established "four nations" approach to British history and challenging the conventional wisdom that – in the scholarly analysis of territorial identity – it is axiomatic that counties cannot be regions, and that regions cannot be nations.[7] Cornwall, it turns out, can be all three! Or, to put it another way, Cornwall for academic observers continues to be an enigma. The purpose of this chapter, then, is to unravel this enigma by appealing to the several "discourses of identity" that underpin it: to see how these discourses have interacted, collided and merged over time to form the Cornish "regional" identity that we recognize – or, more typically, do not recognize – at the beginning of the twenty-first century.

The uncertainty as to Cornwall's precise status is not new. In 1602 Richard Carew in his *Survey of Cornwall* argued that "Cornwall, as an entire state, hath at divers time enjoyed sundry titles, of a kingdom, principality, duchy, and earldom".[8] The twin institutions of the Duchy of Cornwall (vested in the heir to the Crown) and the Stannaries – the latter with its own Tinners' Parliament and separate legal system – afforded Cornwall an "aura of semi-independence" in the medieval and early modern periods, a mechanism of constitutional accommodation within the English state. Moreover, Carew also observed that the Cornish – "together with the Welsh, their ancient countrymen" – were still "fostering a fresh memory of their expulsion long ago by the English". The inquisitive stranger from across the River Tamar border, he said, might sometimes be rebuffed by the Cornish-language phrase "mea navidna cowzasawsnek": I will not speak English.[9]

As Mark Stoyle has shown in his recent work on early modern Cornwall, such sentiment accounted to a considerable degree for Cornish behaviour in the rebellions of 1497 and 1549 and in the Civil War. In supporting the Royalist cause in the latter, Stoyle argues, the Cornish were defending Cornwall against an intrusive English nationalist Parliamentarianism which saw the Cornish as "rebels", "ignorants", "Indians", "Turks", "papists", "atheists" and "pagans". These Roundheads swore they would "give no quarter to any Cornish or Irish" and condemned the "cruel Cornish", the "cursed Cornish", the "perfidious Cornish", raising the frightening spectre of the "Cornish mettal-men [of] heathen . . . Hellish Cornwall".[10] Cornwall, of course, was defeated in the Civil War, and many of the attributes that had so frightened the Parliamentarians – not least the Cornish language – declined or disappeared thereafter.

However, in the aftermath of the Civil War, new forces were already at work in Cornwall, the resurgence of tin mining and the emergence of copper evidence of an incipient industrialisation that would – in the centuries ahead – put Cornwall in the international forefront of deep, hard-rock mining and steam engineering. Intriguingly, just as it has taken the recent work of Mark Stoyle to alert the academic community to the particular place of Cornwall and the Cornish in the history of early modern Britain, so it is only of late that scholars have become more fully aware of the significance and distinctiveness of Cornwall in Britain's "Industrial Revolution". It was not until the 1980s that a new wave of economic historians, historical geographers and political scientists began to argue that industrialisation in the British Isles had promoted regional differentiation rather than national homogeneity. In contrast to an earlier generation of scholars that had assumed cultural, social and political uniformity in Britain as a "natural" outcome of the industrial experience, these new writers concluded that industrialisation both perpetuated and reinforced regional "difference". They argued that the Industrial Revolution gave new meaning to regional identities, the often highly specialized and distinctive forms of industrial activity that had emerged becoming defining cultural icons. As Dai Smith, champion of the socio-economic and cultural history of industrial South Wales, put it: "there was an explosion into industrial pre-eminence of regions *as* regions". [11]

By the 1990s historians were beginning to locate Cornwall within this mosaic of British industrial regions. But, while Cornwall was shown to have much in common with other regions, it was also clear that Cornish identity in the late modern period continued to exhibit distinctive features that differentiated it sharply from these areas: not least an "ethnic" dimension which continued to inform a popular insistence that Cornwall was not part of England. This, in turn, was located within a discourse of "industrial prowess" that reflected Cornwall's technological advance and insisted upon both the global significance of Cornish industrialization and its distinctive qualities.[12]

Four salient features of this discourse of "industrial prowess" can be identified. First of all, and most obviously, was "prowess" itself and the self-confident, even aggressive manner in which it was articulated. In 1839, for example, Thomas Lean – one of Cornwall's many mining engineers – could insist that:

Great as are the advantages which this nation [Britain] in general enjoys from the invention of the steam engine, and the successive improvements which it has received; there is, perhaps, no place in particular, where those advantages have been greater, or more evident, than in Cornwall.

As he explained: "The very existence of its deepest, most extensive, and most productive mines, is owing, not merely to the invention of the steam engine, but to the state of great perfection that machine has been brought in that county". Moreover, Lean added, "the improvements which the engine has, for many years, received, are due to native [Cornish] engineers; whose skill and watchful care, maintain it in its present state, or add continually further improvements".[13] Twenty years later the message was even more confident and expansive, George Henwood – another Cornish mining man – asserting with evident pride that:

The Cornish are remarkable for their sanguine temperament, their indomitable perseverance, their ardent hope in adventure, and their desire for discovery and novelty... to this very cause has science to boast so many brilliant ornaments who claim Cornwall as their birthplace.[14]

Sometimes, indeed, such fulsome assertions of superiority grated on those non-Cornish who read or heard them. As Herman Merivale complained in 1857: "The thorough Cornishman's respect for his own shrewdness and that of his own clan is unbounded, or only equalled by his profound contempt for 'foreigners' from the east".[15]

Part of this sense of "superiority" was based on the distinctive qualities – as the Cornish saw them – of Cornish mining: the second of the features underlying 'industrial prowess'". Contemptuous of coal-mining which they rarely engaged in in Britain or abroad, except as strike-breakers – they emphasized the peculiar characteristics, difficulties and dangers of deep, hard-rock mining and the advanced skills supposedly required to undertake it. Copper and tin became defining "Cornish" minerals – though lead, iron, wolfram and others were also exploited in Cornwall – and were cultural icons in their own right: proudly asserted by the Cornish and readily acknowledged by outsiders. As the nineteenth century wore on, so mining came to encompass more and more of the geographical extent of Cornwall: so much so that by the 1850s it had spread quite literally from Land's End to the Tamar. In 1836, for example, there had been dramatic new copper discoveries near Liskeard, in East Cornwall, shifting the focus of Cornish mining from its traditional West and (to a lesser extent) mid-Cornwall districts, a trend confirmed a few years later by major new finds in the

Tamar valley. At its height, mining employed one third of the Cornish workforce.[16]

"Cornish" technology, too, acquired similar iconic status. High-pressure steam had been pioneered in Cornwall, as the Cornish never tired of reminding the world, and the prefix "Cornish" was itself used in innumerable mining contexts: "Cornish" boilers, "Cornish" stamps (for breaking ore), Cornish kibbles (buckets), "Cornish" captains (managers), even "Cornish" wheelbarrows and "Cornish" shovels. But the greatest source of pride was the "Cornish" beam engine: developed from Trevithick's early high-pressure engines and – after the lapse of Boulton and Watt's restraining patent in 1801 – brought (in Cornish estimations) to "perfection" in Cornwall by a string of engineers who became household names west of the Tamar: Arthur Woolf, Michael Loam, William West, William Sims, Samuel Grose, and very many more. These men vied with one another to achieve ever greater efficiency in their engines, which were used for winding, stamping, the operation of man-engines (to bring men from underground), and pumping. This competitive spirit was reflected in the pages of Thomas Lean's *Engine Reporter*, a journal founded in 1810 to report and record the "duty" achieved by the principal engines at work in Cornwall: "duty" being defined as the number of pounds of water raised one foot high by the consumption of one bushel of coal. The *Engine Reporter* also reflected a high degree of interest in Cornwall in scientific knowledge, an interest exhibited in turn by Cornwall's prestigious nineteenth-century learned societies – the Royal Geological Society of Cornwall, the Royal Cornwall Polytechnic Society, the Royal Institution of Cornwall – the institutional and intellectual expression of a self-confident Cornish identity based on industrial prowess. At a more popular level, such sentiment infused and enthused the many Methodist-inspired self-help and mutual improvement societies that proliferated in Cornwall: such as the St Austell Useful Knowledge Society and the Launceston Philosophical Society. [17]

As Merivale had detected, a further feature of this discourse was its "ethnic" dimension. But this was not merely a question of the Cornish asserting some sort of racial superiority over the "foreigner" from the east. Rather, there had been a determined attempt in the late eighteenth and nineteenth centuries to construct a narrative of "Cornishness" – in effect, a Cornish "ethnic history" – by emphasizing those features that made the Cornish "different" from the English and asserting the River Tamar as an ancient border between Cornwall and England. William Borlase, for example, writing in 1796, believed that from the time Athelstan set the Tamar as the Cornish border in the tenth century, "we are to consider

Cornwall under the Saxon yoke.... the Cornish Britons maintained a perpetual struggle against the Saxons for the full space of 500 years'[18] Similarly, Samuel Drew in 1824 thought Athelstan's intervention "both fatal and final to the independence of the Cornish. This, amidst all the struggles that Cornwall made to preserve her liberty untainted, and that her enemies made to rob her of that inestimable jewel, this was the era of the first subjugation of the Cornish by the English".[19] Although apparently subversive, such perspectives were saved from contemporary political incorrectness by virtue of their emphasis on the Cornish as "Ancient Britons": bolstering rather than threatening the wider discourse of Imperial Britishness within which, perforce, Cornishness was required to exist. In this way, as "Ancient Britons", the Cornish were somehow more "British" than the English: descents of Boudicea and Caractacus – the heroes of Victorian popular history books – and progenitors of Britain's greatness as well as living evidence of the longevity of the British tradition in these islands.

Nonetheless, this sense of Cornish ethnic identity did have a certain exclusivity: heightened by the fact that, in contrast to most other industrial regions in the UK, Cornish industrialisation was not accompanied by substantial in-migration from other areas. Instead, there were significant intra-Cornwall flows of people, a process that enhanced the Cornish sense of ethnic solidarity and territoriality. Between 1841 and 1861, indeed, Cornwall had a higher proportion of native-born than any English county. As late as 1899 the *Cornish Post* newspaper was reminding its readers that "The Cornish miner still speaks of the English as another people living East of the Tamar".[20] This was also a perception shared by the English themselves. At the turn of the twentieth century, W.H. Hudson described "the remote and most un-English county of Cornwall", opining that there were few "Englishmen in Cornwall who do not experience that antipathy or sense of separation in mind from the people they live with, and are not looked at as foreigners".[21] Half a century earlier, Wilkie Collins had said much the same. Cornwall was, he observed, "a county where, it must be remembered, a stranger is doubly a stranger... where the national feeling is almost entirely merged in the local feeling; where a man speaks of himself as Cornish in much the same way that a Welshman speaks of himself as Welsh".[22]

The fourth component of this discourse of "industrial prowess" was its international dimension. As Dudley Baines has observed, in the period 1815–1914 "Cornwall was probably an emigration region comparable with any in Europe".[23] Between 1840 and 1900 almost 250,000 people left Cornwall for destinations overseas, with perhaps a similar number leaving for other parts of the

UK, a period during which the population of Cornwall at no point reached half-a-million. Between 1861 and 1900, 44.8% of the Cornish male population aged 15 to 24 went abroad: a further 29.7% left for other counties. A great many of these emigrants – but by no means all – were miners and their families. Initially, they were responding to the high levels of remuneration their specialist skills could command on the rapidly emerging international mining frontier – in Latin America, the United States, Australia, South Africa – while later, after the crash of Cornish copper in 1866 and the faltering of Cornish tin in the 1870s, they left to escape unemployment at home. One feature of this "Great Emigration", as it was known, was that in mining districts such as Moonta in South Australia and Grass Valley in California, the Cornish re-created Cornish communities with all the usual distinctive features – from Methodism, male voice choirs and Cornish wrestling to pasties and saffron cake. At home, individuals and communities developed sophisticated conduits of communication with these Cornish localities overseas, enabling informed choices to be made between potential destinations for would-be emigrants and facilitating the receipt of "home-pay" – remittances – by those back in Cornwall. Technological transfer accompanied the movement of people, with Cornish beam engines exported to destinations such as Peru, Mexico and New Zealand. The terminology of the North American and Australasian mining industries was dominated by that of Cornwall.[24]

In this way, a vibrant transnational Cornish identity was constructed during the nineteenth century. Inevitably, its touchstone was "industrial prowess" – drawing upon the features discussed above – but it also contributed to the discourse. The disproportional significance of the Cornish in the rapid development of the international mining economy was itself a powerful affirmation of the discourse but of specific importance was the "myth of Cousin Jack". A Cousin Jack was a Cornishman – usually, but not exclusively, a miner. His myth was the belief – perpetrated by the Cornish themselves – that the Cornish were somehow innately endowed with the characteristics of superior miners and that they were uniquely equipped for the challenges and rigours of the international mining frontier. So powerful was this myth that in certain regions – such as South Australia, where the directors of the Moonta copper mine contemplated the qualities of "Cornish nationality"[25] and those at the Burra Burra actively discriminated against miners from other ethnic groups[26] – they came to dominate the emergent local mining industry. In others, such as Grass Valley in California, where they displayed a "prickly sense of self,"[27] the Cornish vigorously asserted their superiority over competing ethnic groups – Irish, Italians, Germans, Croats and so on – as a means of assuring their privileged position in the mines. Here they were aided by the fact that in expressing separate identity they were by no means (unlike other groups) expressing a threat to or deviation from the norms, culture and aspirations of their host societies. On the contrary, as hard-working English-speaking Protestants from an essentially mobile and democratic society back home, they were well suited to the demands of America or Australia and in such countries became model citizens.

The effect of all this in Cornwall itself was to redouble pride in "industrial prowess". In Cornish literature, the theme of the emigrant miner returning home after many years abroad had become familiar by the late nineteenth century. In Charles Lee's 1898 novel *Paul Carah, Cornishman*, the hero returns to his native Cornwall after just such an absence and, moved by the familiar sights and smells of home, declares in an outburst of patriotic passion that there is "no kingdom on earth to come up to Cornwall". Moreover, he cries, there is "no nation fit to stand up in the sight o' the Cornish nation".[28] At such times, assertions of Cornish identity seem almost Imperialist – as they certainly were in W. Herbert Thomas's laudatory poem "All Hail! One and All!", published in Cornwall in 1892:

> *Join hands, ye Cornish lads, across the main!*
>
> *Let Asia clasp Colombia's outstretch'd hand! Come forth,*
> *Australia! Swell the glad refrain! And touch the fringe of*
> *Afric's golden strand! Swift o'er the boundless ocean rings*
> *the call! The mystic girdle round the world is cast!*
> *Shout now with thund'rous voices 'One and All'! [the Cornish motto] All hail!*
> *Old Cornwall! May thy glory last!* [29]

As before, such perspectives also served to complement the contemporary discourse of British imperialism, allowing the assertion of a robust Cornish identity that enhanced rather than challenged existing constructions of "Britishness". Indeed, even pre-dating the growth of the international mining economy, the Cornish had played a distinctive but integral part in Britain's overseas political and commercial expansion – not least in the Royal Navy where in the eighteenth and nineteenth centuries there were disproportionate numbers of Cornishmen both before the mast and as officers. Admiral Edward Boscawen, one of the latter, played an important role in the assertion of British sea-power in the mid-eighteenth century. Boscawen was careful, however, to give preferential treatment to fellow Cornishmen, and was so expansive in his articulation of his own Cornishness that one acquaintance was provoked to speak with teasing irony of "the large continent of Cornwall".[30]

We make take, perhaps, Boscawen's exaggerated sense of Cornwall's worth as typical of a Cornishman of his age. However, it would be an oversimplification to imagine that the boundaries of Cornishness were always as obvious and clear-cut as the discourse sometimes implied, or to suggest that the apparent complementarity in this period of "Cornishness" and "Britishness" meant that there was no room for doubt, collision or conflict in the articulation of varying discourses. For example, discourses of "Britishness" and "Englishness" often overlapped and were entwined, and – although there were sometimes important distinctions between the two – there were also moments when they seemed indistinguishable. It was at such times that the boundary between "Cornishness" and "Englishness" – ostensibly so clear in both popular consciousness in Cornwall and in the constructions of a Cornish "ethnic history" – became distinctly blurred. One response was that typified by the chairman of the West Cornwall Railway in 1859 who, relieved that the Cornish railway system had at last been connected to that of the outside world, exclaimed in a speech in Truro that until that moment Cornwall "was neither within nor without the borders – but now we are part of England (cheers)".[31] Angst and irresolution of a different sort were exhibited in the protestations of one Francis Harvey – writing from the perspective of a Cornish "exile" in South Africa in the 1860s – who both objected to patronizing depictions by "Cockneys" of Cornwall as "other" and "not of England", and yet also appealed to representations of Cornwall that differentiated it from England. He wrote:

> ...it is a fact that Cockneydom, and may be elsewhere, where other blunderers have grown up, Cornwall the brave and truly great, has been of mere slander called 'West Barbary' and 'not of England'; well, be it so, Cornishmen can well afford to smile at all this slang and stupid malignity; may be, Cornwall may justly be proud, as being in all her history, in her internal priceless worth, and in the glorious elements with which she has been served and aided, and honoured every valuable interest of the nation; of being in truth, if 'not of' yet superior by far to England, if really 'not of it'.[32]

However, the real challenge to the discourse of "industrial prowess" in Cornwall as the nineteenth century wore on was not the potential for confusion and uncertainty as to the precise borders of "Cornishness" and Englishness' but rather that industrial prowess was itself under threat. The Cornish beam engine had reached its zenith in the 1850s, new technologies and overseas competition and innovation usurping its position thereafter, this fall from engineering grace matched by the dramatic collapse of the Cornish copper mining industry in the late 1860s and the decline thereafter of Cornish tin. Cornwall was no longer the international centre of mining expertise, and Cornish claims to superiority seemed increasingly hollow. In such circumstances the "myth of Cousin Jack" withered on the vine, while Cornish emigration itself all but dried up in the years immediately after the First World War.

Socio-economically, culturally and politically Cornwall was plunged at the end of the nineteenth century into a "Great Paralysis",[33] as it has been described, a period of inertia and even suffering in which the indigenous Cornish got through by dint of an introspective "making do". However, as opinion leaders reacted to the enormity of the situation in which they found themselves, so they were drawn increasingly to the discourse of "Celticity": to the construction of Cornwall as a "Celtic nation". The idea that Cornwall was "Celtic" was not new. In the 1860s Robert Hunt had echoed the existing conventional wisdom: "England, with many persons, appeared to terminate on the shores of the river Tamar". But he went further, adding that: "[n]othing but what the Briton planted remains, and if tales tell true, it is probable long years mast pass before the Englishman can banish the Celtic powers who here hold sovereign sway".[34] Earlier, in 1859, the Rev. Charles Colwell – Wesleyan minister at Burra Burra in South Australia – had told his Cornish chapel-goers that they, in contradistinction to the Irish with their alternative claims to Celticity, were "the real descendents of the Celts".[35] However, it was not until later in the century and into the twentieth – as Cornwall's swift de-industrialization became so speedily apparent and was so keenly felt – that appeals to Cornish Celticity became commonplace.

Intriguingly, these appeals took two alternative – and yet symbiotic – forms. On the one hand, there was an appeal over the debris of the industrial period (now interpreted as a "blip" in Cornish history) to the times when Cornwall was more "purely Cornish": the pre-Reformation, pre-Industrial Revolution "Celtic-Catholic" Cornwall of the medieval period, when Celtic saints were venerated and the Cornish language spoken. But there was also an appeal to what a post-industrial Cornwall might be like, deploying the discourse of "Celticity" to advocate a tourist industry in which Cornwall's Celtic identity – exotic place-names, holy wells, Celtic crosses – would be a key asset. Henry Jenner, so-called Father of the Cornish Language Revival, in 1904 published his *Handbook of the Cornish Language*, which was to prove a foundation text for the Cornish-Celtic Revival.[36] In the same year the Great Western Railway, anxious to optimise the potential of its main line to Penzance, published *The Cornish Riviera* – written by the popular topographical author A.M. Broadly – in which Cornwall was portrayed as balmy, foreign, quasi-Mediterranean, exotic.[37] Twenty years later, the Great Western was still pursuing the same theme, S.P.B. Mais producing an altogether more ambitious volume of identical title – *The Cornish Riviera* – which informed tourists that Cornwall was "a Duchy which is in every respect un-English ... the Cornish people are not English people". Ile went on: "You may go there [Cornwall] with the idea you are in for a normal English holiday, and find yourself in an atmosphere of warlocks and pixies, miracle-working saints and woe-working witches". Indeed, "you may go there intent only on tennis, and find yourself at the end of a fortnight a devotee of holy wells and Celtic crosses".[38]

As Mais readily acknowledged, he had been helped in his crafting of *The Cornish Riviera* by leading figures in the Cornish-Celtic Revival, and an alliance of sorts had become apparent between these ostensibly very different proponents of Cornish Celticity. The Revivalists themselves had forged ahead with their reconstruction and advocacy of the Cornish language, in 1928 initiating a Gorsedd of bards – Gorseth Kernow – based on the similar Gorseddau of Wales and Brittany – and in 1948 inventing a Cornish National Tartan to complement the Cornish kilt introduced earlier in the century. And yet, as the Gorsedd itself recognised, the Revival in the inter-war period had scarcely touched the "making-do" lives of ordinary Cornish people. It was not until after 1945, in rapidly changing socio-economic circumstances, that the Revival appeared to develop more popular appeal – and then by effectively wedding aspects of Revivalist iconography such as the tartan and the Cornish flag (the black and white cross of St Piran) to existing mediums of Cornish (largely working-class) culture such as brass bands, choirs and rugby football: supporters of the latter now re-invented as the fiercely pro-Cornish "Trelawny's Army". In part, this new synthesis represented a Cornish reaction – perhaps a sharpening of ethnic identity – in response to extensive in-migration in the post-war era in which many people from outside, attracted by romantic tourist images of Cornwall, had been able to take advantage of the relatively low Cornish house prices. Mebyon Kernow – The Party for Cornwall – had been formed in 1951 to press the case for a measure of Cornish self-government and to champion Cornwall's Celtic identity, and although it had enjoyed little electoral success beyond the occasional flurry of local authority victories, it had profoundly influenced the conduct of politics in Cornwall – especially that of the Liberal Democrats.[39]

Although the appeal to the discourse of "Celticity" had been originally a repudiation of that of "industrial prowess", the former adopted in an attempt to fill the void left by the collapse of the latter, the synthesis of Revivalist and popular identity in Cornwall in the years after 1945 suggested that something new was happening. In effect, the apparently erstwhile discourse of "industrial prowess" had coalesced now with the new – the discourse of "Celticity" – to produce a radical alternative: the newly-emergent discourse of the "industrial Celt". At first sight this was a contradiction in terms, for "Celticity" – as much in De Valera's independent Ireland as in Saunders Lewis' vision of future Wales – was the antithesis of industrialisation and encompassed all that was idyllic in an uncomplicated, healthy rural life. However, as Dai Smith and Gwyn A. Williams observed in industrial South Wales and as Mairead Nic Craith showed in urban Northern Ireland, late twentieth-century Celticity was inherently more complex, with industrialisation – and de-industrialisation – emerging as a central component of the modern "Celtic" experience.[40] Amy Hale has offered an insightful summary of the phenomenon in its Cornish context:

> *Many Cornish view the remains of Cornwall's industrial past – such as abandoned tin mines, and to a lesser degree the debris left from china clay mining known as "tips" – as icons of Cornishness of which they are proud . . . Although today the abandoned mines are not icons of the Celtic revival in Cornwall in the same way that the Cornish language and the annual gathering of Cornish bards known as the Gorseth may be, there is no doubt that the remains of native industry are embraced by revivalists and underscore a Cornish sense of ethnic difference – a difference that is often expressed within the discourse of Celticity.*[41]

Moreover, according to Hale, "[t]hese industrial areas are recognized as part of the Cornish heartland, and have acquired great symbolic value by virtue of their importance in Cornish cultural and economic development". As she concludes: "[t]he discarded mine stacks are emblematic of a past Celtic vitality, almost as sacred to some Cornish people as the megalithic monuments" of the prehistoric age.[42]

The identity of early twenty-first century Cornwall, then, has come full circle. Despite the demise of Cornwall's industrial pre-eminence, the newly-fashioned discourse of "the industrial Celtic" had successfully merged and renegotiated elements of "industrial Prowess" with those of "Celticity". For academic observers of late modern Cornwall, this sheds considerable light on the otherwise enigmatic qualities of contemporary Cornish identity. It also helps to explain the persistence into the new millennium of a Cornish consciousness that continues to insist – in certain circumstances at least – that Cornwall is neither county nor region but a nation.

Notes

1. Bill Lancaster, 'An Agenda for Regional History', paper presented at 'Regions & Regionalism in History: International Colloquium', AHRB Centre for North-East England History, Northumbria University, 9–12 September 2004.

2. *Daily Telegraph*, 18 March 2004.

3. See Bernard Deacon, Dick Cole and Garry Tregidga, *Mebyon Kernow and Cornish Nationalism* (Cardiff, 2003).

4. Philip Payton, *Cornwall: A History* (Fowey, 2004), pp. 296–8.

5. Mark Sandford, 'A Cornish Assembly? Prospects for Devolution in the Duchy', *Cornish Studies: Eleven*, ed. Philip Payton (Exeter, 2003), pp. 40–56.

6. Philip Payton, *A Vision of Cornwall* (Fowey, 2002), pp. 176–8.

7. Mark Stoyle, 'Re-discovering Difference: The Historiography of Early Modern Cornwall', *Cornish Studies: Ten*, ed. Philip Payton (Exeter, 2002), pp. 104–15.

8. Richard Carew, *The Survey of Cornwall*, 1602, ed. F.E. Halliday (London, 1953), p. 139.

9. Carew (1953), p.139.

10. Mark Stoyle, *West Britons: Cornish Identities and the Early Modern British State* (Exeter, 2002), pp. 66–90.

11. Dai Smith, *Wales! Wales?* (London, 1984), p. 17.

12. Philip Payton, *The Making of Modern Cornwall: Historical Experience and the Persistence of 'Difference'* (Redruth, 1992); Bernard Deacon, '"The Hollow Jarring of the Distant Steam Engine": Images of Cornwall between west Barbary and Delectable Duchy', *Cornwall: The Cultural Construction of Place*, ed. Ella Westland (Penzance, 1997); and Bernard Deacon, 'The Reformulation of Territorial Identity: Cornwall in the late Eighteenth and Nineteenth Centuries', unpub. Ph.D thesis (Exeter, 2001).

13. Thomas Lean, *On The Steam Engines in Cornwall*, 2 edn (Truro, 1969).

14. Roger Burt (ed.), *Cornwall's Mines and Miners* (Truro, 1972), p.232.

15. Herman Merivale, 'Cornwall', *The Quarterly Review*, 102, 1857.

16. See Payton (1992), pp.71–98.

17. See Payton (1992), pp.71–78.

18. William Borlase, *Antiquities Historical and Monumental of the County of Cornwall* (London, 1754 and 1769), pp. 42–4.

19. Fortescue Hitchins and Samuel Drew, *The History of Cornwall* (Helston, 1824), p.725.

20. *Cornish Post*, 12 October 1899.

21. W.H. Hudson, *The Land's End: A Naturalist's Impression of West Cornwall*, 1908, 2nd edn (London, 1981), p.34.

22. Wilkie Collins, *Rambles Beyond Cornwall, or Notes in Cornwall taken afoot* (London, 1851), p.124.

23. Dudley Baines, *Migration in a Mature Economy: Emigration and Internal Migration in England and Wales, 1861–1900* (Cambridge, 1985), pp.157–9.

24. See Philip Payton, *The Cornish Overseas: A History of Cornwall's Great Emigration* (Fowey, 2005).

25. South Australian Archives (SAA) BRG40/543 *Moonta Mine Proprietors, Minute Books, 1861–91*, 3 May 1875, 7 February 1876.

26. *South Australian Register*, 20 April 1850.

27. Ralph Mann, *After the Gold Rush: Society in Grass Valley and Nevada City, California 1848–1870* (Stanford, 1982), p.179.

28. Charles Lee, *Paul Carah, Cornishman* (London, 1898), pp. 13–4.

29. W. Herbert Thomas, *Poems of Cornwall by Thirty Cornish Authors* (Penzance, 1892), p.iv.

30. Nicholas Rodger '"A Little Navy of Your Own Making": Admiral Boscawen and the Cornish Connection in the Royal Navy', *Parameters of British Naval Power, 1650–1850* ed. Michael Duffy (Exeter. 1992), p.81.

31. Cited in John Corin, *Fishermen's Conflict: The Story of Newlyn* (Newton Abbot, 1988), p.20.

32. Francis Harvey, *Autobiography of Zethar: St Phillockias, Cornu-waille, England* (Durban,1867), p.29.

33. Payton (1992), chapter six.

34. Robert Hunt, *Popular Romances of the West of England*, 1865, 2nd edn (Lampeter, 1993), pp. 22–3.

35. *South Australian Register*, 4 March 1859.

36. Henry Jenner, *A Handbook of the Cornish Language* (London, 1904).

37. A. M. Broadly, The Cornish Riviera (London, 1904).

38. S.P.B. Mais, *The Cornish Riviera*, 3rd edn (London, 1934).

39. See Payton (1992), chapters nine and ten.

40. Smith (1984); Geraint H. Jenkins, *The People's Historian: Professor Gwyn A. Williams, 1925–1995* (Aberystwyth, 1996), p.7; and Mairead Nic Craith, *Plural Identities: Singular Narratives – The Case of Northern Ireland* (Oxford, 2002), p.92.

41. Amy Hale, 'Whose Celtic Cornwall? The Ethnic Cornish Meet Celtic Spirituality', "in David C. Harvey, Rhys Jones, Neil Mclnroy and Christine Milligan (eds)," *Celtic Geographies. Old Culture, New Times* (London, 2002), p.164.

42. Hale (2002), p.164.

Notes on Contributors

Peter Aronsson is Professor of Cultural Heritage and the Use of the Past at Linköping University and Professor of History at Växjö University. He has published extensively in the field of regional cultural history and is currently co-ordinator of an international project comparing national museums.

John Belchem is Professor of Liverpool History at the University of Liverpool. His research interests are in diasporas, migration and identities with reference to Liverpool. He currently holds a Leverhulme Major Research Fellowship.

Ian Farr is Lecturer in German and European History at the University of East Anglia. His research interests are in the history of modern Bavaria as well as modern and contemporary political and social German history.

Graham Ford is Lecturer in European History at the University of Teesside. His recent research and publications are in post-war Bavarian political history and his has published on modern German labour and political history.

Patrick Gilli is Professor of Medieval History at the University of Montpellier III. He has published extensively on the cultural and political history of the Middle Ages in Europe.

Thomas Granier is Lecturer in Medieval History at the University of Montpellier III. He has published extensively on the Medieval history of Naples as well as on the Church in Early Medieval Southern Italy.

A.C. Hepburn retired as Professor of History at the University of Sunderland in 2000. He was Associate Director of the AHRC Centre for North East England History between 2000–2005. He has published extensively on the history of the Modern City as well as on the history of Catholic Belfast.

Matt Holford is a research associate at the University of Cambridge and the National Archives, editing the *Calendar of Inquisitions Post Mortem, 1442–47*.

Michael Keating is Professor of Political and Social Sciences at the European University Institute. His research interests and publications are in comparative European politics; urban and regional politics and nationalism.

Bill Lancaster in Reader in History at Northumbria University. He has published on the history of consumption, regional history and labour history. He was the Director of the AHRC Centre for North East England History and the editor of *Northern Review*.

Ranald Michie is Professor of History at the University of Durham. His research interests are in financial history and he has published extensively on the British financial system and the City of London since 1700.

Philip Payton is Professor of Cornish Studies and Director of the Institute of Cornish Studies at the University of Exeter's Cornwall Campus at Tremough. His principal research interests are in modern and contemporary Cornwall on which he has published widely.

Charles Phythian-Adams is Professor Emeritus and University Fellow at the Centre for English Local History, University of Leicester. He has published extensively on rural, regional and urban history from Roman Britain to the present and his current research interests concern the conceptualisation of English Local History.

Colin Pooley is Professor of Social and Historical Geography at Lancaster University. His research interests are in the social geography of Britain and continental Europe since the eighteenth century.

Brian K. Roberts retired as Professor of Geography at the University of Durham in 2003. His chief research interest is in the interface between historical geography, archaeology and economic history.

Dave Russell is Professor of Professor of History and Northern Studies, Institute of Northern Studies, Leeds Metropolitan University. He has researched and published extensively on the history of popular music, sport and the cultural representation of the North of England.

David Saunders is Professor of Russian History at the University of Newcastle. His research interests are in the Russian Empire and aspects of the Soviet Union. He is currently working on a general social history of the Russian Empire.

Alistair Thompson is Lecturer in Modern European History at Durham University. His principal research interests and publications are in the history of Berlin; imperial German politics; nineteenth century German historians and associational life.

John K. Walton is Professor of Social History at Professor of Social History in the Institute of Northern Studies, Leeds Metropolitan University. His research interests and publications are in the comparative history of leisure, consumption and tourism in Britain and Spain as well as major studies of seaside resorts. He is currently working on a global comparative study of the seaside holiday since the eighteenth century.

Peter Wilson is Professor of History at the University of Hull. He is a specialist in early modern German history and has published extensively in this area. He is currently on AHRC funded leave completing a book on the Thirty Years War.